VISUAL

REPRESENTATIONS

OF SPEECH

SIGNALS

VISUAL

REPRESENTATIONS

OF SPEECH

SIGNALS

Edited by

Martin Cooke, Steve Beet

and

Malcolm Crawford
University of Sheffield, UK

JOHN WILEY & SONS

Chichester · New York · Brisbane · Toronto · Singapore

Other Wiley Editorial Offices

John Wiley & Sons, Inc., 605 Third Avenue,
New York, NY 10158-0012, USA

Jacaranda Wiley Ltd, G.P.O. Box 859, Brisbane,
Queensland 4001, Australia

John Wiley & Sons (Canada) Ltd, 22 Worcester Road,
Rexdale, Ontario M9W 1L1, Canada

John Wiley & Sons (SEA) Pte Ltd, 37 Jalan Pemimpin #05-04,
Block B, Union Industrial Building, Singapore 2057

Library of Congress Cataloging-in-Publication Data

Visual representations of speech signals / edited by Martin Cooke,
  Steve Beet, and Malcolm Crawford.
    p. cm.
  Includes bibliographical references and index.
  ISBN 0 471 93537 9
    1. Speech. 2. Neurolinguistics. I. Cooke, Martin. II. Beet,
  Steve. III. Crawford, Malcolm.
  QP306.V55 1993
  006.4'54—dc20   92-40219
                                                                  CIP

British Library Cataloguing in Publication Data

A catalogue record for this book is available
from the British Library

ISBN 0 471 93537 9

Produced from camera-ready copy supplied by Martin Cooke and Malcolm Crawford,
using FrameMaker 3.0 on NeXT workstations.
Printed and bound in Great Britain by Bookcraft (Bath) Ltd

Contents

Contents

Preface

There is a bewildering array of representations used for the analysis of speech signals, ranging from the traditional spectrogram to those which result from more recent techniques such as time-frequency distributions and auditory models. A direct comparison of these very different representations is rarely possible without implementing them from scratch, since any examples in the literature are usually produced from specific signals designed to show up particular features of the representation.

This book records the result of an ambitious attempt to make good this deficiency by producing large numbers of different representations of the same signals. Each representation reproduced here was presented by a proponent of the respective analysis technique at a European Speech Communication Association (ESCA) Tutorial and Research Workshop, "Comparing Speech Signal Representations", which was held in Sheffield, UK, in April 1992.

All participants were asked to analyse a subset of a small, common database and to present results with similar physical dimensions. This was intended to make it easy to compare the relative resolutions of the various analyses and to characterise their behaviour in a limited range of conditions. Ultimately, over 80 scientists took up this challenge, and this book documents their efforts.

The workshop database consisted of four sentences: one of spontaneous, male speech in a natural acoustic environment (a bar), one of male speech from a standard database, and two versions of a female utterance spoken whilst wearing a Rothenberg mask which provided additional information on the speech production process. One of these versions was the unadulterated microphone signal, while the other had separately recorded background noise added to it, allowing some estimation of the analysis techniques' robustness. These sentences are referred to in the text as 'spont', 'timit', 'clean' and 'dirty', and collectively as the 'Sheffield signals'. They are available for other researchers wishing to compare their analyses with those presented here by application to the editors. The Appendix provides further information about the signals, and includes details of the recording equipment.

The database, although small, was designed to be challenging: the inclusion of female speech (when many algorithms have been developed solely using male speech), the low bandwidth of 'clean' and 'dirty' (due to the Rothenberg mask), and the realistic (i.e. poor) quality of the spontaneous speech all taxed the less robust methods. However, these factors are all present in a real environment, and the sentences were, of course, perfectly intelligible to a human listener.

Different representations of speech signals are often best visualised at different time-scales. For example, those attempting to show the activity in models of the auditory nerve may best be presented as a detailed analysis of perhaps a few tens of milliseconds, whilst others fit naturally into a syllabic time-scale. To support these variations, each participant was provided with the four sentences plus two fragments of each sentence. One fragment consisted of several syllables extracted from the central portion of the signal, whilst the other contained a single diphone from these syllables. The fragments are referred to using the extension '.syl' or '.dip'. So, for example, the signal 'clean.syl' represents the fragment of the 'clean' waveform consisting of a few syllables, whilst 'spont.dip' contains a single diphone from the 'spont' signal. The complete waveform is given the '.wav' extension. The precise portions of each signal which make up the syllable and diphone fragments are detailed in the Appendix.

Participants were encouraged to concentrate on the 'clean' and 'dirty' sentences when performing their analyses. Consequently, most of the representations presented here are of that data.

The book contains five tutorial chapters which provide a wide-ranging introduction to speech analysis methods and representations. Dik Hermes' chapter reviews three generations of pitch determination algorithms and demonstrates their performance on the Sheffield signals. The tutorial of Pat Loughlin and his colleagues provides a glimpse of the world of time-frequency distributions beyond the conventional spectrogram. Katerina Nicolaidis, with other members of the EUR-ACCOR Project, describes the recording and exploitation of articulatory and acoustic signals to supplement the speech waveform. She presents a detailed account of the use of multi-channel recordings in transcribing the 'clean' signal. Tony Robinson reviews artificial neural networks, illustrating their application in tasks such as speech compression, recognition and noise reduction. Malcolm Slaney and Richard Lyon describe two cochlear models — passive long-wave and active short-wave — and present a 'correlogram' representation which serves to summarise the temporal information in these models.

The remaining contributions represent a snapshot of the state-of-the-art in speech analysis and visualisation, covering such diverse topics as temporal decomposition, instantaneous frequency, higher-order statistics and group delay functions. Auditory modelling is well represented along with time-frequency analysis.

Compiling this volume has presented special challenges! In particular, we have attempted to produce displays which have identical physical dimensions to aid in the comparison process. We hope that our struggle to rationalise dozens of different formats has proved worthwhile. We have resorted to scanning figures only when all else failed.

It is a pleasure to acknowledge the contributions of Phil Green and Mike Pont in the workshop organisation, and of Dave Abberley, Luke Boucher, Guy Brown, Gavin Dempster, Ian Gransden, Seyed Mashari, Willem Mevius and Guozhu Wu during the workshop itself. The Department of Computer Science at Sheffield University kindly made a NeXT workstation available for the preparation of this book. We are indebted to Fiona Gibbon and other members of the ACCOR project at Reading University for providing the 'clean' signal, to Malcolm Slaney for making the signals available via FTP, and to ESCA for help in disseminating information about the Workshop. Ros Meredith and Gaynor Redvers-Mutton at John Wiley and Sons deserve mention for their patience and guidance, as does Martin Beavis, whose proofreading skills showed us that there is a lot more to compiling a book than "just" chucking it into a DTP system.

Martin Cooke
Steve Beet
Malcolm Crawford

Contributors

William Ainsworth — Department of Communication and Neuroscience, University of Keele, Keele ST5 5BG, UK
email: co01@uk.ac.kl.gec

Federico Albano-Leoni — CIRASS, Universita di Napoli, via Porta di Massa, 1, 80133 Napoli, ITALY
email: cirass@na.infn.it

Christophe d'Alessandro — LIMSI-CNRS, BP #133, 91403 Orsay Cedex, FRANCE
email: cda@m87.limsi.fr

Paavu Alku — Acoustics Laboratory, Helsinki University of Technology, Otakaari 5 A,
SF-02150 Espoo, FINLAND
email: pia@kolvi.hut.fi

Michael Allerhand — MRC Applied Psychology Unit, 15 Chaucer Road, Cambridge CB2 2EF, UK

J.R. Andrews — Department of Electrical and Electronic Engineering, University Park,
University of Nottingham, Nottingham NG7 2RD, UK
email: eexjra@uk.ac.nott.vax

Ted H. Applebaum — Speech Technology Laboratory, Panasonic Technologies, Inc., Santa Barbara CA 93105, USA
email: ta%stl-sb@uunet.uu.net or ta@stl.panasonic.com

Les Atlas — Interactive Systems Design Lab, Department of Electrical Engineering, FT-10,
University of Washington, Seattle WA 98195, USA
email: les@edu.washington.ee.uw-isdl

P. Basile — CIRASS, Universita di Napoli, via Porta di Massa 1, 80133 Napoli, ITALY
email: cirass@na.infn.it

S.W. Beet — Department of Electronic and Electrical Engineering, University of Sheffield, PO Box 600,
Sheffield S1 4DU, UK
email: el1swb@sunc.sheffield.ac.uk

G. Bloothooft — OTS Research Institute for Language and Speech, University of Utrecht, Trans 10,
3512 JK Utrecht, THE NETHERLANDS

Guy J. Brown — Department of Computer Science, University of Sheffield, Regent Court,
211 Portobello Street, Sheffield S1 4DP, UK
email: g.brown@dcs.shef.ac.uk

J. Caelen — Institut de la Communication Parlée, URA CNRS No 368 INPG & Université Stendhal,
46 Av. Felix Viallet, 38031 Grenoble Cedex, FRANCE

M.F. Cheesman — Hearing Health Care Research Unit, Department of Communicative Disorders,
University of Western Ontario, London N6G 1H1, CANADA

Martin Cooke — Department of Computer Science, University of Sheffield, Regent Court,
211 Portobello Street, Sheffield S1 4DP, UK
email: m.cooke@dcs.shef.ac.uk

Piero Cosi — Centro di Studio per le Ricerche di Fonetica, CNR. P.zza Salvemini, 13, 35131 Padova, ITALY

Malcolm Crawford — Department of Computer Science, University of Sheffield, Regent Court,
211 Portobello Street, Sheffield S1 4DP, UK
email: m.crawford@dcs.shef.ac.uk

K.M. Curtis — Department of Electrical and Electronic Engineering, University Park, University of Nottingham, Nottingham NG7 2RD, UK

Francesco Cutugno — CIRASS, Universita di Napoli, via Porta di Massa 1, 80133 Napoli, ITALY

Paul Dalsgaard — Speech Technology Centre, Institute of Electronic Systems, Aalborg University, 7 Fredrik Bajers Vej, DK 9220 Aalborg, DENMARK
email: pd@dk.auc.stc

C. Demars — LIMSI, BP #133, 91403 Orsay Cedex, FRANCE
email: demars@fr.limsi.m29

Phillip Dermody — National Acoustical Laboratory, 126 Greville Street, Chatswood, Sydney, NSW 2067, AUSTRALIA
email: nal@facet.ee.su.oz.au

P.J. Dix — OTS Research Institute for Language and Speech, University of Utrecht, Trans 10, 3512 JK Utrecht, THE NETHERLANDS
email: paul.j.dix@nl.ruu.let

Alessandro Falaschi — La Sapienza University of Rome, INFO-COM Department, Via Eudossiana 18, 00184 Roma, ITALY

Mauro Falcone — Fondazione Ugo Bordoni, Information Processing Division, Via B. Castiglione 59, 00142 Rome, ITALY

Jing Fang — Interactive Systems Design Lab, Department of Electrical Engineering, FT-10, University of Washington, Seattle WA 98195, USA
email: jfang@edu.washington.ee.uw-isdl

Flemming K. Fink — Speech Technology Centre, Institute of Electronic Systems, Aalborg University, 7 Fredrik Bajers Vej, DK 9220 Aalborg, DENMARK

Jose A.R. Fonollosa — Department of Signal Theory and Communications, Universitat Politecnica de Catalunya, Apdo. 30002, E.T.S.E.Telecomunicacio, 08080 Barcelona, SPAIN

C. Giguère — University of Cambridge, Engineering Department, Trumpington Street, Cambridge CB2 1PZ, UK
email: cg@uk.ac.cam.eng

I.R. Gransden — Department of Electronic and Electrical Engineering, University of Sheffield, PO Box 600, Sheffield S1 4DU, UK
email: el2irg@sunc.shef.ac.uk

P.D. Green — Department of Computer Science, University of Sheffield, Regent Court, 211 Portobello Street, Sheffield S1 4DP, UK
email: p.green@dcs.shef.ac.uk

Brian A. Hanson — Speech Technology Laboratory, Panasonic Technologies, Inc., Santa Barbara CA 93105, USA
email: han%stl-sb@uunet.uu.net

W.J. Hardcastle — Department of Linguistic Science, Speech Research Laboratory, University of Reading, Whiteknights, PO Box 218, Reading RG6 2AA, UK

Dik J. Hermes — Institute for Perception Research/IPO, PO Box 513, NL-5600 MB Eindhoven, THE NETHERLANDS
email: hermes@prl.philips.nl

John Holdsworth — MRC Applied Psychology Unit, 15 Chaucer Road, Cambridge CB2 2EF, UK

B. Horvat — Faculty of Technical Sciences, University of Maribor, Smetanova 17, 62000 Maribor, SLOVENIA

Peter Howell — Department of Psychology, University College London, Gower Street, London WC1E 6BT, UK

Donald G. Jamieson — Hearing Health Care Research Unit, Department of Communicative Disorders, University of Western Ontario, London N6G 1H1, CANADA
email: JAMIESON@UWOVAX.UWO.CA

Contributors

Z. Kacic   Faculty of Technical Sciences, University of Maribor, Smetanova 17, 62000 Maribor, SLOVENIA
email: kacic@uni-mb.si

Richard Katsch   National Acoustical Laboratory, 126 Greville Street, Chatswood, Sydney NSW 2067, AUSTRALIA
email: nal@facet.ee.su.oz.au

Eric Keller   Laboratoire d'Analyse Informatique de la Parole Informatique - Lettres, Université de Lausanne, CH-1015 Lausanne, SWITZERLAND
email: ekeller@ulys.unil.ch

N.R. Kew   Via maccia della sterpara 39, 00044 Frascati, Roma, ITALY
email: nick@mail.esrin.esa.it

I. Kheirallah   Hearing Health Care Research Unit, Department of Communicative Disorders, University of Western Ontario, London N6G 1H1, CANADA

G. Kokkinakis   Wire Communications Laboratory, Department of Electrical Engineering, University of Patras, Patras, GREECE

Stefan Krol   Hearing Health Care Research Unit, Department of Communicative Disorders, University of Western Ontario, London N6G 1H1, CANADA

M.A. de Leeuw   Institut de la Communication Parlée, URA CNRS No 368 INPG & Université Stendhal, 46 Av. Felix Viallet, 38031 Grenoble Cedex, FRANCE

P.J. Loughlin   Interactive Systems Design Lab, Department of Electrical Engineering, FT-10, University of Washington, Seattle WA 98195, USA
email: pat@edu.washington.ee.uw-isdl

Richard F. Lyon   Advanced Technology Group, Apple Computer, Inc., Cupertino CA 95014, USA

A. Marchal   Centre National de la Recherche Scientifique, Institute de Phonetique, URA 261 Parole et Langage, 29 Avenue R Schuman, 13621 Aix-en-Provence, FRANCE

Enrique Masgrau   Department of Signal Theory and Communications, Universitat Politecnica de Catalunya, Apdo. 30002, E.T.S.E.Telecomunicacio, 08080 Barcelona, SPAIN

Seyed Mashari   Department of Computer Science, University of Sheffield, Regent Court, 211 Portobello Street, Sheffield S1 4DP, UK
email: s.mashari@dcs.shef.ac.uk

Pietro Maturi   CIRASS, Universita di Napoli, via Porta di Massa 1, 80133 Napoli, ITALY

Georg Meyer   Department of Communication and Neuroscience, University of Keele, Keele, Staffordshire ST5 5BG, UK
email: cod01@uk.ac.kl.seq1

D.A. Miller   Department of Information Studies, University of Sheffield, Regent Court, 211 Portobello Street, Sheffield S1 4DP, UK

Asuncion Moreno   Department of Signal Theory and Communications, Universitat Politecnica de Catalunya, Apdo. 30002, E.T.S.E.Telecomunicacio, 08080 Barcelona, SPAIN

R. De Mori   School of Computer Science, McGill University, 3480 University Street, Montreal, Quebec, CANADA

J. Mourjopoulos   Wire Communications Laboratory, Department of Electrical Engineering, University of Patras, Patras, GREECE

K. Nicolaidis   Department of Linguistic Science, Speech Research Laboratory, University of Reading, Whiteknights, PO Box 218, Reading RG6 2AA, UK
email: llsnicol@uk.ac.rdg

N. Nguyen-Trong   Centre National de la Recherche Scientifique, Institute de Phonetique, URA 261 Parole et Langage, 29 Avenue R Schuman, 13621 Aix-en-Provence, FRANCE

M. Omologo	Instituto per la Ricerca Scientifica e Tecnologica, 38050 Povo di Trento, ITALY *email*: omologo%irst@it.irst
Andrea Paoloni	Fondazione Ugo Bordoni, Information Processing Division, Via B. Castiglione 59, 00142 Rome, ITALY
Roy D. Patterson	MRC Applied Psychology Unit, 15 Chaucer Road, Cambridge CB2 2EF, UK *email*: roy.patterson@uk.ac.cam.mrc-apu
A. Piccialli	CIRASS, Universita di Napoli, Via Porta di Massa 1, 80133 Napoli, ITALY
James W. Pitton	Interactive Systems Design Lab, Department of Electrical Engineering, FT-10, University of Washington, Seattle WA 98195, USA *email*: yojimbo@edu.washington.ee.uw-isdl
Michael J. Pont	Deptartment of Engineering, University of Leicester, Leicester, UK
Susanna Ragazzini	Fondazione Ugo Bordoni, Information Processing Division, Via B. Castiglione 59, 00142 Rome, ITALY
V.R. Ramachandran	Department of Computer Science and Engineering, Indian Institute of Technology, Madras-600036, INDIA
G. Raicevich	National Acoustical Laboratory, 126 Greville Street, Chatswood, Sydney NSW 2067, AUSTRALIA *email*: nal@facet.ee.su.oz.au
Tony Robinson	University of Cambridge, Engineering Department, Trumpington Street, Cambridge CB2 1PZ, UK *email*: ajr@eng.cam.ac.uk
Jean Rouat	Department des Sciences Appliquées, Université du Quebec a Chicoutimi, Chicoutimi, Quebec G7H 2BI, CANADA *email*: chp0050@uqam.bitnet
Stevie Sackin	Department of Psychology, University College London, Gower Street, London WC1E 6BT, UK
Malcolm Slaney	Advanced Technology Group, Apple Computer, Inc., Cupertino CA 95014, USA *email*: malcolm@apple.com
Ivo Tidei	La Sapienza University of Rome, INFO-COM Department, Via Eudossiana 18, 00184 Roma, ITALY
A. Tsopanoglou	Wire Communications Laboratory, Department of Electrical Engineering, University of Patras, Patras, GREECE
Josep Vidal	Department of Signal Theory and Communications, Universitat Politecnica de Catalunya Apdo. 30002, E.T.S.E.Telecomunicacio, 08080 Barcelona, SPAIN *email*: pepe@TSC.UPC.ES
Hisashi Wakita	Speech Technology Laboratory, Panasonic Technologies, Inc., Santa Barbara CA 93105, USA
P.C. Woodland	University of Cambridge, Engineering Department, Trumpington Street, Cambridge CB2 1PZ, UK *email*: pcw@uk.ac.cam.eng
B. Yegnanarayana	Department of Computer Science and Engineering, Indian Institute of Technology, Madras-600036, INDIA
Keith Young	Department of Psychology, University College London, Gower Street, London WC1E 6BT, UK *email*: ucjtrky@uk.ac.ucl
Yunxin Zhao	Speech Technology Laboratory, Panasonic Technologies, Inc., Santa Barbara CA 93105, USA

PART I

Tutorials

Pitch analysis

Dik J. Hermes

1 INTRODUCTION

One of the most conspicuous features of the normal speech signal is the regularly occurring periodicity at its so-called voiced parts. When first encountered, these clear regularities are so striking that many a young scientist in speech research has thought that it should not be too difficult to measure these periodicities with high degree of reliability (e.g. Noll [84]; Atal [6]; Seneff [100]; Hermes [45]). Indeed, the human eye appears to be a very good estimator of the pitch periods in a plotted speech signal and even now one of the best controls on the outcome of a pitch measurement is comparing it by eye with the periods observed in the oscillogram.

On the other hand, pitch has always been one of the more elusive features of speech research. Many have tried to design pitch-determination algorithms (PDAs) meant for application to the more or less well recorded speech signals of a wide variety of speakers. All have met with the problem that "their" PDA unexpectedly failed for one of the recordings. It has often been rather hard to understand the reason for such failure and, if the student has overcome his reluctance to modify the PDA or to adjust its parameters again, he often found that solving the problem for this particular recording was attended by serious errors in another. Many reasons for such a failure can be given. This paper will refer to some of them. It will be argued, however, that very reliable PDAs are now available for well recorded speech from a single speaker.

In this paper, the term pitch is reserved for something we perceive and the frequency of which can be determined by adjusting the frequency of a pure sine wave until its pitch is the same as the pitch of the signal. For very accurate measurements, the intensity of the sine wave must be specified, too, since the pitch of a sine wave changes somewhat with intensity (Stevens [108]).

A survey will be presented of the principles on which PDAs are based. The improvement in the PDAs over the years will be sketched. This paper will try to show how this progress was made possible by our increasing technical possibilities and the growth of our knowledge of pitch perception and the physiology of the peripheral auditory system. We will try to outline where our knowledge ends and how fundamental the gaps in our knowledge are for the analysis of pitch in speech.

The large number of PDAs will be divided into three generations. The first generation are the PDAs designed to detect the first harmonic or the period of the speech signal in voiced speech segments. Second-generation PDAs are based on or agree with theories of pitch perception. The third generation consists of PDAs which are not only based on knowledge of pitch perception, but also on knowledge of the physiology of the auditory periphery.

This paper will not deal with the details of all these PDAs. An excellent, exhaustive review of PDAs up to 1983 can be found in Hess [48]. For later PDAs, the reader is referred to the literature. Only the principles underlying the various PDAs will be summarised. The

Visual Representations of Speech Signals: Martin Cooke, Steve Beet and Malcolm Crawford (eds.)
© 1993 by John Wiley & Sons Ltd

progress in pitch determination will be sketched and illustrated by means of the four Sheffield utterances 'clean.wav', 'dirty.wav', 'timit.wav' and 'spont.wav'.

2   THREE GENERATIONS OF PDAs

2.1 First generation: period determination

Many of the oldest PDAs are now referred to as 'time-domain' PDAs. The first arose when digital circuitry was still absent and analog electronic devices were used. One simply tried to filter out the first harmonic. For harmonic sounds without first harmonic or with only a very weak one, asymmetric static nonlinearities and low-pass filtering were applied to introduce or enhance the first harmonic. Later time-domain PDAs try to detect the quasiperiodicity of the speech signal. They arose when digital computers began to be used in speech-research institutes and comprise the measurement of zero crossings, peak distances, envelopes, the autocorrelogram, etc. They are quite unexacting and, depending on their application, some perform creditably for well recorded, clean speech. They can be a good choice in real-time applications, where one does not avail oneself of dedicated signal-processing facilities.

Many "time-domain" PDAs, though not those based on autocorrelation, which removes all phase relations, are claimed to lend themselves to determination of the moments of glottal closure. But there is a group of PDAs which is specifically developed not only for determining the moment of glottal closure, but to reconstruct the complete glottal waveform from the speech signal. They are based on a source-filter model of speech production and use linear-predictive-coding (LPC) and sometimes autoregressive-moving-average (ARMA) techniques to reconstruct the glottal-source signal from the speech signal (e.g. Strube [107]; Ananthapadmanabha & Yegnanarayana [3]; Wong *et al.*[124]; Milenkovic [77]; Childers & Lee [17]). They start with a gross estimate of the moments of glottal closure from the LPC residual. The intervals just following these moments are then considered as representing the closed interval of the glottal cycle. A more precise formant analysis is then carried out during this closed interval by means of a pitch-synchronous autocovariance LPC analysis. Next, the speech signal is subjected to another inverse filtering with the newly obtained time-varying inverse filter to obtain the glottal excitation signal. The glottal waveform is then obtained by appropriate integration and deemphasis. In some studies (Krishnamurthy & Childers [60]; Wood & Pearce [125]), this procedure is supplemented by an analysis by means of a laryngograph (Fourcin & Abberton [30]).

Parametric models of the glottal waveform are presented by Fant *et al.* [28] and Fujisaki & Ljungqvist [31]. The estimation of the parameters of such a model is part of more advanced applications (Hedelin [43,44]; Isaksson & Millnert [57]) in which the procedure of determining the closed phase of the pitch period, the formant frequencies and bandwidths, the inverse filter and the glottal waveform is used iteratively until the estimate of the glottal waveform ceases to change.

The possibility to determine the moments of glottal closure is an important feature, which PDAs of the second generation do not have. Because of this property, these PDAs are of relevance to methods like pitch-synchronous overlap-and-add (PSOLA) (Hamon *et al.* [40]). Also if one wants to determine formant frequency and bandwidth very accurately, this can best be done during the closed phase of the glottal cycle, which therefore has to be known.

Though hardly ever mentioned in the literature, the reconstruction of the glottal waveform demands extremely well recorded speech signals. The moment of glottal closure must remain synchronised within the various frequency bands, which means that phase distortions must be known exactly. If the phase of the signal is distorted during recording, an inverse correction filter has to be applied (Hunt [56]). Furthermore, the success of the model depends on the correctness of the inverse filter used to reconstruct the glottal waveform. As mentioned, this inverse filter is best determined during the closed phase of the glottal cycle, but even then hand corrections are often necessary, in sustained vowels as well. In many other speech sounds, such as voiced consonants and nasal vowels, the source-filter model is too simple, leading to serious errors if used to determine the interval between glottal pulses. The suitability of these techniques as a PDA is therefore limited.

The oldest "frequency-domain" PDAs are those based on the *cepstrum*, the inverse Fourier transform of the logarithm of the amplitude spectrum (Noll [84,85]). They have played a very important role in speech analysis. For about two decades cepstrum PDAs were among the most reliable PDAs available, at least for speech signals. The cepstrum PDA is based on a simple linear source-filter model of speech production. The speech signal $s(t)$ is described as a convolution of the periodic glottal-source signal $x(t)$ and the acoustic impulse response of the oral cavity and the mouth $h(t)$, so that

$$s(t) = \int_{-\infty}^{\infty} h(\tau) x(t-\tau) \, d\tau \tag{1}$$

Or, in the frequency domain, $S(f) = H(f) X(f)$. Calculating the absolute value and taking logarithms leads to

$$\log |S(f)| = \log |H(f)| + \log |X(f)| . \tag{2}$$

Now, in speech, the glottal-source signal $x(t)$ has a very broad-band character. It is represented in the amplitude spectrum as a rapidly fluctuating ripple, superimposed on the much less rapidly fluctuating spectral envelope representing the relatively broadly tuned formants. An inverse Fourier transform back to the time domain, giving the cepstrum

$$C_s(\tau) = C_h(\tau) + C_x(\tau) , \tag{3}$$

then gives the characteristics of the acoustic filter $C_h(\tau)$ for short delays (quefrencies in cepstrum jargon), while the source $C_x(\tau)$ is represented by one or two sharp equidistant peaks at longer delays. The highest peak, in most cases the first, gives the estimated pitch period. As calculation of the cepstrum requires two Fourier transforms, its widespread introduction was only possible after publication of the Fast Fourier Transform by Cooley & Tukey [19].

The success of the cepstrum PDAs is based on their close relation to a good, effective speech-production model. It fails, however, for narrow-band signals, though this can to some extent be improved by applying static nonlinearities which introduce higher harmonics (Noll [86]). It has no relevant relation to pitch perception.

2.2 Second generation: PDAs based on pitch-perception theories

In the pitch-perception theory of Schouten [95] and Schouten *et al.* [96], the human pitch extractor was assumed to derive its information from the temporal fine structure of the high, unresolved harmonics. In the early seventies, this theory was replaced by three other pitch-perception theories, Terhardt's virtual-pitch theory [111,112], Goldstein's optimum-processor theory [35] and Wightman's pattern-transformation model of pitch perception [122,123], the first two of which became most influential. In these theories pitch was assumed to arise from harmonic relations between the lower, resolved harmonics. Because of their predictive ability they had a great impact on hearing theory. As demonstrated by De Boer [24] and Houtsma [52], they have much in common. They all start with a signal presentation in the spectral domain. In view of the tonotopic organisation of the basilar membrane, many have considered pitch perception as a central pattern-matching process operating on *place* information from the cochlea. Siebert [101,102] contributed to this place theory of pitch perception by arguing that for the discrimination of a pure sine wave subjects paid almost exclusive attention to place cues, though he recognised that time cues may be necessary for stimuli more complicated than sine waves.

In its original version, Goldstein [35] elaborated his theory only for two adjacent harmonics of equal amplitude. This theory was further developed for nonadjacent harmonics by Gerson & Goldstein [32], to harmonic signals contaminated with components having no harmonic relation to the harmonic complex by Grandori [37] and to dichotic stimuli by Beerends & Houtsma [8,9]. Originally, Goldstein did not pass any judgment on whether place or time cues would be used in pitch perception. In later work, he showed that *time* information in the firing patterns of the auditory-nerve fibres is an adequate basis for auditory frequency measurement (Goldstein & Srulovicz [36]) and combined both views in a central-spectrum model of pitch discrimination (Srulovicz & Goldstein [106]). For want of a crucial experiment, the place vs. time question in pitch perception has remained academic for many years. Many authors claim that the results of their experiments are more in agreement with the time theory of pitch perception. Others advocate a combined theory (Bilsen & Ritsma [12]; Houtsma *et al.* [53]; Srulovicz & Goldstein [106]; Javel & Mott [58]; McFadden [70]).

These pitch-perception theories have resulted in a number of very powerful PDAs. Though neither Schroeder nor Noll mentions any relation to pitch perception, the first PDAs related to pitch perception are those that calculate the harmonic product spectrum (Schroeder [98]) and the harmonic sum spectrum (Noll [87]). It will be shown that these PDAs anticipate PDAs explicitly based on the pitch-perception theories which arose in the seventies. These pitch-perception theories led to Terhardt's virtual-pitch determination algorithms [113,114], the harmonic sieve (Duifhuis *et al.* [27]), the spectral comb (Martin [68,69]) and subharmonic summation (SHS) (Hermes [45]). The harmonic product spectrum $Q(f)$ is defined as

$$Q(f) = \prod_{n=1}^{N} |F(nf)|^2 \tag{4}$$

in which $F(f)$ is the Fourier transform of the appropriately windowed time signal. N is the number of harmonic compressions carried out, which amounts to the number of harmonics taken into account. The harmonic sum spectrum $S(f)$ is defined as

$$S(f) = \sum_{n=1}^{N} |F(nf)|^2. \tag{5}$$

The frequency at which $S(f)$ attains its maximum is that of the estimated pitch. Although these PDAs were recognised as the most robust PDAs (Hess [48]), their wide-spread application was hindered by the numerical necessity to apply a Fourier transform of at least 2048 points. And even then a compression at most of order five was possible. The spectral comb by Martin [68,69] and SHS by Hermes [45] were modifications of Schroeder's and Noll's principles. They chose the harmonic sum spectrum, but they added up not the compressed power spectra, but the compressed *amplitude* spectra. Less weight was given to higher harmonics. In Hermes [45], the lower frequencies were attenuated according to

$$P(f) = W(f) |F(f)| = W(f) A(f). \tag{6}$$

The necessity of calculating a Fourier transform of 2048 points or more was circumvented by substituting the harmonic compression on a linear frequency scale by a harmonic shift on a logarithmic frequency scale,

$$H(s) = \sum_{n=1}^{N} h_n P(s + \log_2 n) \tag{7}$$

where $s = \log_2 f$, $H(s)$ is the subharmonic sum spectrum and h_n ($=0.84^{n-1}$) is the weight attributed to each shifted spectrum in the summation. With this transformation to a logarithmic scale, a Fourier transform of 256 points was enough for compressions of order fifteen. As shown by Hermes [45], SHS is in qualitative agreement with Terhardt's virtual-pitch theory and does not disagree with the optimum processor either, which should not surprise us in view of the close relation between the virtual-pitch theory and Goldstein's optimum processor.

The first deliberate development of a PDA based on pitch theory was developed by Duifhuis *et al.*[27], who implemented Goldstein's optimum processor. Their result became known as the harmonic sieve. Exact implementation of Goldstein's optimum processor was practically impossible, because the maximum likelihood estimation for multicomponent stimuli is numerically too demanding. The stochastic transformation, in practice a Gaussian-shaped widening of the spectral peaks introduced to explain pitch phenomena in tones with nonharmonic partials, is replaced by a rectangular widening, which results in the harmonic sieve. This resolves the numerical maximum-likelihood-estimation problem for multicomponent stimuli. Just as in the optimum processor, no weight was attributed to the amplitude of the components. All peaks contributed according to an all-or-none principle when they obeyed certain audibility conditions based on knowledge of simultaneous masking. It can be shown that replacing the all-or-none principle by a more gradual decrease in the contribution of a component when further away from its exact harmonic position, giving weight to the amplitude of a component and implementing the numerical improvement of the sieve given by Allik *et al.* [2] results in a PDA that is almost the same as the spectral comb or SHS.

The strength of these PDAs comes from their agreement with what we know about pitch perception. Until very recently, they always came out as best, at least in thorough and extensive evaluations including a number of different male and female utterances.

These PDAs are sometimes presented as favouring the place theory of pitch perception. All calculations, pattern matching if you like, are indeed carried out in the frequency domain. However, SHS amounts to first introducing subharmonics for each component in the spectrum and then adding the result. This is very much the same as carrying out a procedure in the time domain as suggested by Van Noorden [120]. Van Noorden added the interval histograms of spike trains of theoretical auditory-nerve fibres stimulated by a harmonic complex signal. The subharmonics in the spectral domain then correspond to higher-order intervals in the time domain.

2.3 Third generation: PDAs based upon the physiology of the cochlea

The most advanced PDAs are those which are based not only on theories of pitch perception, but also on knowledge of the auditory periphery. They are anticipated by Licklider's duplex and triplex theories of pitch perception [64,65]. More recent computational models have been developed by Weintraub [121], Patterson [89], De Cheveigné [25,26], Lazzaro & Mead [63], Slaney & Lyon [104], Meddis & Hewitt [74,75] and by Van Immerseel & Martens [119], who developed the auditory-model-based pitch extractor (AMPEX). Among these, the last, AMPEX, is the only PDA of the third generation which is well evaluated for speech. The pitch-perception model by Meddis & Hewitt [74,75] is of great importance since its power in predicting the results of some crucial pitch-perception experiments was shown to be very substantial. Unfortunately, in its present form, this model does not contain a voiced-unvoiced decision and is unsuitable for application to speech. It would supply a sound basis for developing a very reliable PDA for speech in the future. This model will be indicated by M&H.

The architecture of a pitch meter based on the outputs of modelled auditory filters consists of several stages and is presented in fig. 1.

The first stage mimics the linear filter mechanics of the outer and the middle ear. This is followed by a model of the basilar membrane, which has the form of a bank of bandpass filters simulating the mechanical auditory filters on the basilar membrane. Then follows the transduction stage in which the energy of the vibrating basilar membrane is transformed into a series of firing probabilities and ideally into a simulated train of action potentials or spikes.

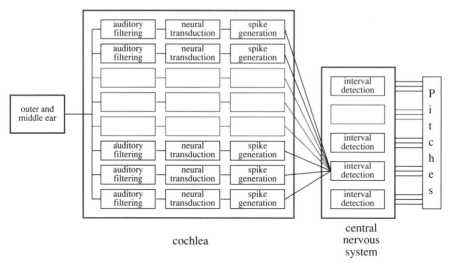

auditory filtering | neural transduction | spike generation

auditory filtering | neural transduction | spike generation

outer and middle ear

auditory filtering | neural transduction | spike generation

auditory filtering | neural transduction | spike generation

auditory filtering | neural transduction | spike generation

interval detection

interval detection

interval detection

interval detection

P i t c h e s

cochlea

central nervous system

Fig. 1   Illustration of the various stages of a third-generation PDA.

This transduction stage comprises a static nonlinearity, in most cases a half-wave rectifier and a compression and a model simulating adaptation in the cochlea (Schroeder & Hall [99]; Meddis [71,72]; Meddis *et al.* [73]; Hewitt & Meddis [50]).

The last stage of the PDAs of this generation is the most speculative. It consists of a procedure which combines input from all frequency channels and aims at finding the interval occurring most often in the various spike trains. In fact, this is the stage about which we know least. In one way or another, all algorithms attempt to detect a common periodicity in the outputs of the auditory filters. An interesting representation, and the only one in which octave and fifth ambiguities are represented in a natural way, is presented by Patterson [89]. In other models, the routines for detecting the periodicities in the auditory-filter outputs remind us of the time-domain PDAs of the first generation. Following Licklider, most use autocorrelation to reveal these periodicities (Weintraub [121]; Lazzaro & Mead [63]; Slaney & Lyon [104]; Meddis & Hewitt [74]). AMPEX uses a modified version of autocorrelation, where the inspiration does not come from pitch-perception theory nor from our knowledge of the cochlea, but simply from the need to speed up computations. De Cheveigné [25,26] then uses the good-old average-magnitude difference function (AMDF) (Ross *et al.* [93]).

This shows how little we know about the central pitch-extraction mechanism. What must surprise us, is how excellent PDAs can be developed on the simple basis of a model calculating interval distributions in the auditory-nerve fibres. Meddis & Hewitt [74,75] have shown how well a number of important pitch-perception phenomena can be simulated with such a model. The good performance of AMPEX has also shown that it can be used as a PDA for pitch analysis in speech and that it outperforms the best previous PDAs. It appears that, for the tasks for which these PDAs were developed, i.e. pitch analysis of speech signals and prediction of pitch in complex tones, precise knowledge about what is going on in the central pitch processor is not necessary. This aspect will be further discussed in the section on outstanding problems in pitch determination.

The predictive power of these PDAs from the third generation stems from two important characteristics. In the first place, they decompose the signal into frequency bands defined by the auditory filters in the cochlea. In the second, they use the *temporal* information in each separate frequency channel. These two features appear to be essential. For instance, in the presence of inharmonic contaminations, the period detectors in inharmonic frequency bands will not produce a maximum at periods corresponding to the period of the harmonic components, but will on average produce a zero outcome. Consequently, adding the autocorrelograms across frequency bands (yielding the *summary autocorrelation function* in M&H) will not be very much disturbed by these inharmonic components. Another important consequence is that the model has no difficulties in dealing with unresolved harmonics. Auditory-nerve fibres tuned to the frequencies of the unresolved harmonics fire in synchrony with the temporal envelope of the signal in these frequency bands. For normal speech this envelope has the same period as the pitch period. Because of this characteristic, Meddis & Hewitt [74] say that their model is in agreement with modern pitch-perception theory in which a new role is given to the unresolved harmonics (Houtsma & Smurzynski [54]). They do not show, however, with what precision their model can predict Houtsma and Smurzynski's results.

In spite of its success in predicting a large number of pitch phenomena, there are some well known properties of the peripheral auditory system, which are absent in the current M&H model. The basilar membrane is modelled as a passive, linear structure. There is no simultaneous masking, and no refractoriness. Furthermore, the implementation of the model is incomplete in details. For instance, the static nonlinearity in the transduction process in the model is the same for all auditory filters, whereas it is known that they are different for different fibres. Meddis and Hewitt themselves can probably supply many more examples of shortcomings like these.

Another, more important disadvantage of M&H is that it has not been tested for speech signals. It might very well be that some parameters, which are of no importance in predicting the pitch of synthetic tones, become crucial in pitch analysis of speech signals. One should not be surprised if application of M&H to speech analysis were to require much more modification and parameter tuning than expected.

The best evaluated PDA for speech remains the AMPEX PDA by Van Immerseel & Martens [119]. A disadvantage of AMPEX can be that many of its features are inspired by speeding up computations, sometimes at the cost of what we know about pitch perception. For instance, the sampling rate in the high-frequency channels is kept so low that the temporal fine structure of the auditory-filter outputs is lost. Also, pitch is determined with an accuracy far below that with which pitch is perceived.

2.4 Other PDAs

Many PDAs have been published which do not fit into one of these classes. In my opinion, there is no reason to put much effort in implementing any of them, as long as there is neither experimental verification of their comparative performance nor any novel theoretical principle underlying them.

The only other "PDA" mentioned here is based not on the speech signal, but on the laryngograph (Fourcin & Abberton [30]). A laryngograph can be the best available instrument for determining the closed phase of the glottal cycle, the moment of glottal closure, the presence of voicing, etc. (Hess & Indefrey [49]; Childers *et al.* [16]). For many applications, however, it is not the perfect pitch meter. For example, in the case of creak a laryngograph will follow the irregular or subharmonic frequency values corresponding to the vibration modes of the glottis. This does not necessarily correspond with the pitch we hear. Another example. If one synthesises LPC-coded speech on the basis of the voiced-unvoiced decision of a laryngograph, one will find the speech quality unacceptably buzzy. Not only will the voiced synthesis of voiced fricatives lead to an incorrect synthesis, at the start and end of many voiced consonants one will also hear a clear buzz. Apparently, speech contains many noisy components at low intensities, so that synthesis can better be unvoiced at these segments.

3   VOICED-UNVOICED CLASSIFICATION

Following Hess [48], an algorithm which determines which segments of speech are voiced and unvoiced will be indicated as a voicing-determination algorithm (VDA). Also following Hess, the VDAs are discussed separately from the PDAs.

The automatic voiced-unvoiced classification of a speech segment is one of the most difficult problems in speech analysis. Only a few papers are specifically dedicated to this important problem (e.g. Atal & Rabiner [7]; Siegel & Bessey [103]; Al-Hashemy & Taha [1]). Even more than in pitch determination, the actual application has a strong effect on the specifications required from a VDA. In a simple source-filter model, for instance, in which the excitation signal consists either of noise or of a pulse train, voiced fricatives should be synthesised unvoiced. For, if voiced fricatives are synthesised with a pulse train as source signal, the result no longer sounds like a fricative. This means that the appropriate VDA should classify voiced fricatives as unvoiced in spite of the clear presence of voicing as well as pitch. If, on the other hand, one wants to study pitch in voiced fricatives, one needs a VDA which classifies voiced fricatives as voiced, of course. In these cases one additionally needs a PDA which is robust for contamination with noise.

Noise is a very important part not only of the unvoiced speech signal, but also of voiced speech. This has already been mentioned for voiced fricatives, where its presence is obvious. But noise can be a substantial part of vowels, too, specifically in breathy voices. These observations have led to speech-analysis-and-synthesis models with mixed excitation (e.g. Makhoul *et al.* [66]; Kang & Everett [59]). This has not yet resulted in very satisfactory results, however. An important problem in this respect is that noise must fulfil very specific conditions if it is to integrate perceptually with the rest of the speech sound. If simple stationary noise is added it is perceived as a separate noise sound and does not improve the quality of the synthesised speech. Important improvements have been made recently in this respect (Carlson *et al.* [15]; Hermes [46]; Childers & Lee [17]).

Another problem relates to the fact that voiced speech does not necessarily have pitch. In creaky voice, clear pitch pulses can be distinguished, so this speech is voiced. But the interval between them can be so irregular that no clear pitch is perceived.

4   COMPARISON OF PDAs FROM THE THREE GENERATIONS

In this section the three generations of PDAs will be compared. The first question that had to be answered was what the perfect result of a PDA should look like. For this, a colleague was asked to produce reference pitch contours and voiced-unvoiced decisions that would be best *when used in LPC synthesis*. This colleague was known to have a perfect ear as far as voiced-unvoiced decisions are concerned. There was no mixed excitation.

As a representative example of a PDA from the first generation we will use the so-called parallel-processor (PPR) PDA by Gold & Rabiner [34]. For some this will naturally raise the objection that there are much better time-domain PDAs now, resistant to contamination with noise, etc. Here it is presented as one of the first relatively reliable PDAs and used to show how much PDAs have improved over the years. SHS (Hermes [45]) was chosen as representative of the second generation. The AMPEX PDA by Van Immerseel & Martens [119] will be presented as representative of the third generation.

The results of these PDAs will be presented on an ERB-rate scale (Patterson [88]), a frequency scale derived from the frequency resolution of the human auditory system. In most intonation research, prominence-lending pitch movements have either been expressed on a linear (e.g. Cooper & Sorensen [20]) or on a logarithmic frequency scale (e.g. 't Hart *et al.* [116]). Experiments by Hermes & Van Gestel [47] showed that the prominences of syllables synthesised in different frequency regions were only perceived as equal when the corresponding excursion sizes were equal on an ERB-rate scale. Hence pitch contours will be displayed on an ERB-rate scale, using the formulae from Glasberg & Moore [33]. Incidentally, since the Bark scale (Zwicker [126]) is linear below 500 Hz, Hermes & Van Gestel showed that pitch movements in different frequency registers do *not* lend equal prominence when equal on a Bark scale.

The pitch contours as measured by PPR, SHS and AMPEX are presented in figs. 2, 3, 4 and 5, together with the reference pitch contours (corr.). A table with the data is presented in Table 1. Pitch was determined every 10 ms. The data clearly show the improvement in pitch determination over the years. Only a few results deviant from this trend will be mentioned. The number of voiced errors by SHS in 'clean.wav' is quite large due to some low-amplitude contamination at the beginning before the start of the speech signal. Simply because in 'dirty.-wav' the signal values are halved, this error is already less. The detrimental effect of the noise in 'dirty.wav' is fatal for PPR. Observe that SHS is best here, except in the number of voiced errors. Also in 'timit.wav' SHS has the most voiced errors, but in this respect PPR outperforms both SHS and AMPEX. In 'spont.wav' pitch determination is best by SHS, except, again, in the number of voiced errors. Observe the low number of pitch measurement errors of both SHS and AMPEX in the presence of contaminating sound in 'dirty.wav' and 'spont.-wav'. This shows that PDAs of the second and the third generation are very robust against contamination with other sounds.

Table 1: Results of three generations of PDAs to 'clean', 'dirty', 'timit' and 'spont'. The figures show the number of frames.

	'clean.wav'				'dirty.wav'			
	PPR	SHS	AMPEX	corr.	PPR	SHS	AMPEX	corr.
correctly voiced	176	197	196	198	152	179	149	198
pitch correct	164	197	195	198	114	165	148	198
pitch incorrect	12	0	1	0	38	14	1	0
unvoiced errors	22	1	2	0	46	19	49	0
correctly unvoiced	141	112	142	157	131	126	155	157
voiced errors	16	45	15	0	26	31	2	0
	'timit.wav'				'spont.wav'			
	PPR	SHS	AMPEX	corr.	PPR	SHS	AMPEX	corr.
correctly voiced	191	204	204	215	29	33	18	41
pitch correct	157	196	201	215	15	29	18	41
pitch incorrect	34	8	3	0	14	4	0	0
unvoiced errors	24	11	11	0	12	8	23	0
correctly unvoiced	165	136	153	165	149	193	231	237
voiced errors	0	29	12	0	88	44	6	0

5   POSTPROCESSING

All PDAs start with the analysis of a time segment of about 20 to 50 ms. Our perception of pitch in speech, however, is not only derived from local information in the speech signal, but also from what comes before and after. In normal speech, pitch is perceived as a continuous, slowly fluctuating contour, even though the voiced segments can be interrupted by unvoiced segments. The imaginary pitch at the voiceless and thus pitchless, parts are apparently interpolated from what comes before and after. Something more extreme occurs when a coded speech utterance is completely synthesised as if it were unvoiced. Even then one often im-

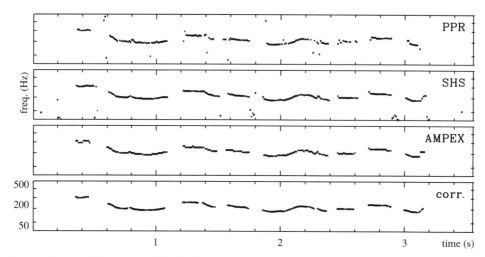

Fig. 2   Results of the various PDAs for the sentence 'clean.wav'.

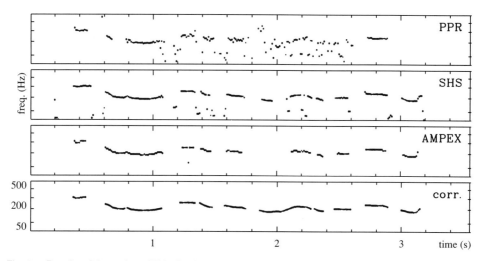

Fig. 3   Results of the various PDAs for the sentence 'dirty.wav'.

agines one perceives a pitch contour, though it is sometimes different from the original. One may listen, for example, to "Whispering Wendy" in the DecTalk text-to-speech system.

Hence, pitch measurements should no longer be considered in isolation. Some restrictions must be imposed on the course of pitch. This will include a prohibition of sudden pitch jumps. Actually, in the displayed pitch contour, pitch measurement errors are most often recognised by discontinuities. Most simple correction algorithms detect them and decide whether they can be resolved by simple harmonic operations on the deviant measurement, e.g., doubling or halving the frequency. Where this is not possible, the original measurements are simply replaced by frequency values interpolated from preceding or following measurements. Many postprocessors operate on this principle.

A more systematic approach is presented by Ney [82,83]. In the PDA that he used, a pitch measurement not only produced one single candidate but also some other candidates which scored less on the basis of the local speech signal. Through these candidates an optimum path

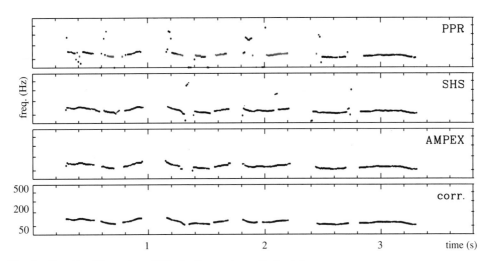

Fig. 4   Results of the various PDAs for the sentence 'timit.wav'.

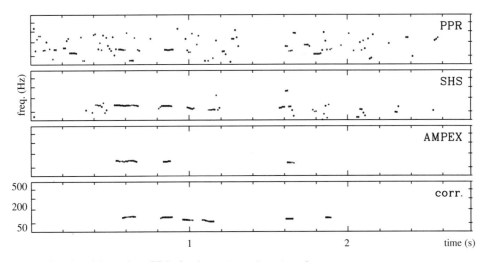

Fig. 5   Results of the various PDAs for the sentence 'spont.wav'.

is selected by dynamic time warping, in such a way that pitch jumps are prohibited. Van Hemert [118] combined this procedure with the harmonic sieve (Duifhuis *et al.* [27]) and showed that many errors, audible in speech synthesis, could be avoided.

Results of applying a simple postprocessor and a dynamic-time-warping (DTW) algorithm to SHS are shown in fig. 6 for 'clean.wav'. Most errors were corrected satisfactorily with these techniques. It should be emphasised, however, that many deviant pitch measurements are not necessarily errors. It happens quite often that, when such an erratic speech segment is listened to in isolation, the very pitch indicated by the PDA is heard. Two situations will illustrate this. The first situation occurs in creaky voices. As has been mentioned above, creak is characterised by clear pitch pulses. Often they are so irregular that no pitch is heard, but creak may also be a consequence of subharmonic vibration modes of the glottis (Titze [117]). This means that the resulting pitch has an exact subharmonic relation to the pitch that the listener expects at these moments. Nevertheless, such subharmonic pitches are often not

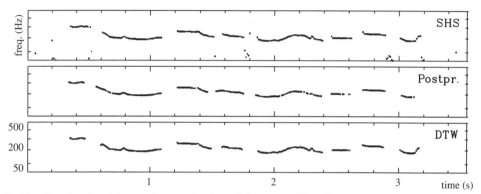

Fig. 6   Results of applying postprocessing to a pitch contour. Note that most errors occurring in
          SHS are corrected by simple postprocessing as well as by dynamic time warping (DTW).

heard, at least not in the context of the whole utterance. Creak is most often perceived as roughness on a continuously perceived pitch contour. However, when listened to in isolation, fragments with creak often have a pitch with corresponds with the pitch displayed by the PDA.

Besides in the presence of creak, where local pitch measurements exhibit sudden breaks and transitions to frequencies lower than expected, it sometimes occurs that PDAs produce intervals at which the estimated pitch equals a higher harmonic. This occurs especially when the second or the third harmonic coincides with the first formant. In many of these cases, listening locally shows that a clearly distinguishable higher harmonic can be heard separately.

Both examples show that the listener has certain expectations about where pitch will be perceived. These expectations can be based on the pitch that is heard before and after. The gender of the speaker can also bring about that pitch is heard at frequencies where it is expected. Looking at a series of pitch measurements then gives the impression of serious errors. This is a difficult problem because, on the other hand, the introduction of sudden pitch jumps in synthesised speech produces an unacceptable result. A similar problem is present in the perception of voicing. Though we do not hear any interruptions in voicing, the correct start of voicing in synthetic speech is very important, e.g., for the quality of stops. Hardly anything is known about the mechanism underlying our perceiving a normal speech utterance as having a smoothly fluctuating, continuous pitch contour. Streaming phenomena, found in the study of auditory scene analysis (Bregman [13]) are of paramount importance here. For want of a quantitative model of these streaming phenomena, it is not yet possible to base the postprocessing of a measured pitch contour on systematic perceptual knowledge.

6   EVALUATION AND CHOICE OF PDAs

The number of published PDAs increases every year. In many cases the authors restrict themselves to presenting positive results for only a few sentences. Only very few PDAs have been properly evaluated for a number of different male and female voices, e.g. Rabiner *et al.* [90], Hermes [45] and Van Immerseel & Martens [119], though none of the authors formulated with what purpose in mind the PDA was developed. Again, a very thorough discussion on the subject is presented by Hess ([48], pp. 133-136, and p. 151).

Two comments will be added to the discussion about the choice and the evaluation of a PDA as presented by Hess [48]. First, PDAs can be used for many different purposes. They can be used for speech coding, speech manipulation, studies of intonation, measurement of voice pathology, cochlear implants, speech enhancement, devices for real-time display of pitch, modelling pitch perception, automatic speech recognition, gender identification and studies on musical performance. Different applications can require different PDAs. For instance, in many cases one only needs to know the pitch, while for other applications, e.g., PSOLA, the position of the pitch pulses must be known. Formant frequencies can most accurately be determined in the closed phase of the glottal cycle, which should therefore be known. For some purposes, very reliable voiced-unvoiced decisions are necessary, while others can do without. Speech segments with creak must sometimes be classified as voiced, sometimes as unvoiced. Various applications require a good performance for speech contaminated with noise. An application to music requires a much more accurate pitch measurement than an application to speech. Finally, a more practical consideration can be whether a PDA has to operate in real time or not.

A second comment is that even a simple form of postprocessing can correct many errors made by a PDA. Sometimes people claim that their PDA is much better than another, whereas closer examination reveals that they differ widely in the amount of postprocessing applied to the unprocessed series of pitch measurements. Such comparison is unfair and only shows that postprocessing is a necessary procedure, particularly in the case of a bad PDA. In comparing the performance of PDAs, each PDA must contain the same amount of postprocessing.

7 PROBLEMS PARAMOUNT IN THE PERCEPTION OF PITCH

In this section some fundamental problems in the study of pitch perception will be formulated. Since it is assumed that the best PDAs will incorporate knowledge of pitch perception, these problems have a direct impact on the implementation of current and future PDAs. Thus, fundamental problems in the study of pitch perception are problems in the measurement of pitch, though it is recognised that PDAs based on this principle can never be used to determine glottal pulses or closed phases in glottal cycles.

7.1 Contributions of harmonics and combination of these contributions

In the pitch theory by Schouten [95] and Schouten *et al.* [96] the human pitch extractor was assumed to derive its information from the temporal fine structure of the high unresolved harmonics. Ritsma [91] and Ritsma & Bilsen [92] confirmed, however, a suggestion by De Boer [23] that pitch was to a large extent determined by the harmonics in the dominant region, i.e. the region of the fourth to the sixth harmonic. Houtsma & Goldstein [51] showed that pitch could arise from only two harmonics of order lower than seven, even if each harmonic was presented to a different ear. Since then, various other attempts have been made to find out to what extent each harmonic contributes to the pitch of a complex tone. Moore, Glasberg & Peters [79,80] measured the influence of mistuning a harmonic on the pitch of a complex tone. Subjects were asked to adjust the frequency of a sine wave to the pitch of the tone. The interpretation of the result was difficult because of great individual differences. The authors could conclude, however, that all harmonics lower than the seventh contributed to pitch, not only the fourth to the sixth, as indicated by the dominant region. Hartmann *et al.* [42] used a different approach. They changed the task of the subjects and asked them to adjust a sine wave not to the pitch of the complex tone, but to the pitch of the separately perceived mistuned harmonic. They concluded that below about 2 kHz, the ability to hear out a mistuned harmonic and adjust a sine wave to its frequency is independent of harmonic number. There were, however, some complicating factors. For instance, a mistuned seventh harmonic was more easily detected at 60 dB than at 30 dB, while the converse was true for the fourth harmonic. And, significantly, the substantial individual differences remained. Darwin & Ciocca [22] studied the effect of onset asynchrony on the contribution of a harmonic to the pitch of a complex tone. They found that the fourth harmonic contributed less to a complex tone when it started 160 ms or more before the remaining harmonics. But, again, significant individual differences were observed.

   In the experiments described above, all harmonics had equal amplitude and only one harmonic was mistuned. This raises two additional questions, very relevant to pitch determination. The first concerns the influence of the amplitude of a harmonic on its contribution to pitch. The second concerns the question of how the contribution of the various harmonics combine. Do they add up, are they multiplied, or what are they? Since no quantitative psychoacoustic experiments have been reported on these questions, no definite answers can be given. In view of the mentioned difficulties in the interpretation of the results with one harmonic, this issue appears to be rather difficult to grasp, especially in the presence of great differences between subjects.

   People who design PDAs simply have to make a choice. As to the relevance of the difference in amplitude of the harmonics, in SHS the lower harmonics are attenuated, which is in line with our decreased sensitivity to lower frequencies. In M&H and AMPEX, the attenuation of lower frequency components corresponds to the mechanical frequency characteristic of the outer and the middle ear. Meddis and Hewitt need this feature to explain the dominant region of pitch perception. Furthermore, in SHS, each harmonic contributes according to its amplitude and not to its power or log-power as originally described by Schroeder [98] and Noll [87]. Informal trials to perform SHS on the basis of the power spectrum led to worse results. The contribution of low-amplitude components was found to be too small. In M&H and AMPEX, the peak value in the correlogram of the auditory-filter outputs determines the contribution of a component, which appears to be leading to good results. Note that the correlogram is a quadratic function, as is its Fourier transform, the power spectrum. In view of the results obtained with SHS, this might not be the best choice. Systematic studies on the importance of these factors are completely lacking, however.

   The second problem relates to the way in which the contributions of the various harmonics are combined. In SHS, M&H and AMPEX, the generated subharmonics are simply added. As to SHS, the frequency at which the resulting subharmonic sum spectrum attains its maximum is the estimated pitch. Besides this absolute maximum, there are very often some additional relative maxima with values which can come very close to the main maximum. In spite of that, no pitch whatsoever is heard at these secondary maxima. This means that the SHS spectrum is not a good representation of the various pitches we perceive. Addition cannot simply be replaced by multiplication, as otherwise the presence of a harmonic with zero amplitude would result in a zero outcome at the desired pitch frequency. Beerends [10] circumvents this problem by substituting every resolved harmonic with a Gaussian-shaped peak, which is zero nowhere. He then introduces subharmonics and combines them multiplicatively. The Gaussian shape of the harmonics and of the introduced subharmonics prevents the occurrence of zeros. In this way his PDA, though never properly tested, appeared to operate quite well for speech signals. The question of how subharmonics combine is further complicated by the finding by Houtsma [52] that analytic pitch becomes stronger for complex tones with spaced harmonics, thus degrading the subject's ability to hear the low pitch of the complex tones. Apparently, the combined contribution of harmonics to pitch depends on their spacing.

   It can be concluded from our results on pitch determination of speech signals that the contribution of individual harmonics should be more or less in agreement with their relative amplitude and that lower harmonics must be attenuated. Within this restriction, much is possible. A PDA can be based both on the addition and on the multiplication of the contributions of the harmonics. What happens in the human pitch processor is largely unknown. We do know, however, that, in actual speech, harmonics can change extremely rapidly and with that, their contribution to pitch. In addition, room acoustics can severely affect the relative amplitudes of harmonics. Apparently, the human pitch processor must be insensitive to rapid changes in the relative amplitudes of the harmonics. Because of this insensitivity, individual differences in the extent to which harmonics contribute to pitch and in how they combine, will not have an important impact on pitch perception in every-day circumstances. In other words, if the aim is to investigate the dependence of pitch on the relative amplitude of the harmonics or how harmonics combine, one should not expect to find strong effects and individual differences are likely to occur.

7.2 Role of unresolved harmonics

An often mentioned problem in modelling pitch perception relates to the role of unresolved, higher harmonics. In its original formulation of the pitch "residue", Schouten [95] and Schouten *et al.* [96] postulated that pitch originated predominantly from the higher harmonics that are not resolved by the auditory periphery. In spite of many later studies which showed that the pitch of a complex tone is almost completely determined by the lower, resolved harmonics, the contribution of the unresolved harmonics could not completely be ruled out (Moore & Glasberg [81], pp. 287-288). This was confirmed by experiments by Houtsma & Smurzynski [54], who showed convincingly that unresolved harmonics contribute to pitch.

Though there is no consistent pitch-perception theory with deals with these unresolved harmonics, third-generation PDAs will probably be in qualitative agreement with the results of Houtsma & Smurzynski [54]. In view of the above-mentioned problems with the studies investigating the contribution to pitch perception of only one resolved harmonic, these models are unlikely to make quantitative predictions on the outcome of experiments like the ones by Houtsma & Smurzynski [54]. Here, it is even more difficult to say something about how the contributions of all these unresolved harmonics combine.

7.3 Variability between subjects

Another important problem in pitch analysis is the variability of the subjects. Here we are not concerned with differences between normal-hearing and hearing-impaired persons, but differences between persons without any hearing complaints. Such differences have already been discussed above in the section on the contribution of harmonics for Moore *et al.* [79,80], Hartmann *et al.* [42] and Darwin & Ciocca [22]. Hartmann *et al.* concluded that the differences found represented "genuine idiosyncratic perceptual effects" (p. 1715). It is hard to say whether this is correct. It is well known that performance in the experimental context of adaptive-forced-choice procedures can vary widely with training level, attention level, motivation, etc. Some researchers have found (*pers. comm.*) that detection thresholds, jnds and d's could change considerably when the financial reward for the subject was made dependent on performance. A very effective measure is to use many subjects simultaneously and to reserve an extra bonus for the best performing subject. These conditions are not fulfilled, at least not reported, in the literature discussed in this paper, but they will certainly have influenced the results presented. My attitude in these matters is then to pay most attention to the best performing subject, because this subject will be the least diverted by experimental circumstances and thus be closest to what is theoretically possible.

In the absence of hearing losses, the idea of individual differences is unattractive. If speech and other sounds are used for communication, a prerequisite is that the communicators perceive the incoming information in exactly the same way. Nevertheless, it cannot be denied that well-defined individual differences exist in sound perception. One of the best known examples is absolute pitch. Musical training will be another important factor in many experimental paradigms. Another difference was found in subjects' tendency to listen "analytically" or "holistically" to a complex tone without a first harmonic (Houtsma & Fleuren [55]). These complex tones varied in whether the virtual pitch or one of the harmonics increased in frequency. If the virtual pitch decreased, one of the harmonics increased and conversely. Houtsma & Fleuren [55] showed that, for low harmonics, most subjects tend to follow the frequency of the moving partial. A small group of subjects consistently followed the virtual pitch, however. For harmonics higher than the sixth, responses were about equally divided between tracking of the moving partial and tracking the virtual pitch.

Without a systematic study of the background underlying these individual differences, it will be very difficult to decide on their impact on the conclusions drawn in many psycho-acoustic studies in which they can be observed. Such studies would need many more subjects than normally used, and consequently, much more training and experimentation. Further-more, I would like to add that studies in animal behaviour usually show results for at least ten animals and often many more. Reporting on the behaviour of only four or five individuals is far below standard.

7.4 Pitch strength, pitch salience?

Another problem with both theoretical and practical implications is the problem of how well a certain pitch is defined perceptually in the presence of other sounds. How strong is the pitch we hear, how "loud"? The problem is that we cannot use the word "loud" here. Loud-ness is a precisely defined concept, for which detailed calculation routines are available (Fletcher & Munson [29]; Zwicker *et al.* [127]; Moore & Glasberg [81]; Glasberg & Moore [33]). In these papers, loudness refers to the whole sound complex and not to the various au-ditory streams we hear. Therefore, the word loudness is not applicable to one single sound source in an auditory image comprising more than one sound. We can assign a loudness value to a whole orchestra, but not to the trumpets or the bassoons. Expressions like "pitch strength" (Hall & Soderquist [38]) and "pitch salience" (Terhardt *et al.* [115]) are used instead. The matter is further complicated, as these words are sometimes used for the uncertainty in *fre-quency* with which pitch is perceived.

The situation is rather unsatisfactory. A simple informal experiment shows that subjects are very well able to match the loudness of a noise source to the amount of noise of a record or a cassette tape, much better than to the loudness of the combined sound as a whole. Actu-ally, in the definition of partial masking, "the reduction in loudness of a test tone in the pres-ence of a masker", it is implicitly assumed that loudness is an attribute of one of the observed sound streams, the test tone and not of the combined sound. It is therefore thought better to assign the attribute loudness to a sound stream in an auditory scene. For other perceptual at-tributes like pitch, duration and timbre, this has always been self-evident.

This affects various applications. If we realise that "loudness" is an attribute of an audi-tory stream, we can ask subjects to match two simultaneous signals in "loudness", or to match a preceding sine-wave or noise sound to one of the streams in a complex sound. This gives us a direct measure of how "loud" we perceive a sound stream, e.g., a higher harmonic, a mis-tuned partial, or a contaminating sound. This can then give us a measure of how well two streams are integrated or segregated (Hermes [46]).

This brings me to a last point, the relation between spectral pitch and virtual pitch. Var-ious other people have already met with some inconsistencies in the concept of virtual pitch (Martens [67]; Hartmann *et al.* [42]). The evidence to distinguish between virtual and spectral pitch is limited (e.g. Hall & Soderquist [39]). In my opinion, there is no reason for distin-guishing between spectral and virtual pitch. Although harmonicity is a very strong cue for perceptual integration, such integration can be incomplete. This means that a harmonic can be heard separately from the other harmonics. Its timbre is then the timbre of a sine wave. There will, of course, be some integration, too, yielding a sound source with the pitch and tim-bre of the complex tone. Listening analytically is then the same as concentrating on auditory objects with the timbre of a sine wave, while listening holistically is all the rest.

This also explains why listening analytically is almost impossible in speech. The first op-tion of the auditory system is integration. Segregation takes time. So, in speech, the system simply does not have the time to segregate the harmonics from each other.

Here, also, if we consider loudness to be an attribute of a stream, this enables us to speak of the loudness of a harmonic and thus determine how much it contributes to pitch. Defined in this way, the louder we hear a harmonic the worse it integrates with the complex, and consequently the less will it contribute to the pitch (and the timbre!) of the complex sound.

7.5 Pitch perception for nonstationary signals

Very little is known about pitch perception of nonstationary signals like speech. Pitch-perception theory is to a large extent based on experiments with signals which are stationary between onset and offset. And even here complications arise. Moore [78] found that frequency resolution becomes less for short tones. Moore *et al.* ([80], p. 481) concluded that, "if we wish to retain the idea that a harmonic sieve is of influence, then we must postulate that the mesh size is large for short-duration tones, and becomes progressively smaller with increasing duration". Furthermore, auditory-filter shapes change with intensity (Glasberg & Moore [33]). For sounds with amplitude and frequency modulation the situation deteriorates further. So what happens in the case of speech is to a large extent unknown. What should astonish us again, is that in the presence of all these uncertainties current PDAs are so reliable for speech.

7.6 Perception of simultaneous pitches

The pitch-determination problem becomes paramount when simultaneous pitches are to be measured. Some early studies showed the importance of pitch as a perceptual cue in the segregation of speech sounds (Darwin [21]; Brokx & Nooteboom [14]; Scheffers [94]). A systematic psychoacoustic study was carried out by Beerends [10]. The study by Scheffers [94] into the perception of concurrent vowels has been further pursued and modelled (Assman & Summerfield [4,5]). Also here, the introduction of Meddis & Hewitt's model appeared to be beneficial (Meddis & Hewitt [76]).

Various systems have now been built to separate concurring speech sound (e.g. Weintraub [121]; Stubbs & Summerfield [109,110]). These systems appear to be able to use pitch information to separate the voices of two simultaneous speakers with widely different pitch ranges, specifically a male and a female voice. In separating voices with pitches crossing each other, they all fail because there is no good algorithm yet to follow one speaker. This would need knowledge of speaker characteristics, one of the most fundamental problems in speech research.

It will be clear that all problems mentioned above for pitch determination in single-speech sounds have a more detrimental effect on the determination of simultaneous pitches. For single-speech sounds, I have already expressed my amazement that many PDAs operate so well, even though we know so little about pitch processing in our central nervous system and about the perception of nonstationary signals such as speech. This lack of knowledge is likely to become fatal when we start to develop PDAs for simultaneous sounds with different (or equal) pitches. Reliable results are only to be expected when we succeed in acquiring systematic knowledge of the perception of simultaneous sounds (Hartmann [41]; Bregman [13]). This knowledge must be integrated into systems which can be tested and further developed. And let me draw attention once again to the first steps made in Sheffield (Cooke [18]).

8 DISCUSSION

The automatic pitch determination of speech signals has made tremendous progress over the last thirty years. Reliable PDAs have been published for most applications involving well recorded speech from a single speaker. In combination with some postprocessing, the error rate will be very low if the proper PDA is selected. The best PDAs are those which combine knowledge of pitch perception with knowledge of the peripheral auditory system. The most difficult problem is the voiced-unvoiced-silence classification. It is hard to predict the direction in which a solution to this problem may be found. We do not know the answer to questions like, when do we hear pitch? We hear voiced consonants, unvoiced consonants, or aspirated consonants, but we do not hear an interrupted pitch contour. The same question can be asked in relation to silence. In stops we do not hear silences, though they are there. Very little is known about the perception of the duration of silent periods in speech.

In conclusion, for well recorded speech signals from a single speaker, pitch determination is no longer very much of a problem. In most cases the correct pitch contour will be obtained. In spite of this, some serious problems remain. There are three important origins for these problems. The first, though perhaps not very important for pitch perception, is that we know very little about the perception of nonstationary signals. The second is that we hardly know anything about the processing of pitch in the central nervous system. The third is that we know very little about the formation of auditory streams. These gaps in our knowledge will become evident as soon as we try to measure the pitch of contaminated speech, pitches of simultaneous speech sounds, repetition pitch (Bilsen [11,12]), edge pitch (Small & Daniloff [105]) and pitches derived from frequency bands with unresolved harmonics.

What then will a PDA of the fourth generation look like? It is hard to tell. It depends on the field of research in which most progress will be made. As mentioned, I expect much from modelling auditory grouping as done in Sheffield. On the other hand, experiments in the central nervous system of animals (e.g. Langner [61]; Langner & Schreiner [62]; Schreiner & Langner [97]) may also give relevant information which could be used in newer PDAs.

For want of knowledge of what will be found in the future, let me give an operational definition. A PDA of the fourth generation will be a PDA which can deal with simultaneous pitches and which can be used for the separation of simultaneous speech sounds, also those with crossing pitch contours.

Acknowledgements: I would to thank Leo Vogten for making the reference pitch contours for 'clean', 'dirty', 'timit', and 'spont', Luc van Immerseel for supplying me with the output of AMPEX to these 'utterances', Berry Eggen for informing me on glottal-waveform reconstruction and Lei Willems for adapting the old parallel processor. Lei Willems and Armin Kohlrausch are additionally acknowledged for their critical comments on the manuscript.

REFERENCES

[1] B.A.R. Al-Hashemy & S.M.R. Taha (1988), 'Voiced-unvoiced-silence classification of speech signals based on statistical approaches', *Applied Acoustics*, **25**, 169-179.

[2] J. Allik, M. Mihkla & J. Ross (1984), 'Comments on "Measurement of pitch in speech: An implementation of Goldstein's theory of pitch perception"' [JASA 71, 1568(1982)], *JASA*, **75**, 1855-1857.

[3] T.V. Ananthapadmanabha & B. Yegnanarayana (1979), 'Epoch extraction from linear prediction residual for identification of closed glottis interval', *IEEE Trans. ASSP*, **27**, 309-319.

[4] P.F. Assman & Q. Summerfield (1989), 'Modeling the perception of concurrent vowels: Vowels with the same fundamental frequency', *JASA*, **85**, 327-338.

[5] P.F. Assman & Q. Summerfield (1990), 'Modeling the perception of concurrent vowels: Vowels with different fundamental frequencies', *JASA*, **88**, 680-697.

[6] B.S. Atal (1968), *Automatic Speaker Recognition based on Pitch Contours*, Dissertation, Polytechnic Institute of Brooklyn, Brooklyn, NY.

[7] B.S. Atal & L.R. Rabiner (1976), 'A pattern recognition approach to voiced-unvoiced-silence classification with applications to speech recognition', *IEEE Trans. ASSP*, **24**, 201-212.

[8] J.G. Beerends & A.J.M. Houtsma (1986), 'Pitch identification of simultaneous dichotic two-tone complexes', *JASA*, **80**, 1048-1056.

[9] J.G. Beerends & A.J.M. Houtsma (1989), 'Pitch identification of simultaneous diotic & dichotic two-tone complexes', *JASA*, **85**, 813-819.

[10] J.G. Beerends (1989), 'A stochastic subharmonic pitch model', in: *Pitches of Simultaneous Complex Tones*, Ph.D. dissertation, Eindhoven University of Technology, 84-100.

[11] F.A. Bilsen (1966), 'Repetition pitch: Monaural interaction of a sound with the repetition of the same, but phase shifted, sound', *Acustica*, **17**, 295-300.

[12] F.A. Bilsen & R.J. Ritsma (1969/1970), 'Repetition pitch and its implication for hearing theory', *Acustica*, **22**, 63-73.

[13] A.S. Bregman (1990), *Auditory Scene Analysis: The Perceptual Organization of Sound*, MIT Press, Cambridge, MA.

[14] J.P.L. Brokx & S.G. Nooteboom (1982), 'Intonation and the perceptual separation of simultaneous voices', *J. Phonetics*, **10**, 23-36.

[15] R. Carlson, B. Granström & I. Karlsson (1991), 'Experiments with voice modelling in speech synthesis', *Speech Comm.*, **10**, 481-489.

[16] D.G. Childers, M. Hahn & J.N. Larar (1989), 'Silent & voiced/unvoiced/mixed excitation (fourway) classification of speech', *IEEE Trans. ASSP*, **37**, 1771-1774.

[17] D.G. Childers & C.K. Lee (1991), 'Vocal quality factors: Analysis, synthesis, & perception', *JASA*, **90**, 2394-2410.

[18] M. P. Cooke (forthcoming), *Modelling Auditory Processing and Organisation*, Cambridge University Press, Cambridge, UK.

[19] J.W. Cooley & J.W. Tukey (1965), 'An algorithm for the machine calculation of complex Fourier series', *Mathematics of Computation*, **19**, 297-301.

[20] W.E. Cooper & Sorensen J.M. (1981), *Fundamental Frequency in Sentence Production*, Springer Verlag, New York.

[21] C.J. Darwin (1981), 'Perceptual grouping of speech components differing in fundamental frequency and onset-time', *Q. J. Exp. Psychol.*, **33A**, 185-207.

[22] C.J. Darwin & V. Ciocca (1992), 'Grouping in pitch perception: Effects of onset asynchrony and ear of presentation of a mistuned component', *JASA*, **91**(6), 3381-3390.

[23] E. De Boer (1956), *On the "Residue" in Hearing*, Ph.D. dissertation, University of Amsterdam.

[24] E. De Boer (1977), 'Pitch theories unified', in: *Psychophysics & physiology of hearing* (eds. E.F. Evans & J.P. Wilson), Academic Press, London, 323-334.

[25] A. De Cheveigné (1986), 'A pitch perception model', *Proc. ICASSP '86*, 897-900.

[26] A. De Cheveigné (1991), 'Speech F0 extraction based on Licklider's pitch perception model', *Proc. Int. Cong. Phonetic Sciences*, **4**, 218-221.

[27] H. Duifhuis, L.F. Willems & R.J. Sluyter (1982), 'Measurement of pitch in speech: An implementation of Goldstein's theory of pitch perception', *JASA*, **71**, 1568-1580.

[28] G. Fant, J. Liljencrants & Q. Lin (1985), 'A four-parameter model of glottal flow', *Speech Transmission Laboratory, Quarterly Progress & Status Report*, **4**, 1-13.

[29] H. Fletcher & W.A. Munson (1933), 'Loudness, its definition, measurement and calculation', *JASA*, **5**, 82-108.

[30] A.J. Fourcin & E. Abberton (1971), 'First application of a new laryngograph', *Medical & Biological Illustration*, **21**, 172-182.

[31] H. Fujisaki & M. Ljungqvist (1986), 'Proposal and evaluation of models for the glottal source waveform', *Proc. ICASSP '86*, 1605-1608.

[32] A. Gerson & J.L. Goldstein (1978), 'Evidence for a general template in central optimal processing for pitch of complex tones', *JASA*, **63**, 498-510.

[33] B.R. Glasberg & B.C.J. Moore (1990), 'Derivation of auditory filter shapes from notched-noise data', *Hear. Res.*, **47**, 103-138.

[34] B. Gold & L. Rabiner (1969), 'Parallel processing techniques for estimating pitch periods of speech in the time domain', *JASA*, **46**, 442-448.

[35] J.L. Goldstein (1973), 'An optimum processor theory for the central formation of the pitch of complex tones', *JASA*, **54**, 1496-1516.

[36] J.L. Goldstein & P. Srulovicz (1977), 'Auditory-nerve spike intervals as an adequate basis for aural frequency measurement', in: *Psychophysics & Physiology of Hearing* (eds. E.F. Evans & J.P. Wilson), Academic Press, London, 337-346.

[37]   F. Grandori (1984), 'Theoretical and experimental analysis of a central optimal processor for pitch of multicomponent inharmonic tones', *Hear. Res.*, **15**, 151-158.

[38]   J.W. Hall III & D.R. Soderquist (1975), 'Encoding and pitch strength of complex tones', *JASA*, **58**, 1257-1261.

[39]   J.W. Hall III & D.R. Soderquist (1978), 'Adaptation of residue pitch', *JASA*, **63**, 883-893.

[40]   C. Hamon, E. Moulines & F. Charpentier (1989), 'A diphone synthesis system based on time-domain prosodic modifications of speech', *Proc. ICASSP '89*, 238-241.

[41]   W.M. Hartmann (1988), 'Pitch perception and the segregation and integration of auditory entities', in: *Auditory Function: Neurobiological Bases of Hearing* (eds. G.M. Edelman, W.E. Gall & W.M. Cowan), Wiley, New York, 623-646.

[42]   W.M. Hartmann, S. McAdams & B.K. Smith (1990), 'Hearing a mistuned harmonic in an otherwise periodic complex tone', *JASA*, **88**, 1712-1724.

[43]   P. Hedelin (1984), 'A glottal LPC-vocoder', *Proc. ICASSP '84*, 1.6.1-1.6.4.

[44]   P. Hedelin (1986), 'High quality glottal LPC-vocoding', *Proc. ICASSP '86*, 465-468.

[45]   D.J. Hermes (1988), 'Measurement of pitch by subharmonic summation', *JASA*, **83**, 257-264.

[46]   D.J. Hermes (1991), 'Synthesis of breathy vowels: Some research methods', *Speech Comm.*, **10**, 497-502.

[47]   D.J. Hermes & J.C. Van Gestel (1991), 'The frequency scale of speech intonation', *JASA*, **90**, 97-102.

[48]   W. Hess (1983), *Pitch Determination of Speech Signals: Algorithms and Devices*, Springer, Berlin.

[49]   W. Hess & H. Indefrey (1987), 'Accurate time-domain pitch determination of speech signals by means of a laryngograph', *Speech Comm.*, **6**, 55-68.

[50]   M.J. Hewitt & R. Meddis (1991), 'An evaluation of eight computer models of mammalian inner hair-cell function', *JASA*, **90**, 904-917.

[51]   A.J.M. Houtsma & J.L. Goldstein (1972), 'The central origin of complex tones: Evidence from musical interval recognition', *JASA*, **51**, 520-529.

[52]   A.J.M. Houtsma (1979), 'Musical pitch of two-tone complexes and prediction by modern pitch theories', *JASA*, **66**, 87-99.

[53]   A.J.M. Houtsma, R.W. Wicke & A. Ordubadi (1980), 'Pitch of amplitude-modulated low-pass noise and prediction by temporal and spectral theories, *JASA*, **67**, 1312-1322.

[54]   A.J.M. Houtsma & J. Smurzynski (1990), 'Pitch identification and discrimination for complex tones with many harmonics', *JASA*, **87**, 304-310.

[55]   A.J.M. Houtsma & J.F.M. Fleuren (1991), 'Analytic and synthetic pitch of two-tone complexes', *JASA*, **90**, 1674-1676.

[56]   M.J. Hunt (1978), 'Automatic correction of low-frequency phase distortion in analogue magnetic recordings', *Acoustic Letters*, **2**, 6-10.

[57]   A. Isaksson & M. Millnert (1989), 'Inverse glottal filtering using a parametrized input model', *Signal Processing*, **18**, 435-445.

[58]   E. Javel & J.B. Mott (1988), 'Physiological and psychophysical correlates of temporal processes in hearing', *Hear. Res.*, **34**, 275-294.

[59]   G.S. Kang & S.S. Everett (1985), 'Improvement of the excitation source in the narrow-band linear prediction vocoder', *IEEE Trans. ASSP*, **33**, 377-386.

[60]   A.K. Krishnamurthy & D.G. Childers (1986), 'Two-channel speech analysis', *IEEE Trans. ASSP*, **34**, 730-743.

[61]   G. Langner (1983), 'Evidence for neuronal periodicity detection in the auditory system of the guinea fowl: Implications for pitch analysis in the time domain', *Exp. Brain Res.*, **52**, 333-355.

[62]   G. Langner & C.E. Schreiner (1988), 'Periodicity coding in the inferior colliculus of the cat I. Neuronal mechanisms', *J. Neurophysiol.*, **60**, 1799-1822.

[63]   J. Lazzaro & C. Mead (1989), 'Silicon modelling of pitch perception', *Proc. Natl. Acad. Sci. USA*, **86**, 9597-9601.

[64]   J.C.R. Licklider (1951), 'A duplex theory of pitch perception', *Experientia*, **7**, 128-133.

[65]   J.C.R. Licklider (1959), 'Three auditory theories', in: *Psychology: A Study of Science. Study 1. Conceptual and Systematic. Vol. 1. Sensory, Perceptual and Physiological Formulations* (ed. S. Koch), McGraw-Hill, New York, 41-144.

[66]   J. Makhoul, R. Viswanathan, R. Schwartz & A.W.F. Huggins (1978), 'A mixed-source model for speech compression and synthesis', *JASA*, **64**, 1577-1581.

[67]   J.-P. Martens (1984), 'Comment on "Algorithm for extraction of pitch and pitch salience from complex tonal signals"' [*JASA*, **71**, 679-688 (1982)], *JASA*, **75**, 626-628.

[68]   Ph. Martin (1981), 'Détection de F0 par intercorrélation avec une function peigne', *Journées d'études sur la parole*, **12**, 221-232.

[69]   Ph. Martin (1982), 'Comparison of pitch by cepstrum and spectral comb analysis', *Proc. ICASSP '82*, 180-183.

[70]   D. McFadden (1988), 'Failure of a missing-fundamental complex to interact with masked and unmasked pure tones at its fundamental frequency', *Hear. Res.*, **32**, 23-39.

[71]   R. Meddis (1986), 'Simulation of mechanical to neural transduction in the auditory receptor', *JASA*, **79**, 702-711.

[72]   R. Meddis (1988), 'Simulation of auditory-neural transduction: Further studies', *JASA*, **83**, 1056-1063.

[73]   R. Meddis, M.J. Hewitt & T.M. Shackleton (1990), 'Implementation details of a computational model of the inner hair-cell/auditory-nerve synapse', *JASA*, **87**, 1813-1816.

[74]   R. Meddis & M.J. Hewitt (1991), 'Virtual pitch and phase sensitivity of a computer model of the auditory periphery. I: Pitch identification.', *JASA*, **89**, 2866-2882.

[75]   R. Meddis & M.J. Hewitt (1991), 'Virtual pitch and phase sensitivity of a computer model of the auditory periphery. II: Phase sensitivity', *JASA*, **89**, 2883-2894.

[76]   R. Meddis & M.J. Hewitt (1992), 'Modeling the identification of concurrent vowels with different fundamental frequencies', *JASA*, **91**, 233-245.

[77]   P. Milenkovic (1986), 'Glottal inverse filtering by joint estimation of an AR system with a linear input model', *IEEE Trans. ASSP*, **34**, 28-42.

[78]   B.C.J. Moore (1973), 'Frequency difference limens for short-duration tones', *JASA*, **54**, 610-619.

[79]   B.C.J. Moore, B.R. Glasberg & R.W. Peters (1985), 'Relative dominance of individual partials in determining the pitch of complex tones', *JASA*, **77**, 1853-1860.

[80]   B.C.J. Moore, B.R. Glasberg & R.W. Peters (1986), 'Thresholds for hearing mistuned partials as separate tones in harmonic complexes', *JASA*, **80**, 479-483.

[81]   B.C.J. Moore & B.R. Glasberg (1986), 'The role of frequency selectivity in the perception of loudness, pitch and time', in: *Frequency Selectivity in Hearing* (ed. B.C.J. Moore), Academic Press, London, 251-308.

[82]   H. Ney (1982), 'A time warping approach to fundamental period estimation', *IEEE Trans. SMC*, **12**, 383-388.

[83]   H. Ney (1983), 'Dynamic programming algorithm for optimal estimation of speech parameter contours', *IEEE Trans. SMC*, **13**, 208-214.

[84]   A.M. Noll (1964), 'Short-time spectrum and "cepstrum" techniques for vocal-pitch detection', *JASA*, **36**, 296-302.

[85]   A.M. Noll (1967), 'Cepstrum pitch determination', *JASA*, **41**, 293-309.

[86]   A.M. Noll (1968), 'Clipstrum pitch determination', *JASA*, **44**, 1585-1591.

[87]   A.M. Noll (1970), 'Pitch determination of human speech by the harmonic product spectrum, the harmonic sum spectrum, and a maximum likelihood estimate', in: *Symposium on Computer Processing in Communication*, (edited by the Microwave Institute), Univ. of Brooklyn Press, New York, **19**, 779-797.

[88]   R.D. Patterson (1976), 'Auditory filter shapes derived from noise stimuli', *JASA*, **59**, 640-654.

[89]   R.D. Patterson (1986), 'Spiral detection of periodicity and the spiral form of musical scales', *Psychology of Music*, **14**, 44-61.

[90]   L.R. Rabiner, M.J. Cheng, A.E. Rosenberg & C.A. McGonegal (1976), 'A comparative performance study of several pitch detection algorithms', *IEEE Trans. ASSP*, **24**, 399-418.

[91]   R.J. Ritsma (1967), 'Frequencies dominant in the perception of the pitch of complex tones', *JASA*, **42**, 191-198.

[92]   R.J. Ritsma & F.A. Bilsen (1970), 'Spectral regions dominant in the perception of repetition pitch', *Acustica*, **23**, 334-339.

[93]   M.J. Ross, H.L. Shaffer, A. Cohen, R. Freudberg & H.J. Manley (1974), 'Average magnitude difference function pitch extractor', *IEEE Trans. ASSP*, **22**, 353-362.

[94]   M.T.M. Scheffers (1983), *Sifting Vowels: Auditory Pitch Analysis and Sound Segregation*, Ph.D. dissertation, University of Groningen.

[95]   J.F. Schouten (1938), 'The residue and the mechanism of hearing', *Proc. Kon. Ned. Akad. Wetenschap.*, **41**, 1086-1093.

[96]   J.F. Schouten, R.J. Ritsma & B.L. Cardozo (1962), 'Pitch of the residue', *JASA*, **34**, 1418-1424.

[97]   C.E. Schreiner & G. Langner (1988), 'Periodicity coding in the inferior colliculus of the cat. II. Topographical organization', *J. Neurophysiol.*, **60**, 1823-1840.

[98]   M.R. Schroeder (1968), 'Period histogram and product spectrum: New methods for fundamental-frequency measurement, *JASA*, **43**, 829-834.

[99]   M.R. Schroeder & J.L. Hall (1978), 'Model for mechanical to neural transduction in the auditory receptor', *JASA*, **55**, 1055-1060.

[100]   S. Seneff (1978), 'Real-time harmonic pitch detector', *IEEE Trans. ASSP*, **26**, 358-365.

[101]   W.M. Siebert (1968), 'Stimulus transformations in the peripheral auditory system', in: *Recognising Patterns* (eds. P.A. Kolers & M. Eden), MIT Press, Cambridge, MA, 104-133.

[102]   W.M. Siebert (1979), 'Frequency discrimination in the auditory system: Place or periodicity mechanisms', *Proc. IEEE*, **58**, 723-730.

[103]   L.J. Siegel & A.C. Bessey (1982), 'Voiced/unvoiced/mixed excitation classification of speech', *IEEE Trans. ASSP*, **30**, 451-460.

[104]   M. Slaney & R.F. Lyon (1990), 'A perceptual pitch detector', *Proc. ICASSP '90*, 357-360.

[105]   A.M. Small Jr. & R.G. Daniloff (1967), 'Pitch of noise bands', *JASA*, **41**, 506-512.

[106]   P. Srulovicz & J.L. Goldstein (1983), 'A central spectrum model: A synthesis of auditory-nerve timing and place cues in monaural communication of frequency spectrum', *JASA*, **73**, 1266-1276.

[107]   H.W. Strube (1974), 'Determination of the instant of glottal closure from the speech wave', *JASA*, **56**, 1625-1629.

[108]   S.S. Stevens (1935), 'The relation of pitch to intensity', *JASA*, **6**, 150-154.

[109]   R.J. Stubbs & Q. Summerfield (1988), 'Evaluation of two voice-separation algorithms using normal-hearing and hearing-impaired listeners', *JASA*, **84**, 1236-1249.

[110]   R.J. Stubbs & Q. Summerfield (1990), 'Algorithms for separating the speech of interfering talkers: Evaluation with voiced sentences, and normal-hearing and hearing-impaired listeners', *JASA*, **87**, 359-372.

[111]   E. Terhardt (1972), 'Zur Tonhöhenwahrnehmung von Klängen. I. Psychoakustische Grundlagen', *Acustica*, **26**, 173-186.

[112]   E. Terhardt (1974), 'Pitch, consonance, and harmony', *JASA*, **55**, 1061-1069.

[113]   E. Terhardt (1979), 'Calculating virtual pitch', *Hear. Res.*, **1**, 155-182.

[114]   E. Terhardt, G. Stoll & M. Seewann (1982), 'Pitch of complex tones according to virtual-pitch theory: Tests, examples and predictions', *JASA*, **71**, 671-678.

[115]   E. Terhardt, G. Stoll & M. Seewann (1982), 'Algorithm for extraction of pitch and pitch salience from complex tonal signals', *JASA*, **71**, 679-688.

[116]   J. 't Hart, R. Collier & A. Cohen (1990), *A Perceptual Study of Intonation: An Experimental Phonetic Approach to Speech Melody*, Cambridge University Press, Cambridge, UK.

[117]   I.R. Titze (1991), 'A model of neurologic sources of aperiodicity in vocal fold vibration', *J. Speech Hear. Res.*, **34**, 460-472.

[118]   J.P. Van Hemert (1988), 'Different time models in pitch tracking', *Proc. Speech '88 (Edinburgh)*, 113-120.

[119]   L. Van Immerseel & J.-P. Martens (1992), 'Pitch & voiced/unvoiced determination with an auditory model', *JASA*, **91**, 3511-3526.

[120] L. Van Noorden (1982), 'Two channel pitch perception', in: *Music, Mind and Brain* (ed. M. Clynes), Plenum Press, London, 251-269.

[121] M. Weintraub (1985), *A Theory and Computational Model of Monaural Auditory Sound Separation*, Ph.D. dissertation, Stanford University.

[122] F.L. Wightman (1973), 'Pitch and stimulus fine structure', *JASA*, **54**, 397-406.

[123] F.L. Wightman (1973), 'The pattern-transformation model of pitch', *JASA*, **54**, 407-416.

[124] D. Wong, J.D. Markel & A.H. Gray (1979), 'Least square glottal inverse filtering from the acoustic speech waveform', *IEEE Trans. ASSP*, **27**, 350-355.

[125] L.C. Wood & D.J.B. Pearce (1989), 'Excitation synchronous formant analysis', *IEE Proc.*, **136**, 110-118.

[126] E. Zwicker (1961), 'Subdivision of the audible frequency range into critical bands (Frequenzgruppen)', *JASA*, **33**, 248.

[127] E. Zwicker, H. Fastl & C. Dallmayr (1984), 'Basic program for calculating the loudness of sounds from their 1/3-oct band spectra according to ISO 532 B', *Acustica*, **55**, 63-67.

Advanced time-frequency representations for speech processing

P. J. Loughlin, L. E. Atlas and J. W. Pitton

1   INTRODUCTION

A common form of processing of acoustic, electronic, and other signals is spectral analysis. In many applications, an estimate of the distribution of signal energy over frequency is desired. From Fourier theory, this distribution is given by the energy spectral density $|S(f)|^2$, in units of energy per unit frequency (e.g. [J/Hz]), where

$$S(f) = \int_{-\infty}^{\infty} s(t)\, e^{-j2\pi ft}\, dt \tag{1}$$

is the Fourier transform of the signal $s(t)$. The energy spectrum is a stationary measure that indicates what frequencies existed in the signal, but not when they occurred. For time-varying (or "nonstationary") processes such as speech, wherein the signal frequency content changes over time, a method to accurately represent this time-varying spectrum is desired. Such is the goal of time-frequency representations. One of the first tools developed to fulfil this need was the spectrogram [42,32].

1.1   What's wrong with the spectrogram?

Since its inception in the mid-1940s, the spectrogram has become one of the preeminent tools for the time-varying spectral analysis of speech. It has provided us with a wealth of information on the nonstationary nature of speech, contributing immensely to our current understanding of speech structure. This success with the spectrographic analysis of speech has also had the circular effect of strongly influencing our expectations of what constitutes a time-varying spectrum; that is, we expect that it should look something like a spectrogram. But is the spectrographic representation of the joint time-frequency characteristics of speech accurate? In many respects, the answer is no. For example, one of the principle uses of the spectrogram is to display the changing formant frequencies of speech. It is expected that it does this accurately, otherwise there would be no validity to quantitative conclusions about the rate of change of the formants. We can indirectly test the accuracy of the spectrographic representation of formant sweeps by measuring the rates from spectrograms of simple, synthetic signals with speech-like characteristics for which we exactly know (*a priori*) the sweep rate.

One such signal to consider is a second-order resonator that linearly sweeps from some frequency f_0 at time t_0 to frequency f_1 at time t_1. Just as a spectrogram peaks along the frequency of a tone or constant frequency resonator, we expect a spectrogram to peak along the "instantaneous frequency" of this sweeping resonator. We would also like this peak to be independent of our choice of window function and size. The instantaneous frequency of this signal is the line in time-frequency given by $\langle f \rangle_t = \beta(t - t_0) + f_0$, where the slope, or sweep rate, is $\beta = (f_1 - f_0)/(t_1 - t_0)$. In order to investigate the accuracy of the spectrogram, we chose a moderate sweep rate ($\beta = 10$ Hz/ms) consistent with formant transition rates seen in diphthongs. The signal was generated by exciting a second-order linear time-varying sys-

Visual Representations of Speech Signals: Martin Cooke, Steve Beet and Malcolm Crawford (eds.)
© 1993 by John Wiley & Sons Ltd

tem, the centre frequency of which swept linearly at the selected rate, with an input pulse train (pulse duration was 0.5 ms) of five uniformly spaced ($T = 10$ ms) pulses. Figure 1 illustrates a narrowband (50 Hz bandwidth) and a wideband (250 Hz bandwidth) spectrogram of this signal, calculated using 40 ms and 8 ms Hanning windows, respectively (the default window lengths for a narrowband and wideband speech spectrogram in the Entropic[1] software package). The vertical axis of each plot is in units of Hz, and the horizontal axis is in seconds.

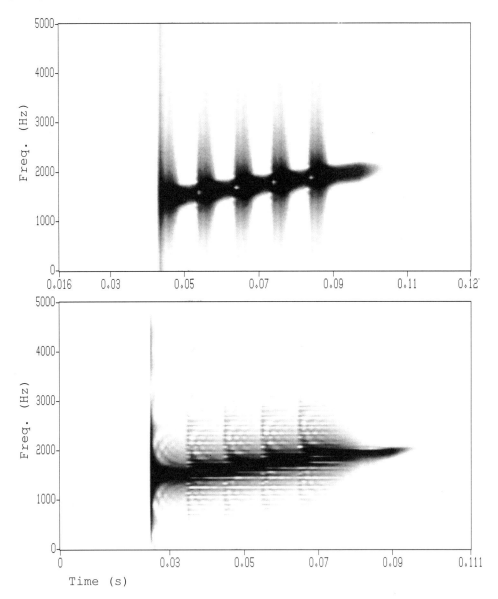

Fig. 1   *top* : wideband spectrogram of a chirping second-order resonator; *bottom* : narrowband spectrogram of the same chirping resonator. Both spectrograms underestimate the true chirp rate of the synthesised signal, and the error is greater (12%) with the narrowband spectrogram. The wideband spectrogram, however, has greater error in its estimate of the instantaneous bandwidth of the resonator.

Measuring the slopes of these spectrograms, we found that the wideband spectrogram underestimated the true sweep rate by 7% and the narrowband spectrogram — which has *better* frequency resolution — underestimated the sweep rate by 12%. These errors are significant: a 12% error in sweep rate is a 120 Hz error in frequency for a sweep over 1 kHz. While these errors may be partially attributed to measurement errors, especially with the narrowband spectrogram where it is difficult to estimate the slope, they nonetheless highlight the difficulty of making accurate estimates of sweep rates from spectrograms. In addition, although the wideband spectrogram yields a better estimate of the instantaneous frequency (sweep rate), it exhibits greater broadening in frequency and therefore gives a poorer estimate of the instantaneous bandwidth (the spread about the estimated slope) than does the narrowband spectrogram. This increased spread can blur (or even hide) other features in a more complicated signal such as speech.

Based on these inaccuracies, which spectrogram — the narrowband or the wideband — is a better representation of the *joint* time-frequency characteristics of this signal (and speech)? For the same signal, we have two very different answers. Similar inaccuracies hold for other signals as well, such as Gaussian-tapered complex linear frequency modulated (FM) chirps [18]. Similar (if not more severe) inaccuracies and discrepancies must also hold for spectrograms of real speech. As an estimate of the true underlying nonstationary structure of speech, the spectrogram is inaccurate, and the degree of inaccuracy depends upon what is measured, the physical properties of the signal, and the size (and type) of window function used.

1.2 Beyond quasi-stationarity

It is important to realise that these trade-offs and inaccuracies are consequences of the *technique* we have chosen to estimate the time-varying spectral features of speech. There is a common misconception that any technique we use to measure a time-varying spectrum will necessarily have these trade-offs in accuracy between time and frequency. Often, the Heisenberg uncertainty principle is inappropriately invoked to support this notion[2]. The trade-offs of the spectrogram, however, are a direct consequence of a quasi-stationary windowing operation that is itself governed by a time/frequency trade-off; namely, the Fourier property that a window and its spectrum cannot both be arbitrarily narrow. But nature did not apply this window to the signal; *we* did in an attempt to estimate the true time-varying spectrum of the signal. There is no fundamental law that prevents us from developing a better technique, that is, one that does not impose its own inaccuracies and trade-offs.

These limitations of the spectrogram apply to other quasi-stationary processing methods as well, such as cepstral coefficients, linear predictive coefficients, and linear, time-invariant filter-banks (indeed, the magnitude-squared output of a linear, time-invariant filter-bank is equivalent to a spectrogram). Any technique wherein the signal is processed via time-invariant methods over *assumed* stationary intervals is by definition quasi-stationary, and subject to the same limitations as the spectrogram. When this assumption is valid, the techniques are quite powerful and useful. But with speech, how can we know with certainty that the assumption is valid? If the only techniques available to assess the nonstationary nature of speech are based on quasi-stationary methods, then we can't! Clearly, at the very least, alternative techniques to the "window, analyse, and shift" approach to speech analysis are necessary to validate the underlying assumptions of current methods[3]. More fundamentally, alternatives to the quasi-stationary approaches to time-varying spectral analysis are required if we wish to accurately represent and understand the *joint* time-frequency characteristics of speech.

1.3 Historical background of time-frequency signal representations

The idea of representing a signal in time-frequency space was put forth by Gabor in 1946 [24], wherein he proposed the expansion of a signal as a double summation of weighted complex modulated Gaussian pulses (or logons). Closely related to the Gabor logon expansion is the spectrogram [42,32] developed at about the same time. Other time-frequency representations that overcome limitations of the spectrogram have been developed (at least one even earlier than the spectrogram!). The first of these was the distribution proposed by Wigner in 1932 [48] as an alternative to the conventional wave equation approach to the study of quantum statistical mechanics. The Wigner distribution was subsequently derived and introduced to the signal processing community by Ville in 1948 [47], and is sometimes referred to as the Wigner-Ville distribution in this community. A thorough analysis of some properties of the Wigner distribution is given in [12]. For the specific case of complex, monocomponent linear frequency modulated (FM) signals, the Wigner distribution is particularly appealing, capable of accurately representing any rate of frequency change. However, when applied to speech (which is multicomponent), the Wigner distribution is extremely difficult to interpret, taking on negative values and indicating energy at frequencies that do not appear in the Fourier energy spectrum. Thus, while the Wigner distribution overcomes the inability of the spectrogram to accurately represent linear FM chirps, it too works well only for certain signals, and has many of its own rather severe limitations. Despite these shortcomings, the Wigner distribution has been used to analyse speech (e.g. [9,46]), although without further postprocessing of the Wigner distribution, the results are quite difficult to analyse and interpret [15]. Invariably, the standard postprocessing methods (e.g. [1,25]) destroy many of the properties that make the Wigner distribution appealing in the first place.

In the years following the classic works of Gabor and Ville, other time-frequency representations were derived (e.g. [41,37,43]), each with its own peculiarities and attributes, and each seemingly unrelated to the others. We note that the motivation behind these approaches to time-varying spectral analysis was not to improve upon the spectrogram, but rather, among other things, to address and develop the fundamental concept of a time-varying spectrum [18]. It was not until 1966, when Leon Cohen [13] introduced the unifying bilinear formulation, that the relationship between all of these seemingly disparate time-frequency representations was made clear. This unified approach allowed instructional comparisons between the many different time-frequency representations to be made (e.g. [23]). More significantly, Cohen's formulation showed how other representations satisfying certain desirable properties could be readily generated.

Direct attempts to preserve many of the desirable properties of the Wigner distribution while simultaneously mitigating its undesirable features led to the development of the exponential distribution by Choi and Williams [11] in 1989 (more commonly known as the Choi-Williams distribution). The significance of their work was that it provided a better understanding of the peculiarities of the Wigner distribution, and presented a sound method to reduce these effects *without sacrificing important properties*. At the same time, Zhao *et al.* introduced the cone kernel time-frequency representation as an alternative to the spectrogram for speech analysis [2,50]. Their contribution — and subsequent work [3-5,33,34] — demonstrated that both the artifact problem of the Wigner distribution and the time/frequency resolution trade-off of the spectrogram could be overcome to yield high-resolution time-frequency displays of speech.

1.4 Overview of the chapter

In this tutorial chapter, we review Cohen's class of generalised bilinear time-frequency representations [13,18] from a speech processing perspective. We begin with the spectrogram, which is perhaps the most easily understood representation (both physically and mathematically), and show how it too can be generalised to the bilinear formulation. Our intent is to introduce in a straightforward manner the general bilinear class to those accustomed to the spectrogram. From this generalisation, it will be seen why the spectrogram has an inherent time/frequency resolution trade-off, and more importantly, how this trade-off can be overcome.

We then proceed with an analysis of some properties proposed for time-frequency representations, and discuss and illustrate their importance from both a theoretical and practical perspective. Examples of four particular bilinear time-frequency representations — the spectrogram, Wigner, Choi-Williams and cone kernel TFRs — are presented for synthetic test signals (tone/chirp combinations) and real speech. It will be seen that no one bilinear TFR performs well for all signals considered, suggesting that different applications can require different TFRs. More fundamentally, it is observed that none of the bilinear TFRs — including the spectrograms — are accurate representations of the joint time-frequency energy distribution of speech.

The chapter closes with a discussion of some of the advances and insights made with the bilinear TFRs, but also offers a critical review of their limitations. It is concluded that, as the bilinear TFRs have overcome some of the limitations of the spectrogram by abandoning the quasi-stationary technique, so too must we move beyond bilinearity to obtain accurate representations of the joint time-frequency energy distribution of speech. An example of our recent results in this area is given.

2   BILINEAR TIME-FREQUENCY REPRESENTATIONS

2.1 The spectrogram and its generalisation

The concept behind the spectrogram is simple: a finite-duration window centred at some time t is applied to the signal to be analysed, and the magnitude-squared of the Fourier transform of the windowed segment is computed. The window is then shifted to a new time t, and another magnitude-squared Fourier transform is computed. Successive window shifts and Fourier transforms thus generate a time-dependent estimate of the energy spectral density.

Mathematically, we can express the sliding window processing of the spectrogram in continuous time and frequency as[4],

$$S(t,f) = \left| \int_{-\infty}^{\infty} s(u)\, h^*(u-t)\, e^{-j2\pi f u}\, du \right|^2 \tag{2a}$$

$$= \left| \int_{-\infty}^{\infty} S(v)\, H^*(v-f)\, e^{j2\pi v t}\, dv \right|^2 \tag{2b}$$

where $*$ denotes the complex conjugate operator, $s(t)$ is the signal, $S(f)$ is its Fourier transform as per eqn. (1), $h(t)$ is a finite-duration unit energy window that tapers to zero (e.g. a Hanning), $H(f)$ is the Fourier transform of the window, and $S(t, f)$ is the spectrogram (in units of a bivariate energy density (e.g. [J/Hz-s])[5]). In speech processing, the window $h(t)$ is typically real; implicit in this processing is the assumption that the signal $s(t)$ is stationary over the duration of the window. If the window duration is too long, this quasi-stationary assumption will be invalid for even moderately nonstationary signals. In these cases, knowledge of the time-varying spectral content of the signal is lost, as can be seen from eqn. (2b): as the duration of $h(t)$ increases, $H(f)$ becomes increasingly impulsive-like, so that the spectrogram approaches the Fourier energy spectrum $|S(f)|^2$ of the signal. The narrowband spectrogram of fig. 1 is an example of this limitation, wherein the spectrogram significantly underestimated the true sweep rate. On the other hand, if the window duration is short enough so that the quasi-stationary assumption is valid for these signals, frequency resolution is degraded because of the Fourier relationship between the window $h(t)$ and its spectrum $H(f)$ (i.e., short windows have broad spectra, and *vice versa*). This effect is seen in the wideband spectrogram of fig. 1.

An alternative view of the source of the time/frequency resolution trade-off of the spectrogram can be formulated by expanding the magnitude-squared expression of eqn. (2a), as such:

$$S(t,f) = \int\limits_{-\infty}^{\infty}\int\limits_{-\infty}^{\infty} s(x)\, s^*(y)\, h^*(x-t)\, h(y-t)\, e^{-j2\pi f(x-y)}\, dx\, dy$$

$$= \int\limits_{-\infty}^{\infty}\int\limits_{-\infty}^{\infty} s\!\left(u+\frac{\tau}{2}\right) s^*\!\left(u-\frac{\tau}{2}\right) h^*\!\left(u-t+\frac{\tau}{2}\right) h\!\left(u-t-\frac{\tau}{2}\right) e^{-j2\pi f\tau}\, du\, d\tau \qquad (3)$$

where in the last step, the linear mapping [31]

$$x = u + \frac{\tau}{2} \qquad\qquad\qquad y = u - \frac{\tau}{2}$$

$$dx\, dy = |J|\, du\, d\tau$$

$$|J| = det \begin{vmatrix} \dfrac{\partial x}{\partial u} & \dfrac{\partial x}{\partial \tau} \\[2mm] \dfrac{\partial y}{\partial u} & \dfrac{\partial y}{\partial \tau} \end{vmatrix} = 1$$

from the xy-plane to the $u\tau$-plane provides a symmetric formulation for the spectrogram.

In expanding eqn. (2a) to this equivalent form, we have mapped the one-dimensional window $h(t)$ of eqn. (2a) to the two-dimensional kernel $h^*(t+\tau/2)\, h\,(t-\tau/2)$ which is a function of time t and lag τ. For a finite length window, for example $h(t) = rect(t/T)$ $(= 0$ for $|t| > T/2$ and 1 otherwise), figs. 2a and 2b illustrate this function in time t, and in time-lag (t,τ), respectively. Note that since $h(t)$ is independent of the lag variable τ, it is unchanging in the lag dimension of the (t,τ) plane (i.e., for any slice through the τ-axis, the result looks the same). Figure 2c illustrates the function $h\,(t-\tau/2)$ in the (t,τ) plane. This function is no longer independent of τ, but is rather shifted by an amount proportional to τ. Thus, for $\tau=\tau_0$, the function $h(t)$ is shifted to the right by $\tau_0/2$, while for $\tau=-\tau_0$, the function is shifted to the left by the same amount; for $\tau=0$, there is no shift, so at this lag value the function is symmetric about $t=0$ (i.e., about the τ-axis). The function $h\,(t-\tau/2)$ thus exhibits a slope of 2 in the (t,τ) plane, as illustrated. Analogously, the function $h^*(t+\tau/2)$ has a slope of -2 in the (t,τ) plane, and the product of the two functions yields the non-zero diamond-shaped kernel support region shown in fig. 2d. This kernel, by eqn. (3), is correlated in time t with the signal function $s\,(t+\tau/2)\, s^*(t-\tau/2)$. The width of the kernel, T, along the t-axis determines the amount of smearing in time that this correlation operation causes: larger T results in a greater loss of time resolution. At the same time, the width of the kernel, 2T, along the τ-axis is inversely proportional to frequency resolution, since this is the dimension in which the Fourier transform of eqn. (3) is performed: larger T improves frequency resolution. It is clear from fig. 2d that, for the spectrogram, the width of the kernel in time t and in lag τ are both proportional to T. Thus, it is impossible to improve frequency resolution (which requires increasing T) without inducing a loss of time resolution in the spectrogram.

Equation (3) can be generalised by replacing the 2-D spectrogram kernel $h^*(t+\tau/2)\, h\,(t-\tau/2)$ with an arbitrary 2-D kernel, $\phi(t,\tau)$. Doing so yields

$$C_s\,(t,f;\phi) = \int\limits_{-\infty}^{\infty}\int\limits_{-\infty}^{\infty} \phi(u-t,\tau)\, s\!\left(u+\frac{\tau}{2}\right) s^*\!\left(u-\frac{\tau}{2}\right) e^{-j2\pi f\tau}\, du\, d\tau. \qquad (4)$$

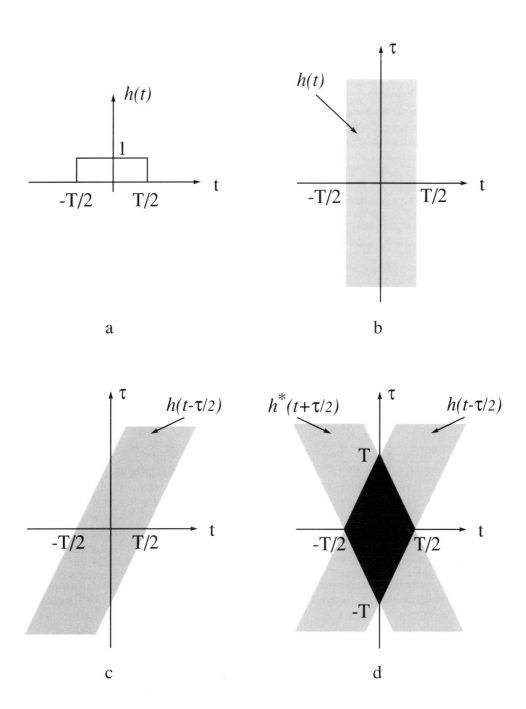

Fig.2 Geometric illustration of the mapping from the spectrogram window $h(t)$ to the spectrogram kernel $h^*(t+\tau/2)\,h(t-\tau/2)$; *a* : A window $h(t)$; *b* : the non-zero support (grey) of $h(t)$ in the (t, τ) plane; *c* : the non-zero support of $h(t-\tau/2)$ in the (t,τ) plane; *d* : the non-zero support (black) of the kernel $h^*(t+\tau/2)h(t-\tau/2)$.

This generalised formulation allows for the construction of an infinite number of bilinear time-frequency representations (TFRs), each of which is uniquely specified by its kernel, $\phi(t, \tau)$ (which, in the bilinear class, is independent of the signal). Equation (4) is a formulation of Cohen's class of generalised bilinear TFRs [13,18].

2.2 Other kernel choices

One goal then, in working with the generalised formulation of eqn. (4), is to find kernels that overcome the limitations of the spectrogram — for example, to find a kernel that avoids the inherent time/frequency resolution trade-off of the spectrogram. Perhaps the most obvious choice one can make for such a kernel is illustrated in fig. 3a. Mathematically, this kernel is given by $\phi(t, \tau) = g(\tau)\delta(t)$ where $\delta(t)$ is the Dirac delta function. This kernel produces the Wigner distribution if $g(\tau) = 1$ for all τ. In practice, $g(\tau)$ is necessarily a finite-duration lag window, and the resulting distribution is referred to as the pseudo-Wigner distribution, where $g(\tau)$ is a product of the form $w(\tau/2)w^*(-\tau/2)$ [12(c)]. Note that for this kernel, time resolution is as sharp as possible because of the Dirac impulse, while frequency resolution can be made arbitrarily fine by increasing the duration T of the lag window.

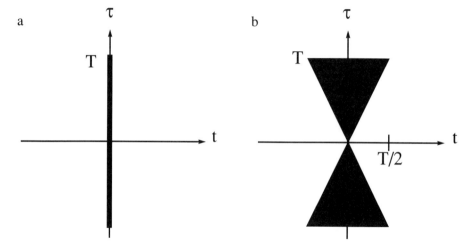

Fig. 3   The non-zero support (black regions) of two kernels that circumvent the time/frequency resolution trade-off of the spectrogram. *a* : the (pseudo) Wigner kernel (for finite T); *b* : a cone-shaped kernel. Note that the width of both kernels along the *t*-axis is independent of T, unlike the spectrogram kernel of fig. 2. Thus, with these kernels, T can be increased to improve frequency resolution without a concomitant loss in time resolution.

A second, although less obvious, choice for a kernel that circumvents the time/frequency resolution trade-off inherent to the spectrogram is illustrated in fig. 3b. For this kernel, the width of the kernel along the τ-axis is again proportional to T (so that frequency resolution is inversely proportional to T), while the width of the kernel along the *t*-axis is independent of T (and is as narrow as the Wigner kernel) so that time resolution is independent of frequency resolution. This kernel is $\phi(t, \tau) = g(\tau)\,rect(t/\tau)$, where $rect(t/\tau)$ is non-zero (and equal to one) only for $|t/\tau| \leq 1/2$. For bounded $g(\tau)$, this kernel is the "cone kernel", [2,50] which has been found to produce time-frequency displays with markedly superior resolution to the spectrogram, while maintaining a desirable "artifact suppression" property[6] similar to that of the spectrogram [3-5,34].

The kernels of fig. 3 are clearly different, and yet both avoid the time/frequency resolution trade-off of the spectrogram. Other factors must therefore be considered in deciding which kernel to use for a particular application. Some of these factors are presented in the form of "desirable" properties (e.g. [12,49,34]) of a time-frequency representation, and it is these properties that dictate the choice of the kernel. To motivate consideration of properties beyond the resolution issue, we consider here a spectrogram and Wigner distribution of some simple signals.

The first of these is a single complex (monocomponent) tone, $s(t) = e^{j2\pi f_0 t}$, for which the Wigner distribution and spectrogram are, respectively,

$$W(t,f) = \delta(f-f_0) \tag{5a}$$

$$S(t,f) = |H(f-f_0)|^2 \tag{5b}$$

where $H(f)$ is the Fourier transform of the spectrogram window $h(t)$. For a two-tone signal $s(t) = e^{j2\pi f_0 t} + e^{j2\pi f_1 t}$, we have

$$W(t,f) = \delta(f-f_0) + \delta(f-f_1) + 2\delta\left(f - \frac{f_0 + f_1}{2}\right)\cos[2\pi(f_0 - f_1)t] \tag{6a}$$

$$S(t,f) = |H(f-f_0)|^2 + |H(f-f_1)|^2 + 2H(f-f_0)H(f-f_1)\cos[2\pi(f_0 - f_1)t]$$

$$\approx |H(f-f_0)|^2 + |H(f-f_1)|^2 \tag{6b}$$

where it is assumed that the spectrogram window $h(t)$ is real and even, and the approximation for the spectrogram holds if the bandwidth of $H(f)$ is much less than the separation of the two tones.

For a single tone, both the spectrogram and the Wigner distribution perform well, although the Wigner distribution is preferred as it directly yields an impulse at the signal frequency and this result is independent of any window function. For the two-tone signal, the Wigner distribution again has impulses at the signal frequencies, but it also indicates oscillating spectral content at the average of the two frequencies. This artifact is a "cross term" that results from the particular nonlinear nature of the Wigner distribution. This cross term causes negative values in the time-frequency plane, thereby hindering an energy density interpretation of the Wigner distribution of this signal. From eqn. (6b), we see that the spectrogram — which is also nonlinear — generates a cross term as well (see [26]), but the placement and amplitude of the spectrogram cross term is such that it does not hinder interpretation of the result. That is, from eqns. (2) and (6b), we note that the spectrogram is always nonnegative, and the cross term is significantly attenuated, and it peaks in the neighbourhood of each signal frequency for sinc-like functions $H(f)$. This latter property is a consequence of the product $H(f-f_0)H(f-f_1)$ coupled with the low-pass, narrowband nature of $H(f)$ [33,34].

3   PROPERTIES

The simple examples above motivate consideration of properties in addition to the time/frequency resolution trade-off. Most, if not all, of the proposed properties stem from the goal of time-frequency representations: to represent the *distribution* of signal *energy* per unit time-frequency. To be a bivariate distribution in the same sense as bivariate distributions in probability, certain fundamental properties must be satisfied. We consider these and other properties next, in the context of time-frequency speech processing.

3.1 Nonnegativity

All true distributions are nonnegative. In signal processing, a TFR is required to be nonnegative if an energy density interpretation in the time-frequency plane is to be valid. As the bilinear TFRs have units of an energy density ([J/Hz-s]), negative values have no physical interpretation. Cohen & Posch [14] have shown that an infinite number of nonnegative time-frequency distributions exist, and they have provided a formulation to generate all members of this class of nonnegative distributions. However, little effort (with the exception of [14,45,35,36]) has been devoted to the synthesis of distributions belonging to the Cohen-Posch class, or to investigating the necessary and sufficient conditions required of the kernel $\phi(t, \tau)$ that ensure nonnegativity for a given signal.

In the class of bilinear TFRs (i.e., those TFRs for which the kernel $\phi(t, \tau)$ is independent of the signal), only the spectrogram is nonnegative for all signals, and it is therefore a *plausible* estimate of the time-frequency energy distribution of speech. Since, to date, most of the advances in time-frequency representations have been in the bilinear class, negative values in a TFR have necessarily been tolerated in order to achieve what some consider to be more important properties (such as the marginals property, to be discussed next). However, the non-negativity property is of paramount importance if the goal is to generate a distribution of energy per unit time-frequency. It is no less important than the marginals property, and sacrificing one for the other does not bring the result any closer to the desired goal.

Nonnegativity guarantees that measurements made from the TFR are sensible. For example, the time-dependent variance in frequency, $\sigma_f^2(t)$, is a likely candidate as a measure of the instantaneous bandwidth of the time-varying speech spectrum, much as the global variance in frequency, σ_f^2, is a measure of the bandwidth of the Fourier speech spectrum $|S(f)|^2$. As a squared real quantity, variance should always be nonnegative. However, TFRs that take on negative values can yield the ridiculous result that $\sigma_f^2(t)$ is sometimes negative [16]. This result does not indicate that the time-dependent variance in frequency is an inappropriate choice as a measure of instantaneous bandwidth. Rather, it shows that a TFR with negative values is fundamentally flawed as a valid distribution of the energy density in time-frequency (this flaw of the other bilinear TFRs does not mean that the spectrogram is the only useful member of the bilinear class, but it does reflect a significant challenge to be met; namely, to find a method to obtain useful, informative nonnegative TFRs that circumvent the quasi-stationary limitations of the spectrogram. A step in that direction has very recently been made in [35]).

3.2 Marginals

As a bivariate distribution of signal energy per unit time per unit frequency, a TFR should accurately reflect the total contribution of temporal and spectral energy. Thus, if we sum the TFR over all time, we should be left with the energy spectral density $|S(f)|^2$, in units of energy per unit frequency (e.g. [J/Hz]). Summing the TFR over all frequency should yield the temporal energy density $|s(t)|^2$, in units of energy per unit time (e.g. [J/s]). These two quantities are the frequency and time marginal, respectively, so named because of their analogy to the marginals of any bivariate distribution. Mathematically, for a TFR $P(t, f)$ that satisfies the marginals, we have:

$$\int_{-\infty}^{\infty} P(t,f)\, df = |s(t)|^2 \tag{7a}$$

$$\int_{-\infty}^{\infty} P(t,f)\, dt = |S(f)|^2. \tag{7b}$$

The time and frequency marginals of the spectrogram are, respectively:

$$\int_{-\infty}^{\infty} S(t,f)\, df = \int_{-\infty}^{\infty} |h(u-t)|^2\, |s(u)|^2\, du \tag{8a}$$

$$\int_{-\infty}^{\infty} S(t,f)\, dt = \int_{-\infty}^{\infty} |H(v-f)|^2\, |S(v)|^2\, dv. \tag{8b}$$

Equation (8a) is readily obtained by integrating eqn. (3), and eqn. (8b) is similarly obtained by integrating the dual frequency formulation to eqn. (3) (which is itself obtained by expanding eqn. (2b) analogously to the expansion of eqn. (2a) in section 2.1). The spectrogram gives smeared versions of the true marginals, a consequence of the quasi-stationary processing of this TFR. Note again the time/frequency resolution trade-off of the spectrogram, as reflected in the marginals: as the duration of $h(t)$ decreases such that $|h(t)|^2$ approaches an impulse, the spectrogram time marginal approaches the desired (true) time marginal, while the spectrogram frequency marginal moves further from the true frequency marginal, and *vice versa*.

What do the marginals imply for time-frequency representations of speech, and why are they important? Equations (8a) and (8b), along with the following figure illustrate their significance. A wideband (250 Hz) spectrogram (fig. 4c) comes closer to yielding the correct time marginal, while a narrowband (50 Hz) spectrogram (fig. 4b) yields a better estimate of the true frequency marginal. As representations of the joint time-frequency characteristics of

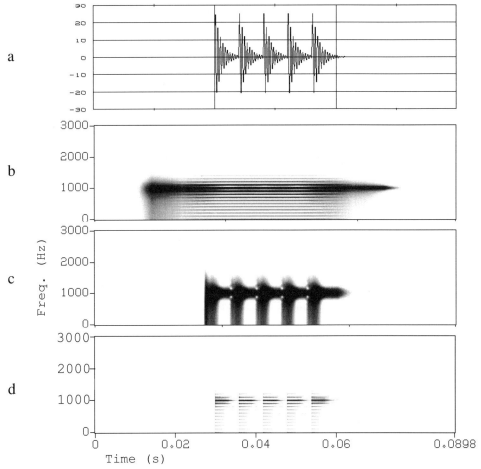

Fig. 4   *a* : time waveform of a synthetic second-order resonator; *b* : narrowband spectrogram; *c* : wideband spectrogram. Which spectrogram is a better representation of the joint time-frequency characteristics of the signal? Paradoxically, both are, but neither is — see text for details. *d* : a joint, nonnegative time-frequency distribution that satisfies the marginals.

the synthetic resonator of fig. 4a, which of the two spectrograms is more accurate? Paradoxically, both are, but neither is. The speech community has long recognised that, taken together, a wideband and narrowband spectrogram complement each other, with each providing different information about the time-frequency characteristics of speech. Indeed, the two have even been combined in an effort to form one image of the joint time-frequency characteristics of speech [10] (the combined picture, however, is still an inaccurate joint representation because it does not satisfy the marginals). As with the synthetic resonator above, the periodic nature of voiced speech has both temporal and spectral characteristics, but a single spectrogram can only approximate these features either in time or in frequency, but not both simultaneously. Imposing the marginal conditions on a distribution, along with nonnegativity, ensures that these features will be jointly and accurately represented, without a concomitant sacrifice in either time or frequency resolution, as illustrated by the joint time-frequency distribution of fig. 4d. This distribution was generated using the method presented in [35,36], and it satisfies the marginals and is nonnegative; we will return to this class of distributions in section 5.

To reflect the importance of the two previous fundamental properties of true distributions, namely nonnegativity and the correct marginals, TFRs that are nonnegative and that satisfy the marginals have been called "proper" time-frequency distributions [14,35]. None of the bilinear TFRs are proper for every signal. As demonstrated by fig. 4d and later in this chapter, proper time-frequency distributions do exist [14], and they more accurately reflect the spectro-temporal characteristics (e.g., energy density, amplitude fluctuations) of signals than do spectrograms (which are always nonnegative, but never proper) [35,36].

3.3 Finite support

If the speech signal is zero over some time interval, then the TFR should also be zero over this interval. Likewise, if the speech spectrum is zero over some frequency band, then the TFR should be zero over this band as well. A TFR exhibiting this behaviour is said to have "strong finite support" in time and frequency, respectively [19,33,34]. Nonnegativity and the correct marginals together guarantee strong finite support [14], although the converse is not true. Strong finite support is a property of all true multivariate distributions, in that a multivariate distribution (e.g. $P(x, y)$) is zero everywhere its marginals ($P_y(x)$, $P_x(y)$) are zero [40].

Classically, finite support has been defined to mean that if a signal is of finite extent in time or frequency, the TFR should have the same finite extent in time or frequency [12(c)]. This classical support property is weaker than strong finite support, as illustrated in fig. 5. Classical (or "weak") finite support does not guarantee strong finite support; however, strong finite support does ensure weak finite support [33,34]. Neither the spectrogram nor the Wigner distribution satisfy strong finite support [17,33,34]. The Wigner distribution does, however, satisfy weak finite support, and a narrowband spectrogram can loosely approximate strong finite frequency support (at the expense of time support); the opposite is true of a (very) wideband spectrogram. The cone kernel TFR was designed to overcome this trade-off of the spectrogram by imposing the properties of classical finite time support, spectral enhancement and cross term attenuation on the kernel [50].

It is important to realise that strong finite support does not mean signal frequencies will appear in the TFR only during those times they actually existed in the signal [34]. Consider the correlationless time-frequency distribution given by[7] $|s(t)|^2 |S(f)|^2$. This distribution clearly satisfies strong finite support — it is zero everywhere the signal or its spectrum are zero — but it does not provide any information as to when signal frequencies actually occurred in the signal. This example demonstrates that, from a time-frequency signal processing framework, other constraints in addition to nonnegativity and the marginals — which together guarantee strong finite support — must be imposed to measure the correlations between

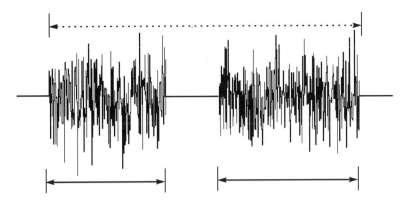

Fig. 5   For the signal above, which consists of two finite-duration bursts and is zero everywhere else, the dashed line delimits the non-zero support of a TFR with weak finite time support. The solid lines delimit the non-zero time support of a TFR with strong finite time support. Note that strong support ensures weak support, but the converse is not true. The analogies are the same for strong finite frequency support and weak finite frequency support.

time and frequency. Considerable work lies ahead in the quest to understand the "local energy" and local time-frequency correlations of time-frequency distributions, and to discover the necessary and sufficient constraints that ensure the accurate representation of these local characteristics.

3.4 Artifact suppression

Returning to eqn. (6), we recall that a significant difference between the spectrogram and the Wigner distribution is in the location and amplitude of the cross term. The major reason that the Wigner distribution has seen little successful application in the time-frequency processing of speech is because of its very poor cross term properties: it is often extremely difficult (if not impossible) to tell whether one is viewing an actual speech feature or an artifactual cross term in the Wigner speech display. Often the view is taken that we would like to find a kernel that yields the Wigner distribution result without all of its problematic cross terms — in effect, we would like to be able to "erase" the oscillating cross term from eqn. (6a), for example. While we can certainly do this (at least for this case), it is important to realise that the result would not be an accurate reflection of the joint time-frequency energy density.

To see why this is so, consider again the complex two-tone signal given earlier. For this signal, the temporal energy density is

$$|s(t)|^2 = 2 + 2\cos\left[2\pi\left(f_0 - f_1\right)t\right]. \tag{9}$$

Note the oscillatory nature of this energy density, much the same as that of the cross term in eqn. (6). As one of the requirements of a TFR is that it should satisfy the time marginal (and thereby accurately reflect the temporal energetic characteristics of the speech signal), this oscillatory nature of the temporal energy density must be reflected in the TFR. Therefore, we really don't want to *remove* the cross term of eqn. (6a), but rather, we want to *move* it to appear only at the true signal frequencies [34], much as the spectrogram of eqn. (6b) can for sinc-like functions $H(f)$. A TFR satisfying these conditions for the complex two-tone signal is

$$P(t,f) = \left(\delta\left(f - f_0\right) + \delta\left(f - f_1\right)\right)\left(1 + \cos\left[2\pi\left(f_0 - f_1\right)t\right]\right). \tag{10}$$

Both the Wigner distribution of eqn. (6a) and the TFR of eqn. (10) have an oscillatory cross term. However, the cross term of the Wigner distribution is like an artifact, appearing at locations in time-frequency inconsistent with the underlying physics of the signal. These artifactual cross terms hinder interpretation of the result. Thus, a desirable property of a physically meaningful TFR is that it suppress *artifactual* cross terms. Traditionally, the view has been that to obtain better interpretability of a TFR, cross terms need to be attenuated, much the way the spectrogram attenuates them, but without sacrificing other properties such as the marginals or finite support (e.g. [11,50,27]). However, the cross terms contain important information, such as relative phase relationships between multiple signal components [27]. It is therefore important to distinguish between suppressing artifacts and universally attenuating cross terms: eqn. (10) has cross terms that are consistent with the physics of the signal and a joint time-frequency energy density interpretation; eqn. (6a) does not, and it is these kinds of artifacts we wish to prevent. By this distinction, artifacts are thus misplaced cross terms. One way to effect artifact suppression then, is to dictate *placement* of the cross terms via appropriate kernel constraints. Recent work in this regard [33,34] has given sufficient conditions on the kernel to achieve desirable cross term placement, and has shown that both the spectrogram and the cone kernel TFRs have analogous cross term placement properties.

To some, the oscillatory nature of the TFR of eqn. (10) may be troubling, and they may conclude that they do not want a "proper" TFR[8] after all, but prefer to see a non-oscillating impulse at each of the signal frequencies. We point out that this desired non-oscillatory response for the two-tone example can be obtained from the proper TFR via the time-conditional distribution. Specifically,

$$P(f \mid t) \equiv \frac{P(t,f)}{P_f(t)} = \frac{1}{2} (\delta(f-f_0) + \delta(f-f_1)) \tag{11}$$

where $P_f(t)$ is the time marginal of $P(t,f)$, given by eqn. (9) for the two-tone signal. Note that if $P(f \mid t)$ is what we really wish to obtain, then what we are after is the *conditional* time-frequency energy density, which can be obtained from a proper joint distribution. The time-conditional distribution would not show the temporal amplitude characteristics of the speech signal, but (ideally) it would accurately track the time-varying frequencies of speech. For finite energy, constant frequency signals, it is reasonable to expect that the "instantaneous energy spectrum" $P(f \mid t)$ is at least proportional to the energy spectral density $|S(f)|^2$.

A second point regarding the oscillatory nature of the TFR of eqn. (10) is that even the spectrogram will exhibit an oscillatory response for the two-tone signal, if the spectrogram window $h(t)$ is chosen such that its spectrum $H(f)$ is approximately constant (and equal to one) for all frequencies. Thus, a (very) wideband spectrogram approximately yields eqn. (9), while a narrowband spectrogram approximately yields eqn. (6b). This behaviour is quite familiar to the speech community, and is one of the trade-offs they endure. This trade-off should not exist with a proper TFR. A proper TFR should jointly reflect the temporal *and* spectral features of the signal. If we are interested in concentrating on frequency changes without the distraction of temporal amplitude fluctuations, then all we need to do is compute the time-conditional distribution from a proper joint distribution (see [35], for example).

4   EXAMPLES

This section serves to illustrate the similarities and differences between four different bilinear TFRs of synthetic signals and speech. The TFRs considered are the spectrogram, the Wigner, the Choi-Williams, and the cone-kernel TFR. Of these, only the spectrogram is nonnegative for the signals considered; nonetheless, despite the lack of a valid energy density interpretation, the other TFRs can be useful and informative beyond the spectrogram in many cases.

The properties of each TFR are readily determined from its kernel [11,12(c),18,33,34]. The continuous time-lag kernels for the four TFRs considered in this section are:

$$\phi_{sg}(t, \tau) = h\left(t + \frac{\tau}{2}\right) h\left(t - \frac{\tau}{2}\right) \tag{12a}$$

$$\phi_{w}(t, \tau) = \delta(t) \tag{12b}$$

$$\phi_{cw}(t, \tau) = \sqrt{\frac{\alpha}{4\pi\tau^2}}\, \exp\left(-\frac{\alpha}{4}\left(\frac{t}{\tau}\right)^2\right) \tag{12c}$$

$$\phi_{ck}(t, \tau) = rect\left(\frac{t}{\tau}\right) \tag{12d}$$

for the spectrogram, Wigner, Choi-Williams and cone-kernel TFRs, respectively, where the chosen window function *h(t)* in eqn. (12a) is equivalent to that in eqn. (2a). Neither the cone-kernel TFR nor the spectrogram satisfy the marginals, while the Wigner and Choi-Williams TFRs do. Conversely, the artifact suppression properties of the spectrogram and the cone-kernel are superior to those of the Wigner and Choi-Williams TFRs. None of the four TFRs satisfies strong finite time support, but the Wigner and cone-kernel TFRs do satisfy weak finite time support. In the frequency dimension, the cone-kernel TFR approximates strong finite frequency support, and the Wigner TFR satisfies weak finite frequency support. The parameter α of the Choi-Williams TFR can be adjusted such that this TFR approximately satisfies weak finite support, at the expense of artifact suppression. Table 1 summarises these properties of the four TFRs.

Table 1: Properties of four bilinear TFRs.

TFR	Non-negative	Marginals	Time Support	Frequency Support	Artifact Suppression
spectrogram	YES	NO[†]	NB/WB trade-off[†]	NB/WB trade-off[†]	GOOD
Wigner	NO	YES	WEAK	WEAK	VERY POOR
Choi-Williams	NO	YES	VARIABLE[‡]	VARIABLE[‡]	VARIABLE[‡]
cone-kernel	NO	NO	WEAK	~STRONG[§]	GOOD

† The spectrogram does not satisfy the marginal or support conditions, but exhibits a narrowband/wideband trade-off between time and frequency.

‡ The parameter α of the Choi-Williams kernel can be adjusted to affect a trade-off between artifact suppression and approximate weak finite support. Small α ($\alpha < 1$) yields fair artifact suppression, but poor support.

§ The cone-kernel TFR does not exactly satisfy strong finite frequency support, but it does closely approximate it [33], [34].

4.1 Methods

Since computations were done on a digital computer using digitised signals, discrete TFRs were necessarily implemented. For the spectrograms, the Entropic Signal Processing spectrogram software was used, with an 8 ms Hanning window and a 256 point fast Fourier transform (FFT) for the wideband (250 Hz) spectrograms. Narrowband (50 Hz) spectrograms used a 40 ms Hanning window and a 1024 point FFT. For the other three bilinear TFRs, custom software was used to compute the discrete TFRs. The continuous kernels were sampled in time *t* and lag τ to obtain discrete kernels $\phi\,[n, k]$, which were then used to compute a discrete TFR analog to the continuous TFR for each of (12b-d) above. The discrete Fourier transform analog to the Fourier transform in lag τ of eqn. (4) was calculated using a 256 point FFT in discrete lag k, with a 256 point discrete Hanning lag window $g[k]$ applied to the discrete kernel $\phi\,[n, k]$. The time-correlation integral of eqn. (4) was implemented in discrete time via a correlation sum over n. Detailed discussions on the implementation and properties of discrete TFRs can be found in [12(b),39,28].

In the case of speech, TFRs were computed from the preemphasised speech signals. Standard first-difference preemphasis was applied to the digitised speech signals to compensate for high-frequency roll-off, via the digital filter $G\,(z)\;=\;1-Az^{-1}$, with $A\;=\;0.94$.

Only the positive frequencies of the spectrum were displayed, from 0 Hz to half the sampling frequency. For those bilinear TFRs that generate negative amplitude values (i.e., all but the spectrogram), these values were set to zero for display purposes. All of the TFR displays used a log-amplitude (dB) grey scale mapping, where the dynamic range of each plot was chosen in accordance with the plotting package[9] specifications to obtain the "best" display for each representation; maximum intensity is black.

4.2 Pulsed Tones

The first nonstationary signal we consider is illustrated in fig. 6. The signal consists of real finite duration tones at different times and frequencies. Two tones turn on simultaneously for 15 ms, one at 1 kHz and a second at 7 kHz. Both tones then turn off for 5 ms. The lower frequency tone then resumes, followed 5 ms later by the 7 kHz tone. After another 15 ms, both tones again cease. We expect that a TFR be zero prior to the start of the signal, after the end of the signal, and during the 5 ms zero gap when both tones are off; that a TFR indicate significant spectral content at only 1 kHz and 7 kHz during the first and last 15 ms of the signal; and that a TFR indicate significant spectral content at only 1 kHz for the first 5 ms following the 5 ms zero gap. An examination of the results in fig. 6 reveals that none of the displayed TFRs exactly matches our expectations, although some do come closer than others. (The vertical dotted and dashed lines delineate time intervals of interest.) The narrowband spectrogram is particularly poor, as is the Wigner distribution with all of its artifactual cross terms. The Choi-Williams TFR attenuates these cross terms, and spreads them over the time-frequency plane, thereby sacrificing weak finite support (but not the marginals). None of the representations preserves strong finite time support (all are non-zero over at least part of the 5 ms zero gap).

4.3 Tone-chirp-tone

Next we consider a signal that linearly ramps in frequency from a steady tone at 1 kHz to a second steady tone at 7 kHz; the ramped transition occurs in 3 ms, so that the sweep rate is 2 kHz/ms. Figure 7 displays the results for the four bilinear TFRs of Table 1. The narrowband spectrogram (fig. 7b) exhibits substantial broadening in frequency and amplitude attenuation during the sweep, and the time duration is much greater than that of the signal. The wideband spectrogram (fig. 7c) does better, although there is still significant frequency broadening during the transition, and the time duration is still greater than that of the signal. The Wigner TFR (fig. 7d) has no frequency broadening during the transition and the time duration of the Wigner result is the same as that of the signal. However, some artifacts are present during the transition, and at 0 and 8 kHz (visible as an oscillatory horizontal black/white line along the top and bottom of the image). The Choi-Williams result (fig. 7e), computed with $\alpha=10$, attenuates the artifacts of the Wigner result and spreads them over the time-frequency plane. As such, it sacrifices the weak support property of the Wigner distribution, but not its marginal property. The transition shows some frequency broadening, but this is still less than the broadening seen in either spectrogram. The cone-kernel TFR (fig. 7f) has the weak time support property of the Wigner result, and yields very narrow spectral lines at

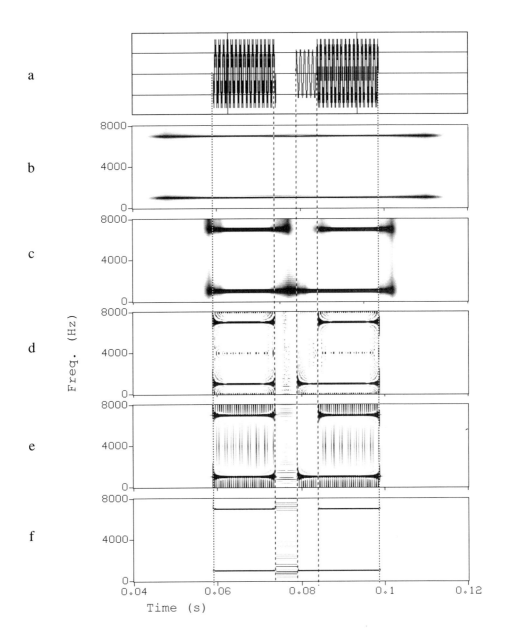

Fig. 6   *a* : Pulsed multi-tone signal; *b* : narrowband spectrogram; *c* : wideband spectrogram;
d : Wigner TFR; *e* : Choi-Williams TFR (α=10); *f* : cone kernel TFR. Vertical dotted lines
delimit the global time support of the signal, while vertical dashed lines delimit local
regions of interest. In particular, none of the TFRs are zero over the 5 ms zero gap in
the signal, and only the Wigner and cone kernel TFRs are zero outside the global time
support of the signal (the Choi-Williams TFR comes very close to satisfying this "weak
time support" property for this choice of α). Note the oscillatory artifactual cross terms of
the Wigner TFR at 0, 4 and 8 kHz, and those of the Choi-Williams TFR, which are
attenuated and spread over the time-frequency plane. None of these TFRs does a
perfect job representing this signal in time-frequency.

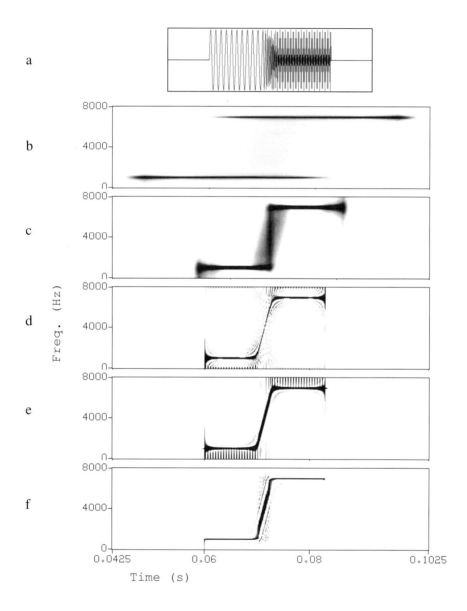

Fig. 7 *a* : tone-chirp-tone signal, where the chirp sweeps 6 kHz in 3 ms; *b* : narrowband spectrogram; *c* : wideband spectrogram; *d* : Wigner TFR; *e* : Choi-Williams TFR (α=10); *f* : cone kernel TFR. The Wigner TFR exhibits no broadening in frequency during the sweep, but does have artifactual cross terms during this transition, and at 0 and 8 kHz. The Choi-Williams TFR has greater broadening during the transition, but this broadening is far less than that seen with either spectrogram. The Choi-Williams TFR also attenuates the cross terms of the Wigner TFR, and spreads them between the signal tones. The cone kernel TFR has very narrow spectral lines at the signal tones, and exhibits about the same frequency broadening as the Choi-Williams TFR during the transition. It also exhibits artifactual cross terms during this transition. None of these TFRs ideally represents this signal.

the tones. The transition exhibits about the same broadening as the Choi-Williams result, but with artifacts extending from the main lobe of the chirp. In short, none of the four bilinear TFRs in either fig. 6 or 7 is ideal, and choosing one over the other is often a matter of personal preference, depending upon the "desirable" properties one wishes to fulfil (although in both figures, the narrowband spectrogram is a particularly poor representation of the time-frequency variations of these signals).

4.4 Speech

We move now to a speech example. Figure 8 illustrates (top to bottom) the time waveform of the utterance "...Susan ca(n't)..." (the 'clean.syl' from the Sheffield data set, downsampled to 10 kHz), followed by a narrowband spectrogram, a wideband spectrogram, the Wigner TFR, the Choi-Williams TFR ($\alpha=10$), and the cone-kernel TFR. With the exception of the wideband spectrogram, the remaining TFRs resolve (to varying degrees of success) the individual harmonics of the formant frequencies. Of the six representations, the best resolution of formants and harmonics is obtained with the cone-kernel TFR in fig. 8f, although the level of some of the harmonics is below the grey level threshold such that they do not appear in the display (compare with the narrowband spectrogram). Unlike a narrowband spectrogram, the cone kernel achieves this improved frequency resolution *without sacrificing time resolution*. This enhanced frequency resolution of the cone kernel results from a lateral inhibition property of the kernel in the frequency dimension [50]. The cross term artifacts of the Wigner TFR (fig. 8d) obliterate the harmonic structure above the first formant in the voicing of "Susan," and all of the harmonic structure in the voiced section of "ca...". The Choi-Williams TFR (fig. 8e) preserves the marginals and reduces these artifacts sufficiently so that more of the harmonic structure of the formants is discernible.

5 BEYOND BILINEARITY

5.1 Shortcomings of the bilinear class of TFRs

The preceding examples demonstrate that limitations of the spectrogram can be overcome by abandoning the quasi-stationary processing of this technique via appropriate kernel selection for the generalised bilinear time-frequency formulation of eqn. (4). Invariably, however, each of the "improved" bilinear TFRs has its own shortcomings. Are these TFRs really any better than the quasi-stationary spectrogram approach? The answer depends on how we quantify "better." For example, recall the opening example of the introduction, wherein it was demonstrated that it is difficult to make accurate measurements of the sweep rate of chirped resonators from spectrograms (the accuracy of the measurements is strongly influenced by the chosen window). The accuracy of the Wigner distribution is much better for this signal. Our measurements indicated an error in the slope of less than 2% (fig. 9); for monocomponent Gaussian-tapered complex linear FM signals (i.e., no resonating amplitude modulation), the Wigner result is perfect (see [18]). However, the Wigner TFR comes with its own severe limitations when applied to speech (i.e., artifactual cross terms) which tend to seriously detract from the improved sweep rate accuracy.

Have the bilinear TFRs provided us with new information about speech that is difficult or impossible to see with spectrograms? The answer is yes. A concrete example of this is given in [4], wherein the cone kernel TFR shows that even over a single pitch period, voiced speech exhibits nonstationarities (in the form of a "spectral peak splitting" observed in the first formant). This peak splitting effect is a manifestation of phase shifts in the signal [38,4], which in voiced speech are probably induced by glottal function. Whether this information is of any importance in speech analysis depends upon the ultimate goal of the analysis. If the goal is to achieve a robust input representation for automatic speech recognition across different speakers, then resolving these phase shifts is arguably detrimental to classifier performance, since glottal function can vary drastically from speaker to speaker for the same

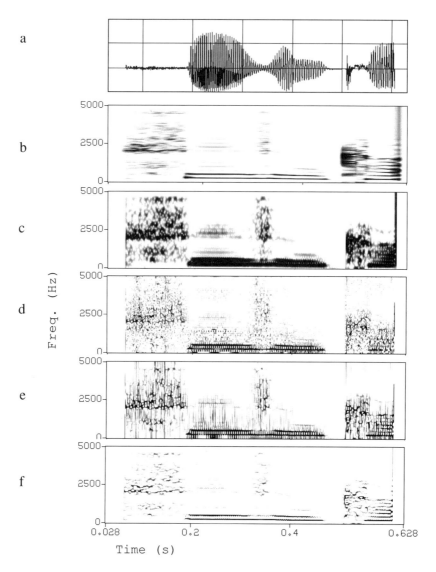

Fig. 8   *a* : speech utterance "...Susan ca(n't)..." from the ESCA Workshop database; *b* : narrowband
spectrogram; *c* : wideband spectrogram; *d* : Wigner TFR; *e* : Choi-Williams TFR (α=10);
f : cone kernel TFR. The cone kernel TFR exhibits frequency resolution on par with the
narrowband spectrogram, but without a concomitant loss of time resolution — note that the
cone kernel result is of the same duration as the speech signal. The Wigner and Choi-
Williams TFRs have better frequency resolution than the wideband spectrogram, but their
artifactual cross terms can obscure information; this problem is more severe with the Wigner
TFR.

utterance. However, if the goal is to achieve a greater fundamental understanding of speech
production, or to determine what cues are important for automatic *speaker* identification, then
this information might be important and useful.

Are the bilinear TFRs better than the spectrogram in that they come closer to yielding
nonnegative distributions without a time/frequency resolution trade-off? Regrettably, no. In

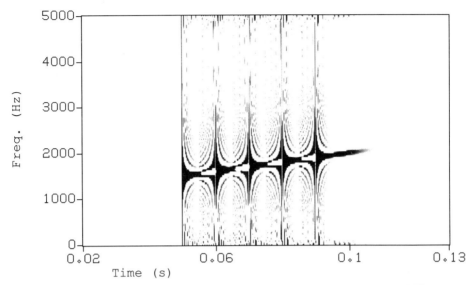

Fig. 9   The Wigner TFR of the chirped resonator example from the introduction. This TFR more accurately estimates the true slope of the sweep rate than the spectrograms of fig. 1. The Wigner result, however, has other problems, such as significant artifactual cross terms and negative values (clipped to zero for display purposes). With real speech, these effects overwhelm the display, thereby detracting from the improved accuracy in sweep tracking. The time axis is different from spectrograms of fig. 1 because of window offsets with the spectrograms; the displayed durations, however, are the same.

the class of bilinear TFRs, only the spectrogram is guaranteed to be nonnegative for all signals. If we are thus unwilling to consider TFRs outside the bilinear class, we are stuck with the spectrogram — and its limitations — as the choice to guarantee nonnegativity in all situations. The negativity of the other bilinear TFRs is their greatest flaw. Speech does not generate "negative energy." How, then, are we to interpret these TFRs? What physical significance can we attach to the amplitude (grey scale) values of these TFRs? Like the spectrogram, they have units of an energy density, but they clearly cannot be accurately measuring the joint time-frequency energy distribution of speech. Arguably, in sacrificing the nonnegativity of the spectrogram, one has gone from reasonable to ridiculous in terms of generating a time-varying energy spectral density of speech.

One of the ultimate goals is to develop TFRs that are nonnegative, satisfy the marginals, have strong support in time and frequency, have artifact suppression at least as good as the spectrogram, and that accurately measure the "local" time-frequency energy density of speech. None of the bilinear TFRs — including the spectrogram — achieve this goal, and *none ever will* because no bilinear TFR can satisfy the marginals and be nonnegative for all (speech) signals, as proved by Wigner in 1971 [48]. To achieve this goal, we must move beyond the bilinear class of TFRs. Efforts in that direction have only recently been undertaken [29,30,6,21,7,8,35,36].

5.2 A step closer

One such effort is reported in [35], and we briefly summarise the authors' work, beginning with the addition of their new "minimum cross-entropy time-frequency distributions" (MCE-TFDs) to Table 1 (repeated here as Table 2 for convenience). Note that, from both a theoretical and physical perspective, the MCE-TFDs are superior to the bilinear TFRs as joint energy densities in time-frequency. To develop these new time-frequency distributions, the

Table 2: Properties of four bilinear TFRs and the MCE-TFD.

TFR	Non-negative	Marginals	Time Support	Frequency Support	Artifact Suppression
spectrogram	YES	NO	NB/WB trade-off	NB/WB trade-off	GOOD
Wigner	NO	YES	WEAK	WEAK	VERY POOR
Choi-Williams	NO	YES	VARIABLE	VARIABLE	VARIABLE
cone-kernel	NO	NO	WEAK	~STRONG	GOOD
MCE-TFD	YES	YES	STRONG	STRONG	GOOD

authors approached the problem as one of inductive inference, wherein a reasonable estimate of the true (but unknown) time-varying energy spectrum is available, along with additional (new) information about the unknown distribution (e.g. we know what the marginals of the unknown distribution should be). The new information is then optimally combined (in a minimum cross-entropy sense) with the prior estimate to obtain an improved estimate of the time-varying energy spectral density. As a reasonable prior estimate of the time-varying energy spectral density, the authors chose a spectrogram, since it can be considered a "blurred" estimate of the true time-frequency distribution of energy. Other prior estimates are possible [35].

We applied the MCE technique to generate an MCE-TFD of the pulsed tones of fig. 6; the result is shown in fig. 10, along with the time signal. Note the strong support of the MCE-TFD, and the amplitude oscillations in time consistent with the sinusoidal nature of the signal. We emphasise that the MCE-TFD is nonnegative and satisfies the marginals. Compare this result with the bilinear TFRs of fig. 6 and Table 2.

An example (from [35]) of this technique as applied to real speech is shown in fig. 11 for the utterance "joy," spoken by a male, and digitised at 8 kHz. Also included in fig. 11 are a narrowband spectrogram of the utterance, and the conditional MCE distributions $P(f \mid t)$ and $P(t \mid f)$. Note that the joint MCE-TFD $P(t, f)$ simultaneously preserves *both* the temporal (amplitude fluctuations and zero crossings) and spectral (shifting formants, etc.) features of the speech signal, unlike the narrowband spectrogram. More striking is the similarity between the time-conditional MCE distribution $P(f \mid t)$ and the narrowband spectrogram. This similarity suggests that a narrowband spectrogram is less like a joint distribution than it is a conditional distribution of the time-frequency energy of speech. The implications of this similarity are that years of experience with spectrograms have provided little insight into the characteristics of *joint* time-frequency distributions of speech. As such, interpretation of joint time-frequency distributions is sure to be unfamiliar.

6 CONCLUSION

The spectrogram, and other quasi-stationary processing techniques, have served — and will continue to serve — the speech community well. With the spectrogram, three important reasons for this utility are that it is easy to implement, readily interpretable, and physically meaningful. But it must be remembered that the spectrogram is an *estimate* of the true time-frequency structure (energy distribution) of speech. The accuracy of this estimation is critical if reliable quantitative measures are to be made. As demonstrated in this paper, the quasi-stationary processing of the spectrogram can introduce significant errors in estimates of

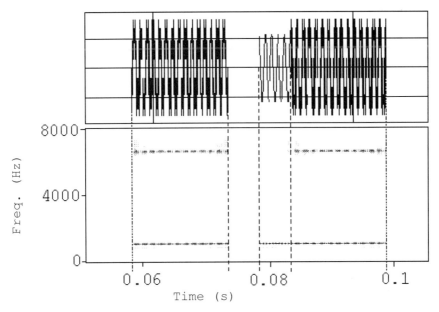

Fig. 10 An MCE-TFD of the pulsed tone example from fig. 6. MCE-TFDs are proper distributions, in that they satisfy the marginals and they are nonnegative. Consequently, they have strong support in time and frequency (note that unlike the TFRs of fig. 6, the MCE-TFD is zero over the 5 ms zero gap). In addition, an energy density interpretation of the result is valid. As a proper distribution of the joint time-frequency structure of the signal, the MCE-TFD above preserves the temporal amplitude oscillations of the time waveform, visible as black/white patterns at the signal frequencies in the time-frequency plane. As in fig. 6, vertical dotted and dashed lines delineate regions of interest.

sweep rate, signal duration, time-varying bandwidth, etc. Careful selection of the spectrogram window can reduce the error of a particular estimate (e.g. sweep rate) to within acceptable tolerance, but this results in increased error in other measures (e.g. instantaneous bandwidth). The spectrogram is incapable of providing simultaneous accurate measures in time-frequency. Efforts to improve upon limitations of the spectrogram by abandoning the quasi-stationary approach have been made. The bilinear class of TFRs is one such effort.

This tutorial has shown how the bilinear TFRs can be obtained as generalizations of the spectrogram. Since the speech processing community is quite familiar with the spectrogram, this approach to the bilinear TFRs was taken to provide them with a greater understanding of the bilinear formulation (eqn. (4)). By then addressing the specific form of the spectrogram kernel in the time-lag plane (fig. 2), it was shown why the spectrogram has a trade-off between resolution in time and frequency, and more importantly, how this trade-off can be overcome (e.g. fig. 3). Other desirable properties of a time-frequency energy distribution were then considered, from both a theoretical and practical (speech processing) perspective.

In addition to the spectrogram, three other bilinear TFRs were considered (the Wigner, the Choi-Williams, and the cone-kernel TFRs), and illustrative examples of their performance for synthetic signals and real speech were provided. It was found that none of these TFRs — including the spectrogram — accurately represented the joint time-frequency energy distribution of the signals considered. In particular, while the spectrogram suffers from limitations imposed by the quasi-stationary processing technique, it is the only bilinear TFR that is nonnegative for all signals. As such, an energy density interpretation of the remaining bilinear TFRs is not possible for speech (and many other) signals. This poses difficulties in interpreting the amplitude values of these distributions, all of which have units of a time-

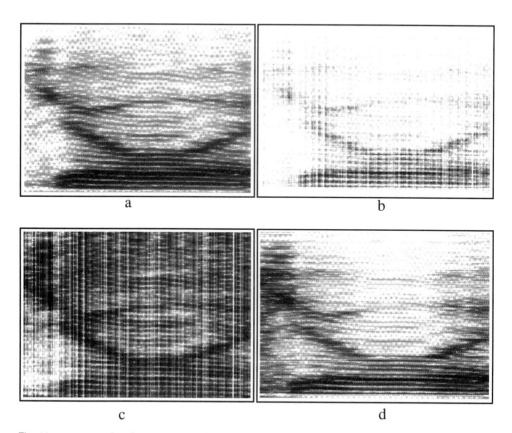

a   b

c   d

Fig. 11   *a* : a narrowband spectrogram of 250 ms of the utterance "joy". Vertical axis spans 0-4 kHz, as in all plots; *b* : a joint MCE-TFD, $P(t,f)$; *c* : the frequency-conditional MCE-TFD, $P(t \mid f)$; *d* : the time-conditional MCE-TFD, $P(f \mid t)$. Note the similarity between the narrowband spectrogram (top left) and the time-conditional MCE-TFD (bottom right). The vertical striations of the frequency-conditional MCE-TFD (bottom left) are suggestive of a wideband spectrogram. Example taken from [35]. Based upon theoretical considerations and other example comparisons between spectrograms and MCE-TFDs in [35], it is concluded that the MCE-TFDs are more accurate representations of the time-frequency energy distribution of speech than are spectrograms. The grey level spans 60 dB. © 1992 IEEE

frequency energy density ([J/Hz-s]). Nonetheless, some of these bilinear TFRs may be useful in speech processing, offering superior time-frequency resolution of formants and bursts over the spectrogram (e.g. the cone-kernel TFR [3,4]).

As the bilinear TFRs solved the time/frequency resolution trade-off and other problems of the spectrogram by dispensing with the quasi-stationary approach, so too must we move beyond bilinearity if we ever hope to achieve an accurate representation of the true time-varying energy spectrum of speech. This task presents a monumental challenge to the time-frequency and speech processing communities, but it can be done. There is no fundamental law of nature that prevents the development of a better time-varying energy spectral estimate to the spectrogram. Concrete proof of this is given by the development of the MCE-TFDs [35, 36], briefly discussed in section 5.2.

The pursuit of this goal is not a trivial theoretical exercise, lacking any real physical or practical significance. If the only tools available to assess the nonstationary energy spectrum of speech are based on quasi-stationary processing, we can never truly know the nonstationary time-frequency structure of speech. Quasi-stationary methods are useful, but limited and inaccurate; we can do better. As the theory of time-varying spectral estimation is continually refined and developed, speech processing may be one of the key areas to benefit. That alone should be sufficient reason to try to do better than the spectrogram. Until we do, we'll never know what we're missing — or worse, misrepresenting.

Acknowledgements: The authors are grateful to Prof. Leon Cohen, Dept. of Physics, Hunter College, City University of New York, for enlightening discussions on time-frequency distributions. The authors also thank Jing Fang of the Interactive Systems Design Lab, Dept. of Electrical Engineering at the University of Washington, for her assistance in computing and displaying the TFRs of section 4. The authors' research was funded by the University of Washington Bloedel Hearing Research Center, Boeing Commercial Airplane Company, the Office of Naval Research, and the Washington Technology Center.

Notes

1 Entropic Signal Processing System, Entropic Speech, Inc., Washington, DC.
2 For discussions of the uncertainty principle and time-frequency distributions, see [18, pp. 970-971], [14, pp. 36-37], [16, p. 31] and references cited therein.
3 Recent work [4] using nonstationary time-frequency analysis reveals that voiced speech has significant nonstationarities over durations shorter than one pitch period.
4 The spectrogram can be expressed either as a correlation between the signal and a window (e.g. [20,44]), as we have done, or as a convolution between the two (e.g. [22]). For the following expansion and generalization of the spectrogram to the bilinear form, the difference between the two expressions is insignificant.
5 Or equivalently in units of [W/Hz]. Thus, the interpretation of the spectrogram can be either that of a bivariate energy density (joules per hertz per sec), or a time-varying power spectral density (watts per hertz).
6 Discussed in section 3.4
7 To be dimensionally correct, the correlationless distribution is technically $|s(t)|^2|S(f)|^2/E$, where E is the total signal energy in joules, so that the distribution has units of [J/Hz-s]. Conventionally, we assume unit energy signals and it is understood that the units of the distribution are [J/Hz-s].
8 We are being rather loose in our use of the term proper here, since in this case the signal is of infinite energy and thus the frequency marginal $|S(f)|^2$ does not exist. However, eqn. (10) can be viewed as a limiting case.
9 The plotsgram routine from the Entropic Signal Processing System, Entropic Speech, Inc., Washington, DC.

REFERENCES

[1] J. Andrieux, R. Feix, G. Mourgues, et al. (1987), 'Optimum smoothing of the Wigner-Ville distribution', *IEEE Trans. ASSP*, **35**(6), 764-768.
[2] L. Atlas, Y. Zhao & R. Marks II (1987), 'Application of the generalized time-frequency representation to speech signal analysis', *IEEE Proc. Pacific Rim Conf. on Comm., Comp. and Sig. Proc.*, 517-520.
[3] L. Atlas, W. Kooiman, P. Loughlin & R. Cole (1990), 'New nonstationary techniques for the analysis and display of speech transients', *Proc. ICASSP '90*, 385-388.
[4] L. Atlas, P. Loughlin & J. Pitton (1991), 'Truly nonstationary techniques for the analysis and display of voiced speech', *Proc. ICASSP '91*, 433-436.
[5] L. Atlas, P. Loughlin & J. Pitton (1992), 'Signal analysis with cone-kernel time-frequency representations and their application to speech', in: *New Methods in Time-Frequency Analysis* (ed. B. Boashash), Longman Cheshire, Sydney, Australia.
[6] R. Baraniuk & D. Jones (1991), 'A radially Gaussian, signal-dependent time-frequency representation', *Proc. ICASSP '91*, 3181-3184.
[7] R. Baraniuk & D. Jones (1991), 'A signal-dependent time-frequency representation, a) Part I: Optimal kernel design; b) Part II: A fast algorithm for kernel design', submitted for publication in *IEEE Trans. Sig. Proc.*

[8] B. Boashash & B. Ristic (1991), 'Time-varying higher order spectra', *Proc. 25th Asilomar Conf. on Signals, Systems and Computers.*

[9] D. Chester, F. Taylor & M. Doyle (1984), 'The Wigner distribution in speech processing applications', *J. Franklin Institute*, **318**(6), 415-430.

[10] S. Cheung & J. Lim (1991), 'Combined multi-resolution (wideband/narrowband) spectrogram', *Proc. ICASSP '91*, 457-460.

[11] H. Choi & W. Williams (1989), 'Improved time-frequency representation of multicomponent signals using exponential kernels', *IEEE Trans. ASSP*, **37**(6), 862-871.

[12] T. Claasen & W. Mecklenbrauker (1980), 'The Wigner distribution - A tool for time-frequency analysis, (a) Part I: continuous-time signals; (b) Part II: discrete-time signals; (c) Part III: relations with other time-frequency signal transformations', *Phil. J. Res.*, **35**, nos. 3-6, 217-250, 276-300, 372-389.

[13] L. Cohen (1966), 'Generalized phase-space distribution functions', *J. Math. Phys.*, **7**(5), 781-786.

[14] L. Cohen & T. Posch (1985), 'Positive time-frequency distribution functions', *IEEE Trans. ASSP*, **33**(1), 31-38.

[15] L. Cohen & C. Pickover (1986), 'A comparison of joint time-frequency distributions for speech signals', *IEEE Proc. Int. Symp. on Circuits and Systems*, **1**, 42-45.

[16] L. Cohen (1986), 'A critical review of the fundamental ideas of joint time-frequency distributions', *IEEE Proc. Int. Symp. on Circuits and Systems*, **1**, 28-33.

[17] L. Cohen (1987), 'On a fundamental property of the Wigner distribution', *IEEE Trans. ASSP*, **35**(4), 559-561.

[18] L. Cohen (1989), 'Time-frequency distributions - A review', *Proc. IEEE*, **77**(7), 941-981.

[19] L. Cohen (1992), 'A primer on time-frequency analysis', in: *New Methods in Time-Frequency Analysis* (ed. B. Boashash), Longman Cheshire, Sydney, Australia.

[20] R. Fano (1950), 'Short-time autocorrelation functions and power spectra', *JASA*, **22**, 546-550.

[21] A. Fineberg & R. Mammone (1991), 'An adaptive technique for high resolution time-varying spectral estimation', *Proc. ICASSP '91*, 3185-3188.

[22] J. Flanagan (1972), *Speech Analysis, Synthesis and Perception*, 2nd ed., Springer-Verlag, NY, ch. V.

[23] P. Flandrin (1984), 'Some features of time-frequency representations of multicomponent signals', *Proc. ICASSP '84*, 41B.4.1-4.

[24] D. Gabor (1946), 'Theory of communication', *Jnl. IEE*, **93**, 429-457.

[25] H. Garudadri, M. Beddoes, A-P. Benguerel & J. Gilbert (1987), 'On computing the smoothed Wigner distribution', *Proc. ICASSP '87*, 1521-1524.

[26] J. Jeong & W. Williams (1990), 'On the cross-terms in spectrograms', *IEEE Proc. Int. Symp. on Circuits and Systems*, 1565-1568.

[27] J. Jeong & W. Williams (1992), 'Kernel design for reduced interference distributions', *IEEE Trans. Sig. Proc.*, **40**(2), 402-412.

[28] J. Jeong & W. Williams (1992), 'Alias-free generalized discrete-time time-frequency distributions', *IEEE Trans. Sig. Proc.* (to appear, November 1992).

[29] D. Jones & T. Parks (1987), 'A high resolution data-adaptive time-frequency representation', *Proc. ICASSP '87*, 681-684.

[30] D. Jones & T. Parks (1990), 'A high resolution data-adaptive time-frequency representation', *IEEE Trans. ASSP*, **38**(12), 2127-2135.

[31] W. Kaplan (1981), *Advanced Mathematics for Engineers*, Addison-Wesley, Reading, MA, 484-490, 523-524.

[32] R. Koenig, H. Dunn & L. Lacy (1946), 'The sound spectrograph', *JASA*, **18**, 19-49.

[33] P. Loughlin, J. Pitton & L. Atlas (1991), 'New properties to alleviate interference in time-frequency representations', *Proc. ICASSP '91*, 3205-3208.

[34] P. Loughlin, J. Pitton & L. Atlas (1993), 'Bilinear time-frequency representations: new insights and properties', , (to appear, February 1993).

[35] P. Loughlin, J. Pitton & L. Atlas (1992), 'An information-theoretic approach to positive time-frequency distributions', *Proc. ICASSP '92*, pp. V-125 - V128.

[36] P. Loughlin, J. Pitton & L. Atlas (1992), 'Minimum cross-entropy positive time-frequency distributions, part I: Theoretical development and examples', submitted for publication in *IEEE Trans. Sig. Proc.* (June 1992).

[37] H. Margenau & R. Hill (1961), 'Correlations between measurements in quantum theory', *Prog. Theor. Phys.*, **26**, 722-738.

[38] W. Music, W. Fox, P. Loughlin, L. Atlas & J. Pitton (1991), 'Shift-keyed signal identification using time-frequency processing', *Proc. 25th Asilomar Conf. on Signals, Systems and Computers.*

[39] A. Nuttal (1989), 'Alias-free Wigner distribution function and complex ambiguity function for discrete-time samples', *Naval Underwater Systems Center, NUSC Tech. Rep. 8533.*

[40] J. Ord (1972), *Families of Frequency Distributions*, Hafner Publishing Co., New York, 56-57.

[41] C. Page (1952), 'Instantaneous power spectra', *J. Appl. Phys.*, **23**, 103-106.

[42] R. Potter, G. Koop & H. Green (1947), *Visible Speech*, Van Nostrand, New York.

[43] W. Rihaczek (1968), 'Signal energy distribution in time and frequency', *IEEE Trans. Info. Theor.*, **14**, 369-374.

[44] M. Schroeder & B. Atal (1962), 'Generalized short-time power spectra and autocorrelation functions', *JASA*, **34**, 1679-1683.

[45] R. Streifel (1991), *Synthesis of time-frequency representations by the method of projections onto convex sets*, Master's Thesis, Dept. of Electrical Engineering, University of Washington.

[46] E. Velez & R. Absher (1989), 'Transient analysis of speech signals using the Wigner time-frequency representation', *Proc. ICASSP '89*, 2242-2245.

[47] J. Ville (1948), 'Theorie et applications de la notion de signal analytique', *Cables et Transmissions*, **2A**(1), 61-74, 1948. Translated from French by I. Selin (1958), 'Theory and applications of the notion of complex signal', RAND Corporation Technical Report T-92, Santa Monica, CA.

[48] E. Wigner (1932), 'On the quantum correction for thermodynamic equilibrium', *Phys. Rev.*, **40**, 749-759. Also see E. Wigner (1971), 'Quantum-mechanical distribution functions revisited,' in *Perspectives in Quantum Theory*, (ed. W. Yourgrau and A. van der Merwe), MIT Press, Cambridge, MA.

[49] W. Williams & J. Jeong (1992), 'Reduced interference time-frequency distributions', in: *New Methods in Time-Frequency Analysis* (ed. B. Boashash), Longman Cheshire, Sydney, Australia.

[50] Y. Zhao, L. Atlas & R. Marks II (1990), 'The use of cone-shaped kernels for generalized time-frequency representations of nonstationary signals', *IEEE Trans. ASSP*, **38**(7), 1084-1091.

Comparing phonetic, articulatory, acoustic and aerodynamic signal representations

K. Nicolaidis, W.J. Hardcastle, A. Marchal and
N. Nguyen-Trong

1 INTRODUCTION

Segmentation and labelling of the speech signal is problematic since there is no one-to-one correspondence between the physical and the linguistic levels of representation (Rossi [23]; Svendsen & Kvale [25]; Glass & Zue [10]). Boundaries between "neighbouring" segments (as defined from a symbolic transcription) are blurred by the speech encoding process. Various approaches have been proposed attempting to relate the symbolic levels (syntactic, phonemic, phonetic etc.) to the acoustic signal for a given utterance (e.g. André-Obrecht [2]; Fourcin *et al.* [8]; Autesserre *et al.* [5]; Arai *et al.* [4]).

Acoustic discontinuities in the speech signal have been in some cases interpreted as the manifestation of articulatory gestures. However, this relationship has not been systematically investigated and we still lack a comprehensive interpretative model of articulatory-acoustic correlations.

One of the aims of the ACCOR project has been to provide a detailed description of the main articulatory and acoustic correlations in coarticulatory processes in seven European languages: Catalan, English, French, German, Irish Gaelic, Italian and Swedish. A cross-language approach has been adopted as a means of differentiating between the major language-independent universal regularities of these processes (due to factors such as the mass, inertia and elasticity of the speech organs, the mechanical linkages between them, and the neuromuscular complexities of the cranial nerve system) and language specific factors such as the phonological rules of the language (Hardcastle & Marchal [16]; Farnetani *et al.* [7]). In order to allow for cross-language comparisons, particular attention has been paid to the design of a suitable multi-sensor database and to the adoption of a common methodology, i.e. standardised investigation tools and normalised measurement procedures at specified locations in the speech signals. In the segmentation and labelling of the database we have adopted a non-linear approach to the annotation of articulatory and acoustic events, based on the evidence provided by the different channels of information: acoustic waveform, airflow traces, linguo-palatal contact patterns, jaw and lip movements (Marchal & Nguyen-Trong [20]).

In this paper, using EUR-ACCOR data on connected speech, we show how this truly multi-level approach leads to a better understanding of articulatory-acoustic mapping.

2 THE ACCOR PROJECT

2.1 Rationale for a cross-language multi-sensor research project

The ACCOR project aims at a detailed description of the complex coordination between the main physiological systems underlying speech production and the resulting acoustic output. The articulatory dimensions under study are: the respiratory system (producing a flow of air), the laryngeal system (modifying the airflow by the valving mechanism of the vocal folds) and the complex system of supraglottal structures in the mouth and nose, such as the tongue, lips, jaw and soft palate shaping the vocal tract into different resonating cavities. Spe-

Visual Representations of Speech Signals: Martin Cooke, Steve Beet and Malcolm Crawford (eds.)
© 1993 by John Wiley & Sons Ltd

cific articulatory processes in the seven languages have been examined with a view to determining how such processes differ according to the different phonological systems. Also, it has been possible to examine the functions of the different motor subsystems in the same speaker.

The cross-language nature of the project has meant considerable attention has had to be paid to the design of a suitable database. Three main scientific goals of the project were considered in the design:

- to test several hypotheses regarding articulatory/phonological interactions in the different languages particularly with a view to differentiating language-specific from language-universal constraints on coarticulatory processes.
- to investigate fundamental issues in speech production theory particularly those relating to coarticulatory processes.
- to provide a unique resource for researchers in speech science and related fields (for further description of these goals see Marchal *et al.* [21]).

2.2 The EUR-ACCOR corpus

The study of coarticulation and its possible implications for the linguistic and neuromotor programming processes would seem *a priori* to exclude the use of nonsense items. On the other hand, although undoubtedly desirable, the analysis of spontaneous speech is problematic in that it is difficult to control all the parameters which may be responsible for coarticulatory effects. The emphasis on cross-language comparison makes this problem even more acute. In the ACCOR project we decided the best compromise was to work in parallel on three different types of speech material; structured VCV nonsense items, real words matching the nonsense items in their VCV structure as closely as possible, and connected speech in the form of a series of short sentences. In addition to providing a basic 'core' component to the corpus the nonsense items provided convenient data for measuring coarticulatory processes and also were a source for an EPG archive of segmental features.

In choosing the items for inclusion in the corpus we were constrained by a number of criteria. Firstly, all items, including the nonsense items, had to comply with the phonological rules of the language. For vowel sounds, it was desirable to cover a range of different tongue postures and different perceptual characteristics. The three 'extreme' vowels /i/, /a/ and /u/ were chosen as these vowels exist as phonemes in each language, and their phonetic manifestations in the different languages are similar. For the consonants, a range of different places and manners of articulation were chosen.

It was decided to focus on VCV sequences for the reasons stated above. This raised the problem of stress placement. Obviously, it would have been preferable if the stress placement were uniform for each language. However, language-specific stress placement rules precluded this possibility if the items were to be produced naturally. In all cases except French stress was placed on the first syllable. In French the more natural placement is on the second syllable. Details of the main sets of material are as follows:

Nonsense items. Vowels /i, a, u/ in isolation. VCV sequences, where C = /p, b, t, d, k, s, z, n, l, ʃ, tʃ/ and the sequences /kl, st/; V = /i/, /a/ (/ə/ when unstressed in English) and /u/. These items are phonotactically permissible in all the languages under investigation, with one or two exceptions, (e.g. /z/ and /ʃ/ do not occur in Swedish, /s/ is restricted in German and /tʃ/ in German and French).

Real words. These match the VCV nonsense sequences above as closely as possible. Thus nonsense item /iti/ is matched by English "meaty", /uti/ in Italian is matched by "muti" etc. It was not possible to obtain a complete set of matching real words for all the languages.

Sentences. A set of short sentences was constructed in each language to illustrate the main connected-speech processes in that language such as assimilations, weak forms, etc.

Thus in English, sentences such as "Fred can go, Susan can't go, and Linda is uncertain" have numerous examples of word-final alveolar stops and nasals which many speakers would assimilate to the place of articulation of following velars when spoken naturally.

3   THE MULTI-SENSOR WORKSTATION

3.1 The experimental set-up

For recording the EUR-ACCOR corpus we have designed a specialised multi-sensor workstation based on a PC which enables simultaneous digital recording of the acoustic signal and a number of additional channels for physiological and aerodynamic data. The hardware and software for a prototype system was developed as part of a collaborative project between the Speech Research Laboratory at Reading and the IBM (UK) Scientific Centre at Winchester (Trudgeon *et al.* [27]; Hardcastle *et al.* [15]). A number of important modifications have been carried out to the system to tailor it to the specific needs of the ACCOR project (Hardcastle *et al.*[13]).

Following a detailed assessment of available instrumentation for investigating physiological and aerodynamic aspects of speech production, we decided to use the following transducers in recording the EUR-ACCOR database: electropalatograph (for measuring the timing and location of tongue contacts with the palate); pneumotachograph with Rothenberg mask (for recording volume velocity of air flow from nose and mouth) and laryngograph (for recording details of vocal fold vibration).

Electropalatography (EPG) is a technique that records details of the timing and location of tongue contacts with the hard palate during continuous speech. In the main versions of the technique currently used the subject wears an artificial plate moulded to fit the upper palate with a number of electrodes mounted on the surface to detect lingual contact. In the Reading EPG system, 62 electrodes are embedded in the surface of the artificial palate (fig. 1). The technique is suitable for investigating those sounds involving measurable amounts of tongue contact with the hard palate.

Electropalatography is a conceptually simple, safe and convenient technique and has now been established in many speech laboratories throughout the world. The wide applicability of the technique and its usefulness as a tool in phonetic descriptive work is reflected in the range of phenomena that have been researched over the years (for a summary, see Hardcastle *et al.* [12]). It has also been extensively used in studies of lingual coarticulation (see Hardcastle *et al.* [14] for a summary of data reduction methods and their use in studies of coarticulation). Also it has proved a particularly useful tool in the diagnosis and treatment of a variety of speech disorders (Hardcastle *et al.* [12]).

Electrolaryngography is a practical, non-invasive technique for detecting vocal fold vibration during the production of voiced sounds and for examining vertical movement of the larynx due to laryngeal or supraglottal adjustments (Abberton *et al.* [1]). For the current laryngograph system, two electrodes are placed at the level of the larynx held by a neckband. A constant voltage is applied and the laryngograph records variations in electrical conductance between the electrodes caused by the opening and closing activity of the vocal folds. During maximum closure current flows at its maximum; when the vocal folds are open there is minimal flow present. In a typical laryngograph Lx waveform, the onset of each steep rise corresponds to the onset of closure of the vocal folds (closing phase), the peak of each cycle corresponds to maximum contact of the vocal folds (maximum closure), the shallow falling phase corresponds to the opening of the vocal folds (opening phase), and the following trough to vocal fold separation (open phase). Variation in voice quality causes changes in the length of these phases. The electrolaryngograph is a convenient, indirect technique for investigating laryngeal activity. It has been used extensively in speech research and as a clinical tool for a

READING EPG SYSTEM

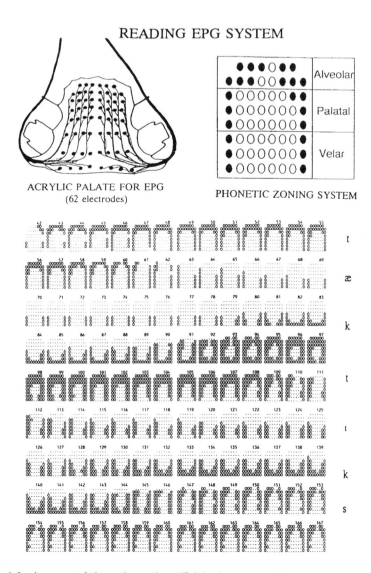

ACRYLIC PALATE FOR EPG
(62 electrodes)

PHONETIC ZONING SYSTEM

Fig. 1 *upper left* : placement of electrodes on the artificial palate; *upper right* : division of electrodes into zones: rows 1-2 alveolar zone, rows 3-5 palatal zone, rows 6-8 velar zone; *lower* : full EPG printout of the word "tactics". In each palatal diagram the alveolar region is at the top, and the velar region at the bottom; lingual contact is indicated by zeros. Interval between frames is 10ms. Notice the double articulation pattern during frames 94-96 with simultaneous closure for velar /k/ and alveolar /t/.

range of speech and hearing pathologies (for a summary, see Abberton *et al.* [1]). Figure 4 shows a typical laryngograph trace.

Pneumotachography is a technique for measuring the volume velocity of the nasal and oral airflow of sounds produced in continuous speech. The pneumotach system marketed by Oral Enterprises Inc. can be used with a hand-held Rothenberg mask. The advantage of using this circumferentially-vented mask is that it minimises sound distortion and the loss of high frequency fidelity by placing the flow resistance in the walls of the mask itself. The mask has a partition separating the nasal and oral parts, and the oral and nasal airflow readings are recorded separately. The flow is calibrated in l/min. against a rotameter. Pneumotachography is an indirect technique since the activity of the velum is not monitored directly but inferred by the airflow output of a particular sound (Anthony & Hewlett [3]). It has proved to be a practical and convenient technique and has been extensively used in speech research and in speech therapy. Figure 4 shows a typical oral airflow trace.

The table below summarises the input types and sampling rates of the standard equipment used to record the database.

Signal	Sampling rate (Hz)	Data bits / sample	Bytes / sample	Data rate bytes/sec
Speech signal	20,000	12	2	40,000
Laryngograph	10,000	12	2	20,000
Oral air flow	500	12	2	1,000
Nasal air flow	500	12	2	1,000
EPG data	200	62	12	2,400
			TOTAL	64,400

Some limited data are also available from an Electromagnetic Transduction System (EMA) for measuring movements of the lips, jaw and tongue. Figure 2 shows a block diagram of the experimental set-up of the multi-sensor workstation.

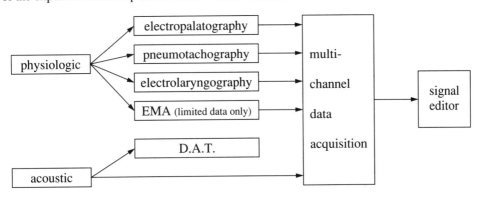

Fig. 2   Block diagram of the experimental set-up of the ACCOR multi-sensor workstation

A number of software programs have been developed for the acquisition and management of the EUR-ACCOR database. These include:

- Multichannel acquisition program (MULTICH). Facilities are included to enable the user to monitor all channels including the EPG, to set the polarities, gains and offsets on the analog channels and to calibrate the analog channels.
- A header program (HED) to produce files which contain subject and experimental details.
- A tape streamer program (SYTOS) to transfer and store the data onto 60MB data cartridges.
- A split program (SPLIT) to identify, order and separate out the data into the various channels.
- An analysis, display and annotation program (EDIT) to perform a variety of functions including attaching labels to relevant events in the data.

- A prototype database management system to allow queries of the type: "Extract all examples of /kl/ clusters in the /i-i/ environment in real words for all male speakers in Italian" (see Pérez *et al.* [22]).

- Edit to database conversion (EDBAS). This program enables the user to create, from annotated data in Edit format, a file of data suitable for export into the PARADOX relational database system for processing of the data.

- Data analysis (PARADOX3) and display (QUATTRO PRO) programs. Various scripts have been written to perform specific routines and calculations in order to manage the data acquired from the Edit annotation points. The spreadsheet program QUATTRO PRO is compatible with PARADOX3 and is used to display the data graphically.

A parallel development in multi-sensor workstation design at Aix-en-Provence has resulted in a new system PHYSIOLOGIA (Teston & Galindo [26]) which enables simultaneous acquisition of up to 16 input channels. Specialised interactive programs have been developed for the display and analysis of the data. It is envisaged that future recordings for the EUR-ACCOR database will be carried out using the more powerful PHYSIOLOGIA system.

3.2 Recording conditions and experimental procedure used

All recordings for the EUR-ACCOR database have been carried out in the Speech Research Laboratory at the University of Reading in a sound-damped studio, fitted with a viewing window. To minimize any extraneous noise, all equipment is outside the room except microphone, EPG multiplexer unit, Rothenberg mask, and laryngograph electrodes. High quality audio recordings are made of the whole recording session with a Sennheiser MKH 40 P48 microphone and Sony DAT (DTC-1000ES). Two different combinations of the instrumentation have been used to date as part of the ACCOR recordings:

- EPG, laryngograph and audio recording.

- EPG, nasal volume velocity of air, oral volume velocity of air, laryngograph and audio recording.

A total of ten repetitions of the full corpus are produced for each subject, i.e. five repetitions with the first instrumental combination and five repetitions with the second combination above. A complete archive of all digital raw data is currently held in Reading on magnetic tape cartridges.

Prior to recording, the experimenter, who is a member of the ACCOR group representing the particular language under investigation, goes through the list of items and sentences with the subject, exemplifying stress placement and tempo, etc. and subsequently monitors the actual recording. The subject is also encouraged to wear the artificial palate for at least a three hour period prior to recording to become accustomed to the feel of the device in the mouth.

3.3 Signal editing

Data may be displayed and analysed using the EDIT software program. The user is presented with a display in which the screen is divided vertically into three partitions. The speech waveform of the selected file is displayed in the middle partition, and the utterance text (from the Utterance field in the header file) is displayed at the top of the middle partition. The user has the option of moving two cursors to delimit an area of the display (which can then, for example, be expanded if desired); this can be done either by keyboard commands or by using a mouse.

The user can obtain various kinds of display in the top and bottom partitions, and perform various analyses and miscellaneous functions, by commands from the keyboard. These include, for example, the display of nasal and oral airflow traces, laryngograph trace and display of linguo-palatal contacts (EPG). When EPG is selected, two palatograms are displayed on the right and the left of the top partition. These are synchronised respectively with the right and left active cursors on the waveform (fig. 3). EDIT provides the facility to play out the displayed speech waveform or selected sections through a digital-to-analog converter.

The edit program also allows the display of various data reduction facilities (described fully in Hardcastle *et al.* [14]). These include:

- contact "totals" in different regions of the palate.
- "centre of gravity" of contact pattern plotted against total number of contacts.
- various numerical indices, e.g. the "asymmetry" index.

EDIT also provides the facility to attach labels ("annotations") to specified instants within the speech data; these can later be used in setting up a database of measurements from the speech data. Annotations are stored, each in the form of a text and speech waveform sample number, in a file with the same name as the appropriate set of speech data, and extension '.ann'. This file is read into memory the first time an annotation command is executed for a given set of speech data, and the annotations thereafter remain in memory while this set of speech data is being edited.

Each signal can be annotated independently of the others. Discontinuities in each trace can be marked according to specific criteria. For instance, in a [kl] sequence (fig. 4), the following landmarks were identified from the different signals: VTT = end of voicing for first vowel (annotated from the laryngograph trace), ACO = beginning of decrease in oral airflow trace indicating onset of approach to /k/ closure (annotated from the oral airflow trace), SRO = onset of [k] release (annotated from the oral airflow trace), LCE = onset of anterior contact for [l] (annotated from EPG), VL = onset of voicing for second vowel (annotated from the laryngograph trace) and LRE = release of [l] closure (annotated from EPG).

4   ANALYSIS AND SEGMENTATION

Segmentation and labelling of large speech databases may serve different purposes:

- Index recordings for fast and efficient retrieval of specific parts of the corpora: sentences, words, syllables, phonemes, phones, etc.
- Align a given transcription with the speech signal.
- Provide a method of relating different levels of representation; orthographic, phonemic, phonetic, acoustic, articulatory, perceptual, etc.
- Extract knowledge on the speech encoding and decoding processes.
- Train phoneme-based speech recognisers.
- Assess the performance of ASR systems.
- Derive prototypes for speech synthesis.

The primary aim of the ACCOR project is to investigate articulatory-acoustic correlations in coarticulatory processes. Given this goal, the major interest has been in relating the phonemic level to the phonetic level through a systematic analysis of the components of the articulatory gestures and the resulting acoustic signal. The different articulatory, aerodynamic and acoustic signals have been annotated so as to allow us to relate in a comprehensive way the symbolic and the physical levels of representation.

The database is annotated manually by trained phoneticians. The uniqueness of this multi-sensor database requires a constant refinement of the criteria used to annotate and label the different signals which are available, i.e. the acoustic waveform, the laryngographic trace, the oral and nasal airflow traces, and the linguo-palatal contacts. In future, we intend to adopt a semi-automatic procedure to help with the processing of the remaining data from a total 12.5 Gbyte archive.

A further aim of annotating our data has been to provide us with a knowledge database to test various hypotheses concerning the speech encoding process.

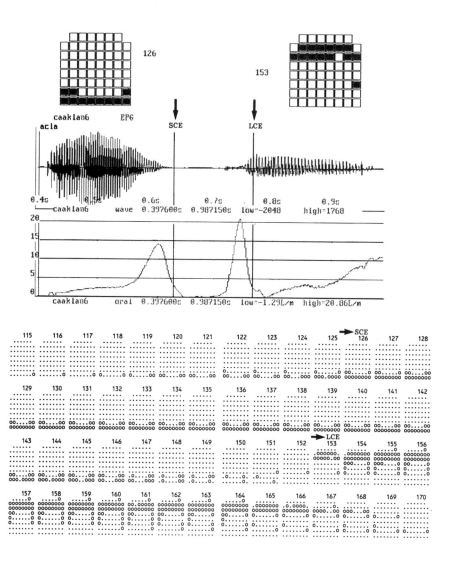

Fig. 3 Typical EDIT display of the sequence "akla" spoken by an Italian subject. The acoustic waveform is shown in the centre of the display. The two cursors can be moved through the utterance with the *upper left* EPG pattern corresponding to the left hand cursor and the *upper right* to the right hand one. Two annotations are marked in the position of the cursors: SCE = constriction at the velar region for the [k], and LCE = constriction at the alveolar region for the [l] (both annotations are based on EPG). The bottom trace shows the oral airflow trace. The calibration scale (in litres per minute) can be changed in multiples of ten to suit the utterance under investigation. Below the screen display is a computer printout of the EPG patterns occurring in the sequence "akla" (sampled at 5 ms intervals).

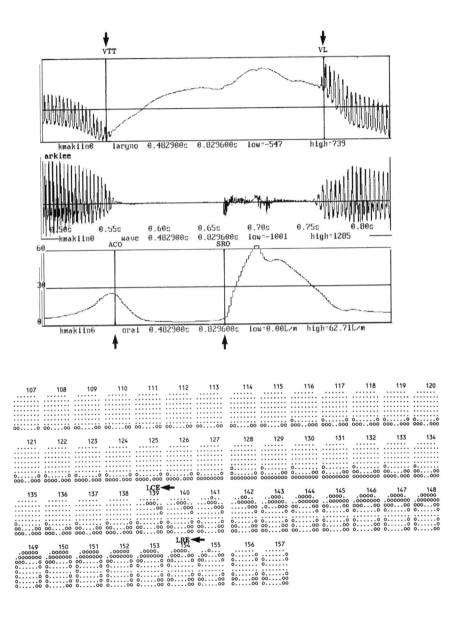

Fig 4   Typical EDIT display of the [kl] sequence of the nonsense word /akli/ spoken by an English subject showing: *top* : laryngograph trace; *middle* : acoustic waveform; and *bottom* : oral airflow trace; with labelled annotation points inserted at specific locations. Below the screen display is a computer printout of the EPG patterns occurring in the sequence /akli/ (sampled at 5ms intervals). The annotations based on the different channels are: VTT = end of voicing for the first vowel (annotated from the laryngograph trace), ACO = beginning of decrease in oral airflow trace indicating onset of approach to /k/ closure (annotated from the oral airflow trace), SRO = onset of [k] release (annotated from the oral airflow trace), LCE = onset of anterior contact for [l] (annotated from EPG), VL = onset of voicing for second vowel (annotated from the laryngograph trace), and LRE = release of [l] closure (annotated from EPG).

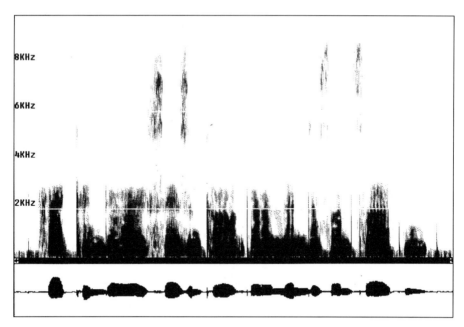

Fig. 5   Wideband spectrogram of the sentence "Fred can go, Susan can't go, and Linda is
uncertain" produced by an English female speaker.

4.1 Principles of annotation

Speech production is a complex process relying on coordinated gestures. In essence, it is a non-linear mechanism, such that articulatory gestures overlap (Löfqvist [19]), and that resulting events can be associated with more than one phonetic symbol. In view of the above, the annotation of our database has relied upon the following two principles:

- the principle of non-linearity.
- the principle of independence of information from the different channels.

Each of these principles have been stated for rather straightforward reasons. At first, it seems evident that we cannot consider a speech signal to be a linear concatenation of segments, without implicitly assuming that coarticulation is just an accommodation process, devoted to facilitating transitions from one segment to the next. Looking for acoustic boundaries between non overlapping segments presupposes that coarticulation involves a spreading of features along a unidimensional representation of speech. This assumption has given rise to the so-called translation theory, which presents the classical view of coarticulation. Our proposal would be to adopt a less restricting method than the linear one, and to locate successive articulatory events rather than segmental boundaries of any kind. It seems to us that this method could lead to proper "annotation" which would not preclude *a priori* non-linear assumptions about coarticulation.

We have adopted a methodological principle according to which different channels would be annotated independently of each other. For example, in a case where we observe a double velar/alveolar closure in a /kt/ stop sequence and no trace of release of the first in the acoustic signal, we cannot simply annotate at one level only (Gibbon *et al.* [11]). Annotation is based on the identification of discontinuities in each signal independently. It is absolutely essential to adopt such a principle in a study which is precisely concerned with a systematic investigation of the correlations between different levels of representation.

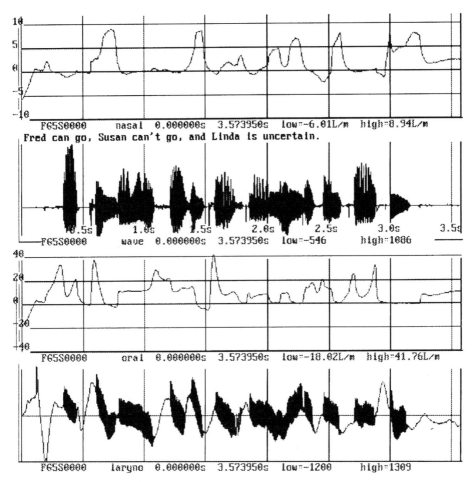

Fig. 6   EDIT screen display of the sentence "Fred can go, Susan can't go, and Linda is uncertain" produced by an English female speaker, showing nasal airflow, acoustic waveform, oral airflow and laryngograph trace.

Discontinuities are interpreted as indications of oncoming gestures from and towards articulatory goals. They correspond to turning points on the different traces and they are marked in the temporal domain according to precisely defined criteria. These gestures may of course have different temporal extents in the different articulatory dimensions under investigation. This further motivates the adoption of a non-linear approach to segmentation.

4.2 Analysis

The sentence to be analysed is "Fred can go, Susan can't go, and Linda is uncertain" produced by an English female speaker with a Southern English accent. The sentence, from the ACCOR database, was constructed and selected because it potentially contains a number of connected speech processes such as assimilations, reductions, deletions etc. For instance, there is a variety of final alveolar consonants that can be assimilated to the place of articulation of the next stop. This reflects the natural production of similar utterances in natural spontaneous conversational speech. Spontaneous speech was not recorded for the ACCOR database due to the limitations imposed by the experimental set-up and the number of variables involved which make comparisons between languages extremely difficult.

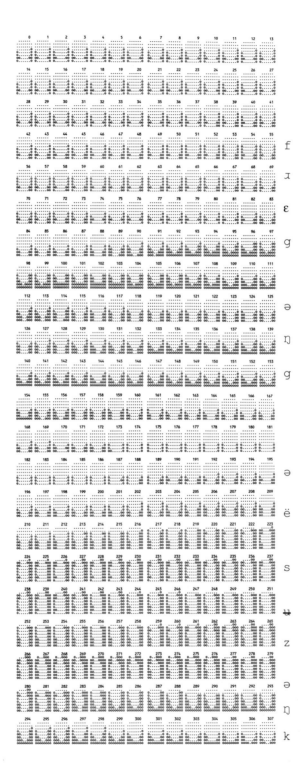

Fig. 7   (continued)

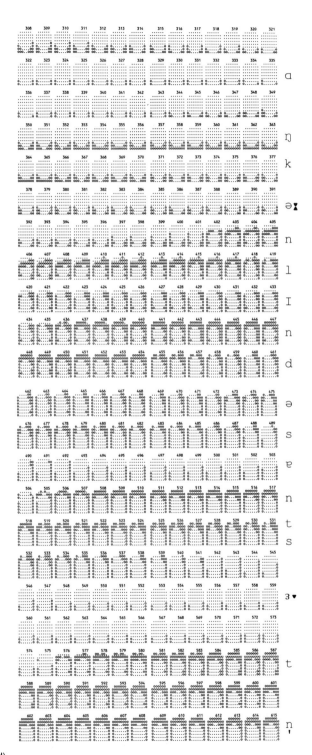

Fig. 7   (continued)

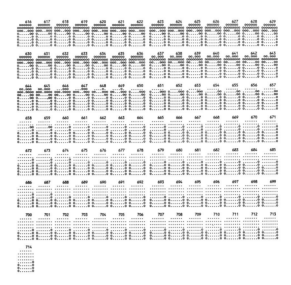

Fig. 7   Full EPG printout of the sentence "Fred can go, Susan can't go, and Linda is uncertain".
Interval between frames is 5 ms.

Figure 5 shows a wideband spectrogram of "Fred can go, Susan can't go, and Linda is uncertain"; the EDIT screen display of the complete sentence and the corresponding full EPG printout appear in figs. 6 and 7 respectively. There is an evident attenuation of the higher frequencies in the spectrogram which is caused by the mask used for the oral and nasal flow recordings.

We will proceed by analysing the three grammatically defined clauses individually, i.e.

   i   Fred can go (figs. 8, 9)

   ii   Susan can't go (figs. 10, 11)

   iii and Linda is uncertain (figs. 12, 13)

and using as data the spectrograms, the acoustic waveforms, the EPG, the aerodynamic and laryngographic signals. We will focus mainly on those parts of the utterance where we can identify interesting connected speech phenomena and where the various channels indicate some underlying articulatory activity not easily identifiable from the spectrogram or the acoustic waveform only. The time from the beginning of the utterance (given in parentheses) and/or the EPG frame number [given in square brackets] will be given for every event identified.

(i) Fred can go

The first landmark on the spectrogram is the occurrence of friction at (0.265) (line 1 on the spectrogram and acoustic waveform, figs. 8, 9). The oral airflow trace shows increased oral airflow output (fig. 9). The relatively long duration of friction (80 ms) and the lack of a long falling F3 transition at the beginning of the following vowel indicate that part of the approximant [ɹ] must be voiceless and produced with friction. EPG linguo-palatal contact patterns show that there is no change in lingual activity during the period of friction [53-69] (fig. 7). The tongue appears to have anticipated the position for the approximant at the onset of friction. There is some lingual movement (slight retraction) at the end of friction and the beginning of voicing [68-70].

At the end of the vowel /ɛ/ the lack of a clear change in F2 transition makes it difficult to determine the place of articulation of the following stop. Lingual contact changes at [88] (fig. 7) leading to a constriction for the stop. This is coupled with a drop in oral airflow and a reduction in amplitude on the acoustic waveform at the same point. Complete constriction occurs at [92] (fig. 7) at the velar place of articulation. Phonemically an alveolar stop would be indicated here. From the EPG data, however, there is no evidence of any contact at the alveolar place of articulation. Moreover, there does not appear to be any residual or incomplete movement to this place. It is evident from the EPG data that the alveolar segment has been fully assimilated to the velar place of articulation of the following stop.

The release of the velar stop is accompanied by a rapid increase in oral airflow (0.551) (line 4 on the oral airflow trace, fig. 9). There is also some escape of nasal flow shortly after the release of the EPG constriction (0.560) [112] (line 1 on the nasal airflow trace, fig. 9) which often characterises strongly aspirated stops.

A further increase in nasal airflow occurs at (0.616) [123] (line 2 on the nasal airflow trace, fig. 9). The peak coincides with complete constriction for the nasal (0.665) [133] (line 3 on the nasal airflow trace in fig. 9; and fig. 7) and at the same time the oral airflow trace reaches the baseline. There is evidence therefore that there is anticipatory nasality during the vowel [ə] as shown by the nasal airflow trace. This might not be readily apparent from the spectrogram although an examination of spectral slices during the vowel shows some attenuation in the intensity of the higher frequencies especially after the rapid increase in nasal airflow (line 2 on the nasal airflow trace, fig. 9).

EPG contact data show that the nasal segment is articulated at the velar place of articulation, being assimilated to the place of articulation of the following velar stop.

The nasal airflow starts dropping towards the end of the closure at (0.749) [149] (line 4 on the nasal airflow trace, fig. 9). There is also a reduction in amplitude evident at the laryngograph trace and the acoustic waveform caused by the activity of the velum and its effect on the intraoral pressure. The drop in intensity at the end of the nasal, as seen on the spectrogram, approximately 10 ms before the release indicates that the duration of the oral velar stop is indeed very short. However, it is sufficient to cause an audible release (0.772) (line 9 on the acoustic waveform and line 6 on the oral airflow trace, fig. 9) which is followed by an increase in oral airflow.

EPG contact patterns show a retracting movement of the tongue after the release of the velar closure. This ends at [174] which corresponds to the end of the F2 transition at the beginning of the diphthong. There is some steady state period following with no evident tongue movement [175-186]. At [187] the onset of some gradual contact build-up is also reflected at the onset of the final transition of the diphthong.

(ii) Susan can't go

An increase in oral airflow at the end of the diphthong indicates the approach to the following fricative starting at (1.085) [216] (line 1 on the spectrogram and acoustic waveform, figs. 10 and 11). The characteristic two-peak pattern occurring with fricatives can be seen on the oral airflow trace and is also present in the following fricative occurrences in the utterance.

EPG contact patterns show that the articulation of this fricative does not involve very close constriction at the alveolar zone. The decrease in linguo-palatal contact [242-244] (fig. 7) is accompanied by a decrease in the airflow trace. This corresponds also to the start of the voicing for the vowel (1.211) (line 3 on the acoustic waveform and line 1 on the laryngograph trace, fig. 11). The tongue remains in a high position for the following vowel [242-264] (1.211-1.322) indicating a close central [ʉ]. At [264] (fig. 7) there is already a considerable amount of contact anticipating the following fricative (build-up of contact starting at [259]).

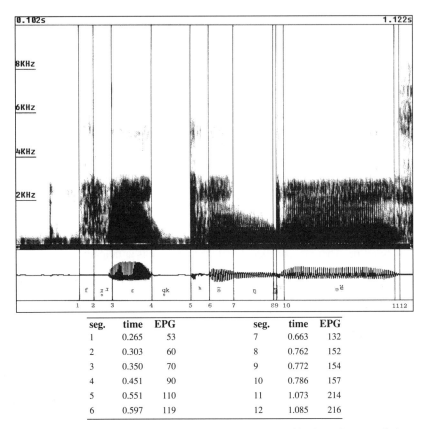

seg.	time	EPG	seg.	time	EPG
1	0.265	53	7	0.663	132
2	0.303	60	8	0.762	152
3	0.350	70	9	0.772	154
4	0.451	90	10	0.786	157
5	0.551	110	11	1.073	214
6	0.597	119	12	1.085	216

Fig. 8   Wide-band spectrogram of the utterance "Fred can go" with phonetic transcription and segmentation lines marked numerically. The key below gives times (from the beginning of the utterance) and EPG frame numbers corresponding to the segmentation lines.

A two-peak pattern can be seen for the [z] but the volume velocity is much less for this voiced fricative. A reduction in amplitude is also evident on the laryngograph trace and acoustic waveform during the production of this fricative. Additionally, there is some increase in the nasal volume velocity starting towards the end of the first (low) peak on the oral airflow (1.342) [268] (line 1 on the nasal airflow trace, fig. 11). This increase is in anticipation of the following nasal but may also serve to facilitate voicing during the fricative. EPG contact patterns show a more constricted articulation for the voiced fricative compared to the preceding voiceless fricative.

The nasal airflow gradually rises during the following vowel and reaches its peak at the complete constriction (1.426) [285] (line 2 on the nasal airflow trace, fig. 11; and fig. 7) while the oral airflow reaches the baseline at this point. We observe from the EPG patterns the realisation of a velar stop, i.e. a complete assimilation of the underlying /n/ [285] (fig. 7). Again, there is some anticipatory nasality during the vowel which may not be easily identifiable from the spectrogram. An assumed nasal formant at approximately [900 Hz] can however be seen at the end of the vowel.

An increase in the nasal airflow occurs after the beginning of the open vowel [ɑ] of "can't" at (1.601) [320] (line 4 on the nasal airflow trace, fig. 11) when retraction of the tongue also occurs. A further increase occurs after the end of the vowel (1.759) [351] (line 5 on the nasal airflow trace, fig. 11). At the same point the laryngograph trace and the spectro-

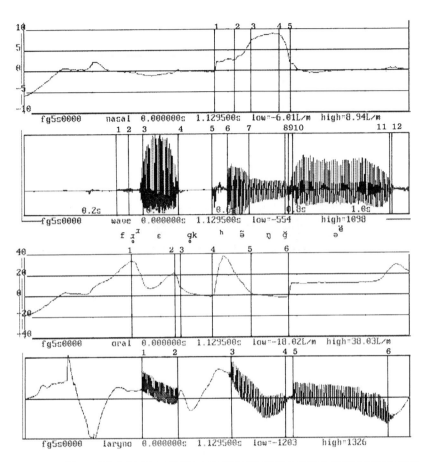

acoustic waveform			nasal airflow			oral airflow			laryngograph signal		
seg.	time	EPG	seg.	time	EPG	seg.	time	EPG	seg.	time	EPG
1	0.265	53	1	0.560	112	1	0.311	62	1	0.343	68
2	0.303	60	2	0.616	123	2	0.444	88	2	0.448	89
3	0.350	70	3	0.665	133	3	0.460	92	3	0.605	121
4	0.451	90	4	0.749	149	4	0.551	110	4	0.762	152
5	0.551	110	5	0.779	155	5	0.665	133	5	0.786	157
6	0.597	119				6	0.772	154	6	1.064	212
7	0.663	132									
8	0.762	152									
9	0.772	154									
10	0.786	157									
11	1.073	214									
12	1.085	216									

Fig. 9   EDIT screen display of the utterance "Fred can go" showing nasal airflow, acoustic waveform, oral airflow and laryngograph trace. Segmentation lines are included separately for each channel and correspond to the major discontinuities in each signal (see text for full description). They are numbered separately for each channel, and the corresponding times and EPG frame numbers are provided below.

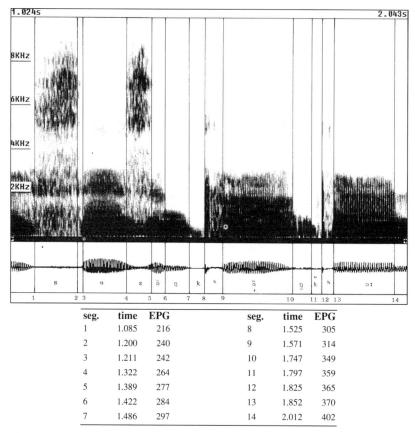

seg.	time	EPG	seg.	time	EPG
1	1.085	216	8	1.525	305
2	1.200	240	9	1.571	314
3	1.211	242	10	1.747	349
4	1.322	264	11	1.797	359
5	1.389	277	12	1.825	365
6	1.422	284	13	1.852	370
7	1.486	297	14	2.012	402

Fig. 10 Wide-band spectrogram of the utterance "Susan can't go".

gram show several wider-spaced, open pulses characteristic of creaky voice. Laryngographic and nasal airflow data therefore show that nasal creak occurs at (1.747-1.797) [349-359] for 50 ms. EPG contact data additionally show that there is no alveolar gesture for the two underlying alveolar segments. Instead constriction occurs at the velar place of articulation.[353] (fig. 7) shortly after the onset of the nasal creak. It is evident that the two underlying segments [n] and [t] coalesce and assimilate into a velar place of articulation. Laryngealisation is typical in this position in English. A drop in the nasal airflow at the end of the nasal creak indicates the presence of an oral velar stop following the [ŋ].

There is a reduction of the sequence /əʊə/ where the three vocalic elements are all reduced to a [ə] lasting for approximately 160 ms (1.852-2.012) [370-402].

(iii) and Linda is uncertain

Some slight anticipatory nasal airflow is present at the end of the [ə] vowel with a major rise at (2.001) [400] (line 1 on the nasal airflow trace, fig. 13) during the approach to the nasal. At the same time the oral airflow drops. Constriction is formed at the alveolar place of articulation as shown in the EPG data. The nasal airflow continues during both [n] and [l]. A boundary between [n] and [l] is not clear on the spectrogram but a major discontinuity is present at (2.051) (line 2 on the spectrogram and the acoustic waveform, figs. 12,13). Airflow data, however, show that there is nasal airflow throughout the [nl] sequence. Segmentation

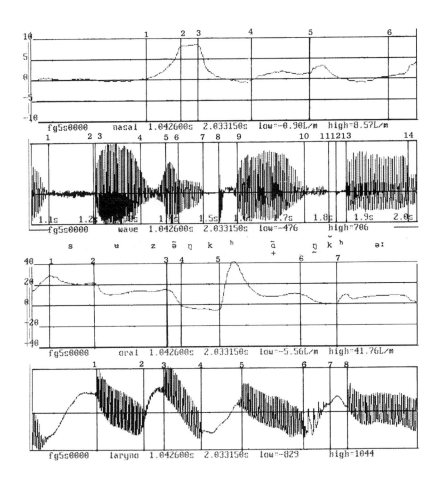

	acoustic waveform			nasal airflow			oral airflow			laryngograph signal	
seg.	time	EPG	seg.	time	EPG	seg.	time	EPG	seg.	time	EPG
1	1.085	216	1	1.342	268	1	1.085	216	1	1.211	242
2	1.200	240	2	1.426	285	2	1.200	240	2	1.328	265
3	1.211	242	3	1.472	294	3	1.389	277	3	1.380	276
4	1.322	264	4	1.601	320	4	1.426	285	4	1.477	295
5	1.389	277	5	1.759	351	5	1.525	305	5	1.580	316
6	1.422	284	6	1.963	392	6	1.731	346	6	1.740	348
7	1.486	297				7	1.825	365	7	1.797	359
8	1.525	305							8	1.852	370
9	1.571	314									
10	1.747	349									
11	1.797	359									
12	1.825	365									
13	1.852	370									
14	2.012	402									

Fig. 11   EDIT screen display of the utterance "Susan can't go".

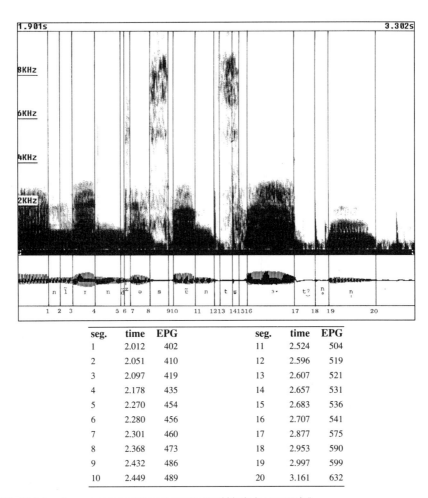

seg.	time	EPG	seg.	time	EPG
1	2.012	402	11	2.524	504
2	2.051	410	12	2.596	519
3	2.097	419	13	2.607	521
4	2.178	435	14	2.657	531
5	2.270	454	15	2.683	536
6	2.280	456	16	2.707	541
7	2.301	460	17	2.877	575
8	2.368	473	18	2.953	590
9	2.432	486	19	2.997	599
10	2.449	489	20	3.161	632

Fig. 12 Wideband spectrogram of the utterance "and Linda is uncertain".

of the two phones would therefore be problematic. The boundary, if any, could be decided on the basis of EPG data, instead, at point [406] (fig. 7) where one lateral electrode goes off. This pattern is typical for a lateral indicating that the lateral seal has been broken and that air is escaping laterally. Since the velum is lowered in this case, however, the production of the lateral is fully nasalised.

Very little nasal airflow is present during the following vowel [i] and there is no clear evidence of presence of nasality from spectral slices at different points during the vowel. This can be attributed to the fact that the vowel is close.

Nasal airflow is present throughout the following cluster (2.178-2.280) but the release of the [d] is oral. Energy falling at the end of the cluster and the shape of the last 3-4 pulses indicate that the duration of the [d] is very short (2.270 -2.280 = 10 ms approximately).

Following the release of the voiced [d] some noise appears on the spectrogram. Examination of the EPG patterns at the time of release [455] (fig. 7) shows a typical alveolar fricative pattern which indicates that the release is slightly affricated [d^z].

The tongue remains relatively high and front during the following [ə] in anticipation of the following [s]. This is reflected in the high F2 formant (1988 Hz approximately).

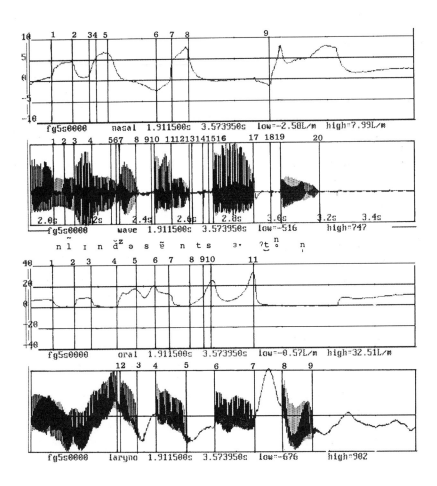

	acoustic waveform					nasal airflow			oral airflow			laryngograph signal	
seg.	time	EPG	seg.	time	EPG	seg.	time	EPG	seg.	time	EPG	seg.	time	EPG
1	2.012	402	11	2.524	504	1	2.001	400	1	2.001	400	1	2.280	456
2	2.051	410	12	2.596	519	2	2.094	418	2	2.094	418	2	2.297	459
3	2.097	419	13	2.607	521	3	2.160	432	3	2.160	432	3	2.370	474
4	2.178	435	14	2.657	531	4	2.194	438	4	2.280	456	4	2.450	490
5	2.270	454	15	2.683	536	5	2.255	451	5	2.368	473	5	2.582	516
6	2.280	456	16	2.707	541	6	2.461	492	6	2.449	489	6	2.705	541
7	2.301	460	17	2.877	575	7	2.530	506	7	2.516	503	7	2.877	575
8	2.368	473	18	2.953	590	8	2.596	519	8	2.596	519	8	2.997	599
9	2.432	486	19	2.997	599	9	2.953	590	9	2.657	531	9	3.124	624
10	2.449	489	20	3.161	632				10	2.688	537			
									11	2.877	575			

Fig. 13 EDIT screen display of the utterance "and Linda is uncertain".

Some anticipatory nasality is evident on the nasal airflow trace during [e]. Nasal flow also carries over during the fricative following the [n]. Airflow data show that as the nasal flow drops the oral flow increases very gradually. At the sharp increase in oral flow at (2.657) [531] (line 9 on oral airflow trace, fig. 13; and fig. 7) the maximum constriction is released and there is evidence of relatively high intensity fricative noise. The increased constriction evident on the EPG and the initial gradual increase in flow give rise to the perception of a stop segment (often produced with incomplete closure in connected speech) before the fricative.

The approach for the last alveolar oral stop starts at [575] at which point there is a drop at the oral airflow trace. The release for the [t] is nasal as indicated by the nasal airflow trace (2.953) [590] (line 9 on the nasal airflow trace, fig. 13). The nasal airflow continues during the following nasal which is a syllabic [n̩]. The phoneme [ə] has been elided. It is also possible that a [ʔ] is produced simultaneously with the alveolar stop prior to the nasal. The presence of a burst on the spectrogram and increased vertical movement of the larynx indicate the possible presence of a glottal stop in this position.

4.3 Segmentation and transcription

The segmentation criteria and the annotations used are described in this section. Information from all levels of representation is used and the reader might find it useful to refer to the analysis section above for a more detailed description of the activity of the different subsystems at different points during the utterance and of the connected-speech processes occurring.

For practical reasons, the following discussion on annotation assumes the phoneme as the segment for which landmarks are identified. However, the actual phonetic realisation of each phoneme is also provided. An overall phonemic and phonetic transcription of the utterance is also given in order to point out the differences between the reference underlying level and the actual realisation of the utterance.

/f/: The overall friction lasts for 80 ms. Part of the friction (0.303-onset of voicing) belongs to the following /r/. The annotations are taken from the onset of the friction to the end of the high intensity in the higher frequencies (0.303) [60] (line 2, fig. 8) evident on the spectrogram where the lip is assumed to release contact from the teeth. There are no evident discontinuities on the rest of the channels.

/r/: Most of the approximant is voiceless. The right boundary is taken shortly after the onset of voicing at the point where EPG shows tongue retraction [70] (0.350). F3 seems to become fairly stable after this point. Phonetic realisation [ɹ̥ᴵ].

/ε/: Beginning is taken at (0.350) at the onset of the main F2 and F3 structure and the end at the termination of the F2, F3 at (0.451).

/d/ and /k/: There is complete assimilation of /d/ to the following velar /k/. The duration of the closure (0.451-0.551) is taken from the end of the vowel to the moment of release as indicated from the spectrogram, the acoustic waveform and the oral airflow trace. The duration is longer than for a target /k/. When annotating from the oral airflow data it is often useful to consider the onset of the approach to the closure which coincides with a constriction in the EPG data and a reduction in amplitude on the acoustic waveform. This effectively captures the onset of the gesture towards the realisation of the segment. Considering the onset of closure at the point where the oral airflow reaches the baseline is not always useful since there might be some secondary coarticulatory airflow initiated by the movement of the tongue during the actual closure (Barry & Kuenzel [6]). Complete constriction as shown from the EPG data occurs at [92] (0.459) and the release occurs at [112] (0.560). It is not always reliable to use the EPG data alone when annotating the closure phase of a stop since complete constriction might occur behind/in front of the last/first row of electrodes and release might occur first laterally and then centrally. Phonetic realisation [g̊kʰ] (this transcription is used to reflect the longer duration of the closure, and the lower airflow peak, at the end of the /ε/ vowel than would be expected with a target /k/). Aspiration at the release occurs for 46 ms (0.551-0.597).

/ə/: Duration (0.597-0.663 = 66 ms). The nasal airflow trace (fig. 9) indicates this vowel is nasalised [ə̃].

/n/: Assimilated to the place of the following velar stop. Onset at (0.663) (line 7, fig. 8) from the spectrogram. Complete constriction from the EPG at [133] (0.665) coincides with the top of a sharp rise in the nasal flow (line 3 on the nasal airflow trace, fig.9) and the low point on the oral airflow (line 5 on the oral airflow trace, fig. 9). The right boundary is taken two pulses before the release (0.762) (line 8 on the spectrogram and the acoustic waveform, figs. 8, 9) where the intensity drops and there is evidence of a change in the shape of the pulses in the acoustic waveform. Nasal flow drops from (0.749) [149] to (0.779) [155]. Phonetically [ŋ].

/g/: Very short duration of approximately 10 ms. Release on the EPG is at [155], one frame after acoustic release (line 9, fig. 8) and oral airflow rises (line 6 on oral airflow trace, fig. 9)

/əu/: Duration of 287 ms (0.786-1.073). Annotation points were defined by the beginning and end of the F2 transitions. F1 and F2 values suggest phonetically [ə̈].

/s/: Annotated at onset and end of friction in the higher intensities (1.085-1.200 = 115 ms). It is difficult to annotate from the EPG data since constriction is often gradual. The peak on the airflow trace corresponds to the onset of the friction. The second peak corresponds closely to the end of the friction and soon after there is a release in the constriction for the fricative on the EPG data [240] (1.200) (line 2 on oral flow trace, fig. 11; and fig. 7).

/u/: Duration from (1.211-1.322), i.e. 111 ms, as annotated from the spectrogram. The tongue is relatively close for this vowel as shown on the EPG data. Phonetically [ʉ].

/z/: Annotated at the onset and end of the higher frequencies on the spectrogram (1.322-1.389). It is difficult to annotate from the acoustic waveform since the drop in amplitude is very gradual and there is no significant change in the shape of the pulses. The amplitude in the laryngograph trace drops between (1.328-1.380) [265-276] (lines 2, 3 on the laryngograph trace, fig. 11). At [265] (fig. 7) there is already a lot of contact in the alveolar region and at [277] there is release of the maximum contact for the /z/. The laryngograph trace does not therefore capture the approach to the gesture. Annotation from the oral airflow is difficult since the first peak can not be easily defined. There is some build-up in nasal airflow during the fricative beginning at (1.342) (line 1 in the nasal airflow trace, fig. 11).

/ə/: (1.389-1.422) annotated at onset and end of the formant structure on the spectrogram. The vowel is fully nasalised [ə̃] as evident from the nasal airflow trace which peaks at the end of the vowel (line 2 on nasal airflow trace, fig. 11).

/n/: Assimilated to the place of the following velar stop. Annotated from the spectrogram at (1.422-1.486 = 64 ms). It can be annotated from the EPG closure to the end of voicing (1.426-1.486 = 60 ms) [285-297]. Phonetically [ŋ].

/k/: Annotated from the spectrogram and the acoustic waveform (1.486-1.525 = 39 ms). The release of the oral airflow also occurs at the same point (1.525) (line 5 on the oral airflow trace, fig. 11). There is aspiration at the release (1.525-1.571) for 46 ms. The laryngograph trace shows clearly the lack of voicing during the closure. Phonetically [kʰ].

/ɑ/: From (1.571-1.747 = 176 ms) as annotated from the spectrogram and the acoustic waveform. The presence of nasal flow indicates this vowel is nasalised [ɑ̰̃].

/n/ and /t/: There is no realisation of the alveolar gesture for the two phonemes which coalesce and are realised as nasal creak lasting from (1.747-1.797). Laryngealisation is indicated by the presence of irregular cycles on the acoustic waveform and the laryngograph trace. EPG data show the presence of velar closure during the period of the nasal creak [353]. The presence of a [ŋ̰] is therefore indicated by the EPG data.

/g/: Completely voiceless velar stop from end of nasal creak (1.797) to the release on the spectrogram and oral airflow (1.825) (line 12 on the spectrogram and 7 on the oral airflow trace, figs. 10, 11). Aspiration from (1.825-1.852). Phonetically [kʰ].

/əʊ/: The diphthong and the following /ə/ from underlying /ənd/ are reduced to a long /əː/ lasting for 160 ms (1.852-2.012).

/n/ and /l/: There is presence of nasal airflow for both segments which last 85 ms (2.012-2.097). At [406] one lateral electrode goes off and the characteristic EPG pattern for the lateral is formed. The boundary could be taken at this point, i.e. /n/ (2012- 2.031 = 19 ms) based on the EPG data. Acoustic data show a discontinuity at (2.051).

/ɪ/: Duration of 81 ms (2.097-2.178) annotated at the beginning and end of the formant structure. Very little anticipatory and carryover nasal airflow present. The nasal airflow drops rapidly at (2.094) (line 2 on the nasal airflow trace, fig. 13) and rises rapidly at (2.160) (line 3 on the nasal flow, fig. 13).

/n/: The left boundary is taken immediately after the vowel but the right boundary is problematic. It is taken at the end of the drop of intensity and 10 ms before acoustic release (2.178-2.270).

/d/: The right boundary is taken at the release (2.270-2.280 = 10 ms). It corresponds with increase in airflow (line 4 on oral airflow trace, fig. 13). EPG data show a fricative pattern immediately after the release. The presence of noise on the spectrogram after the release also indicates that it is slightly affricated (2.280-2.301 = 21 ms). Phonetically [d̆ᶻ].

/ə/: The right boundary is taken at the end of the formant structure from the spectrogram (2.301-2.368 = 67 ms). EPG contact pattern data show that the tongue remains relatively high and front during the articulation of this vowel and this is reflected in the high F2 frequency present (1988 Hz).

/s/: Annotated from the presence of high frequencies on the spectrogram (2.368-2.432 = 64 ms). A period of voicelessness follows (2.432-2.449) just before the onset of the vowel.

/e/: Duration from (2.449-2.524). There is some nasal airflow towards the end of this vowel.

/n/: Annotation from the spectrogram (2.524-2.596 = 72 ms). Annotation from the EPG onset of the gesture to release of the contact in the alveolar region [504-518] (2.524-2.595 = 71 ms). This coincides closely with nasal trace lines 7 and 8 (fig. 13).

/s/: Initially there is increased constriction and low oral airflow which indicates the presence of a [t] before the [s]. The onset of the fricative may be taken at the sharp rise of oral airflow where there is evidence of a reduction in tongue palate contact (2.657) [531] and a burst on the acoustic waveform. The fricative is followed by a short period of voicelessness for 24 ms.

/ʒ/: From 2.707-2.877 (= 170 ms), annotated from the spectrogram and the acoustic waveform.

/t/: Approach starts at [575] for the stop and there is a gradual drop in oral airflow (line 11 on the oral airflow trace, fig. 13). The vertical movement of the larynx seen on the laryngograph trace indicates the presence of a glottal stop overlapping with the alveolar /t/. The nasal airflow rises at (2.953) [590] corresponding to a small burst on the acoustic waveform and the spectrogram and indicating a nasal release; phonetically [ʔt̚n̥]. The duration from the onset of silence to the onset of voicing for the following /n/ is (2.877-2.997).

/n/ The voicing for this syllabic [n̩] lasts till (3.161).

Phonemic transcription

/ˈfrɛd kən gəʊ // ˈsuzən ˈkɑnt gəʊ // ənd ˈlɪndə ɪz ənˈsɜtən /

On the basis of previous work on phonological processes in conversational speech (Shockey & Nicolaidis [24]) we would expect the following processes to occur (In the above transcription we assume that vowel reduction has already taken place in "can" and "and"):

i   Partial or complete assimilation of the alveolar /d/ to the following velar /k/. Alternatively both gestures may occur but they overlap.

ii Assimilation of the alveolar nasal to the velar place of articulation of the following velar stop: n > ŋ. A syllabic /ŋ̩/ may also occur: /kŋ̩g/.

iii The alveolar nasal may become syllabic in [suzn̩] and [ɛnsɜtn̩].

iv The alveolar plosive may be realised as a glottal stop or laryngealisation before a boundary: [t > [ʔ]/ _ #].

v   Dropping of the [d] in final -nd clusters, i.e. ənd > ən.

vi Devoicing of word final [z], i.e. lindəs.

vii A glottal stop may coincide with the alveolar plosive before a nasal stop, i.e. /ʔt̪n/ in "uncertain".

In our analysis we have found evidence for process (i) in "Fred can", (ii) in "can go" and "Susan can't", (iii) in "uncertain", (iv) in "can't", (v) in "and", (vi) in "Linda's", (vii) in "uncertain". Examination of the spectrogram, acoustic waveform, EPG, laryngograph and oral and nasal airflow traces has shown a variety of additional phonetic and idiosyncratic processes. In particular, the nasal airflow trace has shown the presence of nasal airflow during the production of several vowels preceding a nasal. Also, EPG data have indicated the presence of velar closure during the production of the nasal creak, for instance.

This multi-level analysis has therefore provided further insight in the processes present. The phonetic output as indicated by the different channels of information is transcribed below.

Phonetic transcription

[ˈfɹ̩ɪɛgkʰə̃ŋ̆gə̈ˈsʉzə̃ŋˈkʰɑ̃ŋkʰə̃ɪnˈl̃ɪnd̆ᶻəsẽnˈtsɜ•ʔtə̊n]

5   DISCUSSION

The main observations we can draw from the multi-channel analysis of the reference sentence may be summarised as follows:

i   A noticeable right-to-left assimilatory processes involving oral and nasal stops (d > g, n > ŋ). The systematic comparison of the information provided by the different channels of information indicated that there was absolutely no trace left of the underlying phoneme. This has important implications for automatic alignment of a given phonemic transcription onto a speech signal. It is necessary in cases of discrepancy to take into account the phonological assimilatory processes as manifested at the articulatory and acoustic level. A system would fail if such representations were not present. An abstract level of representation containing information such as speaker-specific socio-idiolectal phonological rules as well as speaking rate, style, etc. is necessary for successful recognition.

ii Nasalisation which anticipates or carries over into the actual realisation of the nasal segment. A comparison of the nasal and oral airflow is of particular interest since it indicates indirectly the movements of the velum and the control of the velopharyngeal port.

iii Complete or partial overlap of phonologically consecutive segments, e.g. /nt/ > [ŋk] in "can't go". The need for additional channels of information can be best illustrated in such cases of overlap where spectral information may not be sufficient in depicting the underlying organisation and sequence of segments.

The non-linear multi-level approach adopted in the ACCOR project is particularly well adapted to the investigation of the simultaneous activity of the different motor subsystems and the resulting acoustic output. This activity can give a precise view of the timing relationships of the different components of the phonatory and articulatory gestures. As such it proves a unique tool in the investigation of the temporal organisation of the speech production process. In particular, it gives us a better insight into the complementary fine-tuned coordination of antagonistic and synergistic actions co-occurring for the achievement of a given articulatory goal. For instance, we have been able to show the relationships which exist between the establishment of a constriction in the vocal tract and the modifications to the oral volume velocity. The consequences on the voicing were also evident in the laryngographic trace. A further example of such coordination between the velar and lingual subsystem was evident in the gradual lowering of the velum giving rise to gradual increase in the nasal airflow prior to the realisation of nasal consonants.

This approach facilitates the systematic mapping of articulatory activity to the acoustic output. It is interesting to notice that discontinuities on the one level do not necessarily correspond to discontinuities on the other. However, when we observe a major discontinuity in the acoustic signal we can refer to the different articulatory signals and interpret it more directly as a consequence of a particular articulatory gesture. Multi-channel data are most useful in the precise examination of the timing relationships between articulatory and acoustic events.

The above analysis has illustrated that a one-level annotation may not be sufficient and conclusive. Segmentation from the acoustic signal is based on delimiting the extent of the "phase of predominance" of the segment (Fowler [9]). A vowel in a CVC sequence, for example, is annotated at the onset or end of the formant pattern, i.e. where it dominates in the acoustic signal. The full extent of the underlying gestures, however, releasing the constriction sufficiently so that the formant structure can dominate are not captured. The vowel extent measured is therefore smaller than the actual extent of the underlying gestures for the vowel. The full extent of the underlying component gestures which coarticulate with neighbouring segments may not therefore be captured when delimiting the phase of prominence. Additional channels of information including oral/nasal airflow and other articulatory data often indicate the full extent of the underlying gestures (e.g. onset of constriction at the velar place of articulation is often evident in the EPG data and is accompanied by a decrease in oral airflow; initiation of velar movement is shown by increased nasal airflow). A multi-level approach is therefore essential in the investigation of the behaviour of the different subsystems and in the precise examination of the timing relationships of the underlying gestures during the production of continuous speech. Our data would then prove particularly suitable for the testing of various hypotheses from current models of speech production. As a long-term perspective the systematic comparison between articulatory gestures and the acoustic signal could lead to the development of a more comprehensive speech production theory. This multi-sensor data can be further used to attempt to reconstruct the vocal geometry from the signal.

In our description of the articulatory, aerodynamic and acoustic signals for the sentence "Fred can go, Susan can't go, and Linda is uncertain" we have alluded to the necessity to test some hypotheses by examining other dimensions of the speech production process. For instance, our discussion about the variations in the direction of the nasal airflow trace relies on the assumption that it reflects relatively linearly the vertical movements of the velum. This needs to be substantiated by additional data where we would record simultaneously the actual displacements of the velum and the resulting modifications of the nasal airflow. Also, EPG provides us with very valuable data on the organisation of lingual palatal contacts but we lack information about precise tongue placement and displacement when there is no contact. We have therefore started to extend our database by collecting data with electromagnetic devices such as the Articulatograph and the Movetrack simultaneously with the EPG recordings

(Hoole *et al.* [17]). With these techniques, we can additionally analyse the lips and jaw component which has to be taken into account when considering the vocal tract aperture (Hoole *et al.* [18]). Although a long-term and difficult enterprise, such an approach appears to be a promising way to continue in order to form better models of speech production.

6 CONCLUSION

Speech production is the result of the execution of coordinated gestures. The acoustic signal as such, although the output of this coordinated activity, does not explicitly depict the underlying organisation of articulatory gestures. The original feature-spreading theory considered speech as a linear concatenation of segments. In the ACCOR project, simultaneous examination of the activity of various motor subsystems and the resulting acoustic output has provided supporting evidence towards a non-linear based speech production theory.

We have shown in this paper that our approach to segmentation and labelling could shed some light on the issue of "missing data", i.e. the apparent discrepancy between different levels of representation and the absence of some direct correspondence between one symbolic unit (e.g. a segment) and a given physical signal, either acoustic or articulatory.

For the investigation of coarticulation, a nonlinear method of annotation (preferred to segmentation which refers directly to the concept of segment) gives a better picture of coproduction. This approach reveals important aspects of speech processes, of the timing relationships among different motor subsystem activities, and of the dynamic properties of the articulatory gestures. It furthermore provides a sound basis for distinguishing between universal regularities and language-specific constraints. This nonlinear procedure enables a unified interpretation of contradicting results obtained from different scholarly-oriented segmentation operations.

A systematic comparison of the activity of the different motor subsystems and the resulting acoustic signal based on this nonlinear methodology should lead to the development of an interpretative model of articulatory-acoustic correlations.

Acknowledgements: We acknowledge financial support from The European Economic Commission DGXIII under the auspices of ESPRIT II Basic Research Action (ACCOR project 3279). Thanks are due to Andy Butcher, Linda Shockey and Fiona Gibbon for helpful comments on the manuscript. We would also like to acknowledge Peter Davies for his work on the software and documentation reported in this paper.

REFERENCES

[1] E.R.M. Abberton, D.M. Howard & A.J. Fourcin (1989), 'Laryngographic assessment of normal voice: a tutorial', *Clinical Linguistics and Phonetics*, **3**(3), 281-296.

[2] R. André-Obrecht (1988), 'A new statistical approach for the automatic segmentation of continuous speech signals', *IEEE Trans. ASSP*, **36**(1), 29-40.

[3] J.K.F. Anthony & N. Hewlett (1984), 'Aerometry', in: *Experimental Clinical Phonetics* (eds. C. Code & M. Ball), London, Croom Helm, 79-106.

[4] K. Arai, Y. Yamashita, T. Kitahashi & R. Mizogucchi (1990), 'A speech labelling system based on knowledge processing', *Proc. ICSLP '90*, 1005-1008.

[5] D. Autesserre, G. Pérennou & M. Rossi (1989), 'Methodology for the transcription and labelling of a speech corpus', *J. Int. Phonetic Assoc.*, **19**(1), 2-15.

[6] W. Barry & H. Kuenzel (1975), 'Co-articulatory airflow characteristics of intervocalic voiceless plosives', *J. Phonetics*, **3**, 263-282.

[7] E. Farnetani, W.J. Hardcastle & A. Marchal (1989), 'Cross-language investigation of lingual coarticulatory processes using EPG', *Proc. Eurospeech '89*, 429-432.

[8] A.J. Fourcin, G.Harland, W. Barry & V. Hazan (eds) (1989) *Speech Input-Output Assessment; Multi-Lingual Methods and Standards*, Chichester: Ellis Horwood.

[9] C.A. Fowler (1985), 'Current perspectives on language and speech production: A critical overview', in: *Speech Science* (ed. R.G. Daniloff), Taylor & Francis, London, 193-278.

[10] J.P. Glass & V. Zue (1988), 'Multilevel acoustic segmentation of continuous speech', *Proc. ICASSP '88*, 429-432.

[11] F. Gibbon, W.J. Hardcastle & K. Nicolaidis (1991), 'Temporal and spatial coarticulation in /kl/ sequences: a cross-linguistic investigation', *ESPRIT II, BRA/ACCOR Periodic Progress Report III*.

[12] W.J. Hardcastle, F.E. Gibbon & W. Jones (1991), 'Visual display of tongue-palate contact: Electropalatography in the assessment and remediation of speech disorders', *Brit. J. Disorders of Communication*, **26**, 41-74.

[13] W.J. Hardcastle, F.E. Gibbon & K. Nicolaidis (1991), 'Multi-channel data acquisition and analysis system', *ESPRIT II, BRA/ACCOR Periodic Progress Report II*, vol. 3, 15.

[14] W.J. Hardcastle, F.E. Gibbon & K. Nicolaidis (1991), 'EPG data reduction methods and their implications for studies of lingual coarticulation', *J. Phonetics*, **19**, 251-266.

[15] W.J. Hardcastle, W. Jones, C. Knight, A. Trudgeon & G. Calder (1989), 'New developments in electropalatography: A state of the art report', *Clinical Linguistics & Phonetics*, **3**, 1-38.

[16] W.J. Hardcastle & A. Marchal (1990), 'EUR-ACCOR: A multilingual articulatory and acoustic database', *Proc. ICSLP '90*, 1293-1296.

[17] P. Hoole, N. Nguyen,W.J. Hardcastle & A. Marchal (1991), 'Reduction and parametrization of EPG and EMA data for the investigation of articulatory/acoustic correlations', *ESPRIT II, BRA/ACCOR Periodic Progress Report III*.

[18] P. Hoole, N. Nguyen & W.J. Hardcastle (1991), 'Articulatory, and acoustic analysis of coarticulation in lingual fricatives', *ESPRIT II, BRA/ACCOR Periodic Progress Report II*.

[19] A. Löfqvist (1990), 'Speech as audible gestures', in: *Speech Production and Speech Modelling* (eds. W.J. Hardcastle & A. Marchal), Kluwer, Dordrecht, 289-322.

[20] A. Marchal & N. Nguyen-Trong (1990), 'Nonlinearity and phonetic segmentation', *JASA*, Suppl. 1, **87**, 79-82.

[21] A. Marchal, W.J. Hardcastle, P. Hoole, W. Farnetani, A. Ni Chasaide, O. Schmidbauer, I. Galiana-Ronda, O. Engstrand & D. Recasens (1991), 'EUR-ACCOR: the design of a multichannel database', *Proc. XIIth ICPhS.*, vol. 5, 422-425.

[22] J.C. Pérez, I. Alfonso & F. Casacuberta (1991), 'The ACCOR database: Design of the DB management system', *ESPRIT II, BRA/ACCOR Periodic Progress Report II*, vol. 3, 10.

[23] M. Rossi (1990), 'Automatic segmentation, why and what segments?', *Proc. ICSLP '90*, 237-240.

[24] L. Shockey & K. Nicolaidis (1991), 'Connected speech processes in English', *ESPRIT II, BRA/ACCOR Periodic Progress Report II*, vol. 3, 15.

[25] T. Svendsen & K. Kvale (1990), 'Automatic alignment of phonemic labels with continuous speech', *Proc. ICSLP '90*, 997-1000.

[26] B. Teston & B. Galindo (1990), 'Design and development of a workstation for speech production analysis', *Proc. VERBA*, 400-408.

[27] A. Trudgeon, C. Knight, W.J. Hardcastle, G. Calder & F. Gibbon (1988), 'A multi-channel physiological data acquisition system based on an IBM PC, and its application to speech therapy', *Proc. Speech '88 (7th Fase Symposium)*, 1093-1100.

Artificial neural networks: the mole-grips of the speech scientist

Tony Robinson

1   INTRODUCTION

The aim of this paper is to give an overview of artificial neural networks (ANN) with application to speech processing. The first half of the paper starts off at a very general level by describing the whole range of tasks, models and techniques within the field. This is then narrowed down to the back-propagation algorithm for feed-forward and feedback networks. The second half covers a range of speech processing tasks, giving examples of the use of artificial neural networks.

2   BACKGROUND

2.1 What are artificial neural networks?

The field of artificial neural networks, or *connectionism*, covers a wide variety of techniques and models [17,10,18,25,9,16,32]. In general, artificial neural networks are used to model a task by adapting internal parameters. Due to the nonlinear nature of many artificial neural networks, iterative techniques are often employed to perform the parameter adaptation, which can then be reasonably viewed as a "learning" process. Tasks are usually specified in terms of modelling a data set.

The models consist of a large number of simple *processing elements* (*computational neurons, nodes* or *units*) that in number can be used to generate non-linear mapping functions to do useful tasks. Each processing element computes a simple function of the other processing elements to which it is connected, and this result (activation) is made available to other units. The pattern of interconnection of the processing elements leads to a range of architectures:

- Strictly *feed-forward networks* are those where an ordering of the processing elements exists such that the output of one processing element is only dependent on the input of elements with a lower index. Thus the state of the network can be determined by computing the activations of the processing elements in order.

- If feedback is allowed, then the network becomes a dynamical system. Such *recurrent networks* can be formulated in terms of discrete time [1,30] or continuous time [26]. The feedback may be either used to settle to a fixpoint for a given input, or may change as a function of the changing input.

These two architectures are shown in fig. 1. Units are shown as circles, and connections between units as arrows. The architecture of the feed-forward network is one layer of *hidden units* and two layers of *weights*.

2.2 Are artificial neural networks real neural networks?

Whilst the field of artificial neural networks has doubtless been inspired by the information processing that occurs in real neural networks, artificial neural networks can at best be considered a poor approximation of the real thing. Some of the key areas where neural com-

Visual Representations of Speech Signals: Martin Cooke, Steve Beet and Malcolm Crawford (eds.)
© 1993 by John Wiley & Sons Ltd

Feed-forward network   Recurrent network

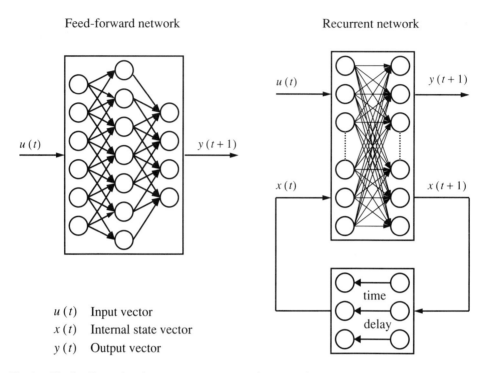

u (t)   Input vector
x (t)   Internal state vector
y (t)   Output vector

Fig. 1   The feedforward and recurrent error propagation networks.

putation (whether performed by real or artificial neural networks) differs significantly from
symbolic processing are:

  • Massively parallel operation
  • The use of many simple processing elements
  • The use of distributed representations
  • Robustness to failure of a single unit.

One of the main differences between the neural processing of man and machine is that of
scale. Current artificial neural network technology uses about $10^{?}$ processing elements
whereas the brain has about $10^{??}$ neurons. This difference is vast and thus it is difficult to justify a model of human information processing using artificial neural networks. However, if
the sights are lowered to that of modelling simple animal behaviour, then it is possible to
match the number and interconnectivity of the neurons of simple insects with today's silicon
hardware.

2.3 What can artificial neural networks compute?

One property of the current generation of artificial neural networks that has received
much attention is the formulation of models that can represent any arbitrary nonlinear function [11]. However, the property of representation is very different from being able to learn
the function from example, and even in the cases where this is possible, there is not necessarily any guarantee that a trained network will produce an appropriate output for an unseen input.

As in any function approximation technique, it remains important to have a good model
of the task in order to specify a sensible network architecture and cost function to minimise.

One of the most important considerations is fitting the number of free parameters used to specify the model to the size of the training set available. With insufficient free parameters an adequate model cannot be formed, and with too many, arbitrary inappropriate features can be modelled as well.

2.4 How do artificial neural networks compute?

There are two common types of processing element employed in artificial neural network:

i   The first computes the distance from any point in the input space to a hyperplane, and outputs a nonlinear function of that distance, normally such that the points on one side of the plane have a high output, and the points on the other side have a low output. Thus the input space is carved up into regions which may correspond to some pattern class or feature.

ii The second computes the distance to another point in the input space and outputs a nonlinear function of the distance. This is normally high for the area near the central point and low for points further away. The technique of radial basis functions falls into this class, where the centre of the basis function is often placed on a training example, the radius of the basis function giving the sphere of influence of the node. This methodology has the advantage of forcing a smooth function of the input space, which is often desirable. In addition, if the basis functions are fixed, a linear mapping to the output space is easily computed.

Although this simple technique is often sufficient, radial nodes have a more general applicability [30]. For example, consider the two dimensional problem in fig. 2 where the task

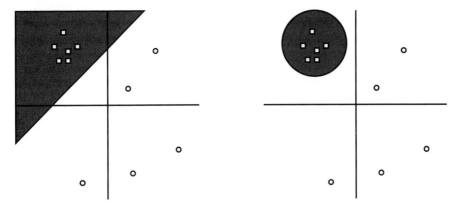

Hyperplane solution   Radial basis function solution

Fig. 2   Partitioning the input space with different types of network

is to partition the input space such as to separate the regions containing squares and circles. Here a network consisting of hyperplane nodes gives quite a different decision boundary to one consisting of radial basis functions. The problem was deliberately chosen so that either solution seems reasonable, although physical constraints on the input space may favour one or other type of processing in a real-world task.

2.5 A few rivals to artificial neural networks

If the problem is simple enough, there is no need to invoke a complex tool to solve it. For instance, if a linear function can perform the required mapping, then it is likely that standard linear techniques are more appropriate [16]. Similarly, if there are sufficient training examples to populate the input space to the resolution required, then averaging over a radius of resolution will give an acceptable solution.

In many interesting real-world tasks, the form of the solution is not known, and there are insufficient examples to use simple partition and average techniques. It is therefore necessary to use a more complex form of smoothing in the input space. The technique of k nearest-neighbours does this very neatly by averaging over the k training patterns that are closest to the probe input. This has the advantage of fine resolution in the densely populated areas, whilst maintaining a sufficient number of data points to maintain the accuracy of the result. The search for the nearest neighbours can be made fast using kD trees, and it is possible to hard limit the size of the tree for the continuous learning case [19].

However, it can be argued that if high-order correlations exist in the input data, then any technique that uses a simple distance metric in the input space will not be able to exploit this information.

2.6 What are the main forms of artificial neural network?

In addition to the use of feedback discussed earlier, classification of artificial neural network techniques can be done in terms of the types of task and the training procedures used.

Tasks:

i   The *associative memory* task is to recall the closest training pattern given a partial or corrupted input. As pointed out in [17], some care must be taken when using this style of computation, since if the distance measure is well defined, then the network can perform no better than simply searching the training set.

ii The task of *prediction* is to form an internal model of the process sufficient to generate the next point in a series. The fields of system identification and control have long been applied to linear models and are now being applied to non-linear systems [23, 2].

iii Perhaps the most common task that artificial neural network models are applied to is that of *classification*. This is because many classification tasks require the construction of complex decision surfaces. Whilst classification merely requires a decision as to which class a given input most probably belongs, a powerful extension is to estimate the probability density function over all classes. Simple classification can be performed by picking the class with the maximum *a posteriori* probability, but in addition the network may be used as a component in a larger classifier that incorporates other probabilistic evidence, such as a Markov model [29].

Training procedures:

i   In the *supervised learning* task, the data set consists of typical input/output pairs. The aim here is to adapt the internal parameters to minimise some cost function dependent on the distance between the output of the network and the target given by the data.

ii The *reinforcement learning* task is similar to that of supervised learning, but in this case only the distance between the actual and ideal outputs is available as a training signal. As there is much less information available, the task is correspondingly harder.

iii The third type of task, *unsupervised learning*, is when there is no information at all about the ideal output for a given input. Instead, learning is guided by a general principle or format for the outputs, such as minimising the information loss through the model.

2.7 Back-propagation for multi-layer perceptrons

Back propagation [37, 31] is a gradient descent technique for cascades of nonlinear but differentiable functions. It can be applied to learn the set of weights associated with an artificial neural network consisting of multiple layers of processing elements, as illustrated in fig. 1. Such models are known as *multi-layer perceptrons* (MLPs) and normally consist of weighted-sum nodes with sigmoidal activation functions. For a given set of inputs, x_j and a set of weights, w_{ij}, the outputs of a standard feed-forward network are given by:

$$net_i = \sum_{j=0}^{i-1} w_{ij} x_j \qquad x_i = \frac{1}{1 + e^{-net_i}} \, . \tag{1}$$

The Euclidean distance measure is often used on the outputs:

$$E = \frac{1}{2} \sum_{all\,patterns} \sum_i (o_i - t_i)^2 \, . \tag{2}$$

Differentiating this error measure with respect to the output of all units gives the *error signal*. This may be done directly for units in the output layer, and indirectly using the chain rule for all other units. Differentiating the error measure with respect to the weights and summing over all patterns gives the direction of steepest descent. Changing the weights by a small amount in the direction of steepest descent minimises the error measure and so adjusts the internal parameters so as to better model the target input/output pairs.

2.8 Practical issues

In practice, several modifications have to be made to get reasonable learning performance from the back-propagation algorithm. Perhaps the most fundamental is that strict gradient descent is not a practical learning algorithm in that it assumes infinitesimal changes in weight space on each iteration. More desirable is to make as large a change as possible on every iteration. A simple method, known as adding *momentum*, applies a first-order filter to the gradient signal. Thus changes in dimensions with oscillatory trajectories are damped in relation to changes in non-oscillatory dimensions. More sophisticated methods exist and generally repay the effort involved in implementing them [4,13,6].

There are two extremes to the frequency at which the gradient information is used to update the weights. At one end is true gradient descent, which requires that the partial gradients are summed over all pattern classes. The other extreme is to update the weights on the basis of one pattern alone. If the number of patterns is small and covers the whole of the pattern space, such as the "exclusive or" toy problem, then summing over all patterns is a good technique. However, real-world tasks require a large amount of training data to specify a model accurately, but a much smaller amount to make a poorer approximation. Iterative learning techniques have to refine poor approximations, and during the initial training it is sufficient to only see part of the training set. This is taken to the extreme in *stochastic gradient descent* which maintains a per-pattern update throughout the training. For linear systems there are schedules for decreasing the gradient weighting in order to ensure convergence. In the middle ground, it is possible to either gradually increase the number of patterns used to estimate the gradient over, or maintain per-pattern updating but increase the momentum smoothing factor to eventually average over the whole training set. Finally, it should be noted that strict gradient descent will find the first local minimum, which may be not be a good solution. The use of stochastic gradient methods may add sufficient noise to escape shallow minima.

The architecture and number of connections in a network are a critical part of the model design. Too many or too few layers and the required mapping may take too long to train, if at all. Most researchers using the basic architecture have settled on one hidden layer and two layers of adjustable weights. This leaves the size of the hidden layers, and hence the number of free parameters in the model: too few, and the model won't even fit the training data; too many and overfitting will occur so that poor generalisation is seen. One easy way to limit the effects of overfitting is to keep back a proportion of the training data, and test on this data periodically. Training stops when performance ceases to increase on the *cross-validation set*.

It is very important to use the right cost function, or error measure when parameter fitting any model. In the case of artificial neural networks, this is closely related to a sensible choice of the activation function on the output units. Three simple cases may be identified:

i In the case where the model is known to have a strong linear component, then it is important to be able to model that. This means having linear output units and direct connections from the input units to the output units. Under the assumption of a Gaussian distribution of the predictor error, then minimising the mean squared error maximises the mutual information between the target values and the predicted values.

ii If the outputs are to be interpreted as the estimation of independent probabilities, then the information difference between the target and actual output distributions is given by the cross entropy distance measure:

$$E = -\sum_i (t_i \log(x_i) + (1 - t_i) \log(1 - x_i)). \tag{3}$$

iii Similarly, if outputs are to be taken as a probability density function over N classes, then the use of the *softmax* activation function [3] on the outputs ensures that the total sums to unity. A sensible distance measure is then to maximise the log likelihood of the occurrence of the target class:

$$x_i = \frac{e^{net_i}}{\sum_i e^{net_i}} \qquad E = -\sum_i t_i \log\left(\frac{t_i}{x_i}\right). \tag{4}$$

These are only examples, and the general principle is to pick a network architecture and cost function that best fits the task to hand.

2.9 Recurrent networks

For problems with sequential input, it is important to exploit the known structure in order to make a good model of the system. The simplest method is to truncate the series, giving the *sliding window* approach. This may be sufficient if the information needed is known to decay rapidly outside the input window. However, this technique can only deal with finite context and equal weighting is given over the whole window. Increasing the context available rapidly increases the number of parameters to be estimated, which decreases model accuracy.

Common computations need to be shared for accuracy of parameter estimation and for run-time efficiency. This may be achieved within the sliding window framework by tying the weights from every frame of input to the hidden layer. The same thing can be done for a range of hidden layer units, and this architecture is known as a time delay neural network [36]. The use of shared weights can be seen as incorporation of prior knowledge that subsections of the complete network should perform the same computations. A related way of incorporating prior knowledge into network design is to specify a range of values that the weights may adopt, or to specify the form of the probability density function [24].

A more efficient way of sharing computations is to employ feedback. This may be achieved in a number of ways, which can be divided into supervised and unsupervised methods for estimating the internal state. Historically, most connectionist research has concentrated on the supervised methods:

i   Conceptually the simplest method is *back-propagation through time* [31]. Here the network is expanded in time, and at the end of the sequence the target values are presented and the gradient signal calculated by back-propagating the error signal in time. This has the disadvantage that no learning takes place until the end of the sequence, and therefore requires some approximations to deal with non-terminating sequences. Nevertheless, this is still a very useful technique.

ii To avoid the unrolling of the network in time, it is possible to limit the recurrence to *output feedback* [15]. However, this method cannot deal with feeding back information that is not present in the output.

iii An approximation to back-propagation through time can be made by truncating the error signal after one time step. If the hidden units of one time frame are presented to the network input at the next time frame, then some context information is fed forward in time. This network architecture is known as the *simple recurrent network* [5]. However, the truncation of the gradient signal can lead to problems in convergence, and there is no gain in reduced computational requirements over back-propagation through time.

iv A neat method of achieving local learning in time is to limit the feedback to a fraction of the past value of the unit. This scheme is known as Focused Back-propagation [21].

v   Another approach is to place the burden of the feedback with the link connecting the units. This is normally taken to be a time-independent multiplicative function, but generalising this to a linear IIR filter gives recurrent behaviour. Such *globally-feedforward locally-recurrent networks* [2] have the advantage that the dynamics can be analysed by linear systems theory.

vi Yet another approach is to carry a set of partial derivatives forward in time from which the error signal can be calculated. This *real-time recurrent learning* [30, 38] has the appeal of a simpler structure than maintaining past inputs, although in practice the required computation is much larger.

vii Finally, the *recurrent cascade-correlation* [7] achieves fast sequential learning by detecting correlations in the input and state units which are likely to be exploitable in forming the output.

Unsupervised recurrent networks deserve a mention, for their potential if not for their current degree of development. Here the aim is to form a dynamical system such that the internal state retains the maximum amount of information from past inputs. In the linear case, this may be achieved with *anti-Hebbian learning* [8,27] which is an iterative technique to perform principle component analysis on the input. Under the appropriate assumptions, the information loss is minimised when the output spans the subspace of maximum variance. One approach to the non-linear case is to try to unpack the current state into the last input and last state. Such a *state compression network* [30] has been found useful for simple problems. Another approach is to try use all but one state output to predict the remaining value. Non-linear decorrelation can be driven by the difference in these values, which forms the basis of *history compression* [33].

Feedback in recurrent networks adds stability problems during training. Many of the approximations used to speed up the training of non-recurrent networks fail when the parameters to be adapted occur to high-order powers in the gradient descent procedure. However, when used with care, these networks have the power to represent complex non-linear dynamical systems.

3 SPEECH APPLICATIONS

This section gives a brief overview of the application of artificial neural net techniques to speech processing (e.g. [20]). Further details can be found in the proceedings of the IEEE International Conference on Acoustics, Speech and Signal Processing (ICASSP), as well as the series Advances in Neural Information Processing (published by Morgan Kaufmann), the proceedings of the IEEE workshops on Neural Networks for Signal Processing, and many other publications.

3.1 Prediction

The autoregressive model of linear prediction is widely used in all areas of speech processing. Here the output of the model, $y(t)$, is a weighted sum of past outputs plus an error term, $x(t)$, which defines an IIR filter:

$$y(t) = x(t) + \sum_{i=1}^{N} a_i \, y(t-i).$$ (5)

A closed form solution to calculating the coefficients, a_i, exists via Durbin's algorithm or the covariance method [28].

Similarly, for a moving average model, an FIR filter may be defined:

$$y(t) = \sum_{i=0}^{M} b_i \, x(t-i).$$ (6)

For many speech applications it is better to use the closed form solution for parameter reestimation. However, gradient-based techniques have a place, for instance in the continuous estimation of the inverse response of a telephone channel for modem applications.

Locally recurrent networks [2] have been shown to be able to model non-linear dynamical processes with lower prediction error than the equivalent linear system. These have an interpretation in terms of the transient response of internal linear synapses.

Radial basis functions and multi-layer perceptrons have been used in place of the standard linear predictive coder and found to give lower mean squared error [23,39]. However, there are the disadvantages that no inverse model exists, stability conditions are not known, and good quantisation schemes for the predictor parameters have yet to be formulated.

3.2 Compression

Artificial neural networks have been proposed to perform the data compression task by presenting the input as the desired output. If the network has an intermediate layer whose dimensionality is less than that of the input and output, then this forces a lower dimensional representation of the input. The linear case with the squared error cost function is well understood, the compressed representation is the subspace of the input which has maximum variance. This can be found using principle component analysis. The closed form solution is to calculate the covariance matrix of the zero-meaned input. The desired dimensions are those of the eigenvectors associated with the largest eigenvalues. Anti-Hebbian learning [8, 27] can find this subspace using stochastic gradient descent. The use of an extra linear layer to orthogonalise the outputs of hidden units has been found to considerably speed up back-propagation training [34]. This has been attributed to the fact that for a quadratic error surface, the direction of steepest descent only points towards the minimum if the gradient is aligned with one of the parameter axes.

3.3 Noise Reduction

Tamura has applied multi-layer perceptrons to the task of mapping a speech waveform, corrupted by additive noise, to the clean waveform [35]. The mapping was performed in the time domain, using least mean squares as the distance measure. The resulting speech was judged to be more intelligible than that processed using spectral subtraction which is commonly used for noise compensation in speech recognition.

3.4 Speaker Adaptation

Several researchers have applied multi-layer perceptrons to the task of voice normalisation so that any speaker can be mapped onto a standard voice which is used to train a recogniser. For example Huang *et al.* [12] used dynamic programming to align the two speakers, then used vector quantisation to give coarse classification of types of speech. Multiple networks were trained, one for each type of speech. The resulting recognition rate on a large vocabulary task after 40 adaptation sentences was as good as the speaker-independent performance.

3.5 Speech Recognition

Speech recognition has received the most attention of all the applications to speech. This is because there is a large gap between machine and human performance, which makes the area a challenging one, and also because most researchers now agree that the best way to tackle the task is to fit the parameters of a general model to a large body of training data.

Approaches can be categorised by the method of dealing with time variation. For medium vocabulary, isolated word recognition, the beginning and end of the word can be determined, and pattern matching techniques applied. Commonly, dynamic time warping or the related technique of hidden Markov models is used. Both these techniques use dynamic programming to align the unknown word with a template. It is not obvious how to incorporate this process of alignment into an artificial neural net approach, but some success has been achieved with using linear time warping or dynamic programming.

More interesting is the task of large vocabulary connected speech recognition where no reliable cues to the endpoints of words exist, and where the vocabulary size is such that it is necessary to build pronunciation models. The task then becomes that of recognising a sequence of sub-word units, and being able to build these into word strings constrained by a grammar. The established technique in this area is that of hidden Markov models which associates a state occupancy probability with all points in the input space. Multi-layer perceptrons have been shown to be good estimators of the Markov model emission probabilities [29].

Context is important in speech recognition at all levels of representation. On short timescales, co-articulation changes the pronunciation of phonemes due to physiological constraints on the rate of change of the articulators. On a longer time scale, we can expect the voice characteristics of the speaker to be constant, and so recognition should occur in the context of the estimated speaker characteristics. Hidden Markov models attempt to incorporate these context effects by considering first- and second-order differences of the acoustic vector. The same effect may be achieved by using many consecutive frames as input to a sliding-window multi-layer perceptron [36,29], or the use of recurrent networks [30].

3.6 Language Modelling

Comparatively little work has been done on language modelling using artificial neural net techniques. Perhaps this is because of the lack of a good framework to represent the sequential nature of the task. The use of multi-layer perceptrons as probability estimators for Markov models looks promising as a way of estimating stochastic grammars. Given a word string $W = w_0, w_1, w_2, ..., w_{n-1}$ which occurs with probability $Pr(w)$, the problem is to find a good model for $Pr(w)$. Expanding gives:

$$Pr(W) = Pr(w_0, w_1, w_2, ..., w_{n-1}) \qquad (7)$$

which is

$$Pr(w_0) Pr(w_1 \mid w_0) Pr(w_2 \mid (w_0, w_1)) \dots Pr(w_{n-1} \mid (w_0 \dots w_{n-2})) \tag{8}$$

A popular assumption is to limit the dependency to the last three words [14]:

$$Pr(w) \approx Pr(w_0) Pr(w_1 \mid w_0) \prod_{i=2}^{n} Pr(w_i \mid w_{i-1}, w_{i-2}) \tag{9}$$

Practical difficulties arise from the need to make good estimates of probabilities when the count of occurrences in the training set is small or zero. Using word categories instead of words is one way of smoothing. Connectionist language modelling via probability estimation has been recorded with a performance as good as that of standard trigram techniques [22].

4 CONCLUSION

Although artificial neural net techniques are obviously not the solution to every problem, the examples given show that they can be usefully applied to a range of speech-processing problems. The technology is just a way of performing parameter estimation for non-linear models, and whilst blind application may give a low-manpower solution to a problem, forming a good model is normally more important. The iterative techniques involved mean that the models normally take longer to train, although there are potential benefits of large-scale parallelism given suitable hardware. In problems where the exact specification of a good solution is not known and a sensible neural net architecture can be found, these techniques can provide the best approach to obtaining a good solution.

REFERENCES

[1] L. B. Almeida (1987), 'A learning rule for asynchronous perceptrons with feed back in a combinatorial environment', *Proc. IEEE 1st An. Int. Conf. Neural Networks*, II, 609-618.

[2] A. D. Back (1992), *New Techniques for Nonlinear System Identification: A Rapprochement between Neural Networks and Linear Systems*, PhD Thesis, Department of Electrical Engineering, University of Queensland.

[3] J. S. Bridle (1989), 'Probabilistic interpretation of feedforward classification network outputs, with relationships to statistical pattern recognition', in: *Neuro-computing: Algorithms, Architectures and Applications* (eds. F. Fougelman-Soulie & J. Hérault), Springer-Verlag, New York, 227-236.

[4] L. W. Chan & F. Fallside (1987), 'An adaptive training algorithm for back propagation networks', *Computer Speech & Language*, **2**(3/4), 205-218.

[5] J. L. Elman (1988), 'Finding structure in time', *Technical Report CRL-8801, Center for Research in Language, UCSD*.

[6] S. E. Fahlman (1988). 'Faster-learning variations on back-propagation: An empirical study', *Proc. Connectionist Models Summer School*, Morgan Kaufmann.

[7] S. E. Fahlman (1991), 'The recurrent cascade-correlation architecture', *Technical Report CMU-CS-91-100, School of Computer Science, Carnegie Mellon University*.

[8] P. Földiák (1989), 'Adaptive network for optimal linear feature extraction', *Int. Joint Conf. Neural Networks*, vol. I, 401-405.

[9] J. Hertz, A. Krogh & R. Palmer (1991), *Introduction to the Theory of Neural Computation*, Addison-Wesley.

[10] G. E. Hinton (1987), 'Connectionist learning procedures', *Technical Report CMU-CS-87-115, Computer Science Department, Carnegie Mellon University*.

[11] K. Hornik, M. Stinchcombe & H. White (1989), 'Multilayer feedforward networks are universal approximators', *Neural Networks*, **2**, 359-366.

[12] X. D. Huang, K. F. Lee & A. Waibel (1991), 'Connectionist speaker normalization and its application to speech recognition', *Proc. IEEE Workshop on Neural Networks for Signal Processing*, 357-366.

[13] R. A. Jacobs (1988), 'Increased rates of convergence through learning rate adaptation', *Neural Networks*, **1**, 295-307.

[14] F. Jelinek (1991), 'Up from trigrams! The struggle for improved language models', Proc. European Conf. on Speech Technology, 1037-1040.

[15] M. I. Jordan (1986), 'Serial order: A parallel distributed processing approach', *ICS Report 8604, Institute for Cognitive Science, University of California, San Diego.*

[16] T. Kohonen (1988), *Self-organization and Associative Memory*, 2nd ed., Springer-Verlag, New York.

[17] R. P. Lippmann (1987), 'An introduction to computing with neural nets', *IEEE ASSP Magazine*, **4**(2), 4-22.

[18] J. Makhoul (1991), 'Pattern recognition properties of neural networks', *Proc. IEEE Workshop Neural Networks for Signal Processing*, IEEE, Piscataway, NJ, 173-187.

[19] A. W. Moore (1990), *Efficient Memory-based Learning for Robot Control*, PhD thesis, Cambridge University Computer Laboratory. Available as TR 209.

[20] D. P. Morgan & C. L. Scofield (1991), *Neural Networks and Speech Processing*, Kluwer Academic Publishers.

[21] M. C. Mozer (1989), 'A focused backpropagation algorithm for temporal pattern recognition', *Complex Systems*, **3**, 349-381.

[22] M. Nakamura & K. Shikano (1989), 'A study of english word category prediction based on neural networks', *Proc. ICASSP '89*, 731-734.

[23] M. Niranjan & V. Kadirkamanathan (1991), 'A nonlinear model for time series prediction and signal interpolation', *Proc. ICASSP '91*, 1713-1716.

[24] S. J. Nowlan & G. E. Hinton (1991), 'Soft weight-sharing', in: *Advances in Neural Information Processing Systems 4*, Morgan Kaufmann.

[25] Y. H. Pao (1989), *Adaptive Pattern Recognition and Neural Networks*, Addison-Wesley.

[26] B. A. Pearlmutter (1990), 'Dynamic recurrent neural networks', *Technical Report CMU-CS-90-196, School of Computer Science, Carnegie-Mellon University.*

[27] M. D. Plumbley (1991), *On information theory and unsupervised neural networks*, PhD thesis, Cambridge University Engineering Department, 1991. Available as CUED/F-INFENG/TR78.

[28] L. R. Rabiner & R. W. Schafer (1978), *Digital Processing of Speech Signals*, Prentice Hall, Englewood Cliffs, NJ.

[29] S. Renals, N. Morgan & H. Bourlard (1991), 'Probability estimation by feed-forward networks in continuous speech recognition', *Proc. IEEE Workshop on Neural Networks for Signal Processing*, Princeton, NJ

[30] A. J. Robinson (1989), *Dynamic Error Propagation Networks*, PhD thesis, Cambridge University Engineering Department.

[31] D. E. Rumelhart, G. E. Hinton & R. J. Williams (1986), 'Learning internal representations by error propagation', in: *Parallel Distributed Processing: Explorations in the Microstructure of Cognition. Vol. I: Foundations*, (eds. D. E. Rumelhart & J. L. McClelland), chapter 8, Bradford Books/MIT Press, Cambridge, MA.

[32] D. E. Rumelhart & J. L. McClelland (1986), *Parallel Distributed Processing: Explorations in the Microstructure of Cognition. Vol. I: Foundations*, MIT Press, Cambridge, MA.

[33] J. H. Schmidhuber (1992), 'Learning complex, extended sequences using the principle of history compression', *Neural Computation*, **4**, 234-242.

[34] F. M. Silva & L. B. Almeida (1991), 'Speeding-up backpropagation by data orthonormalization', *Proc. ICANN '91 (Espoo, Finland)*, vol. 2, Elsevier Science, Amsterdam, 1503-1506.

[35] S. Tamura (1989), 'An analysis of a noise reduction neural network', *Proc. ICASSP '89*, 2001-2004.

[36] A. Waibel, T. Hanazawa, G. Hinton, K. Shikano & K. J. Lang (1989), 'Phoneme recognition using time-delay neural networks', *IEEE Trans. ASSP*, **37**(3), 328-339.

[37] P. J. Werbos (1974), *Beyond Regression: New Tools for Prediction and Analysis in the Behavioral Sciences*, PhD thesis, Harvard University.

[38] R. J. Williams & D. Zipser (1988), 'A learning algorithm for continually running fully recurrent neural networks', *ICS Report 8805, Institute for Cognitive Science, University of California, San Diego*.

[39] L. Wu & F. Fallside (1992), 'Fully vector quantised neural network- based code-excited non-linear predictive speech coding', *Technical report, Cambridge University Engineering Department.* Submitted to *IEEE Transactions on Signal Processing*.

On the importance of time — a temporal representation of sound

Malcolm Slaney and Richard F. Lyon

1   INTRODUCTION

The human auditory system has an amazing ability to separate and understand sounds. We believe that temporal information plays a key role in this ability, more important than the spectral information that is traditionally emphasised in hearing science. In many hearing tasks, such as describing or classifying single sound sources, the underlying mathematical equivalence makes the temporal versus spectral argument moot. We show how the nonlinearity of the auditory system breaks this equivalence, and is especially important in analysing complex sounds from multiple sources of different characteristics.

The auditory system is inherently nonlinear. In a linear system, the component frequencies of a signal are unchanged, and it is easy to characterise the amplitude and phase changes caused by the system. The cochlea and the neural processing that follow are more interesting. The bandwidth of a cochlear "filter" changes at different sound levels, and neurons change their sensitivity as they adapt to sounds. Inner hair cells (IHC) produce nonlinear rectified versions of the sound, generating new frequencies such as envelope components. All of these changes make it difficult to describe auditory perception in terms of the spectrum or Fourier transform of a sound.

One characteristic of an auditory signal that is undisturbed by most nonlinear transformations is the periodicity information in the signal. Even if the bandwidth, amplitude, and phase characteristics of a signal are changing, the repetitive characteristics do not. In addition, it is very unlikely that a periodic signal could come from more than one source. Thus the auditory system can safely assume that sound fragments with a consistent periodicity can be combined and assigned to a single source. Consider, for example, a sound formed by opening and closing the glottis four times and filtering the resulting puffs of air with the vocal resonances. After nonlinear processing the lower auditory nervous system will still detect four similar events which will be heard and integrated as coming from a voice.

The duplex theory of pitch perception, proposed by Licklider in 1951 [11] as a unifying model of pitch perception, is even more useful as a model for the extraction and representation of temporal structure for both periodic and nonperiodic signals. This theory produces a movie-like image of sound which is called a correlogram. We believe that the correlogram, like other representations that summarise the temporal information in a signal, is an important tool for understanding the auditory system.

The correlogram represents sound as a three-dimensional function of time, frequency, and periodicity. A cochlear model serves to transform a one-dimensional acoustic pressure into a two-dimensional map of neural firing rate as a function of time and place along the cochlea. A third dimension is added to the representation by measuring the periodicities in the output from the cochlear model. These three dimensions are shown in fig. 1. While most of our own work has concentrated on the correlogram, the important message in this chapter is that time and periodicity cues should be an important part of an auditory representation.

Visual Representations of Speech Signals: Martin Cooke, Steve Beet and Malcolm Crawford (eds.)
© 1993 by John Wiley & Sons Ltd

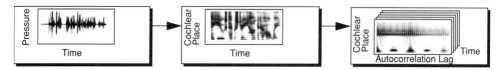

Fig. 1   Three stages of auditory processing are shown here. Sound enters the cochlea and is transduced into what we call a cochleagram (*middle*). A correlogram is then computed from the output of the cochlea by computing short time autocorrelations of each cochlear channel. One frame of the resulting movie is shown in the rightmost box.

This chapter describes two cochlear models and explores a structure which we believe can be used to represent and interpret the temporal information in an acoustic signal. Section 2 of this chapter describes two nonlinear models of the cochlea we use in our work. These two models differ in their computational approach and are used to illustrate the robustness of the temporal information in the output of the cochlea. Over the past forty years there have been several ways to summarise this information at the output of the cochlea [11, 22, 36]. Since these representations produce such similar pictures we describe them all with the term correlogram. Correlograms, their computation and implementation, are the subject of Section 3 of this chapter. Finally, Section 4 describes the use of correlograms for sound visualisation, pitch extraction, and sound separation.

2   NONLINEAR COCHLEAR MODELS

Two different computational models of the cochlea are described in this work: the older model [12,30] which we refer to as the "passive long-wave model", and the newer model [14], which we refer to as the "active short-wave model". The two models differ in their underlying assumptions, approximations, and implementation structures, but they share three primary characteristics (not necessarily implemented independently or in this order):

- Filtering: A broadly tuned cascade of low-pass filters models the propagation of energy as waves on the basilar membrane (BM).

- Detection: A detection nonlinearity converts BM velocity into a representation of IHC receptor potential or auditory nerve (AN) firing rate.

- Compression: An automatic gain control (AGC) continuously adapts the operating point of the system in response to its level of activity, to compress widely varying sound input levels into a limited dynamic range of BM motion, IHC receptor potential, and AN firing rate.

The several differences between the models are largely independent of each other, so there is a large space of possible models in this family. The main differences between the two models we have experimented with are:

- The passive long-wave model is based on a popular one-dimensional (long-wave) hydrodynamic approximation with a lightly damped resonant membrane [37]; the active short-wave model is based on a two-dimensional hydrodynamic approximation (emphasising the short-wave region) with active undamping and negligible membrane mass [15].

- Our passive long-wave model is implemented with complex poles and zeros, while the filters in the active short-wave model have only complex poles. These decisions are based on rational filter approximations to the different underlying hydrodynamic simplifications.

- The passive long-wave model uses time-invariant linear filters followed by a variable gain to functionally model the AGC. The active short-wave model varies the filter pole Q over time to effect a gain variation and to model the mechanical AGC in terms of active adaptive hydrodynamics.

Both models are motivated by the desire to compute a representation of sound that is approximately equivalent to the instantaneous firing rates of AN fibres. By assembling the firing rates versus time for a large number of fibres with different best frequencies (BF), we construct a picture called the "cochleagram". The cochleagram is useful as a visual representation of sound, and as a numerical input to other sound processing functions, such as automatic speech recognition.

The cochleagram has a wealth of fine time structure or "waveform synchrony" driven by the temporal structure of the incoming sound. The extraction and representation of the important perceptual information carried in the temporal structure on the AN is the main topic explored in this chapter. Nevertheless, for the display of cochleagrams, we often just smooth away the details via a low-pass filter, in order to reduce the bandwidth enough to fit a signal of some duration (e.g. a sentence) into the resolution of the display medium. These "mean-rate" cochleagrams would be rather flat looking if they really represented mean AN firing rates. Instead, we follow Shamma [29] in using a first-order spatial difference (a simple lateral inhibitory network or LIN) to sharpen the cochleagram response peaks due to spectral peaks.

2.1 Modelling approach

Sound waves enter the cochlea at the oval window, causing waves to travel from the base to the apex along the BM. The speed at which waves propagate and decay is a function of the mechanical properties of the membrane and the fluid, and of the wave frequency. The most important property that changes along the BM is its stiffness. As a wave of any particular frequency propagates along the BM from the stiff basal region toward the flexible apical region, its propagation velocity and wavelength decrease, while its amplitude increases to a maximum and then rapidly decreases due to mechanical losses. The amplitude increase is due to the energy per cycle being concentrated into a smaller region as the wavelength decreases, and, in the case of an active model, to energy amplification in the travelling wave.

For both one-dimensional and two-dimensional hydrodynamic models, a technique known as the WKB approximation allows us to describe the propagation of waves on the BM one-dimensionally, using a local complex-valued "wave-number." The wave-number k (the reciprocal of Zweig's λ parameter [37]) may be thought of as a reciprocal wavelength in natural units, or a spatial rate of change of phase in radians/metre. But, it can also have an imaginary part that expresses the spatial rate of gain or loss of amplitude.

In general, k depends on frequency (ω) and on the parameters of the wave propagation medium (for example, stiffness, mass, damping, height, width). We allow parameters of the medium to depend on x, the distance along the BM measured from the base. Thus the wave-number is expressed as a function of frequency and x, *viz.* $k(\omega, x)$. The equation that describes the wave medium and lets us find k from the frequency and the parameters at location x is known as the dispersion relation, and may be derived from some approximation to the hydrodynamic system. The popular long-wave approximation [38] is simplest, but is only valid when the wavelength is very long compared to the height of the fluid chambers of the cochlea. A better approximation to physical (or at least mathematical) reality results from a 2D or 3D model of the hydrodynamics [25,37]. Different models lead to different solutions for $k(\omega, x)$ [37].

The WKB approximation says, roughly, that we can describe wave propagation along the x dimension by integrating the rate of change of phase and relative amplitude indicated by k. In a uniform medium, a (complex) wave traversing a distance dx is multiplied by

$$\exp[ik(\omega, x)\, dx]. \tag{1}$$

According to WKB, in a nonuniform medium, as a wave traverses a region from x_1 to x_2, it is multiplied by

$$\exp\left[i \int_{x_1}^{x_2} k(\omega, x)\, dx \right]. \tag{2}$$

The WKB approximation also includes an amplitude correction factor. This factor depends on whether the wave being propagated represents pressure or displacement and ensures the wave amplitude correctly accounts for energy as the wavelength changes. In the short-wave region, under an assumption of constant BM mass and width, no amplitude correction is needed for the pressure wave. On the other hand, an amplitude increase proportional to k is needed for the BM displacement or velocity wave. In the long-wave region, pressure amplitude decreases as $k^{-1/2}$, while displacement and velocity increase as $k^{3/2}$. In the general 2D case, and for more general mass and stiffness scaling, amplitude scaling is more complex [15]. For our models, we choose *ad hoc* stage gains near unity that provide plausible correction factors and lead to good-looking results.

We model wave propagation using a cascade of filters by noting that the exponential of an integral is well approximated by a product of exponentials of the form

$$\exp[ik(\omega, x)\, dx] \tag{3}$$

for a succession of short segments of length dx. We then only need to design a simple filter

$$H_i(\omega, x) = \exp[ik(\omega, x_i)\, dx] \tag{4}$$

for each segment of the model corresponding to BM location x_i. For short enough segments, the filter responses will not be too far from unity gain and zero phase shift, and will themselves be well approximated by low-order causal rational transfer functions (i.e. by a few poles and/or zeros).

The conversion of mechanical motion into neural firings is performed by the IHCs and neurons of the AN. IHCs only respond to motion in one direction and their outputs saturate if the motion is too large. Thus a simple model of an IHC is a half wave rectifier (HWR), while more complicated models might use a soft saturating HWR such as

$$\frac{1}{2}(1 + \tanh(x + a)). \tag{5}$$

Even more realistic models of IHC and AN behaviour take into account local adaptation, refractory times, and limited firing rates [19]. Our work is more interested in the average firing rate of a number of cells so we do not need this level of detail. Both cochlear models described in this chapter use a simple HWR as a detector.

All IHC models share the important property of acting like detectors. This means that they convert the pressure wave with both positive and negative values into a signal that retains both the average energy in the signal and the temporal information describing when each event occurs. Over a period of several cycles, the average pressure at a point on the BM will be zero. But by first using a HWR, or other hair cell model, the average will be related to the energy in the signal yet the fine time structure is preserved. This temporal information will be important later when trying to group components of a sound based on their periodicities [12].

Such a nonlinearity is an important part of understanding the perception of sounds with identical spectra but different phase characteristics. One such set of sounds was studied by Pierce [24]. In his study, carefully constructed sounds with identical spectra but different phases were shown to have different pitches. A simple HWR detector is sufficient to turn the phase differences into envelopes whose periodicities explain the different pitches.

Finally, a model of adaptation, or AGC, is necessary. In its simplest form, the response to a constant stimulus will at first be large and then as the auditory system adapts to the stimulus the response will get smaller. There are many types of adaptation in the auditory system that respond over a large range of time scales. Some of these adaptations affect the mechanical properties of the BM and thus change the wave propagation equation.

The interaction of sound levels and wave mechanics is clear in the iso-intensity mechanical response data of Rhode [27], Johnstone [10], and Ruggero [28]. Typical data are shown in fig. 2. In all cases, the peak of resonant response is blunted at high sound levels, resulting in an increased bandwidth, a shift in best frequency, and a reduced gain for frequencies near the characteristic frequency (CF). These effects are qualitatively in agreement with the result due to reducing the pole Q in our active short-wave model. Our passive long-wave model, on the other hand, keeps the mechanics constant and applies a pure gain variation before the IHC. Models that rely on the place of maximum response cannot realistically count on the cochlea to map a consistent frequency to a particular place. Using a lateral inhibition network to shift the response peak closer to the sharp cutoff edges gives a more consistent mapping.

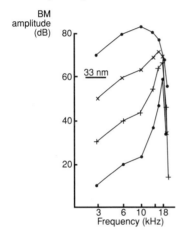

SPL	$Q_{3\,dB}$	CF
80dB	1	10k
60dB	2.7	16k
40dB	4.8	17k
20dB	8.3	17k

Fig. 2   Mössbauer data shows the nonlinearity of the cochlea. This data, measured by Johnstone, shows the motion of the BM at four different sound levels. Note that the response is most highly tuned at the lowest sound levels. Adapted from [10] with permission.

2.2 The passive long-wave model

Our passive long-wave model was designed by Lyon [12] based on a long-wave analysis of the cochlea by Zweig [37]. The implementation of this model is described by Slaney [30]. This model uses a cascade of second-order sections to approximate the complex, frequency-dependent delay and attenuation a wave encounters as it travels down the BM. This model uses a HWR as a detector and four stages of a multiplicative AGC to model adaptation.

The transfer function for a stage of the model is based on an approximation to the long-wave solution for a short section of the BM. The transfer function, or ratio of complex output amplitude to input amplitude, over a length dx of the BM is a function of frequency, ω, and is written

$$\frac{P_0}{P_i} = A(\omega)\, e^{ik(w)\,dx} \quad \text{with} \quad k(\omega) = \frac{c}{\sqrt{\omega_R^2 + i\,\omega\,\omega_R^2/Q - \omega^2}} \tag{6}$$

where $A(\omega) \approx 1$. When the wave-number k is real-valued, the transfer function contributes just a phase change and there is no change in amplitude. Negative imaginary values of k cause the exponential's magnitude to be less than one and the wave to decay. The resulting transfer function, as a function of sound frequency, for a small section of the cochlea with ω_R near 5.8 kHz is shown in fig. 3.

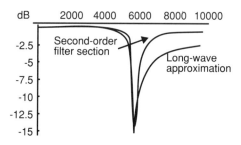

Fig. 3   The frequency response of a small section of a long-wave model of the BM is compared to an approximation based on a second-order filter. A large number of these sections are combined to form the overall low-pass filter characteristic of the cochlea.

The parameters ω_R and Q are local parameters for each small section of BM being modelled in the cascade. The resonance frequency, ω_R, changes exponentially from $2\pi \cdot 20$ kHz at the base of the cochlea to approximately $2\pi \cdot 20$ Hz at the apex. The transfer function in Eqn. (6) is a notch filter, and when the response is combined from the base to any point along the BM the result is a low pass filter (LPF).

Equation (6) describes the transfer function for a pressure wave traversing a section of length dx. Pressure is converted to BM velocity by the local BM impedance, which is essentially a simple resonator described by the same ω_R and Q. We approximate the transfer function and the accompanying resonator using a biquadratic filter (two poles and two zeros). The resulting structure is computationally efficient and an adequate model of the cochlea for our purposes. This structure is shown in fig. 4.

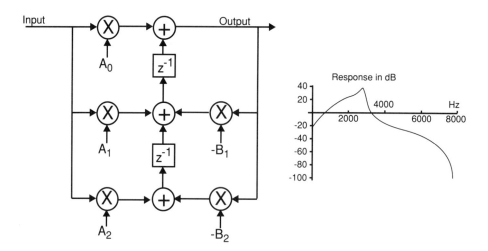

Fig. 4   A single stage of the cascade-parallel model is implemented with the second-order section shown on the left. The frequency response for one typical stage is shown in fig. 3. The BM is simulated by combining stages into a cascade. The typical response, including a differentiator to convert to velocity, is shown on the right.

The bandwidth and centre frequency of the notch varies as a function of the characteristic frequency corresponding to each position along the BM. The bandwidth of the poles is given by the expression

$$BW = \frac{\sqrt{f_{break}^2 + CF^2}}{Q_{hi}} \qquad (7)$$

and corresponds roughly to a critical band. Model parameters Q_{hi} and f_{break} specify the high-frequency limit of the pole Q, and the frequency that separates the nearly constant-Q and constant bandwidth regions. Filter stages are cascaded, with centre frequencies from high to low, so that the centre frequency of each stage falls a small fraction of the bandwidth below the centre frequency of the previous stage.

The filter Q_{hi} and the percentage of filter overlap are parameters of our long-wave model; no one value is correct for all situations. Instead, depending on the use, we often choose one of two values. If we are computing a cochleagram then we use a Q_{hi} of 8, which yields unrealistically sharp filters but produces a picture with good frequency-domain resolution. If instead we are looking at the periodicities of the signal by computing a correlogram, we can use a more realistic bandwidth and a Q_{hi} of 4. To keep the same number of channels per octave, we step the narrow filters by a factor of 25% of BW and the wide filters by 12.5% of BW (overlap 75% and 87.5% respectively).

An important step in a cochlear simulation is a model of adaptation. In our passive cochlear model this function is performed by time-varying gains in an AGC loop. To simulate adaptation the AGC is operating at a point where it is sensitive to new sounds. After an increased sound loudness is detected, the gain is turned down. The structure of this multiplicative AGC is shown in fig. 5. Four of these stages, each with a different time constant, are used to model the range of adaptation rates found in the auditory system.

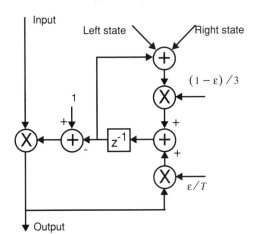

AGC	Target	Time constant
First	0.0032	640 ms
Second	0.0016	160 ms
Third	0.0008	40 ms
Fourth	0.0004	10 ms

Fig. 5   The structure of the AGC used in the cascade-parallel model of the cochlea. Four of these stages are combined, each with a different value for the time constant (ε) and output target value (T), to make the complete adaptation model. In the passive long-wave model of the cochlea, the AGC follows the detector, so only positive values are seen.

While the passive long-wave model does a reasonably good job of calculating a cochleagram, it differs from the physiology in two areas. Most importantly, there is evidence that an active mechanical mechanism is part of the cochlea and serves not only to amplify low-level travelling waves but also to sharpen the iso-response mechanical tuning curves. Incorporating the AGC into the mechanical properties of the cochlea tends to compress the range of signal levels that need to be represented by neural circuits. This point is minor for high-precision floating-point computer implementations but is critical for the representation and for neurons, which have a limited dynamic range.

2.3 The active short-wave model

The second model we use in our work is based on two-dimensional hydrodynamics and includes negative damping to model the mechanical amplification of low-level signals by active outer haircells. This approach has been described by Lyon and Mead [14,15] in terms of analog circuits. We have implemented their approach digitally, and extended it to include a coupled AGC loop that adapts the filters.

Though the model is based on a full two-dimensional analysis, we characterise it as a short-wave model to emphasise the importance of the short wavelength near the response peak, and to clearly contrast it with our long-wave model. Because of the short-wave behaviour and the form of the active undamping and higher-order loss mechanisms we have used, it is possible to get a reasonably sharp response peak even with no BM mass [15]. This massless approach is not possible in a passive long-wave model. Finding a more realistic version of this class of model requires more data on BM mechanics and outer hair cell (OHC) micromechanics.

Like the passive long-wave model, our active short-wave model is built with a cascade of second-order filter sections that model-pressure wave propagation. But in the short-wave model, the filter stages adapt in response to the sound level by lowering their pole Q when the local wave energy is high. The filters have unity gain at DC, for lossless propagation of low-frequency waves. When the pole Q is greater than 0.707 (the usual case), each filter has a frequency range over which its gain is greater than unity, implying active amplification. With quiet sounds, the Q values for each stage can be as high as 2. This results in gain peaks for the cascade near 2^{10} (60 dB), depending on parameters such as the filter overlap and step factor. Adjusting the Q values between 0.707 and 2 can change the overall filter cascade's peak gains by about 60 dB in response to sound levels over a 100 dB range.

The active cochlea has negative damping. This corresponds to a positive imaginary part of the wave-number k and causes energy to be added to propagating waves. A wave of a particular frequency would grow without bound if the damping did not become positive at some place as the wave propagated. The curve of gain versus place for a particular frequency is also reflected in the curve of gain versus frequency at a particular place. Each filter stage needs to have a gain greater than unity followed by a falloff toward zero; a pair of poles is the simplest way to approximate this shape qualitatively.

In simple dynamic systems, damping is used to quantify the rate at which energy is dissipated over time. Negative damping in a dynamic system, or in a simple second-order filter, results in an instability. But with a propagating wave, damping quantifies the rate of energy dissipation per distance. Negative damping in a uniform medium would be unstable, but in a cochlea with changing parameters, each region can have negative damping for a range of frequencies, and positive damping for higher frequencies, with no instability. The negative damping of a section of the wave medium is captured via the WKB approximation as a gain greater than unity.

In the cochlea, there must be a physical limit to the amount of energy that can be added to a wave by active outer hair cells. Therefore, at high sound levels the system must become passive, corresponding to reducing all the Q values to 0.707 or less in our model. Changing the Q values between the small-signal and large-signal limits results in an overall compressive behaviour, in agreement with compression seen in the actual cochlear mechanics [16].

In the cochlea, the level of OHC activity is probably controlled both by a fast local nonlinearity and by a slower feedback loop involving the cochlear efferents and the olivary complex. The degree of feedback and activity is not the same at all places, but is dependent on the signal spectrum. We model this control loop using a set of parallel time-space smoothing filters similar to those used in the coupled AGC of our long-wave model. Following the IHC detection nonlinearity, four filters with different time constants and space constants add their outputs. This sum is added to a minimum damping parameter to compute a filter stage's pole damping. The wide range of possible loop characteristics, nonlinearities, and binaural effects that no doubt occur in the olivary complex have not been explored, but this *ad hoc* AGC gives good compression and qualitatively correct shifts in *CF*, bandwidth, and phase. Due to the spatial coupling and the fact that cascaded stages interact, there is also a qualitatively reasonable two-tone suppression effect, as there was in the long-wave model [13]. The structure of this active and adaptive model is shown in fig. 6.

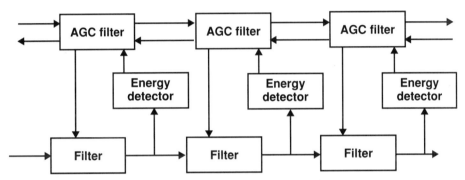

Fig. 6　A more realistic model of the cochlea uses energy detectors that control the parameters of the cochlear filters. The AGC filters integrate the energy over time and space and control the damping of the BM filters.

The digital implementation of the active short-wave model uses a novel second-order filter structure, shown in fig. 7, in which one coefficient directly controls the pole damping, or $1/Q$ [35]. This allows us to connect the output of the AGC loop filters to the cascaded filter stages, without a block to convert pole *CF* and *Q* to filter coefficients. The *CF* parameter directly controls the pole frequency, and is a design parameter that is held constant for each stage. The separation of frequency and damping is exact only in the limit of low pole frequencies, and is usable with care up to only about half of the Nyquist frequency. Thus the high-frequency end of the short-wave model is not as high as it is for the long-wave model, for a given sound sample rate.

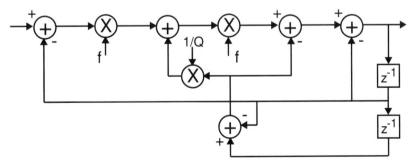

Fig. 7　This structure is used to implement a single stage of our model of the hydrodynamics of the cochlea. Unlike the structure shown in fig. 4, the centre frequency and the filter damping, or $1/Q$, can be controlled directly.

2.4 Pictures

A time-frequency representation is often used to analyse and display speech signals. Four representations of the utterance 'clean.wav' are shown in figs. 8 and 9. Figure 8 shows the conventional wide- and narrowband spectrograms using the short-time Fourier transform. These two spectrograms use two different window sizes and thus differ in their resolution in the time and frequency domains.

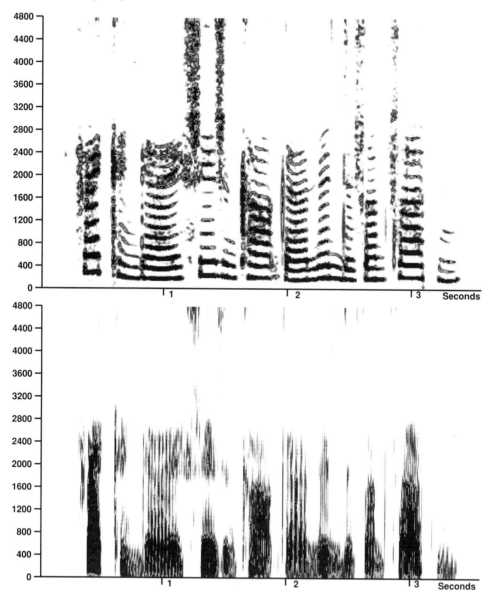

Fig. 8   Narrow- (top) and wideband (bottom) spectrograms of the Sheffield 'clean.wav' utterance, "Fred can go, Susan can't go, and Linda is uncertain". These spectrograms were computed with the Signalyze™ program for the Macintosh using bandwidths of 20 and 200 Hz, respectively.

Figure 9 shows two cochleagrams of the same utterance. The cochleagram, much like the spectrogram, is a function of time along the horizontal axis and cochlear place, or frequency, along the vertical axis. The darkness of the picture at each point represents the LIN-enhanced average of the auditory nerve firing rate at each position along the BM. The spectrograms and cochleagrams show a remarkable similarity. The most noticeable differences in the pictures are the change in the scaling of the frequency axis and some enhancement of the onsets in the cochleagrams.

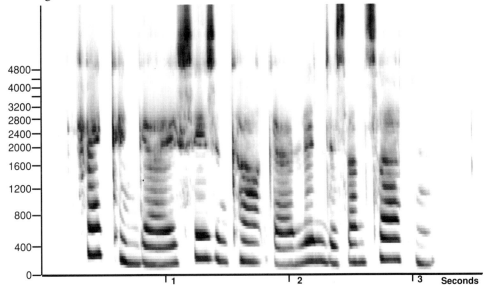

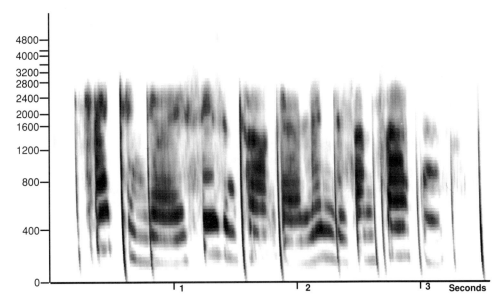

Fig. 9   Passive long-wave (top) and active short-wave (bottom) cochleagrams of the Sheffield 'clean.wav' utterance. The passive long-wave cochleagram was computed using the default MacEar parameters and "df=100 tau=1". The active short-wave cochleagram was computed using "df=100 tau=1 gain=.001".

A more important difference can not be seen in these pictures. Because of the limited space on the printed page, each pixel in these cochleagrams represents the average cochlear firing rate over a period of approximately 5 ms. But the cochlea and the IHCs are exquisitely sensitive to the time structure of each component of the sound. Fig. 10 shows an expanded view of the diphthong "rea" from the word greasy. At this time scale each glottal pulse and each waveform peak is visible. One can still follow the formant tracks, but in addition the glottal pulses that trigger the formant information allow one to group frequency channels that come from the same source.

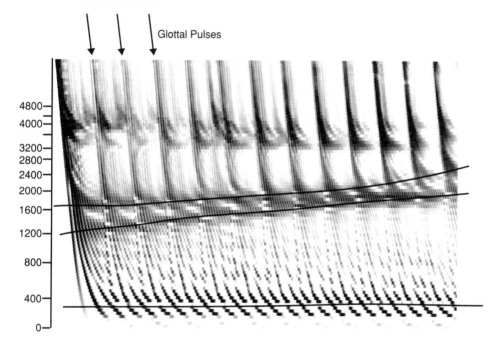

Fig. 10 Expanded cochleagram of the diphthong "rea" in greasy from the Sheffield 'timit.dip' utterance. The first three formant tracks are shown (the lowest formant is excited with two harmonics). The vertical lines, each of which represents a glottal pulse, are tilted slightly due to the natural delay through the cochlea.

We argue that this temporal information is important. Conventional models of audition base all performance on a suitably narrow resolution in the frequency domain. We feel this is unrealistic since the bandwidth and centre frequency of the mechanical system change with level. Instead, if the auditory system is based on the temporal information in the signal then the performance of the system is relatively insensitive to each filter's bandwidth and centre frequency. The correlogram is one way to capture the temporal structure in the cochlear output and is the subject of the remainder of this chapter.

3   REPRESENTING TIME — THE CORRELOGRAM

We use the correlogram to summarise the temporal information in the sounds we hear. This chapter argues that the correlogram is biologically plausible and serves as a representation that higher-level processes can use to form auditory objects. The cochlea separates a sound into rather broad frequency channels yet retains the timing of the original sound. How is it that the brain extracts this information from the acoustic signal and uses it to group sounds?

The first step is to gather evidence of events that repeat. There are many ways to do this and in this section we will describe a range of techniques from those that are biologically plausible to those that can be efficiently implemented on a digital computer. We use the term correlogram, literally "picture of correlations", to describe the resulting sequence of images. While other researchers have described different implementations, we believe that each of these representations have the same goal: to represent the time structure of a signal.

In its ideal form, a correlogram is computed by measuring the short-time autocorrelation of the neural firing rate as a function of cochlear place, or best frequency, versus time. Since an autocorrelation is itself a function of a third variable, the resulting correlogram is a three-dimensional function of frequency, time, and autocorrelation delay. For display, we assemble a frame of data, all autocorrelations ending at one time, into a movie which is synchronised with the sound.

An idealised structure to compute the correlogram is shown in fig. 11. Sound enters the correlogram array from the cochlea, a picture is computed, and is then sent to higher level structures in the brain.

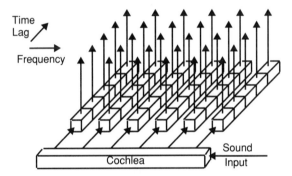

Fig. 11   This structure can be used to measure the temporal information in a sound. Sound enters the cochlea on the bottom right and is analysed into broad frequency channels. Each channel is then correlated with itself and the resulting picture is passed to higher structures in the brain for further processing.

We cannot show a correlogram on paper but we can show individual frames and talk about the significant features. More examples are available in a video report we have published [31]. Figure 12 shows several correlogram frames and illustrates how the correlogram changes as the pitch and formant frequencies of the sound change. Distance along the BM is shown on the vertical axis of a correlogram. Since each section of the BM is most sensitive to a single frequency the vertical axis of a correlogram roughly corresponds to frequency, with the base of the cochlea, or the part that is most sensitive to high frequencies, at the top and the apex, or the low frequency portion, at the bottom.

Autocorrelation time delay, or lag, is shown on the horizontal axis of a correlogram. The width of a correlogram is chosen to include time delays long enough to include the lowest expected pitch. Generally this is at least 10 ms.

The activity of the correlogram is displayed as darkness in the image. As in a conventional spectrogram, dark areas represent autocorrelation lags and cochlear frequencies where there is a large response.

Voiced sounds, as shown in fig. 12a-c, best show the utility of the correlogram. Strong vertical lines at particular autocorrelation lags indicate times when a large number of cochlear channels are firing with the same period. This is a strong indication of a pitch which has a frequency inversely related to the autocorrelation lag. When the pitch increases, as shown between fig. 12a and b, the dominant line moves to the left, to a lag equal to the reduced period.

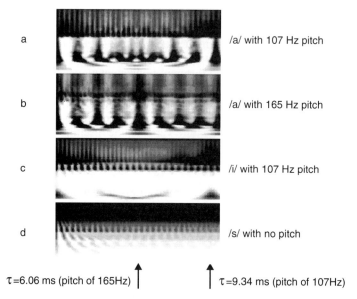

a   /a/ with 107 Hz pitch

b   /a/ with 165 Hz pitch

c   /i/ with 107 Hz pitch

d   /s/ with no pitch

τ=6.06 ms (pitch of 165Hz) ↑   ↑ τ=9.34 ms (pitch of 107Hz)

Fig. 12   Four frames of a correlogram of a voice. The first three frames (a-c) are voiced sounds. When the pitch is raised the vertical structures become closer together (frames a and b). As the formant frequencies change the horizontal bands move (frames a and c). Finally, if the sound is unvoiced (frame d) then there is no vertical structure.

Horizontal bands are indications of large amounts of energy within a frequency band. The correlogram frames shown in fig. 12a-c illustrate how the correlogram changes as the vowel /a/ is changed to /i/. Note that the first formant drops while the second and third formants move much higher. Finally, only voiced sounds have a pitch. Unvoiced sounds, like the letter /s/, do not contain any periodic information and thus the correlogram is uniformly black for all BM channels that contain energy. This is shown in fig. 12d.

An autocorrelation of $x(t)$ is defined by the following integral:

$$R_{xx}(\tau) = \int_{-\infty}^{\infty} x(t)\,x(t-\tau)\,dt. \tag{8}$$

For dynamic signals, we are interested in the periodicities in the signal within a short window ending at time t. This short-time autocorrelation can be written

$$R_{xx}(\tau,t) = \int_{0}^{\infty} x(t-s)\,x(t-s-\tau)\,w(s)\,ds = [x(t)\cdot x(t-\tau)]^*w(t) \tag{9}$$

where $w(t)$ is an arbitrary causal window which limits the autocorrelation to a neighbourhood of the current time. As indicated by the convolution form above, one way to calculate such a running autocorrelation is to filter the instantaneous correlation through a smoothing filter whose impulse response is a window [11].

A slightly different definition is useful on a digital computer. By windowing the data first, we can implement the correlation using a fast Fourier transform (FFT) algorithm and reduce the computations by an order of magnitude or more. Now assume

$$w(t) = 0 \quad \text{for } t < 0 \text{ and } t > T \tag{10}$$

and form a windowed signal ending at a particular time t:

$$y_t(s) = x(t-s)\,w(s). \tag{11}$$

The windowed autocorrelation can now be written

$$R_{xx}(\tau, t) = \int_0^T y_t(s)\, y_t(s + \tau)\, ds = F^{-1} \|F(y)\|^2 \tag{12}$$

where F and F^{-1} indicate the forward and the reverse Fourier Transform. This equation can be rewritten to make it more like eqn. (9):

$$R_{xx}(\tau, t) = \int_0^T x(t - s)\, w(s)\, x(t - s - \tau)\, w(s + \tau)\, ds. \tag{13}$$

The correlogram is also a function of BM position or frequency. Using eqn. (9), we can write the following equation for the correlogram as a function of the cochlear firing rate $x_f(t)$ at the position along the BM most sensitive to a sinusoid of frequency f. The most general form of the correlogram is written

$$C_f(\tau, t) = \int_0^\infty x_f(t - s)\, x_f(t - s - \tau)\, w(s)\, ds. \tag{14}$$

Autocorrelations are often normalised so that the value for zero lag is equal to one. Such normalisation reduces the dynamic range required for display, but completely eliminates any indication of the relative power in different frequency channels. Since autocorrelation doubles the dynamic range required to represent varying signal levels, we partially normalise by the square root of the power. This serves as a compromise so that a correlogram can be displayed with a dynamic range comparable to the cochleagram. This is written

$$\hat{C}_f(\tau, t) = \frac{C_f(\tau, t)}{C_f(0, t)^{1/2}}. \tag{15}$$

Since the autocorrelation of a nonnegative function is also nonnegative, the resulting normalised correlogram will have values between 0 and a maximum value that we scale for the display technology.

The correlogram as described above is a continuous function of time, frequency, and autocorrelation lag. We have already sampled the auditory input as a function of time and the BM as a function of place or frequency. Sampling the auditory input means that only discrete time lags are possible in the autocorrelation without interpolating to a higher sample rate.

Still, the value of the correlogram at any one frequency and lag changes at every sample time. There is no way to display 16000 or more correlogram frames per second, so instead we subsample the correlogram to a more manageable rate of 10 to 30 frames per second. Thus to prevent temporal aliasing it is necessary to low-pass filter the correlogram. The easiest way to accomplish this filtering is to choose the correlogram window so that it is an appropriate lowpass filter. Without much biological evidence to base a window length on, we instead choose a Hamming window twice as long as the frame sampling interval. This serves to average the correlogram over a long enough interval to prevent aliasing.

There are many ways to measure periodicities and implement a correlogram. The correlograms in this chapter were computed on a digital computer using an FFT to efficiently implement the correlation operation. But there is little reason to think that neurons would use an FFT. Instead a direct solution, like that shown in fig. 13 is more plausible. In this implementation a neural delay line, perhaps using a combination of axonal delays and neural resonators, delays a copy of the signal. For each time delay, a neuron fires when both the delayed and undelayed inputs are active at nearly the same time. A second neuron then sums the number of coincidences and remembers them over a small window in time. This second neuron can be called a leaky integrator or lowpass filter. Structures similar to the correlator shown in fig.

13 have been found in the owl [5] for doing binaural cross-correlation and in the bat [34] for echo location.

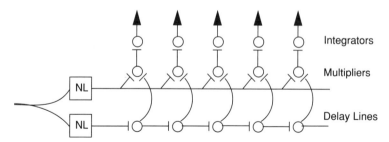

Fig. 13   This simple structure, first proposed by Licklider [11] in 1951, can be used by the brain to calculate a correlogram. For each time lag, delayed (bottom line) and undelayed versions of the auditory signal are multiplied together and integrated. The two boxes labelled NL are optional non-linear processing steps.

While the correlogram was first proposed in 1951, only recently has it become feasible to explore the use of the correlogram with multiple seconds of sound. Using an FFT on a Cray YMP supercomputer we can compute one second of a correlogram with about a second of CPU time. The same calculation takes about a half hour on a small personal computer.

An even more efficient implementation is possible using analog silicon VLSI as described by Lyon [17]. Using low-power sub-threshold CMOS transistors, the chip computes a real-time video correlogram from a microphone input. This implementation combines a cascade of analog filters, simulating the cochlear transmission line, with an array of CCD (charge-coupled device) delay lines. At each position in the correlogram array (frequency versus lag) there are four CCD gates, a transistor multiplier, a capacitor to sum the current output, and video scan-out circuitry. A separate gate array generates the video timing and addresses the correlogram pixels in the proper order. The two chips produce a recognisable correlogram, not as precise as the digital versions, but which can be computed using a single 9 volt radio battery for power.

There are many ways to compute variations of a correlogram. One way to describe these implementations is shown in fig. 13. This is a generalisation of the basic correlator described above and includes two optional nonlinearities that modify the neural input. In a method proposed by Patterson [23], only the nonlinearity in the undelayed signal path is present. This nonlinearity is an adaptive peak picker and produces a binary output when it sees a major peak. As each peak occurs the delayed input signal is transferred to the leaky integrators. An approach first described by Weintraub [36] uses identical nonlinearities in each path. Each nonlinearity replaces the original waveform with an impulse train that represents the location of each peak in the waveform. In addition, the impulses of the signal are scaled by the energy in the original peak. In both cases, the large amounts of data that are combined to form a single frame of a correlogram help to average out the noise caused by these approximations.

Another technique which might be used to generate a correlogram is to model chopper cells in the cochlear nucleus [8] and to count their output spikes. Chopper cells prefer to fire at a fixed rate and tend to lock to sound periodicities. It is easy to imagine that these cells could be used to measure the periodicities in an auditory signal. We have not yet tried to generate a correlogram using this approach.

4   APPLICATIONS

Let us review our progress to date. We believe we have a good understanding of how to make a cochlear model. The models we describe here are a severe simplification of the complex behaviour of the cochlea, designed to preserve the aspect most relevant to auditory processing. This we believe is the temporal information in the signal. While there are many details that remain to be worked out, one can now choose any number of models that can be used to model various aspects of the cochlea.

One aspect that is clear, at least to us from our review of cochlear mechanics, is that the tuning curves cannot be sharp enough to account for all the exquisite properties of the human auditory system. Yet the system is quite good at preserving the temporal information in the signal. Even above 3 kHz, where phase locking to high frequencies is lost, auditory nerves preserve the envelope and thus the timing of the glottal pulses. The correlogram is one way to capture this temporal information.

Given a temporal representation of sound one certainly wonders what it is good for. This section describes the use of the correlogram as a tool for visualisation, a model of pitch perception, and our efforts to perform sound separation using this representation.

4.1 Sound visualisation

The most striking property of a correlogram movie is that the visual and acoustic experiences are so similar. It is intuitively appealing to be able to see sounds in much the same way that we hear them. It is, of course, hard to share this kind of experience in a book, but we can illustrate some of the things we have seen.

A simple example is provided by "Strike Note of a Chime," Demonstration Number 24 from the Acoustical Society of America's *Auditory Demonstrations* CD [9]. Bells are interesting because they are inharmonic, with several different mechanical modes. Each mode corresponds to a resonance at a different frequency and the inharmonic relationship between these resonances accounts for the rich sound associated with a bell.

Figure 14 shows several frames of a correlogram of a bell. At first, there are many harmonics and the sound is quite rich. Different overtones decay at different rates as is seen in the second and third frames. Finally after two seconds, or the last frame, there are only two (inharmonic) components left.

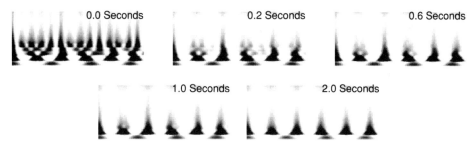

Fig. 14 Correlogram of the "Strike Note of a Chime". Five frames show the different decay rates of the resonating modes of an orchestral chime. This example is Demonstration 24 from the *Auditory Demonstrations* CD [9].

4.2 Pitch

Pitch is an obvious quantity to measure with a correlogram. Licklider originally proposed the correlogram as a pitch model and only recently has it been studied and compared to human performance [20,21,32]. The results closely match the published literature for all experiments except those based on loudness changes.

Pitch is measured from a correlogram as shown in fig. 15. After the correlogram is computed, evidence for a pitch at each lag is found by summing across channels. The resulting function is called a summary correlogram. It measures how likely a pitch would be perceived with the given time delay. Inverting this time delay gives the resulting pitch frequency.

It is important to realise that pitch is not a single-valued function. Pitch is conventionally defined as "that attribute of auditory sensation in terms of which sounds may be ordered on a musical scale". But, for many sounds any number of frequencies can be called the pitch. Most engineering solutions reduce pitch to a single-valued quantity, but the correlogram pitch detector described in fig. 15 estimates the likelihood that a pitch exists at the corresponding time delay. If a single pitch estimate is desired then one solution is to choose the largest peak and call this the pitch.

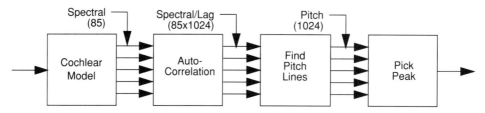

Fig. 15   Human pitch perception can be modelled with this correlogram technique. After computing the correlogram, a summary correlogram is computed (third box) by summing the correlation across channels, or along vertical lines. The numbers in parentheses show the typical amount of data at each time step.

Figure 16 shows the processing involved in a pitch detector we have built [32].This pitch detector adds two additional *ad hoc* stages to improve the system's performance with real-world sounds. We have not found these stages to be necessary with synthetic sounds, but with real sounds we have found they improve the performance of our pitch detector. Fortunately, neither step is hard to implement with neural circuits.

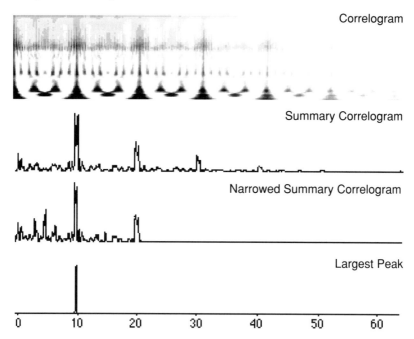

Fig. 16   Pitch of a vowel. Data processing steps in a correlogram pitch detector are illustrated here. After computing the summary or integrated correlogram, sub-harmonics are considered using the narrowed autocorrelation technique. Finally, if desired, the highest peak can be chosen and considered the pitch.

To compute a pitch, a correlogram of the sound is first nonlinearly filtered to emphasise the vertical structures in the correlogram. This is equivalent to biasing the pitch detector so that it will emphasise sounds that are harmonic. The summary correlogram is computed, and then a final stage of sub-harmonic processing is performed. In our pitch detector this is implemented using the narrowed-autocorrelation idea proposed by Brown [3]. This type of processing is equivalent to the sub-harmonic analysis proposed by Hermes [7] and the pitch spiral proposed by Patterson [22].

In our pitch detector, a single pitch value is independently chosen at each frame time (30 times a second). This pitch detector has no history so it is quite happy to choose a completely different pitch at each frame. Humans do not work this way: instead we use the pitch at recent times to help us to choose the most likely pitch in the future. The result is that if two pitches are equally likely then this pitch detector will oscillate between the two possible choices. A better choice would be to model the dynamics of pitch perception, perhaps based on the data for pitch just noticeable difference (JND) as a function of time interval [1].

Figure 17 shows the pitch measured from a sound with an ambiguous pitch, the continuous Shepard tones by Jean-Claude Risset from the ASA *Auditory Demonstrations* CD (Demonstration 27, [9]). In this example the pitch is heard to constantly fall. But analysis by correlogram shows that at each frame a number of pitches are possible, each separated by an octave. Our pitch detector is happy to oscillate between likely pitches but humans tend to follow a single pitch track, perhaps over many octaves.

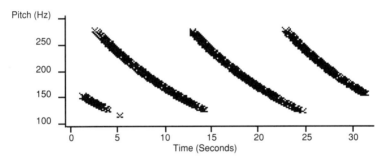

Fig. 17   Pitch of the continuous Shepard tones. Note that the correlogram pitch detector described in this chapter does not enforce any frame-to-frame coherence. Thus it is equally likely to choose either pitch if the summary correlogram assigns the two periods similar magnitudes.

4.3 Sound Separation

Our ultimate goal with correlogram processing is to understand how humans separate the sounds in our environments. Even with a monaural recording we are quite good at separating out the vocals from an instrumental track, hearing a bird as a separate object outdoors, or even listening to a single conversation in a noisy room.

There are many cues [2] that we use to group pieces of a sound into a whole auditory object. Some of the cues we have studied are onsets, pitch, and common modulation. A good example of the power of common modulation is the Reynolds-McAdams oboe [18,26]. In this sound a single oboe sound was analysed into its even and odd frequency harmonics. Then the harmonics were put back together, but each set of harmonics was independently jittered. At first, the harmonics are fixed and the sound is heard as the original oboe sound. After a few seconds the vibrato is turned on and the two sets of harmonics are heard as separate objects. The odd harmonics sound like a clarinet since clarinets have most of their energy in the odd harmonics. The even harmonics go up an octave in pitch and sound like a soprano.

Figure 18 shows correlogram frames that represent this sound. Over time the movie shows the even harmonics moving left and right. The odd harmonics are moving independently and the original oboe sound splits into two sounds. The pitch tracks for the two sets of harmonics are shown in figure 19. At this time we do not know whether this grouping is based on detection of the FM modulation or synchronous onset detection in the correlogram domain.

More work needs to be done to build models of sound separation that take into account the dynamics of the auditory system. The correlogram can quantify the short-term periodicities (less than 25 ms) in the signal but does not capture the information at longer time scales. For example, a voiced signal can be thought of as a vocal tract signal modulated by the glottal pulses. The correlogram does a good job of representing the amplitude modulation or pitch of the voiced signal as activity in a spatial map. But modulatens with even lower frequencies, such as the 6 Hz tremolo of a human voice, are not explictly represented. Higher-level models of the auditory processing will need to represent these longer time scales in order to understand the dynamics of real sounds.

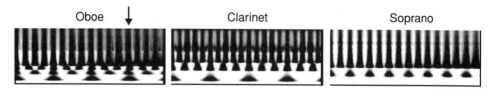

Fig. 18   Three frames illustrating the correlogram of the Reynolds-McAdams oboe. The left frame shows the correlogram of the combined sound (even+odd harmonics) when the sets are slightly inharmonic. Note that the rightmost pitch line (at arrow) is no longer straight. The middle frame shows the correlogram of just the odd harmonics, or the clarinet. The right frame shows the correlogram of the even harmonics, or soprano. When this sound is played for human listeners, the independent vibrato clearly causes the sound to split into two objects.

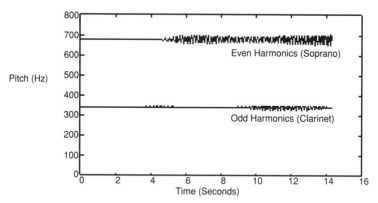

Fig.19   Pitch of the odd harmonics (clarinet, bottom) and even harmonics (soprano, top) are shown here as a function of time. At first, the harmonics are held fixed and the original oboe sound is heard. After three seconds the independent vibrato is turned on and the sound separates into a clarinet and a soprano.

Acknowledgements: Over the years many of our colleagues have helped us as the ideas presented here evolved. We especially want to acknowledge the discussions we have had with the people at the Hearing Seminar at Stanford's CCRMA, and at Caltech's computational and neural systems group. We would specifically like to thank our colleagues Bill Stafford, Daniel Naar, Richard Duda, and Steve Greenberg for their support and encouragement.

REFERENCES

[1] J. 't Hart, R. Collier, & A. Cohen (1990), *A Perceptual Study of Intonation: An Experimental-Phonetic Approach to Speech Melody*, Cambridge University Press, Cambridge, UK.

[2] A. S. Bregman (1990), *Auditory Scene Analysis*, MIT Press, Cambridge, MA.

[3] J. Brown & M. S. Puckette (1989), 'Calculation of a 'narrowed' autocorrelation function', *JASA*, **85**(4), 1595-1601.

[4] L. H. Carney & T. C. T. Yin (1988), 'Temporal coding of resonances by low-frequency auditory nerve fibers: single-fiber responses and a population model', *Journal of Neurophysiology*, **60**(5), 1653-1677.

[5] C. E. Carr & M. Konishi (1990), 'A circuit for detection of interaural time differences in the brain stem of the barn owl', *Journal of Neuroscience*, **10**(10), 3227-3246.

[6] R. O. Duda, R. F. Lyon & M. Slaney (1990), 'Correlograms and the separation of sounds', *Proc. Twenty-fourth Asilomar Conference on Signals, Systems, and Computers (Pacific Grove, CA)*, Maple Press, 457-461.

[7] D. J. Hermes (1988), 'Measurement of pitch by subharmonic summation', *JASA*, **83**(1), 257-264.

[8] M. J. Hewitt, R. Meddis & T. M. Shackleton (1992), 'A computer model of a cochlear-nucleus stellate cell: responses to amplitude-modulated and pure-tone stimuli', *JASA*, **91**(4), 2096-2109.

[9] A. J. M. Houtsma, T. D. Rossing & W. M. Wagenaars (1987), *Auditory Demonstrations*, Woodbury, NY: Acoustical Society of America.

[10] B. M. Johnstone, R. Patuzzi & G. K. Yates (1986), 'Basilar membrane measurements and the travelling wave', *Hearing Research*, 22, 147-153.

[11] J. C. R. Licklider (1951), 'A duplex theory of pitch perception', *Experentia*, **7**, 128-133. Also reprinted in *Pysiological Acoustics* (ed. E. D. Schubert), Dowden, Hutchinson and Ross, Inc. Stroudsburg, PA, 1979.

[12] R. F. Lyon (1982), 'A computational model of filtering, detection, and compression in the cochlea', *Proc. ICASSP '82 (Paris)*, 1282-1285.

[13] R. F. Lyon & L. Dyer (1986), 'Experiments with a computational model of the cochlea',*Proc. ICASSP '86 (Tokyo)*, 1975-1978.

[14] R. F. Lyon & C. Mead (1988), 'An analog electronic cochlea', *IEEE Trans. ASSP*, **36**(7), 1119-1134.

[15] R. F. Lyon & C. Mead (1989), *Cochlear Hydrodynamics Demystified*, Caltech Computer Science Technical Report, Caltech-CS-TR-88-4.

[16] R. F. Lyon (1990), 'Automatic gain control in cochlear mechanics', in: *The Mechanics and Biophysics of Hearing* (ed. P. Dallos, C. D. Geisler, J. W. Matthews, M. A. Ruggero & C. R. Steele), Springer-Verlag, New York.

[17] R. F. Lyon (1991), 'CCD correlators for auditory models', *Proc. Twenty-fifth Asilomar Conference on Signals, Systems & Computers (Pacific Grove, CA)*, 775-789.

[18] S. McAdams (1984), *Spectral fusion, spectral parsing and the formation of auditory images*, Technical Report STAN-M-22, Center for Computer Research in Music and Acoustics, Department of Music, Stanford University, Stanford, CA.

[19] R. Meddis, M. J. Hewitt & T. M. Shackleton (1990), 'Implementation details of a computation model of the inner hair-cell/auditory-nerve synapse', *JASA*, **87**(4), 1813-1816.

[20] R. Meddis & M. Hewitt (1991), 'Virtual pitch and phase sensitivity of a computer model of the auditory periphery. II. Phase sensitivity', *JASA*, **89**(6), 2883-2894.

[21] R. Meddis & M. J. Hewitt (1991), 'Virtual pitch and phase sensitivity of a computer model of the auditory periphery. I. Pitch identification', *JASA*, **89**(6), 2866-2682.

[22] R. D. Patterson (1987), 'A pulse ribbon model of monaural phase perception', *JASA*, **82**(5), 1560-1586.

[23] R. D. Patterson, K. Robinson, J. Holdsworth, D. McKeown, C. Zhang & M. Allerhand (1991), 'Complex sounds and auditory images', in: *Auditory Physiology and Perception* (ed. Y. Cazals, L. Demany & K. Horner), Oxford: Pergamon, 429-446.

[24] J. R. Pierce (1991), 'Periodicity and pitch perception', *JASA*, **90**(10), 1889-92.

[25] O. F. Ranke. (1950), 'Theory of operation of the cochlea: A contribution to the hydrodynamics of the cochlea', *JASA* , **22**, 772-777.

[26] R. Reynolds (1983), *Archipeligo*, New York: C. F. Peters.

[27] W. S. Rhode (1971), 'Observations of the vibration of the basilar membrane in squirrel monkeys using the Mössbauer technique", *JASA*, **49**, 1218-1231.

[28] M. A. Ruggero (1992), 'Responses to sound of the basilar membrane of the mammalian cochlea', *Current Opinion in Neurobiology,* **2**, 449-456.

[29] S. Shamma (1985), 'Speech processing in the auditory system I: The representation of speech sounds in the responses of the auditory nerve', *JASA*, **78**(5), 1612-1621.

[30] M. Slaney (1988), *Lyon's Cochlear Model*. Apple Computer Technical Report #13. Corporate Library, 20525 Mariani Avenue, Cupertino, CA 95104.

[31] M. Slaney & R. F. Lyon (1991), *Apple Hearing Demo Reel*. Apple Computer Technical Report #25. Corporate Library, 20525 Mariani Avenue, Cupertino, CA 95104.

[32] M. Slaney & R. F. Lyon (1990), 'A perceptual pitch detector', in: *Proc. ICASSP '90 (Albuquerque, NM)*, 357-360.

[33] C. R. Steele & Larry A. Taber (1979), 'Comparison of WKB calculations and experimental results for three-dimensional cochlear models', *JASA*, **65**, 1007-1018.

[34] N. Suga (1990), 'Cortical computational maps for auditory imaging', *Neural Networks*, **3**(1), 3-21.

[35] C. D. Summerfield and R. F. Lyon (1992), 'ASIC implementation of the Lyon cochlear model', in: *Proc. ICASSP '92 (San Francisco, CA)*, 673-676.

[36] M.l Weintraub (1985), *A Theory and Computational Model of Auditory Monaural Sound Separation*, Ph.D. Dissertation, Electrical Engineering Department, Stanford University, Stanford, CA.

[37] G. Zweig, R. Lipes & J. R. Pierce (1976), 'The cochlear compromise', *JASA*, **59**, 975-982.

[38] J. J. Zwislocki (1950), 'Theory of the acoustical action of the cochlea', *JASA, ***22**, 778-784.

PART II

Specialised Representations

Speech analysis by means of a physiologically-based model of the cochlear nerve and cochlear nucleus

6

William Ainsworth and Georg Meyer

1 INTRODUCTION

Speech sounds are transmitted via the cochlear nerve to the cochlear nucleus, the first stage of information processing in the mammalian auditory system. While the cochlear nerve transmits a relatively homogeneous signal representation, the cochlear nucleus contains cells that are adapted morphologically and physiologically to extract very specific features from the signal representation at the nerve level.

A physiologically-based computational model of the processing of sounds by the cochlear nerve and nucleus has been developed. The first stage is a series of filters based on simulated reverse correlation functions as measured in the cochlear nerve (de Boer [2]; Carney & Yin [3]). The output of these filters is then processed by a stage adding a human audiogram and an absolute hearing threshold across the array of channels. This array of signals is then processed by a model of hair cell transduction (Meddis [5,6]) and finally spikes are generated by a probabilistic spike generator.

The resulting spike trains are processed by tonotopically organised arrays of models of cochlear nucleus neurones. Two populations in the cochlear nucleus have been shown to extract two very different features from the input signals. Onset chopper (onset-C) units extract very precise temporal features, the envelope pitch (Palmer & Winter [12]); another population, consisting of transient choppers (chop-T), extracts mainly spectral information (Blackburn & Sachs [1]). The responses of these units to the Sheffield stimuli (in both cases the syllables 'susan ca') are described here.

2 THE COCHLEAR NERVE MODEL

The cochlear nerve model is a phenomenological model, simulating spike trains as measured in the cochlear nerve. Single cochlear nerve fibres transmit a composite of both spectral and temporal information to higher centres. Both representations are far from ideal, the fibres have limited dynamic ranges and cannot phase lock into frequencies above 5 kHz. The degree of phase locking deteriorates from 1 kHz onwards. Recent work (e.g. Winter *et al.* [14]) has shown that cochlear nerve fibres have varying thresholds and dynamic ranges. The model takes account of this by generating two populations of cochlear nerve responses:

- *low-threshold fibres*: These fibres have thresholds matched to behavioural hearing thresholds, high spontaneous rates (50 spikes/s) and a small dynamic range of 20 dB.

- *high-threshold fibres*: The thresholds of this population are 15 dB above those of low threshold fibres. The spontaneous rate is 15 spikes/s and the dynamic range is 40 dB.

The model is based largely on work by Meddis [5,6] and Carney & Yin [3] and will not be discussed further here.

Visual Representations of Speech Signals: Martin Cooke, Steve Beet and Malcolm Crawford (eds.)
© 1993 by John Wiley & Sons Ltd

3   THE COCHLEAR NUCLEUS MODEL

The cochlear nucleus model is based on tonotopically organised arrays of isopotential nodes. Each node receives excitatory inputs from a limited range of simulated cochlear nerve fibres as well as excitatory or inhibitory inputs from local interneurons. The input connections and the membrane characteristics of single units determine the response patterns. Arrays of units are created by connecting inputs with systematically increasing frequencies to a given node (fig.1). A detailed discussion can be found in Meyer & Ainsworth [9].

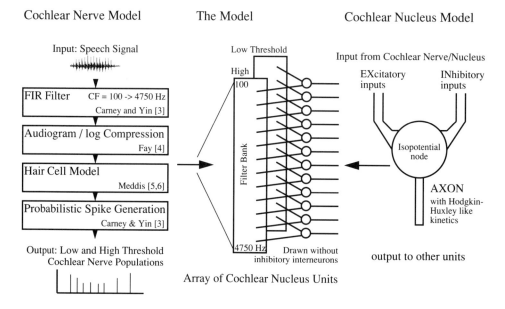

Fig. 1   Schematic processing diagram.

3.1 Transient Chopper Response

All chopper responses are characterised by a regular response to pure high-frequency tones and noise. Some units give a sustained regular discharge — sustained choppers (chop-S). Others respond with a transient regular discharge, followed by irregular activity — transient choppers (chop-T). Spectral cues are maintained in chop-T units over amplitude ranges which exceed the dynamic range of single cochlear nerve fibres (Blackburn & Sachs [1]). The large dynamic range is a result of the convergence of cochlear nerve fibres with a range of thresholds onto a single unit. Chop-T units themselves have very limited dynamic ranges (dB), so that a simple convergence of the two populations of nerve fibres would not produce realistic results. The low-threshold fibres alone would be able to drive the unit to saturation.

The units are prevented from saturating by lateral inhibition from high-threshold nerve fibres. Each projection neuron receives excitatory inputs from a narrow frequency range of both low- and high-threshold fibres and inhibitory inputs from the high-threshold fibres with characteristic frequencies 2 Bark above and below the excitatory inputs. As the sound level increases, more and more inhibitory inputs are activated and pull the membrane potential down. The result is a good spectral representation over a wide range of intensities. Figure 2 (left) shows the rate code for /u/ (150-200 ms of 'clean.syl') in both low-threshold cochlear nerve and chop-T units. The difference between nerve and nucleus responses is marked, but not dramatic because the signal is scaled to 50 dB for the data reported here (physiological data: Palmer & Evans [11]). The inhibitory input causes the units which would respond with

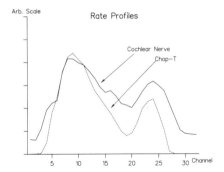 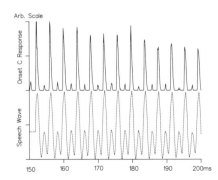

Fig. 2   *left* : Low-threshold nerve and chop-T place code for 150-200 ms of 'clean.syl'.
right : Syllable data 150-200 ms ('clean.syl') and onset-C response for all channels.

chop-S characteristics to give typical chop-T responses (Meyer [7]). The regular discharge pattern exhibited by all chopper responders is due to membrane properties (Oertel *et al.* [10]) rather than explicit processing. Most chopper units phase lock into frequencies below 1 kHz, so that the timing of the low-frequency harmonics is retained.

When a tonotopically organised array of these units is presented with the Sheffield syllable "susan ca", the output resembles a wideband spectrogram (fig. 3). Both the formant peaks and noise components and the timing of the fundamental are represented in the image. A striking difference between the chop-T and the cochlear nerve representation is the absence of spontaneous activity which makes the spectral information stand out much more clearly.

Transient choppers phase lock into low-frequency and amplitude-modulated stimuli. Here the fundamental frequency is clearly encoded, particularly in the low-frequency channels. The "chopping" in the response is evident in the noise burst of the plosive /k/ in the 'clean' speech example. In the medium-frequency range a prominent peak in the response marks the onset of the burst, followed by regular discharges. In noise the response is seriously impaired, particularly in the high-frequency region. Chopper units respond to any stimulus type, so that noise is transmitted "faithfully" to higher centres.

3.2 Onset chopper response

Onset choppers respond most strongly at the onset of pure high-frequency tones. The neurons encode signal amplitude over a very wide frequency range as well as extracting the envelope pitch of synthesised vowels (physiological data: Palmer & Winter [12]; model: Meyer & Ainsworth [9]). The units' principle of operation is coincidence detection over a population of 100 fibres with a wide range of characteristic frequencies (5 Bark).

There are considerable delays across the tonotopic axis in the encoding of timing in the cochlear nerve that are due to the basilar membrane and phase delay across frequency. For coincidence detection to work, these delays have to be removed. A conceivable neural mechanism for doing this is dendritic delay: synapses are organised such that low frequency connections are closer to the soma than the high-frequency inputs that have longer group delays associated with them (Rall [13]).

The current model is an isopotential node so that dendritic delays cannot be simulated; the cross-frequency delays consequently are removed by time shifting the input channels. To work as a coincidence detector model, single excitatory post-synaptic potentials have to be short — here half-widths of 0.7 ms. Figure 2 (right) shows the response of 26 channels of onset C units summed into one trace, compared with the stimulus. It is evident how well the envelope pitch is encoded.

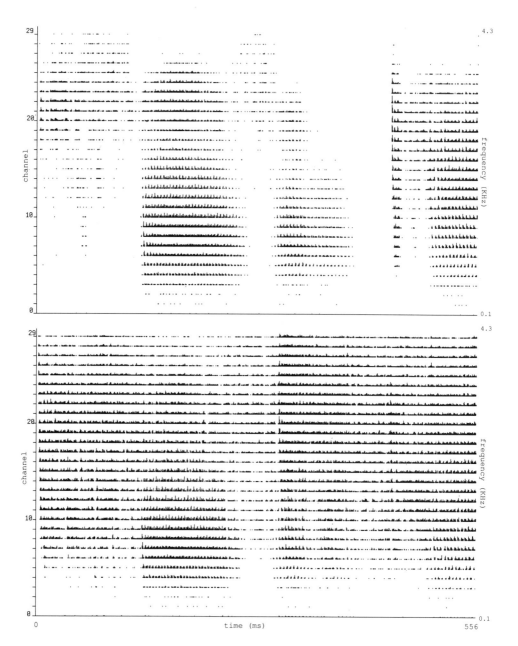

Fig. 3   Response of an array of transient choppers to *upper* 'clean.syl' and *lower* 'dirty.syl'.

When tonotopically organised arrays of these units are stimulated with the test syllable the following picture emerges (fig.4).

- Low-frequency channels show very well timed spikes. The figure was constructed by repeating the utterance 100 times; each time with a different (probabilistic) cochlear nerve input. The time of spike occurrence is virtually fixed and locked into the fundamental frequency for the voiced part of the utterance.

Fig. 4　Response of an array of onset choppers to *upper* 'clean.syl' and *lower* 'dirty.syl'.

- The high-frequency sounds, particularly at the end of the utterance encode the timing of the positive going deflections of the signal.

- The plosive burst triggers a prominent response throughout the spectrum. The fine time structure is not caused by the signal, but the "chopping" at the onset of the response.

- The spectral resolution of the units is poor. This is not surprising as each unit has a receptive field stretching over 5 Bark.

- The high-frequency noise components elicit virtually no response. The coincidence detection mechanism prevents low-amplitude noise being transmitted. Onset C units react strongly to high-intensity noise — with increased noise levels coincidences across frequency bands become more common. The pitch coding is maintained in the low-frequency channels.

The response pattern in noise is seriously degraded in the high-frequency region. Impulsive noise bursts cause strong discharges. This is particularly evident in the first fricative and during the second vowel.

REFERENCES

[1] C.C. Blackburn & M.B. Sachs (1990), 'The representation of the steady-state vowel sound /ɛ / in the discharge patterns of cat anteroventral cochlear nucleus neurons', *J. Neurophys.*, **63**, 1191-1212.

[2] E. de Boer (1969), 'Reverse correlation II. Initiation of nerve impulses in the inner ear', *Proc. Kon. Ned. Acad. Wet.*, **72**, 129-151.

[3] L.H. Carney & T.C.T. Yin (1988), 'Temporal coding of resonances by low-frequency auditory nerve fibres: single fibre responses and a population model', *J. Neurophys.*, **60**(5): 1653-1677.

[4] R.R. Fay (1988), *Hearing in Vertebrates: A Psychophysics Data Book*, Hill-Fay Assoc., Winnetka, 347-384.

[5] R. Meddis (1986), 'Simulation of mechanical to neural transduction in the auditory receptor', *JASA*, **79**(3), 702-711.

[6] R. Meddis (1988), 'Simulation of auditory-neural transduction: further studies', *JASA*, **83**, 1056-1063.

[7] G. Meyer (1992), 'CNet - point neuron simulator', Internal report, CNS Keele.

[8] G. Meyer & W.A. Ainsworth (in press), 'Modelling response patterns in the cochlear nucleus using simple units', in: *Advances in Speech, Hearing and Language*, JAI Press.

[9] G. Meyer & W.A. Ainsworth (1992), 'Processing speech in models of the cochlear nucleus', Royal Society Discussion Meeting (poster).

[10] D. Oertel, S.H. Wu & J.A. Hirsch (1988), 'Electrical characteristics of cells and neuronal circuitry in the cochlear nuclei studied with intracellular recordings from brain slices', *Auditory Function, An. Symp. Neurosciences Institute*, 313-336, J. Wiley & Sons.

[11] A.R. Palmer & E.F. Evans (1982), 'Intensity coding in the auditory periphery of the cat: responses of cochlear nerve and cochlear nucleus neurons to signals in the presence of bandstop masking noise', *Hearing Res.*, **7**, 305-323

[12] A.R. Palmer & I.M. Winter (in press), 'Coding of fundamental frequency of voiced speech sounds and harmonic complexes in the cochlear nerve and ventral cochlear nucleus', *NATO Adv. Res. Workshop*.

[13] W. Rall (1977), 'Core conductor theory and cable properties of neurons', *Handbook of Physiology: Section 1*, **1**, 39-97.

[14] I.M. Winter, D. Robertson & G.K. Yates (1990), 'Diversity of characteristic frequency rate-intensity functions in guinea-pig auditory nerve fibres', *Hearing Res.*, **45**, 191-202.

Representation of frequency variations in time in speech signals

Federico Albano-Leoni, Francesco Cutugno and Pietro Maturi

1   INTRODUCTION

Our aim in this paper is to show an example of the application of a method which we have previously presented [1,2] to the Sheffield speech material. This method was conceived in order to make it possible to describe phenomena of frequency variations in time (such as formant transitions in VC or CV groups or in diphthongs) in the form of absolute numerical values. Thus we can avoid the classical qualitative descriptions generally employed in phonetic analysis such as "rising", "falling", "constant", "steep", which are of very little use for statistics and for a closer analysis of the data.

The little space available does not allow us to present the method here separately from its application to the data, so the operations performed will be briefly described and explained step by step in the following paragraphs with direct reference to the particular measures obtained for the signals used for the application.

2   MATERIALS AND METHODS

The materials we decided to use for the present paper are the clean and noisy diphones ('clean.dip', 'dirty.dip'), consisting of the sequence [kʰɑ] isolated from the word "can't", and the spontaneous diphone ('spont.dip'), consisting of the sequence [bɪ] isolated from the word "bitter". For each of the three items only the portion containing the formant transitions was taken into account. This portion was analysed spectrographically, by means of a Sensimetrics SpeechStation produced by Ariel Corporation. An LPC analysis at 18 coefficients was performed every 2 ms starting from the first period of the consonant-vowel transition down to the last measurable point; the peak frequency values of F1, F2, F3 were measured for each frame (see Table 1).

The values so obtained were then used to build time/frequency scatter-graphs schematically reproducing the formant patterns. For this and the following operations a software spreadsheet was used. Starting from the input data, the software calculated a second-degree polynomial curve for each of the formants, transforming their graphic representation from the previous scatter-graphs into the best-fitting parabolic curves (see figs. 1-3), and obtaining thus a symbolic representation of formant transitions[1]. Statistics performed on a large amount of data [3] show that the correlation between the experimentally measured points and the parabolic curves is fairly good. In our opinion, this makes a second-degree linear regression suitable for the description of the phenomena observed.

In the formants analysed, the correlation coefficient R proved to be very high in 'clean' and very low in 'dirty', just as one would expect. The values for 'spont' are also fairly high, but not as much as for 'clean'. We think this may have some relation with the noise contained in the spontaneous diphone, but this should be checked through more measurements on larger data sets.

Visual Representations of Speech Signals: Martin Cooke, Steve Beet and Malcolm Crawford (eds.)
© 1993 by John Wiley & Sons Ltd

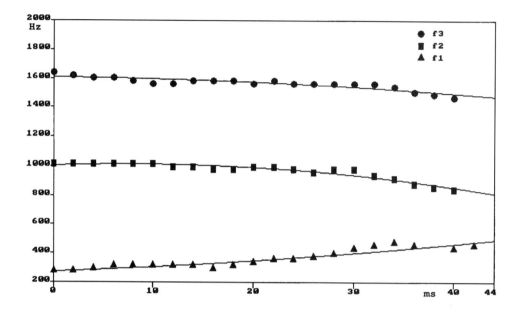

Fig. 1 Experimental data measured for F1,F2 and F3 and parabolic curves for 'clean.dip'.

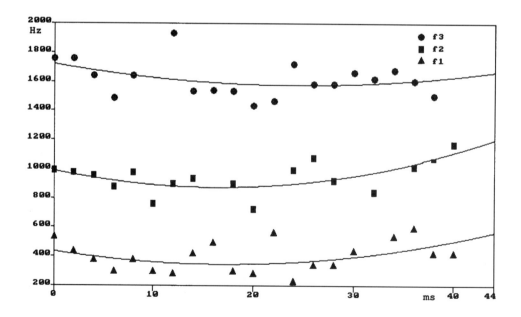

Fig. 2 Experimental data measured for F1,F2 and F3 and parabolic curves for 'dirty.dip'.

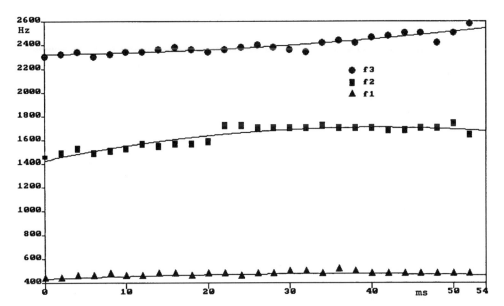

Fig. 3 Experimental data measured for F1,F2 and F3 and parabolic curves for 'spont.dip'.

We now define, for each transition, a parabolic function expressed by the formula:

$$y = ax^2 + bx + c \qquad (1)$$

where x = time and y = frequency. Table 2 lists the values calculated for the formants in the sequences observed and the respective correlation coefficient with the experimental data.

Starting from the a and b coefficients we calculate the derivative of the parabola. The derivative ideally expresses the slope of the curve at any point in time. The derivative y' is expressed by the function

$$y' = 2ax + b. \qquad (2)$$

Here we have chosen to calculate the derivatives at the instant when the first vocalic period starts[2]. In this case, the slope is equal to the coefficient b in the parabolic equation.

We can now represent each of the formant transitions studied here with only one number, i.e. with the coefficient b in the parabolic function, which is also the expression of the derivative, and hence of the slope of the curve, at the point $t = 0$ (see Table 3).

3   GENERAL COMMENTS

The present application of the method to the Sheffield data is obviously not meant here to yield any general information about English phonetics. Rather, we consider it an occasion to present this system to an international scientific audience. Moreover, we have no statistics yet about English CV sequences to compare these results with. However, some comments are in order.

First, there is a very remarkable difference between the 'clean' and 'dirty' sequences at all stages of the analysis, from the single values of the formant frequencies measured down to the coefficients calculated and to the slope. Even more importantly, the error measured with 'dirty' is too high for the regressions to be reliable at all. All that means, according to our interpretation, is that the noise has disturbed the signal in such a deep way that practically all segmental information contained in the formant structure was lost. This corresponds to the perceptual fact that the isolated diphone is no longer recognisable, and that the message is only recoverable when the whole sentence is listened to.

Second, it is impossible at present to relate the English data to our previously gathered Italian data, both because of the huge difference in quantity (three items versus several hundreds) and because of the phonetic differences between the English diphones [kʰɑ] and [bɪ] and the nearest Italian ones [ka] and [bi].

Our method was applied [3] to a large database of data with various vowels [a, i, u] in many consonantal contexts (all Italian stops and fricatives), and it was possible to draw some interesting statistical conclusions about the effects on formant transitions of both the place of articulation and voice quality. Only a comparably large number of sequences could give analogous results for English.

Other kinds of interpolation could also be used, e.g. exponentials or splines. Our group is presently working on the application of various interpolation tools. Our aims are to reduce the standard regression error, and to interpret the acoustic data so obtained as an objective description of the articulatory movements occurring during speech production.

Notes

1   A discussion could be opened here about the statistical relevance of this kind of interpolation. Apart from its simple use, the parabola also implies a description of formant transitions according to a two-variable nonlinear model. Some further implications on the physical interpretation of data could be drawn as well.

2   By contrast, in VC sequences the most suitable point in time for the calculation of the curve slope will be the last point of the transition.

REFERENCES

[1] F. Albano-Leoni, F. Cutugno & P. Maturi (1990), 'Un metodo per la descrizione delle variazioni della frequenza nel tempo', *Riv. Ital. di Acustica*, **3**(4), 61-67.

[2] F. Albano-Leoni, F. Cutugno & P. Maturi, 'Eine Methode zur Beschreibung der Frequenzvariationen in der Zeit', *Forum Phoneticum*, in press (German version of [1]).

[3] G.Rispoli & R.Savy (1992), 'Un' analisi acustica della coarticolazione di vocale e consonante in relazione al tratto di sonorità', in: *Atti del XX Convegno Nazionale dell'A.I.A.*, Roma, 373-378.

Table 1: Formant values measured for the diphones 'clean', 'dirty' and 'spont'.

t = 0 corresponds to 55 ms in the original signal for 'clean' and 'dirty', and 60 ms for 'spont'.

time (ms)	'clean.dip'			'dirty.dip			'spont.dip'		
	F1	F2	F3	F1	F2	F3	F1	F2	F3
0	273	1015	1640	527	996	1757	430	1445	2300
2	273	1015	1621	429	976	1757	430	1484	2324
4	292	1015	1601	371	957	1640	450	1523	2344
6	312	1015	1601	292	878	1484	450	1484	2304
8	312	1015	1582	371	976	1640	469	1504	2324
10	312	1015	1562	292	761	---	449	1523	2344
12	312	996	1562	273	898	1933	449	1562	2344
14	312	996	1582	410	937	1532	469	1543	2363
16	292	976	1582	488	---	1542	469	1562	2383
18	312	976	1582	292	898	1533	449	1562	2363
20	332	996	1562	273	722	1435	469	1582	2344
22	351	996	1582	556	---	1464	469	1719	2363
24	351	976	1562	222	996	1718	449	1719	2383
26	371	957	1562	332	1074	1582	469	1699	2402
28	390	976	1562	332	918	1582	469	1699	2383
30	429	976	1562	429	---	1660	488	1699	2363
32	449	937	1562	527	839	1621	488	1699	2344
34	468	917	1542	585	1015	1679	469	1718	2421
36	449	878	1503	410	1054	1601	507	1699	2441
38	429	859	1484	410	1171	1504	488	1699	2422
40	449	839	1464	332	1093		469	1699	2461
42							469	1680	2480
44							469	1680	2500
46							469	1699	2500
48							469	1699	2421
50							469	1738	2500
52							469	1641	2578

Table 2: Second-degree regressions calculated for the transitions.

	Equation	R	Std. Err. (Hz)
'clean.dip'			
F1	$y = 0.08x^2 + 2.6x + 273.5$	0.90	21
F2	$y = -0.15x^2 + 2.4x + 1005$	0.91	15
F3	$y = -0.05x^2 - 0.6x + 1968$	0.88	19
'dirty.dip'			
F1	$y = 0.30x^2 - 10.4x + 434.5$	0.30	91
F2	$y = 0.40x^2 - 14.3x + 991.1$	0.46	81
F3	$y = 0.02x^2 - 11.7x + 1720$	0.26	110
'spont.dip'			
F1	$y = -0.05x^2 + 2.9x + 443$	0.76	10
F2	$y = -0.20x^2 + 16.3x + 1428$	0.86	33
F3	$y = -0.10x^2 - 0.6x + 2323$	0.84	27

Table 3: Slopes calculated at t=0 for the transitions (in Hz/ms).

	'clean.dip'	'dirty.dip'	'spont.dip'
F1	+ 2.6	+ 10.4	- 2.9
F2	+ 2.4	- 14.3	+ 16.3
F3	- 0.6	- 11.7	- 0.6

Auditory-based wavelet representation

Christophe d'Alessandro

1 INTRODUCTION

This paper presents briefly the auditory-based wavelet representation (AWR). The adaptation of an auditory frequency scale to the wavelet representation was proposed in d'Alessandro & Beautemps [3] and discussed for speech in d'Alessandro & Beautemps [2]; a speech representation model, closely related, to AWR was proposed in d'Alessandro [1]. The reader is referred to these papers for more information and references on these methods.

The wavelet representation is a linear nonparametric representation method, closely related to linear filtering. It provides a local time-frequency description of the signal: at the analysis stage, wavelet coefficients are obtained by correlation between the wavelets and the signal, and at the synthesis stage the signal is reconstructed as a discrete weighted sum of wavelets. These two points (speech analysis using a spectrographic format, and speech synthesis using wavelets) will be discussed in relation to the Sheffield data. Displaying the wavelet coefficients provides auditory-based wavelet spectrograms (AWS). Different types of AWS are discussed.

Compared to models of the auditory periphery, AWS can be considered as a somewhat simplified functional representation of the first stage of analysis (i.e. cochlear filtering). The aim is not to provide a refined auditory model, but to propose an auditorily-justified tool in acoustic-phonetics.

Another application of AWR is speech synthesis. AWR gives a complete resynthesis scheme. For speech synthesis or modification, it is possible to reduce this redundant representation to its most important components. Resynthesis from AWS and reduced AWS indicates those of the acoustic speech parameters that seem more perceptually relevant. Section 2 presents a brief description of the methods. Section 3 discusses of these methods in relation to the Sheffield data.

2 DESCRIPTION OF THE METHODS

2.1 Overview of AWR

AWR may be interpreted in terms of linear filtering, both at the analysis and at the synthesis stages. These wavelets are defined on a set of points in the time-frequency domain, and are weighted by a set of coefficients which are dependent on the analysed signal.

To interpret the representation, the wavelets must be localised functions both in time and frequency. In other words, they are chosen with a main spectro-temporal maximum, and with negligible values outside a (small enough) time-frequency domain. One can therefore interpret the local behaviour of the signal by comparison with the analysing wavelets, and one can consider AWR as a decomposition of a signal on a discrete set of time-frequency points.

The AWS examples presented here were obtained using a critical-band (Bark scale) finite impulse response (FIR) filterbank. The prototype wavelet was a Hamming window. The filterbank used constant 1 Bark, 6 dB bandwidth filters. In each band, analysing wavelets (re-

Visual Representations of Speech Signals: Martin Cooke, Steve Beet and Malcolm Crawford (eds.)
© 1993 by John Wiley & Sons Ltd

lated to the impulses responses of the filters) were obtained by contraction/dilation and modulation of the Hamming window.

2.2 Amplitude, phase and filtered instantaneous frequency AWS

As wavelet analysis is equivalent to filtering, one can display multi-band filtered signals using amplitudes and phases of the wavelet coefficients. This display is fairly different from a classical spectrogram because of the linear (instead of bilinear) nature of the analysis, and because of the frequency scale. We prefer here a spectrographic format where only the coefficients with positive phases are plotted (i.e. half-wave filtered signals). This spectrographic format provides several representations of the important features of speech signal (dominant frequencies and periodicity). As complex coefficients are computed at the analysis stage, in each band, computation of the time-derivative of phase provides instantaneous frequencies of the filtered signal. Dominant frequencies are enhanced on these spectrograms.

2.3 Reduced AWS

The ability of the representation to retain relevant acoustic parameters may be checked using resynthesis. The first type of resynthesis is direct resynthesis: the sum of all the weighted wavelets. The quality obtained with resynthesised signals is perfect, excepted for a little bandwidth reduction, as the chosen wavelets are not ideal bandpass filters. A reduced resynthesis scheme, using only the wavelets present at dominant time-frequency points was defined. Local energy concentrations in time and frequency were detected using linear predictive analysis and short-time Fourier analysis, and peak picking. Fourier wavelets (i.e. with constant resolution) were selected on these frequency tracks, and a signal was resynthesised using only this reduced wavelet representation. These reduced resynthesised signals are perceptually identical to resynthesised signals.

One step forward in AWS reduction is to synthesise the signal directly from the acoustic parameters extracted from the AWS. This reduction was performed using the following parameterisation: sinusoidal representation of the F0-F1 area, formantic representation (using dominant frequencies and temporal envelope modulations) above. The quality obtained is excellent, although the reduced synthetic signal sounds a bit different from the direct resynthesised signal. The reduced signal is not identical with the original signal because of the nonlinear relationship between the acoustic parameters used for synthesis (temporal envelopes, dominant frequencies) and speech production parameters (formants, F0). Therefore, the parameters used for synthesis are only approximations of the true speech parameters. This approximation is good enough to preserve the general quality, but not to give identical signals.

3   APPLICATION TO THE SHEFFIELD DATA

3.1 Sheffield data

Owing to the limited space available for diagrams, we limited analyses to sound examples referred to as 'timit.syl', 'clean.syl' and 'dirty.syl'.

'Timit' : this example is a well-recorded sentence, uttered by a male American speaker, and sampled at 16 kHz. Formants are clearly visible, both on wideband spectrograms and AWS. This example was judged easy to read by an expert in (American English) spectrogram reading. Fig. 1 shows 'timit.syl' in AWS format; an instantaneous frequency AWS corresponding to fig. 1 is shown in fig. 2, and a reduced AWS in fig. 3.

'Clean': the quality of this example is rather poor, due to the recording conditions. The signal is low-pass filtered at 2.8 kHz. Without any prior knowledge, this sentence appeared difficult to understand both for French and American listeners in our laboratory. The spectrogram reading experiment was also not completely successful, because it appeared difficult to find the formant frequencies and motions, and because of the unusual phonetic realisations of

some vowels. Figure 4 shows 'clean.syl' in AWS format, and an instantaneous frequency AWS corresponding to fig.4 is given in fig. 6.

'*Dirty*': Figure5 shows 'dirty.syl' in AWS format, and an instantaneous frequency AWS corresponding to fig.5 is given in fig. 7.

3.2 AWS reading

The acoustic features that are apparent on AWS are dependant both on the acoustic signal produced by the vocal apparatus, and on the time-frequency resolution of the analysis. Analyses of quasi-periodic signals, like voiced speech, indicate the following:

- Below a frequency threshold, individual harmonics are resolved. This threshold is dependant both on F0 and critical bandwidth. In each band a time-varying sinusoid is obtained, whose amplitude and phase are set according to vocal tract and source amplitudes and phases, and whose frequency is F0 times the harmonic number.

- Above this threshold, two or more harmonics merge into a single filter, but formants are resolved (i.e. a single band contains at most one formant). The signal is therefore an amplitude and frequency modulated sinusoid, resulting from beats between the harmonic components. Unfortunately, the relationship between amplitude and frequency modulation of the waveform in a band, and the underlying speech production parameters (F0, formants, etc.) is nonlinear, and generally not analytically tractable. Nevertheless, one can prove analytically, at least for two components beating in a band, that the average period of amplitude modulation equals 1/F0, and that the mean of frequency excursion during a fundamental period is a local maximum of the spectral envelope.

- Above another frequency threshold, two or more formants merge into a single filter. The beats pattern is very complex, resulting in a spectral mass on AWS, with an amplitude modulation frequency greater than F0, and a rather wide frequency modulation.

For speech parameters, generally speaking, the first point above corresponds to the F1 region, the second point to F2 and F3, and the final point to the region above F3.

4 CONCLUSIONS

In this paper an auditory-based wavelet representation was introduced for speech analysis and synthesis.

The auditory spectrograms obtained are somewhat different to classical spectrograms; it is not clear that they will prove better for phoneme identification. Generally speaking, AWS show less contrast than spectrograms, because it is a signal decomposition and not an energy distribution. Other auditory-like processing might be applied after this first stage of analysis, to enhance contrast. For instance lateral inhibition may enhance spectral contrast and short-term adaptation may enhance temporal contrast.

On the other hand, both reading and resynthesis indicates that the acoustic parameters which are visible on AWS could give a more complete description of the speech signal than those visible on spectrograms: F0 and parameters related to voice quality are visible. It is well known that voice quality (naturalness, speaker individuality, etc.) is difficult to assess precisely using spectrograms. AWS could work better here. For AWR reduced synthesis, the accurate estimation of speech parameters from the wavelet coefficients is a difficult problem, as soon as several harmonics merge in a single band.

This representation takes advantage of the interplay between perception and production in speech analysis. It might provide another tool for studying several open questions such as:

how is F1 perceived in relation to F0, what is the influence of higher formants on vowel quality, and what is the perceptual relevance of (the amplitudes and phases of) lower harmonics?

Acknowledgements: I would like to thank Denis Beautemps for programming the analysis-synthesis system, Lori Lamel for help in spectrogram readings and phonetic transcriptions, and both of them for fruitful discussions.

REFERENCES

[1] C. d'Alessandro (1990), 'Time-frequency speech transformation based on an elementary waveform representation', *Speech Comm.*, **9**, 419-431.

[2] C. d'Alessandro & D. Beautemps (1991), 'Justification perceptive du spectrographe auditif', *Proc. XIIth Int. Cong. Phonetic Sciences*, vol. 5, 86-89.

[3] C. d'Alessandro & D. Beautemps (1991), 'Transformation en ondelettes sur une échelle fréquentielle auditive', *Proc. XIIIth GRETSI Symp.*, 745-748.

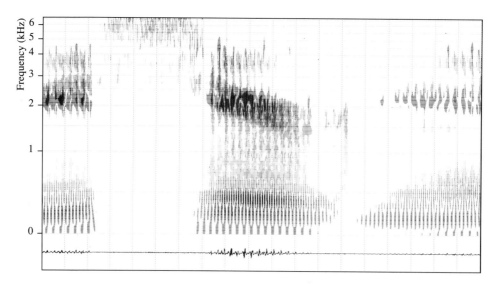

Fig. 1   AWS of 'timit.syl'.

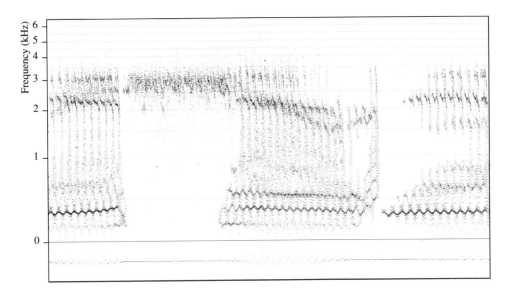

Fig. 2   Instantaneous frequency AWS of 'timit.syl'.

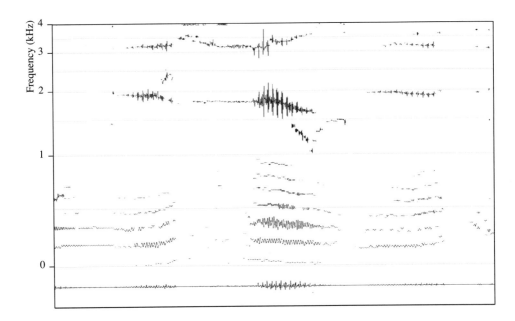

Fig. 3   Reduced AWS of 'timit.syl'.

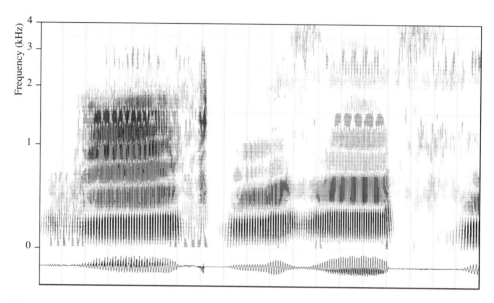

Fig. 4   AWS of 'clean.syl'.

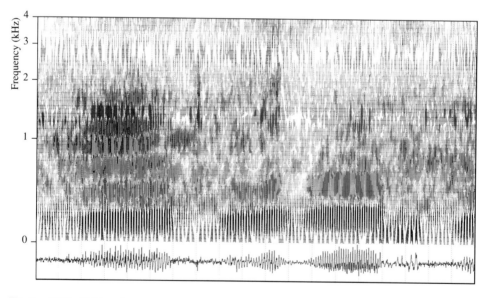

Fig. 5   AWS of 'dirty.syl'.

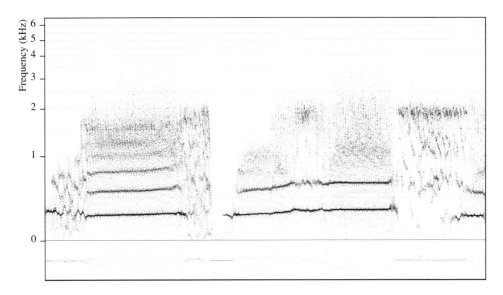

Fig. 6   Instantaneous frequency AWS of 'clean.syl'.

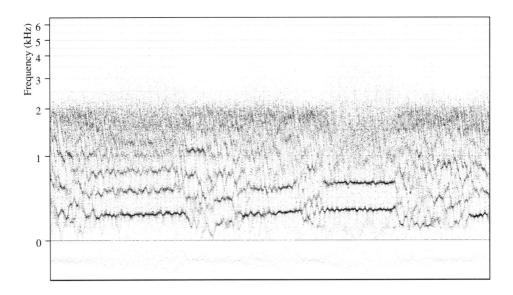

Fig. 7   Instantaneous frequency AWS of 'dirty.syl'.

Estimation of the glottal excitation of speech with pitch-synchronous iterative adaptive inverse filtering

Paavu Alku

1   INTRODUCTION

The source of voiced speech, the glottal pulseform, has been a subject of research for several decades. Due to the complexity of the human speech production mechanism the computation of the glottal excitation is not easy. Therefore many methods have been developed during the past years in order to obtain reliable estimates for the glottal source. Among these techniques inverse filtering is one of the most frequently used.

Although many different inverse filtering techniques have been developed for glottal wave analysis (e.g. [5,6]), the basic idea in all of these is the same. Models for the vocal tract and lip radiation effects are first formed. The estimate for the glottal source is then obtained by filtering the speech signal through the inverses of the vocal tract and lip radiation models. A widely used inverse filtering technique was presented in [7]. In Rothenberg's method the glottal flow is computed by inverse filtering the volume velocity waveform at the mouth. The recording is performed with a circumferentially vented pneumotachograph mask. The parameters of the inverse filter are adjusted manually. Another widely applied inverse filtering technique, the-closed phase covariance analysis (CP analysis), was presented in [8]. The idea in the CP-technique is that the vocal tract is estimated during the time when there is no glottal excitation. The estimation of the vocal tract is computed automatically with linear predictive coding (LPC) using the covariance criterion from the speech samples during the closed phase of the glottal cycle. Determination of the position of the closed phase is difficult. Therefore, electroglottography (EGG) has been used in order to make the closed phase analysis more reliable [4]. However, the analysis of voices where the closed phase of the glottal cycle is short or does not exist at all cannot be performed accurately with the CP technique.

In this paper a new inverse filtering technique, pitch-synchronous iterative adaptive inverse filtering (PSIAIF), is used to estimate the glottal excitation. In comparison to Rothenberg's method the PSIAIF algorithm has two benefits: the method is completely automatic and noninvasive (i.e. no mask is required during the recording of speech). The estimation of the closed phase of the glottal cycle is not needed at all in the PSIAIF method. Hence, the analysis can be performed also on those speech signals that are created by a source with no glottal closed phases.

The structure of the algorithm is presented in section 2. The results that were obtained when the Sheffield data (signals 'clean.wav' and 'dirty.wav') were analysed are discussed in section 3. In the description of the results emphasis is placed on the presentation of the figures leaving the verbal discussion short.

2   METHOD

2.1   General

The PSIAIF algorithm is based on a speech production model [3] that consists of three separated parts: the glottal excitation, the vocal tract, and the lip radiation effect. The model

Visual Representations of Speech Signals: Martin Cooke, Steve Beet and Malcolm Crawford (eds.)
© 1993 by John Wiley & Sons Ltd

is linear and no interaction is assumed between the three different parts. The lip radiation effect is modelled in the PSIAIF algorithm with a fixed differentiator. Hence, in the estimation of the glottal excitation the computation of the second part of the model, the vocal tract, is most essential.

The estimation of the glottal pulseform with the PSIAIF algorithm is based on a previously developed method, iterative adaptive inverse filtering (IAIF) [1]. The role of the IAIF algorithm is important in the new PSIAIF method. Hence, a short description is first given about the function of the IAIF method. The new algorithm, the PSIAIF method, is then presented in section 2.3.

2.2 Iterative adaptive inverse filtering (IAIF)

The computation of the glottal pulseform in a pitch asynchronous manner with the IAIF method was presented in [1]. By referring to the block diagram of fig. 1 the function of the IAIF method is as follows. First, an average effect of the glottal excitation to the speech spectrum is estimated by applying first order LPC analysis to the speech signal that is to be analysed (block 1). After eliminating the estimated glottal contribution by inverse filtering (block 2) a model for the vocal tract is formed (block 3). A first estimate for the glottal excitation signal, $g_1(n)$, is obtained by cancelling the effects of the vocal tract and lip radiation by inverse filtering (blocks 4 and 5). A new estimate for the effect of the glottal source is then computed (block 6). A new model for the vocal tract is obtained (block 8) by again first cancelling the effect of the source (block 7). Finally, the glottal pulseform is obtained by eliminating from the original speech signal the effects of the vocal tract and lip radiation (blocks 9 and 10).

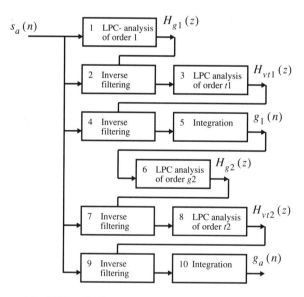

Fig. 1   Block diagram of the IAIF method.

2.3 Pitch-synchronous iterative adaptive inverse filtering (PSIAIF)

The IAIF-algorithm described in the previous section is used as a sub-method when the glottal excitation is estimated with the PSIAIF algorithm. In the PSIAIF method the speech signal is analysed twice with the IAIF algorithm. The first analysis is pitch asynchronous. Its result is used in order to determine the positions of frames for the second IAIF analysis, which is computed one fundamental period at a time. In the pitch-synchronous analysis the estimation of the vocal tract can be computed more accurately than in the pitch-asynchronous case.

The block diagram of the PSIAIF method is shown in fig. 2. The speech signal to be analysed is denoted $s(n)$. The final result, the estimate for the glottal pulseform, is denoted $g(n)$.

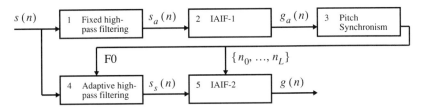

Fig. 2   Block diagram of the PSIAIF method.

The function of each of the blocks is as follows:

- *Block 1*: The speech signal is high-pass filtered in order to remove undesirable fluctuations of the resulting glottal waveform. Fluctuations of the glottal waveform, if the low-frequency components are not removed, result from integration that is used as the last block of the IAIF algorithm (block 10 in fig. 1). As a high-pass filter we have used a linear phase FIR whose cutoff frequency is fixed to 30 Hz. The filter has 2047 coefficients.

- *Block 2*: The output of the high-pass filter, signal $s_a(n)$, is analysed with the IAIF method as described in section 2.2. The autocorrelation method together with Hamming-windowing is used in all of the LPC analyses. The analysis is computed pitch asynchronously using a frame whose length is long enough to span several fundamental periods.

- *Block 3*: The glottal waveform given by the IAIF-1 stage is analysed (see [2] for details) in order to determine time instants of maximal glottal openings, denoted $\{n_0, ..., n_L\}$. The fundamental frequency, F0, is determined as an inverse of the largest distance between two consecutive maximal glottal openings that were found from one frame of $g_a(n)$.

- *Block 4*: The original speech signal is high-pass filtered with a linear phase FIR, whose cutoff frequency is adjusted to (F0 – 10 Hz). This high-pass filtering removes effectively the low-frequency "noise" components that, especially when silent voices are analysed, distorts the resulting glottal pulseform.

- *Block 5*: Signal $s_n(n)$ is analysed with the IAIF algorithm pitch synchronously using frames that span between two consecutive maximal glottal openings. If the length of the frame is short (below 40 samples) the covariance criterion is used in all of the LPC-analyses of the IAIF 2 structure. The output of block 5 is the final result, the estimate for the glottal excitation.

3   RESULTS AND CONCLUSIONS

The PSIAIF algorithm was used in the estimation of the glottal pulseform by analysing signals 'clean.wav' and 'dirty.wav'. The analysis was computed from seven segments that were cut from the original sentences. Each of the segments consisted of one vowel as shown in Table 1.

The sampling frequency of the signals was decreased from the original value of 20 kHz to 8 kHz. By referring to fig. 1 the following parameters[1] were used.in both the pitch-asynchronous and pitch synchronous IAIF stages: t1 = t2=12, g2 = 4 (after we noticed the cutoff

Table 1

segment	vowel	word	first index	last index
1	e	Fred	6847	8889
2	ae	can	11918	15327
3	o	go	15622	21441
4	u	Susan	24167	26366
5	a	can't	31347	34873
6	i	Linda	41951	43465
7	a	uncertain	48965	50372

around 3 kHz in 'clean.wav' the analysis was computed with smaller parameters, viz. t1 = t2 = g2 = 4; however, this did not affect the resulting pulseforms greatly). Since the utterance was spoken by a female speaker, the covariance criterion was used in all of the LPC analyses of the IAIF-2 stage. If the LPC analysis gave an inverse filter that had zeros outside the unit circle they were replaced by their mirror image partners inside the unit circle.

The results that were obtained when the above-mentioned seven segments were analysed are shown in figs. 3-9. In these figures the original signals that were cut from 'clean.wav' and 'dirty.wav' and downsampled are shown by curves (a) and (c), respectively. The glottal waveforms obtained from the clean data are shown by curves (b) and the results obtained from noisy speech are shown by curves (d). In general it can be observed that the pulseforms correspond quite well with *a priori* knowledge about a typical female glottal pulseform. The overall shape of the glottal pulseform is quite smooth in all of the results. The length of the closed phase was very short; in most cases the glottis started to open immediately after the time instant of minimum flow. No significant differences were found between the shapes of excitations of different vowels. By comparing the results obtained from signal 'clean.wav' to those computed from 'dirty.wav' it can be observed that the PSIAIF algorithm is fairly immune to noise. This can be seen clearly from fig. 8, for example, where curve 8(c) shows a segment that was severely distorted by noise. However, the corresponding glottal wave estimate, curve 8(d), is still quite similar to the one, curve 8(b), that was computed from clean samples.

REFERENCES

[1] P. Alku, E. Vilkman & U.K. Laine (1991), 'Analysis of glottal waveform in different phonation types using the new IAIF-method', *Proc. XIIth Int. Congress of Phonetic Sciences '91*, **4**, 362-365.

[2] P. Alku (1991), 'Glottal wave analysis with Pitch Synchronous Iterative Adaptive Inverse Filtering', *Proc. EUROSPEECH '91*, 1081-1084.

[3] G. Fant (1960), *Acoustic Theory of Speech Production*, Mouton, The Hague.

[4] A.K. Krishnamurthy & D.G. Childers (1986), 'Two-channel speech analysis', *IEEE Trans. ASSP*, **34**, 4, 730-743.

[5] M.R. Matausek & V.S. Batalov (1980), 'A new approach to the determination of the glottal waveform', *IEEE Trans. ASSP*, **28**, 6, 616-622.

[6] M.V. Mathews, J.E. Miller, & E.E. David, Jr. (1961), 'Pitch synchronous analysis of voiced sounds', *JASA*, **33**, 2, 179-186.

[7] M. Rothenberg (1973), 'A new inverse-filtering technique for deriving the glottal air flow waveform during voicing', *JASA*, **53**, 6, 1632-1645.

[8] D.Y. Wong, J.D. Markel & A.H. Gray, Jr. (1979), 'Least squares glottal inverse filtering from the acoustic speech waveform', *IEEE Trans. ASSP*, **27**, 4, 350-355.

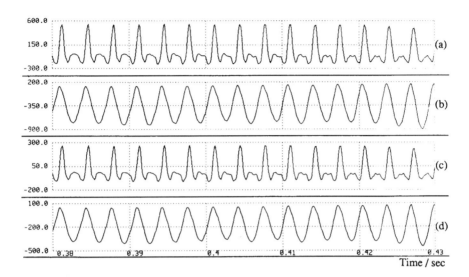

Fig. 3   Segment no. 1: *a* : clean speech signal; *b* : glottal waveform computed from curve a;
c : speech signal with added noise; *d* : glottal waveform computed from curve c.

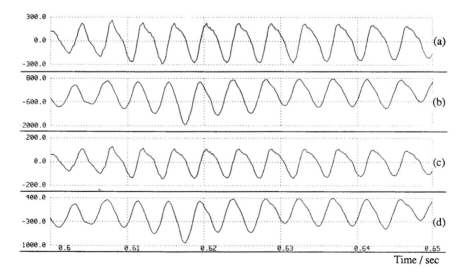

Fig. 4   Segment no. 2: *a* : clean speech signal; *b* : glottal waveform computed from curve a;
c : speech signal with added noise; *d* : glottal waveform computed from curve c.

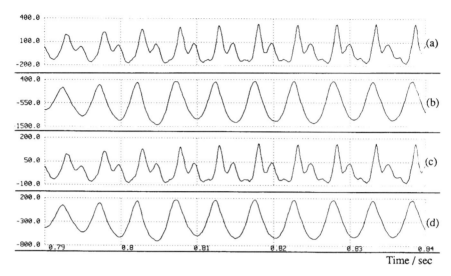

Fig. 5   Segment no. 3: *a* : clean speech signal; *b* : glottal waveform computed from curve a;
c : speech signal with added noise; *d* : glottal waveform computed from curve c.

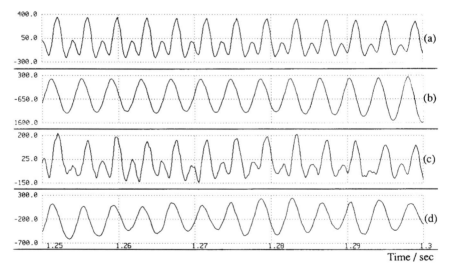

Fig. 6   Segment no. 4: *a* : clean speech signal; *b* : glottal waveform computed from curve a;
c : speech signal with added noise; *d* : glottal waveform computed from curve c.

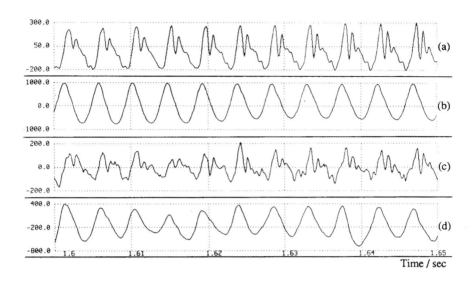

Fig. 7   Segment no. 5: *a* : clean speech signal; *b* : glottal waveform computed from curve a;
c : speech signal with added noise; *d* : glottal waveform computed from curve c.

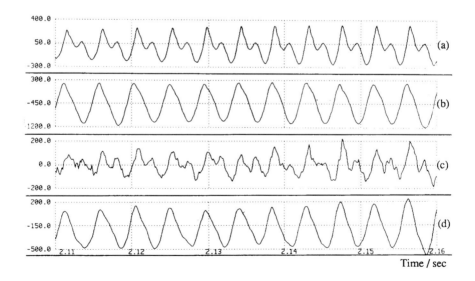

Fig. 8   Segment no. 6: *a* : clean speech signal; *b* : glottal waveform computed from curve a;
c : speech signal with added noise; *d* : glottal waveform computed from curve c.

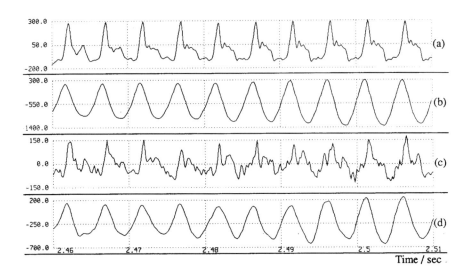

Fig. 9   Segment no. 7: *a* : clean speech signal; *b* : glottal waveform computed from curve a;
c : speech signal with added noise; *d* : glottal waveform computed from curve c.

Analysis and synthesis: a hybrid solution for speech parameter extraction

10

J. R. Andrews and K. M. Curtis

1 INTRODUCTION

In the age of rapid technological progress, society is not only becoming increasingly demanding but also more aware of what it wants. The public are requesting higher quality products and services. This is very apparent in the field of man-machine communication where natural sounding speech is much sought after. It has long been established that human-computer interaction needs to be vastly improved, with the cumbersome keyboard being the focus of attention.

There are basically two aims of speech research. One is to find an effective form of coding for recognition, so as to aid the human-to-machine communication side. The other is to develop a comprehensive form of parameterisation for synthesis, for the modelling of the human vocal system. This is to produce a voice with a high degree of naturalness. Various products are currently available, ranging from public announcement systems, to aids for the blind and vocally handicapped [3].

High-quality speech synthesisers are readily obtainable, such as the Klatt cascade/parallel synthesiser [8] and the Holmes parallel formant synthesiser [5]. There are also a plethora of well established speech analysis methods, e.g. cepstral [4], LPC coding[6], and the more recently developed group delay techniques [9]. Unfortunately there seems to be a gap in the combination of highly accurate speech analysis to high-quality speech synthesis systems.

We propose a complete system, which addresses both problems of accurate formant analysis and synthesis, in order to produce high-quality natural sounding speech. The formant description of a speech sound is widely accepted as the most practical and comprehensive analysis method, as it leads to a quick and thorough understanding of a speech sound. The entire system uses a formant tracking algorithm based on the group delay (GD) function, integrated with a highly programmable parallel formant speech synthesiser [1]. Each section is realised on the most suitable processing system, thus facilitating optimised performance [2].

The two component parts are connected via a novel highly adaptive phase locked loop technique. This produces high accuracy by matching the extracted synthesis parameters to the formant synthesiser output. The complete system is designed for the analysis/synthesis of any language and work has already been carried out on German demisyllables.

2 SYSTEM DESCRIPTION AND ANALYSIS ALGORITHM

The hybrid system described here, comprises of a supervisor which controls and links the two separate processing units. The total system is contained in a PC and utilises two processors on add-in boards. A Motorola M56000 DSP board was chosen to perform the highly accurate formant frequency tracking, as it is ideally suited to carry out the FFT frequency analysis, due to the sequential nature of the algorithm itself.

First, segments of speech are preprocessed to produce a minimum phase signal. This preprocessing reduces the effects of phase wrapping. This also gives a certain freedom in the

Visual Representations of Speech Signals: Martin Cooke, Steve Beet and Malcolm Crawford (eds.)
© 1993 by John Wiley & Sons Ltd

subsequent analysis, as the analysis window has to be aligned with the signal's phase. The GD function, *the negative derivative of the phase of the FFT spectrum*, is calculated to identify the formant frequencies present. This method provides high resolution due to the additive nature of the phase spectrum and can identify closely coupled or weak (e.g. nasal) formants and is not dependent on the synthesis model as in LPC analysis, where the number of coefficients determines the spectral resolution of the analysis. A 1024 point FFT is used on n time pitch periods of the speech signal (n is typically 2 or 3), with the rest of the samples in the 1024 points, set to zero. Figure 1 depicts the complete analysis and synthesis approach when using the system to carry out copy synthesis.

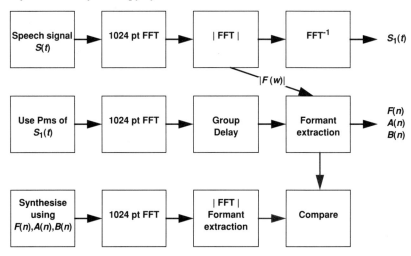

Fig. 1   Analysis with feedback loop for copy synthesis.

The GD data along with FFT magnitude spectrum is passed to the transputer network for formant tracking. Each formant frequency is then calculated and tracked in parallel, by the transputers along with the formant's amplitude and bandwidth. The network of transputers can track up to seven formants, thus leading to a complete description of the speech sound. This is particular suited to both female and child speech production.

The procedure of using the GD data and the FFT magnitude data enables accurate extraction of formant frequencies, amplitudes and bandwidths. The GD data is used to calculate the formant frequencies. As the preprocessing and GD provides a smoothed spectral envelope all harmonic components are removed. Thus to identify the formant frequencies a number of simple peak-picking algorithms are employed. Peaks from the GD data are identified and firstly sorted in order of size. These are then passed through a number of algorithms which decide which represent the formant frequencies. The formant amplitudes and bandwidths are computed using the formant frequencies obtained from the GD information and the FFT magnitude data. This approach was used as additional algorithms are required to calculate the amplitudes and bandwidths using the GD data only [10].

These raw formant frequencies with their associated amplitudes and bandwidths are then fed to the synthesiser section of the system, which firstly performs appropriate modifications to this data, converts the frequency information to synthesiser parameters and subsequently controls the speech synthesiser.

A parallel design was selected for the synthesiser, as it has been shown by Holmes that this can produce both good vocalic and non-vocalic sounds [5]. It has been demonstrated that to realistically synthesise high-quality male or female speech more than five resonators are needed [7]. Therefore the synthesiser [1] developed here can have up toseven resonators in parallel to describe any speech sound precisely. As the synthesiser's structure is inherently of a parallel nature then a parallel processor architecture offers the best solution to the synthesiser's implementation. The synthesiser is mapped onto a multi-transputer network for real-time performance.

The formant information fed to the synthesiser, via the adaptive link, produces output. The frequency spectrum of the original speech segment is compared to the synthesised one and appropriate alterations are carried out on the formant data and the segment is resynthesised. This feedback is used to tune the synthesiser's parameters to the natural formant data, thus optimising the quality of the synthesiser's output. This process is utilised in two ways. Firstly, it is used to copy synthesise, for the evaluation of both the analysis and synthesis elements of the system, and, secondly, it is used to build up a "tuned" database of synthesis units for unrestricted text-to-speech conversion. The proposed synthesis units are demisyllables which contain the transition from vowel to consonant cluster. Demisyllables were selected since they retain the natural coarticulation present between sounds. They also require a small number of simple rules in the concatenation process. Therefore this simplifies the synthesis process and provides the most natural sounding speech.

3   RESULTS

The analysis provides the formant frequencies, amplitudes and bandwidths of a speech segment in a noise-free environment, such as an anechoic chamber. Therefore just the analysis of the clean signals are considered. First of all the speech signal /k{/ (SAMPA from the 'clean.dip' file) was analysed. This signal was sampled at 20 kHz, but with a low filtered cut-off at 2.8 kHz. Figure 2 displays the formant magnitude history of the /k{/ waveform. The cutoff can be clearly seen and it was felt that to achieve higher quality the entire spectral content of this signal was required. The spectra of two segments within the demisyllable are then shown in greater detail, with analysis frames of 9 ms (two pitch periods). Figure 3(a) is the frequency analysis of the plosive burst of /k/ which is 10.6 ms long and fig. 3(b) shows the same analysis for the middle part of vocalic section /{/.

This speech signal was subsequently run through the adaptive algorithm for re-synthesis. This involved two pitch period segments for each frame of the analysis and synthesis. The resolution of the group delay is high and it has picked out all the relevant formant information accurately, and via the phase locked loop this data supplied to the synthesiser has accurately re-synthesised the sound, as shown in the formant tracks in fig. 4. Figure 5 depicts the three dimensional view of the re-synthesised waveform. The speech segment under analysis was sampled at 20 kHz, using 9 ms frames and 1024 point FFTs are employed in the subsequent analysis.

Two opposing factors have to be considered here, in order to obtain accurate frequency analysis. On the one side there is frequency resolution and on the other the duration of the speech segment under consideration. A 1024 point FFT was used to provide a resolution of 10 Hz and a duration of 9 ms to make sure of not averaging the formants over a changing waveform.

4   CONCLUSIONS

This work demonstrates a new adaptive method for addressing the problem of high-quality analysis and synthesis of speech. Both parts of this system have been tackled separately using optimised mapping techniques and structures. This is a very important part as this helps to achieve real-time system performance. We now require complete systems for analysing and synthesising natural sounding speech. The unique combination of the two highly accurate speech processing components, via an adaptive technique, provides a new comprehensive approach to the whole field of speech processing. The results here have been based on a copy

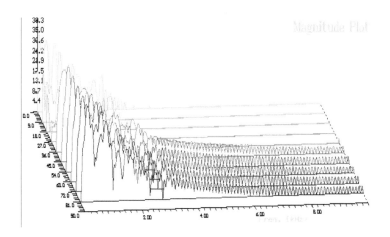

Fig. 2   Frequency plot of /k{/ from 'clean.dip'.

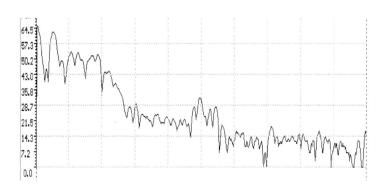

Fig. 3   FFT magnitude spectrum of plosive burst /k/ from 'clean.dip'.

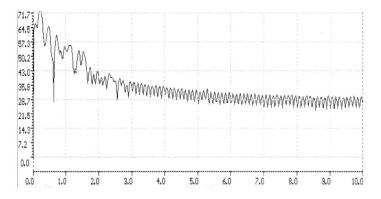

Fig. 4   FFT magnitude spectrum of vocalic section /{/ from 'clean.dip'.

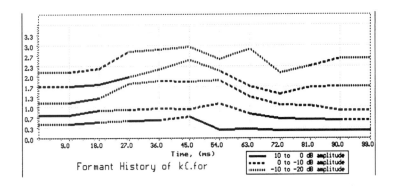

Fig. 5   Formant tracks for waveform /k{/ from 'clean.dip'.

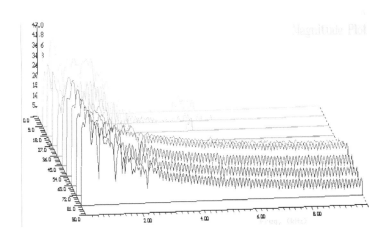

Fig. 6   Frequency plot of resynthesised /k{/'.

synthesis technique which can easily be applied to setting up a database for unrestricte speech synthesis. Work is presently being carried out on creating a formant-coded Germa demisyllable inventory, utilising several speech segments for each demisyllable. The grou delay function is currently being extended for the extraction of the pitch period from t speech segment.

Acknowledgements: Mr. J.R. Andrews wishes to thank the SERC who provided his studentship.

REFERENCES

[1] K.M. Curtis, G.M. Asher, S. Pack & J.R. Andrews (1991), 'A highly programmable formant speech synthesizer utilising parallel processors', *Proc. ICSLP '90 (Japan)*, 817-820.

[2] K.M. Curtis & J.R. Andrews (1991), 'Control flow: a technique for optimising processing structure', *Proc. 9th IASTED International Symposium (Austria)*, 322-325.

[3] anon (1988), 'An Introduction for the Hal System Version 1.12 & 1.18', Dolphin Systems 198

[4] F. Fallside & W.A. Woods (1985), *Computer Speech Processing*, Prentice Hall International, Englewood Cliffs, NJ, 74-77.

[5] J.N. Holmes (1985), 'A parallel-formant synthesizer for machine voice output', in: *Computer Speech Processing* (eds. F. Fallside & W.A. Woods), Prentice Hall International, Englewood Cliffs, NJ, 163-187.

[6] J.N. Holmes (1988), *Speech Synthesis and Recognition*, Van Nostrand Reinhold, New York, 66-69.

[7] W.J. Holmes, J.N. Holmes & M.W. Judd (1990), 'Extension of the bandwidth of the JSRU parallel-formant synthesizer for high quality synthesis of male and female speech', *Proc. ICASSP '90 (Alberquerque)*.

[8] D.H. Klatt (1987), 'Review of text-to-speech conversion for English', *JASA*, **82**(3), 737-793.

[9] H.A. Murthy, K.V. Madhu Murthy & B. Yegnanarayana (1989), 'Formant extraction from Fourier transform phase', *Proc. ICASSP '89 (Glasgow)*, 484-487.

[10] B. Yegnanarayana (1978), 'Formant extraction from linear prediction phase spectra', *JASA*, **63**(6), 1638-1640.

Perceptually-based dynamic spectrograms

Ted H. Applebaum and Brian A. Hanson

1   INTRODUCTION

Spectral transitions play an important role in human auditory perception. Temporal derivative features (delta cepstrum [2], or regression features [3]) are computational correlates of spectral transitions. These features have been shown to greatly enhance the performance of speech-processing tasks such as speech recognition [1-4] and speaker identification [8]. However, little has been published about the way in which these features contribute to the representation of speech. To better understand the characteristics of temporal derivative features, dynamic and perceptually-based dynamic spectrograms were introduced in [4]. Dynamic spectrograms enhance the representation of speech events through time differentiation. Perceptually-based dynamic spectrograms combine time differentiation with other psychophysically motivated speech transformations to emphasise perceptually salient aspects of the signal.

2   BACKGROUND

Due to the improvement of speech recognition performance they provide, temporal derivative spectral features of some kind are now almost universally incorporated into the speech representations used for automatic speech recognition [2]. Nevertheless there is little standardisation of these features, and their contribution to improved recognition is still poorly understood.

Our previous work has focused on finding speech representations for robust speaker-independent recognition of speech produced in noise. Both additive noise and noise-induced speech production effects (Lombard effect) have been considered. Use of time derivatives of cepstral coefficients derived from linear prediction (LPC) or perceptually-based linear prediction (PLP) [6] analysis has been shown to be effective for recognition of noisy or noisy-Lombard speech [4]. Time derivatives out to the third derivative have been found to increase recognition rates for recognition of noisy-Lombard speech [3]. More recent work [1] has isolated separate factors which contribute to the improved recognition performance when the speech representation is augmented with these time-derivative features.

Spectral and temporal derivative features can be represented visually, using colour or separate monochrome images to distinguish the sign of the derivative. Dynamic spectrograms and perceptually-based dynamic spectrograms were developed as tools to evaluate and understand the behaviour of the time-derivative features, but are also useful ways of examining speech.

Dynamic spectrograms, based on linear prediction analysis, relate directly to standard wideband spectrograms (i.e. both are representations of log power versus frequency). They are therefore more readily interpretable by one familiar with standard spectrograms than are perceptually-based dynamic spectrograms.

Visual Representations of Speech Signals: Martin Cooke, Steve Beet and Malcolm Crawford (eds.)
© 1993 by John Wiley & Sons Ltd

Perceptually-based dynamic spectrograms, based on PLP analysis, emphasise perceptually significant features. We believe, from our earlier work on word recognition, the time derivatives of the PLP spectrum are relatively invariant under changes in speech due to varying noise conditions. PLP combines autoregressive modelling with psychophysically motivated speech transformations: Bark-spaced filterbank processing, equal-loudness compensation, and third root compression (simulating the intensity-loudness power law).

Early versions of the perceptually-based dynamic spectrogram appeared in [4]. Extensions and additional displays are included with this paper.

3 METHOD

A progression of speech representations will be presented, with illustrative examples of the 'clean.syl' speech segment from the Sheffield data set. The original 20 kHz sampling rate data were low-pass filtered and downsampled by 2 to match the 10 kHz sampling rate for which the PLP filters are designed.

Figure 1 is a standard wideband spectrogram of the 'clean.syl' example speech segment, and represents the log magnitude spectrum on a "frequency versus time" grey scale display. It uses a 9-bit FFT to estimate the spectrum over a 40 ms Hamming window. This analysis is repeated for each 2 ms time frame shift.

3.1 Static features

All of the remaining speech representations are based on a 12th-order all-pole model (LPC or PLP), expressed by its cepstral expansion, which is the Fourier expansion of the model log spectrum [7]

$$S = \ln \frac{\sigma^2}{|A(e^{j\theta})|^2} \approx \sum_{k=-L}^{L} c_k \, e^{-jk\theta} \tag{1}$$

where σ is a gain factor, A is the model polynomial and θ is the normalised frequency $2\pi f/f_s$. For speech-recognition purposes we obtain an adequate representation with $L = 12$ terms.

The static LPC-CEP spectrogram shown in fig. 2 uses 12th-order LPC analysis to estimate the spectrum over a 200 ms Hamming window. This analysis is repeated for each 10 ms time frame shift. As in the wideband spectrogram, the vertical axis is linear in frequency from 0 to 5kHz.

The static PLP-CEP spectrogram (fig. 3) substitutes 12th-order PLP analysis for the LPC analysis used in fig. 2. The vertical axis of the figure is linear in Barks, emphasising the low frequency region. As a result of the critical-band integration step in PLP analysis, the spectral peaks are wider and more continuous than in the LPC-CEP representation.

In the previous figures only the positive portion of the log spectrum was plotted, since the peaks of the magnitude spectrum have the most perceptual significance. For the spectral or temporal derivatives of the log spectrum, which are considered below, both the positive and negative extremes have perceptual significance. The following speech representations will be shown in two panels to simultaneously display the positive (upper) and negative (lower) portions of the derivatives of the log spectrum.

The static PLP-RPS spectrogram (odd symmetry) shown in fig. 4 represents the spectral derivative with respect to frequency [5] of the PLP-CEP spectrum shown in fig. 3. This is implemented by weighting the cepstral coefficients (c_k) by their index (k):

$$S'_O = \frac{\partial S}{\partial \theta} \approx -j \sum_{k=-L}^{L} k \, c_k \, e^{-jk\theta} \, . \tag{2}$$

Because the cepstral coefficients are even symmetric with respect to the index $(c_{-k} = c_k)$ the series coefficients (kc_k) of eqn. (2) are odd symmetric (therefore eqn. (2) can be expressed as a sine series). This representation yields a complicated display (fig. 4) as the peaks of the spectrum can generate both positive (top) and negative (bottom) extrema in the display. An alternative, even symmetric representation may defined as in eqn. (3):

$$S'_E \approx \sum_{k=-L}^{L} |k|\, c_k \, e^{-jk\theta} . \tag{3}$$

The corresponding even symmetric static PLP-RPS spectrogram is shown in fig. 5.

The RPS distance measure [5], which has been used in speech recognition tasks to compare test and reference spectra, is the Euclidean distance between two index-weighted cepstral vectors (eqn. (4)). The even and odd symmetric representations are equivalent with respect to this distance measure, as the squaring operation removes symmetry considerations. Hence either of the representations (eqn. (2) or eqn. (3)) may be used to display what is being compared in the RPS distance:

$$d_{RPS}\left(c^{TEST}, c^{REF}\right) = \sum_{k=1}^{L} \left(k\left(c_k^{TEST} - c_k^{REF}\right)\right)^2 . \tag{4}$$

We will use the even symmetry representation (eqn. (3)) as a basis for all of the following dynamic features because the even symmetry representation of PLP-RPS tracks extrema rather than locations of rapid spectral change and is observed to be generally positive, yielding clearer displays when time-differentiated.

3.2 Dynamic features

Dynamic features are the time derivatives of the spectrum, and can be numerically approximated by regression over a finite time length. These features are characterised by the order of the derivative (i.e. order of the regression function), the time length over which the derivative is calculated and the number of spectral analysis frames included in the calculation [1]. The notation used here is $R_r(T)$ for regression feature of order r and time length T, with the number of frames determined by the 10 ms frame rate.

Increasing the number of analysis frames used in calculating the dynamic features smooths the representation by linearly combining more data values. Such temporal smoothing has been found to improve word recognition rates [1] and speaker verification scores [8]. At fixed analysis frame rate the time length and number of frames are proportional. For speech recognition the first temporal derivative is usually calculated over 50 to 100 ms [2].

Experiments on automatic word recognition at a fixed 10 ms frame rate [1,3,4] have shown that integration over longer time intervals gives higher recognition rates, especially for recognition of Lombard or noisy-Lombard speech by a system trained with clean speech. The benefit from additional smoothing due to increasing the time length of the R_1 feature to longer than 200 ms more than compensated for any resulting loss of temporal resolution. Compare, for example, the PLP-RPS R_1 (90 ms) spectrogram of fig. 6 with the smoother PLP-RPS R_1 (210 ms) spectrogram of fig. 7.

The second temporal derivative is calculated by weighting the cepstral coefficients by a quadratic weighting function [1]. Although adding the second temporal derivative to cepstrum-based speech representations significantly improves automatic speech recognition rates, the visual display of the second derivative feature is less readily interpretable than that of the first derivative feature. The PLP-RPS R_2 (250 ms) spectrogram shown in fig. 8 is a typical second derivative feature display.

4 SUMMARY

The index-weighted (RPS) cepstral coefficients from perceptually-based linear prediction analysis, and their first few temporal derivatives, are effective features for representing speech in speech recognition or speaker identification tasks. They have been found to be particularly robust to the distortion of test speech by additive noise or the Lombard effect. The parameters of these features may be adjusted to optimise the speech representation for a particular speech processing problem.

Perceptually-based dynamic spectrograms are visual displays of these features, which use two-colour (or pairs of monochrome) images to represent the positive and negative portions of the spectral and temporal derivatives of the auditory spectrum. Further experience in interpreting these displays is expected to yield improvements to the underlying speech representation, and may additionally be useful for visually examining speech produced in noise.

REFERENCES

[1] T. H. Applebaum & B. A. Hanson (1991), 'Trade-offs in the design of regression features for word recognition', *Proc. EUROSPEECH '91*, 1203-1206.

[2] S. Furui (1990), 'On the use of hierarchical spectral dynamics in speech recognition', *Proc. ICASSP '90*, 789-792.

[3] B. A. Hanson & T. H. Applebaum (1990), 'Features for noise-robust speaker-independent word recognition', *Proc. Int. Conf. Spoken Lang. Processing (ICSLP), (Kobe)*, 1117-1120.

[4] B. A. Hanson & T. H. Applebaum (1990), 'Robust speaker-independent word recognition using static, dynamic and acceleration features: experiments with Lombard and noisy speech', *Proc. ICASSP '90*, 857-860.

[5] B. A. Hanson & H. Wakita (1987), 'Spectral slope distance measures with linear prediction analysis for word recognition in noise', *IEEE Trans. ASSP*, **35**, 968-973.

[6] H. Hermansky, B. A. Hanson & H. Wakita (1985), 'Low-dimensional representation of vowels based on all-pole modelling in the psychophysical domain', *Speech Communication*, **4**, 181-187.

[7] A. H. Gray Jr. & J. D. Markel (1976), 'Distance measures for speech processing', *IEEE Trans. ASSP*, **24**(5), 380-391.

[8] J. S. Mason & X. Zhang (1991), 'Velocity and acceleration features in speaker recognition', *Proc. ICASSP '91*, 3673-3676.

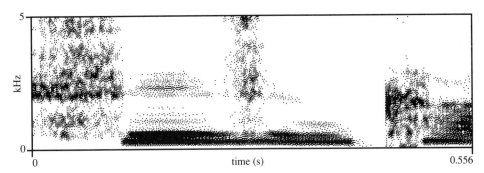

Fig. 1   Wideband spectrogram of 'clean.syl' ("Susan ca[n't]").

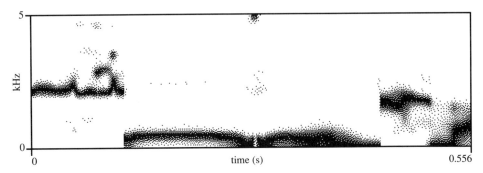

Fig. 2   Static LPC-CEP spectrogram of 'clean.syl'.

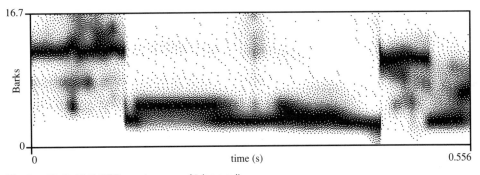

Fig. 3   Static PLP-CEP spectrogram of 'clean.syl'.

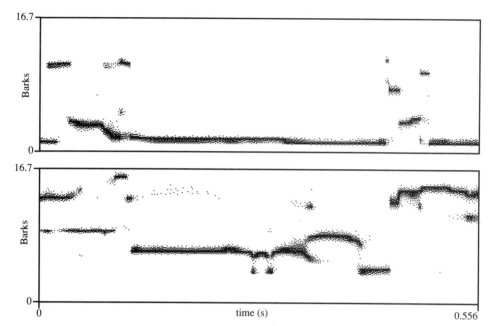

Fig. 4   Static PLP-RPS spectrogram [odd symmetry] of 'clean.syl'. This and all the following figures
consist of two parts. The upper and lower panels represent the positive and negative
components of the spectrogram, respectively.

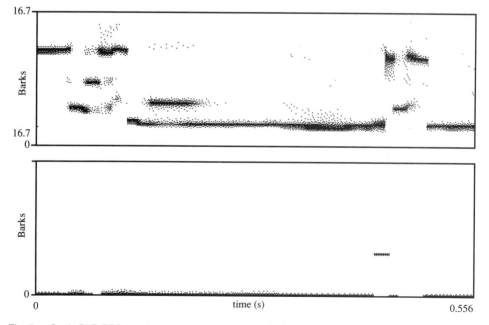

Fig. 5   Static PLP-RPS spectrogram [even symmetry] of 'clean.syl'.

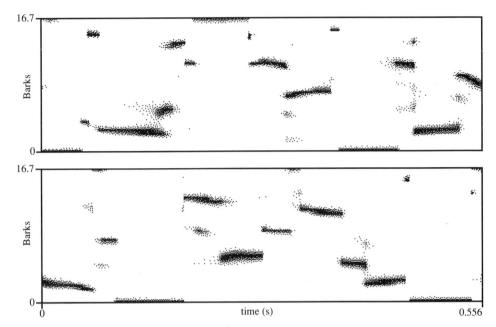

Fig. 6 R_1 (90 ms) PLP-RPS spectrogram of 'clean.syl'.

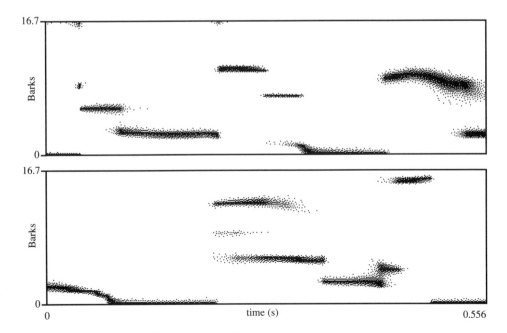

Fig. 7 R_1 (210 ms) PLP-RPS spectrogram of 'clean.syl'.

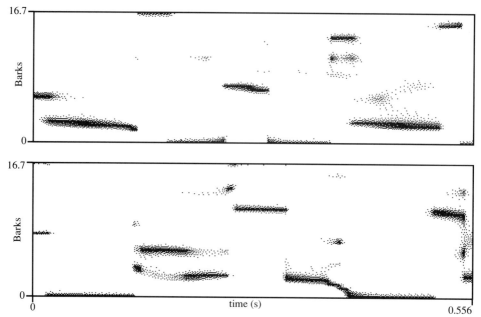

Fig. 8 R_2 (250 ms) PLP-RPS spectrogram of 'clean.syl'.

Advantages of general quadratic detectors for speech representations

L. Atlas and J. Fang

1 INTRODUCTION

The precise analysis of pitch periods, formants, and other features, such as energy, of speech is potentially useful in the design of speech coding and recognition systems. Among these features, accurate pitch determination is considered to be one of the most difficult tasks in speech processing. One reason that pitch and other features are difficult to analyse is that the tools of linear time-invariant systems (LTI) are not totally applicable to nonlinear operations, such as magnitude-squaring or thresholding. Empirical studies of systems with these nonlinear operations have been an essential part of the past progress in speech representations. However, mathematical analysis of these systems is difficult, if not impossible. Systems which are quadratic in the signal, such as Teager's model [6,8] or our own past work in quadratic time-frequency representations (e.g. [9]), are amenable to analysis and, as we show, have potential for new applications in the representation of speech.

Our concepts of quadratic detectors provide a structure which integrates frequency filtering (e.g. a bandpass filter) with energy detection (e.g. a magnitude-squared detector). When formulated in discrete-time, they are related to and, in fact, subsume Teager's energy model. Thus, they are generalised detectors which have coefficients that are designed for specific applications. These detectors have frequency selectivity which arises from the same design techniques as conventional linear filters (e.g. standard FIR filter design techniques). However, the temporal response of these detectors can allow a rise time which is essentially instantaneous. In other words, the trade-off between time and frequency resolution which is required in linear systems does not have to apply to quadratic processing.

In this paper, we review our quadratic detector formulation, link it to time-frequency representations and show how a quadratic detector could be beneficially used for pitch tracking in noise. Other recent work [1] has shown the utility of quadratic detectors for speech stop-burst classification and telephone pitch representation.

2 THE QUADRATIC DETECTOR

A standard linear energy detector, consisting of a one-dimensional linear time-invariant (LTI) filter followed by a magnitude-square and possibly a smoothing filter, is commonly applied to both time-varying and time-invariant signals. For example, many filterbank analysers use this form of detector at each channel's output. Although the conventional magnitude-square introduces a quadratic operation, a trade-off between time and frequency resolution must exist due to the LTI filter. However, once the detector is generalised, this trade-off does not have to exist [2].

Mathematically, the output $E_L[n]$ of a signal $x[n]$ from the conventional linear detector (a linear bandpass filter followed by a magnitude square) can be expressed as

Visual Representations of Speech Signals: Martin Cooke, Steve Beet and Malcolm Crawford (eds.)
© 1993 by John Wiley & Sons Ltd

$$E_L[n] = \left| \sum_k x[n-k] h_L[k] \right|^2 \tag{1}$$

where $h_L[k]$ is impulse response of a linear bandpass filter. For a real signal and impulse response the magnitude square is expanded as

$$E_L[n] = \sum_k \sum_l x[n-k-l] x[n-k+l] h_L[k+l] h_L[k-l]. \tag{2}$$

It is important to note that the product $h_L[k+l] h_L[k-l]$ is actually a *separable* kernel of the general class $h_G[k,l]$. Namely, if we redefine eqn. (2) to be

$$E_G[n] = \sum_k \sum_l x[n-k-l] x[n-k+l] h_G[k,l] \tag{3}$$

then this new formulation can either encompass the magnitude-squared formulation of eqn. (1), or it can go beyond it when $h_G[k,l] \neq h_L[k+l] h_L[k-l]$. A simple version of this more general case, where $h_G[k,l] = \delta[k] h[l]$ and where $\delta[k]$ is the unit pulse function, results in the quadratic detector [1] which does not require the LTI time-frequency trade-off:

$$E[n] = \sum_{m=0}^{M-1} x[n+m] x[n-m] h[m] \tag{4}$$

where $h[m]$ is an M-point set of *quadratic filter coefficients*. These coefficients can be chosen using standard FIR filter design procedures and $E[n]$ will have a magnitude response to single or swept sine waves which corresponds to [1]:

$$|H(e^{j\omega})|^2 = \left| \sum_{m=0}^{M-1} h[m] e^{-j\omega m} \right|^2. \tag{5}$$

Note that a conventional LTI definition of frequency response will not hold for the quadratic formulation in eqns. (4) and (5). However, the response to single sine waves swept from $-\pi$ to π will uniquely characterise the detector of eqn. (5).

For real signals such as speech, the quadratic detector can be viewed in filtering sense as

$$y[n] = y[n,m]\big|_{m=0}$$
$$= \sum_{m=0}^{M-1} r[n,k-m] h[m]\big|_{k=0} \tag{6}$$
$$= r[n,m]^* h[m]\big|_{m=0}$$

where $*$ is convolution and $r[n,m]$ is instantaneous autocorrelation defined as

$$r[n,m] = x[n+m] x[n-m]. \tag{7}$$

Equation (6) implies taking the zero-lag sample from the convolution of instantaneous autocorrelation and impulse response (i.e. a filter with impulse response $h[m]$ is applied to instantaneous autocorrelation for each time point n and then only the zero-lag sample is kept).

The quadratic detector can also be viewed in a time-frequency sense as

$$y[n] = Y[n,f]\big|_{f=0}$$
$$= \sum_{m=0}^{M-1} r[n,m] h[m] e^{-j2\pi f m}\big|_{f=0} \tag{8}$$
$$= R[n,f]^* H[f]\big|_{f=0}$$

where $Y[n,f]$ and $R[n,f]$ are time-frequency representations, by taking Fourier transforms in m on the quadratic detector output $y[n,m]$ and the instantaneous autocorrelation $r[n,m]$, respectively. Equation (8) indicates that the quadratic detector output $y[n]$ is taking the zero frequency output of pseudo-Wigner distribution $Y[n, f]$ [3]. In the frequency domain, equivalence between eqns. (6) and (8) can be shown by:

$$R[n,f]^* H[f]|_{f=0} = \int_{-\infty}^{\infty} R[n, 0 - f'] H[f'] \, df'$$

$$= \int_{-\infty}^{\infty} R[n, f'] H[f'] \, e^{j2\pi f'0} df' \tag{9}$$

$$= r[n, m]^* h[m]|_{m=0} \, .$$

Equations (8) and (9) link the quadratic detector viewed in the time domain to Cohen-class quadratic time-frequency representations [6]. As shown in [1], the discrete time version of Teager's model is subsumed in the quadratic detector of eqn. (2) and links can also be made to Gardner's quadratic techniques [5] and second-order Volterra series filter [7].

3   PREPROCESSING FOR PITCH TRACKING

Pitch determination plays an important role in many speech analysis and recognition algorithms. However, the variability and irregularity of speech and speaking environments can cause difficulty in pitch determination. Noisy environments are especially difficult since low frequencies are commonly masked and even lost. Purely linear techniques are unable to recover the missing fundamental frequency yet nonlinear techniques, such as a quadratic detector, can potentially regenerate the missing frequency from its harmonics. Our results, which will be shown below, will mainly illustrate how the quadratic detector enhances the time-domain representation of speech.

3.1 Methods

Signals 'clean.wav', 'dirty.wav' and 'spont.wav' were used in the experiments. Two processing techniques were applied: one was a standard linear energy detector which was a linear bandpass filter followed by a magnitude-square and a smoothing filter (eqn. (1)); the other was a quadratic detector (eqn. (4)) which was comprised of a quadratic bandpass filter cascaded with a quadratic smoothing filter and then normalised. The same filter coefficients were used in both the linear energy detector and the quadratic detector.

A simple pitch tracker was used in some of the experiments: a peak is only considered a pitch peak if it is larger that all other points in the neighbourhood N points to the left and N points to the right, where N is a rough estimate of the smallest possible pitch period. This rule does not allow two pitch peaks closer than N points. This method worked reasonably well even in cases where the pitch period is several times larger than N.

3.2 Results

In fig. 1, the filter coefficients were calculated by a frequency sampling technique with a filter length of 127, a bandwidth of 400 Hz, and a bandpass filter centre of 400 Hz. With preprocessing by the quadratic detector, the extra pitch peak in the waveform of the noisy utterance caused by the broadband noise was removed. The outputs of quadratic detector [(h) and (i)] also showed smaller errors in pitch peak position than was achieved with the noisy utterance without preprocessing [(f) and (g)].

In figs. 2i and 2ii, the same set of filter coefficients were used with a linear energy detector. The important observation about the quadratic detector shows that it can gain frequency selectivity without the usual linear system requirement of smoothing temporal response. The comparison also shows that in the vocalic regions of the waveform, the quadratic detector can provide better temporal resolution and presumably more accurate waveform features.

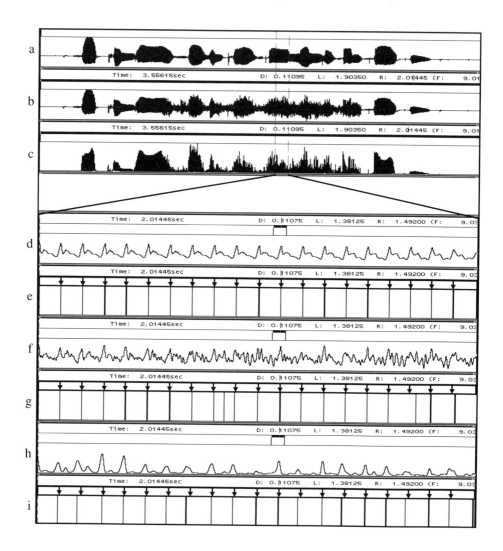

Fig. 1   Performance of quadratic detector on pitch tracking. *a*, *b*, and *c* are waveforms of
'clean.wav', 'dirty.wav', and the output of quadratic detector on 'dirty.wav'. *d*, *f*, and *h* are
zoomed displays of waveforms corresponding to a, b, and c, respectively. *e*, *g*, and *i* are
pitch positions of d, f, and h, respectively. The arrows above each pitch display are the pitch
positions of 'clean.wav' shown in d.

In fig. 3, a quadratic detector was used for spontaneous speech corrupted by noise in the
environment of a public house ('spont') and comparisons are made to the linear technique.
The coefficients were again calculated by frequency sampling with a filter length of 127, a
bandwidth of 400 Hz, and a bandpass filter now centred at 450 Hz. For this spontaneously
spoken speech, the quadratic detector showed advantages similar to those seen in the laboratory speech in figs. 1 and 2.

4   CONCLUSION

A generalised quadratic detector formulation has been defined and linked to the theory which underlies quadratic time-invariant transformations and quadratic time-frequency representations. A simple formulation was provided to achieve frequency selectivity without the usual linear system requirement of smoothing temporal response. The nonlinear effects of these detectors provide a new form of preprocessing for pitch tracking of real speech in noisy environments. In [1] we also showed potential advantages for stop burst and telephone bandwidth speech representations.

Quadratic detectors may have more general signal processing applications and our work is also directed toward their analysis and design for factory sensor, automatic transient classification, and communications applications.

Acknowledgements: We wish to thank Prof. Ron Cole of Oregon Graduate Institute for his helpful comments and Mr. Christian Roehr of our lab for providing the pitch tracker. This research was supported by the Boeing Commercial Airplane Company and the Washington Technology Center.

REFERENCES

[1] L. Atlas & J. Fang (1992), 'Quadratic detectors for general nonlinear analysis of speech', *Proc. ICASSP '92*, II-9—II-12.

[2] L. Atlas, J. Fang, P. Loughlin & W. Music (1991), 'Resolution advantages of quadratic signal processing', *Proc. SPIE Int. Sym. Conf. 1566 (San Diego, CA)*, 134-143.

[3] T. Classen & W. Mecklenbrauker (1980), 'The Wigner distribution. Part 3', *Phillips J. of Res.*, **35**, 277-300.

[4] L. Cohen (1989), 'Time-frequency distributions - a review', *Proc. IEEE*, **77**, 941-981.

[5] W. A. Gardner (1988), *Statistical Spectral Analysis,* Ch. 10, Prentice Hall, Englewood Cliffs, NJ.

[6] J. Kaiser (1990), 'On a simple algorithm to calculate the 'energy' of a signal', *Proc. ICASSP '90*, 381-384.

[7] M. Schetzen (1980), *The Volterra and Wiener Theory of the Nonlinear Systems,* J. Wiley and Sons, New York.

[8] H. M. Teager (1980), 'Some observations on oral air flow during phonation', *IEEE Trans. ASSP,* **28**, 599-601.

[9] Y. Zhao, L. Atlas & R. Marks (1990), 'The use of cone-shaped kernels for generalized time-frequency representations of nonstationary signals', *IEEE Trans. ASSP,* **38**, 1084-1091.

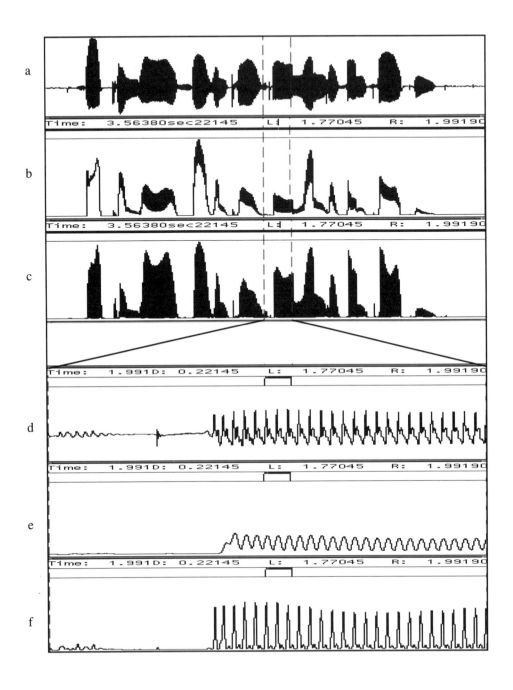

Fig. 2i   'clean.wav' : comparison of conventional linear energy detector and quadratic detector as preprocessing for pitch tracking of speech in noise; *a-c* are the time waveform, the output of a conventional linear energy detector, and the output of a quadratic detector. *d-f* show zoomed displays of vocalic regions for the three waveforms a-c, respectively. Figure 2ii shows the noisy speech, 'dirty.wav'.

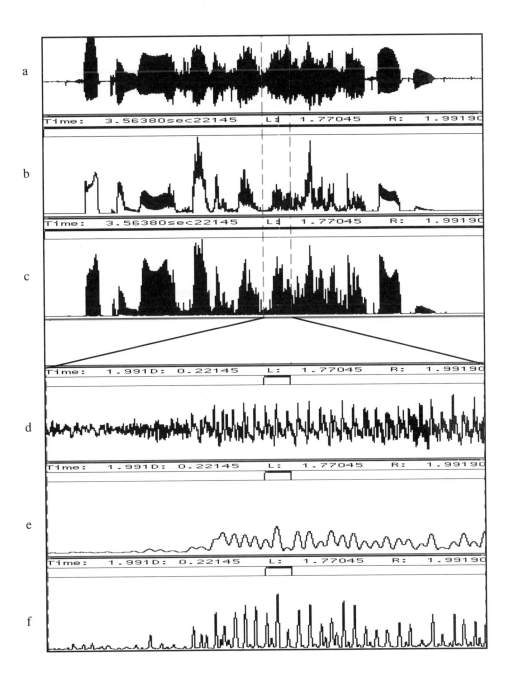

Fig. 2ii   'dirty.wav' : comparison of conventional linear energy detector and quadratic detector as preprocessing for pitch tracking of speech in noise; *a-c* are the time waveform, the output of a conventional linear energy detector, and the output of a quadratic detector. *d-f* show zoomed displays of vocalic regions for the three waveforms a-c, respectively. Figure 2ii shows the noiseless speech, 'clean.wav'.

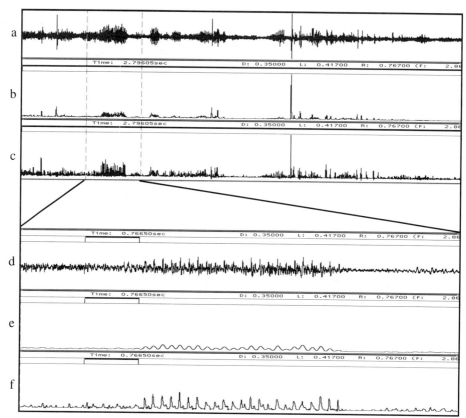

Fig. 3   Comparison of conventional linear energy detector and quadratic detector as preprocessing
for pitch tracking for 'spont.wav'. *a-c* are the time waveform, the output of a conventional
linear energy detector, and the output of a quadratic detector. *d-f* show zoomed displays of
vocalic regions for the three waveforms a-c, respectively.

The time-scale transform method as an instrument for phonetic analysis

P. Basile, F. Cutugno, P. Maturi and A. Piccialli

1 INTRODUCTION

Non-parametric techniques [1] such as the short-time Fourier transform (STFT) bear a particular significance in phonetic analysis as they allow us to make as few *a priori* assumptions as possible about the given signal. This allows us to verify existing models or to suggest new models. We propose in this work an attempt to compare the traditional Fourier analysis with a time-scale technique, namely the wavelet transform (WT). We show that such comparisons can cast new light on the problem of the representation and interpretation of speech signals. Although nonparametric techniques do not require in their definitions any general *a priori* assumptions about the signals to be analysed, it is important to note that they do require some specific assumptions about the signal in order to derive a meaningful representation, and that such assumptions depend on the signal model itself (e.g. an estimate of the value of the fundamental frequency is necessary in order to fix the filter bandwidth in the STFT).

2 DEFINITIONS

The short-time Fourier transform of a signal $x(t)$ can be defined as follows [3,4]:

$$X(T, \omega) = \int_{-\infty}^{\infty} x(t)\, h(t - T)\, e^{-j\omega t}\, dt \tag{1}$$

where $h(t)$ is an adequate weighting function, compactly supported (also known as the *analysis window*). This equation, as is well known, can be seen from two equivalent, though conceptually and operationally different, points of view. First, it can be viewed, at a fixed t', as the local spectrum of $x(t')$ seen through the sliding window $h(t)$, i.e. an amplitude-frequency representation (spectrogram). Second, it can be considered as the output of a constant-bandwidth filterbank, whose bandwidth is inversely correlated to the length of the window $h(t)$. Conversely, the wavelet transform (WT) is defined as follows [2]:

$$W(T, a) = \frac{1}{\sqrt{a}} \int_{-\infty}^{\infty} g^*\left(\frac{t - \tau}{a}\right) x(t)\, dt \tag{2}$$

where $g(t)$, the analysing wavelet, defines a family of functions, $g(t - T/a)$, whose time and frequency localisation vary depending on the scale factor a. In fact, for any value of a, $g(t - T/a)$ defines a bandpass filter, the centre frequency of which is inversely correlated with a. A change of a simultaneously involves both the centre frequency and the bandwidth so that the ratio $\Delta f/f$ (or $Q = $ bandwidth/central frequency ratio) remains constant.

The main difference between the two analysis methods, when employed in a phonetic environment, is that the WT representation is unique and relies exclusively on the choice of analysing wavelet, whereas the STFT retains its duality (narrowband and wideband analysis are both necessary for a correct investigation [4]) no matter which analysis window is chosen. In the STFT, moreover, an *a priori* estimation of the fundamental frequency is required [3,4] to

Visual Representations of Speech Signals: Martin Cooke, Steve Beet and Malcolm Crawford (eds.)
© 1993 by John Wiley & Sons Ltd

select the appropriate bandwidth of the analysis filter. Another main difference, strictly linked to the previous one, is that the STFT is a constant-bandwidth analysis method, whereas the WT is a constant-Q analysis method. This means that the WT enhances the frequency resolution at lower frequencies and the time resolution at higher frequencies.

Although one can choose an analysing wavelet which results in an orthogonal family of functions, our aim is to choose a wavelet which determines a Q approximately similar to the Q of the human ear. Because of the difficulty in creating such an orthogonal wavelet, we decided to use here an analysing wavelet which is a modification of the one proposed in [2]. Our wavelet has a finite time support and a constant Q of 0.3. That means that a band with central frequency of 1 kHz has a bandwidth of 300 Hz. The ratio between the centre frequencies of two adjacent bands is $1/12$ octave, which guarantees a very good overlap between bands. We think that the wavelet transform offers at least three very important advantages:

i   The WT representation gives information about both the harmonic structure (at lower frequencies) and the formant structure (at higher frequencies) of the signal in the same sonogram, which is more practical than the traditional recourse to narrow- and wideband sonograms. Moreover the WT sonogram always shows the first two or three harmonics of the signal, independently of the value of the fundamental frequency and its variations. The STFT, on the other hand, can become inaccurate if the pitch varies significantly along the signal.

ii   One obtains a signal representation which is certainly more similar to the analysis performed by the ear, which is based on approximately the same principles.

iii   The WT shows signal discontinuities of the signal well: good frequency localisation at lower frequencies corresponds to a poor time localisation, but conversely at higher frequencies there is good time resolution. This can produce, in the diagrams, a triangular spot marking the onset and offset of vowels and other discontinuities, the broad bases of the triangles resulting from the poor time definition at lower frequencies. The point where the apex of the triangle meets the x-axis can be assumed to be the exact time location of the phenomenon.

The most usual representation of the results of a WT analysis is a time-frequency graph with a logarithmic frequency scale. Here we show both this kind of representation and a linear one, which we prefer as it allows a better visual comparison with the STFT of the same signal. Moreover, we feel that the log-scale graphs do not give a sufficiently good resolution at medium and higher frequencies, while a much better resolution is obtained with the linear scale.

3   MATERIALS

The signals we have analysed for the present paper are the 'clean' syllable (figs. 1,2,3,4) and the 'clean' diphone (figs. 5,6,7,8). For each signal we obtained a linear-scale representation of a WT sonogram, a logarithmic-scale representation of a WT sonogram, a narrow-band STFT sonogram and a wideband STFT sonogram.

REFERENCES

[1]   P. Flandrin (1987), 'Some aspects of non-stationary signal processing with emphasis on time-frequency and time-scale methods', in: *Wavelets: Time-Frequency Methods and Phase Space* (eds. J.M. Comb, A. Grossmann & Ph. Tchamitchian), Springer-Verlag, Berlin, 68-97.

[2]   R. Kronland-Martinet & A. Grossmann (1991), 'Application of time-frequency and time-scale methods (Wavelet transforms) to the analysis, synthesis, and transformation of natural sound', in: *Representation of Musical Signals* (eds. G. De Poli, A. Piccialli & C. Roads), MIT Press, Cambridge, MA, 43-85.

[3]   M.R. Portnoff (1980), 'Time-frequency representation of digital signals and systems based on short-time Fourier analysis', IEEE Trans. ASSP, **28**(1), 55-69.

[4] M.R. Portnoff (1981), 'Short-time Fourier analysis of sampled speech', IEEE Trans. ASSP, **29**(3), 364-373.

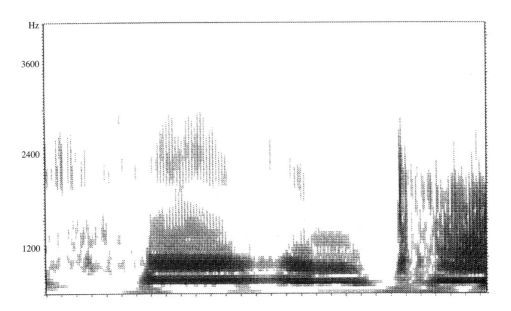

Fig. 1   'clean.syl': WT sonogram with linear frequency scale.

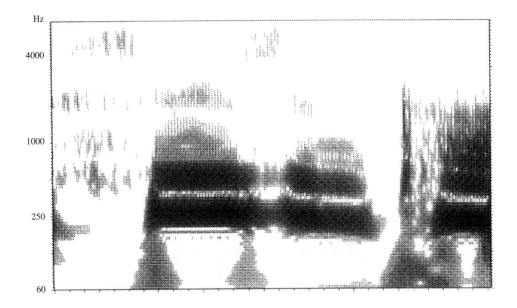

Fig. 2   'clean.syl': WT sonogram with log frequency scale.

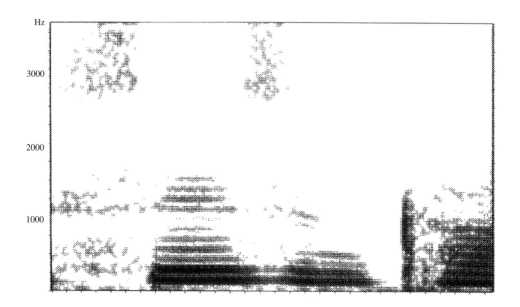

Fig. 3   'clean.syl': STFT narrow-band sonogram.

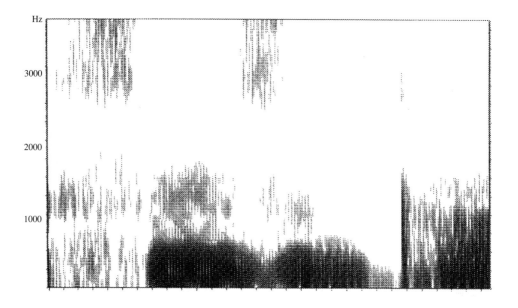

Fig. 4   'clean.syl': STFT wide-band sonogram.

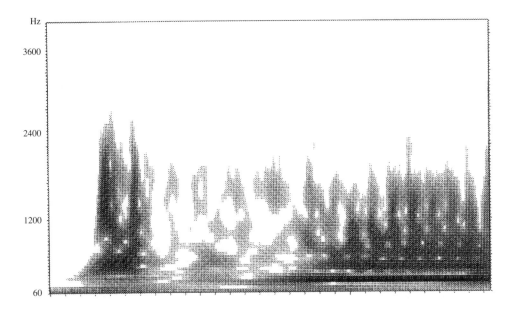

Fig. 5   'clean.dip': WT sonogram, linear frequency scale.

Fig. 6   'clean.dip': WT sonogram, log frequency scale.

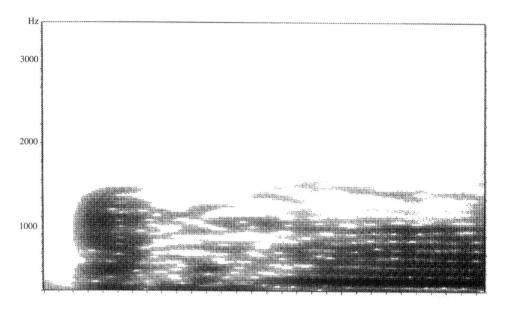

Fig. 7   'clean.dip': STFT narrow-band sonogram.

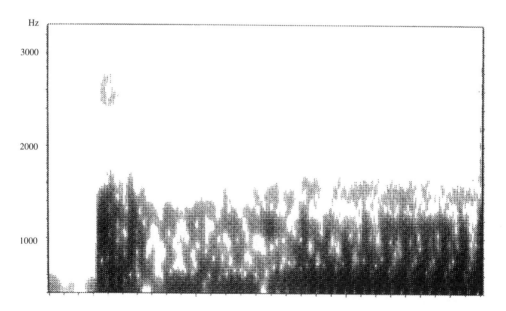

Fig. 8   'clean.dip': STFT wide-band sonogram.

Time and frequency resolution in the reduced auditory representation

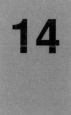

S. W. Beet and I. R. Gransden

1 ABSTRACT

The reduced auditory representation (RAR) was developed for use in automatic speech recognition (ASR), but differs from most other auditory analyses in that it evaluates four separate parameters at each point along a model of the basilar membrane (BM). Together, these parameters represent the detailed structure of the neural firing patterns in a concise and regularly sampled form, suitable for presentation to existing recognition algorithms.

This paper uses the standard test utterances provided for the workshop to demonstrate how the temporal and spectral resolution offered by the RAR can be modified to preferentially resolve acoustic events of specified bandwidth and duration.

2 INTRODUCTION

The RAR was designed to characterise the output of the auditory periphery in a form which meets the requirements of current speech recognisers [1]. In so doing, it provides a fuller description of the input signal than more conventional front-end processors. Several changes have been made since it was last described in any detail [2], not least by the division of the original amplitude parameter into two separate parameters, one of which is (paradoxically) independent of global signal amplitude. Other changes have been made to mimic the frequency-dependent nature of human loudness perception (in terms of sensitivity and dynamic range) and to further improve the RAR's resolution (both in time and frequency).

3 THE STRUCTURE OF THE RAR

The task of modelling the auditory system can be simplified somewhat by observing that all the information encoded in the neuron firings must be present in the displacement of the BM, and that the neural firing patterns are very closely related to that displacement. Thus, the RAR only explicitly simulates the response of the BM, extracting parameters related to characteristics of the subsequent neuron firings without simulating the neurons themselves.

The mechanical filtering of the BM is simulated with a cascade/parallel filterbank similar to that developed by Lyon [5]. However, the filters' bandwidths and centre frequencies are selected according to Moore and Glasberg's ERB-rate scale [6].

Each element in the BM model has a narrow transfer function, so, in general, the displacement represented by that element's output contains only a restricted range of frequencies. Such a narrowband signal can be represented as a sinusoid, modulated in amplitude and frequency. Thus it can be characterised in terms of these two parameters, both of which should be slow to change because of the narrow signal bandwidth.

Unfortunately, despite the preceding rationale, only the most apical (low-frequency) parameter values change slowly enough to be considered stable on a phonetic time scale. Rather than sampling at a sub-phonetic rate and developing a completely new approach to ASR, it has been found expedient to average these "instantaneous" parameters over successive over-

Visual Representations of Speech Signals: Martin Cooke, Steve Beet and Malcolm Crawford (eds.)
© 1993 by John Wiley & Sons Ltd

lapping time-frames. The blurring of events due to the averaging process is minimised by including a weighting function which enhances acoustically important events (onsets and spectral discontinuities) while obscuring the less significant parts of the signal. The information lost by this process is not perceptually critical since it is only acute at the basal (high-frequency) end of the model where the ear is less sensitive to rapid modulation in any case.

In practice, the RAR characterises the amplitude and phase of the BM outputs with four parameters: intensity, adaptation, frequency and delay. It is not suggested that all four are essential to represent the signal, but it is not yet known which (if any) are redundant. All four are clearly visible in simulated neural firing patterns.

3.1 The amplitude parameters

The peak intensity of a neural firing pattern occurs during bands of synchronous activity (phase locking), and its magnitude is largely determined by the signal amplitude (the larger the signal, the more neurons become phase-locked). The signal power is therefore used to estimate this parameter.

On the other hand, the probability of a neuron firing during a particular synchrony band is simply the proportion of the total neuron population exhibiting phase-locking (as given by the intensity parameter) multiplied by a factor reflecting the effects of lateral inhibition and firing rate adaptation. Rather than evaluate this product, since the intensity has already been found, the adaptation factor is calculated separately. This forms a further parameter indicating the presence of discontinuities in time or frequency, but which is independent of global signal amplitude. Both these parameters are encoded on a logarithmic scale, so their "product" is merely a linear combination of the encoded values.

3.2 The phase parameters

The temporal derivative of phase is used to form an estimate of the dominant frequency, while the ratio of spatial to temporal derivatives is also calculated, giving the phase delay between adjacent elements in the model. This parameter is especially good at revealing resonant peaks in the signal spectrum.

3.3 The averaging process

Each of the parameters is averaged using a weighting which reflects the strength of the neural evidence for the reliability of the local estimate. The form of weighting is roughly as described in [2], but in the case of the adaptation parameter, an intensity weighting is used, while the delay weighting now includes a term proportional to the square of the local frequency estimate. This improves the numerical stability of the resulting parameter values.

The averaging process also includes a windowing operation, which has been extended since [2] to include a spatial dimension. The new windowing operation effectively integrates the local instantaneous parameter estimates after they have been passed through a spatio-temporal filter. This approximates to the matched filter which would optimise the response to signals of a bandwidth and duration similar to the "phonetically important" features in a speech signal. In the case of a standard ASR algorithm, this would imply about 400 Hz and 12.5 ms, respectively, although a more "intelligent" system which could make use of pitch information, would probably use values nearer 40 Hz to resolve pitch harmonics or 1.25 ms to separate individual pitch events.

Design of this "matched" filter should be based on the response of each parameter to a wavelet of appropriate dimensions for each frequency of interest. This response will depend on the exact form of the wavelet, so in the examples reproduced here, an approximate formula has been used instead. The optimal window is (unlike those conventionally used in signal analysis) highly asymmetrical: the temporal response in any given section of the model has a rapid attack, followed by a near-exponential decay. The frequency response is also asymmetrical because of the shape of the BM transfer function. Windows such as these (with abrupt leading edges) are obviously desirable, since they give a sharper response to onsets. The exponential decay ensures that response is insensitive to temporal shifts within the averaging window.

A suitable window function is given in equation (1), but this has infinite extent and so is impractical. The equation is readily modified, however, so that it reaches zero at a finite frequency, ω_1, for all times, t, and at a finite time, t_1, for all frequencies, ω. This criterion is satisfied by equation (2), where the values of k_ω and k_t are chosen to give the appropriate degrees of frequency and time resolution:

$$W_{\infty,\infty}(x,t) = (\omega - \omega_0)^2 (t - t_0)^2 \exp[k_\omega(\omega - \omega_0) + k_t(t - t_0)] \tag{1}$$

$$W_{\omega_1,t_1}(x,t) = \sin^2\left(\pi\frac{\omega - \omega_0}{\omega_1 - \omega_0}\right)\sin^2\left(\pi\frac{t - t_0}{t_1 - t_0}\right)\exp[k_\omega(\omega - \omega_0) + k_t(t - t_0)]. \tag{2}$$

A useful side-effect of the introduction of spatial averaging (or rather, matched filtering), is that an arbitrary frequency scale can be imposed on the resulting data vector. This is achieved simply by choosing the nominal wavelet frequencies to coincide with evenly-spaced points on the desired scale. The examples shown here (figs. 1-4) were produced with a linear frequency scale, unlike those in earlier publications [1,2]. Further examples were presented in Beet & Gransden [3].

It should also be noted that the intensity parameter in these examples only covers a dynamic range of about 60 dB, which is quite modest compared with that of the human ear. This is purely for display purposes, and the RAR is normally calculated so as to accurately reflect the true (frequency-dependent) dynamic range and sensitivity of the ear.

The other parameters cover a more modest (and predictable) range, and so do not need to be modified prior to visual presentation.

4   CONCLUSIONS

The recent changes to the details of the RAR analysis have improved its numerical properties and its ability to resolve phonetically significant events.

By extending the averaging window to include a spatial dimension, the data can be fed directly to a continuous-pdf HMM recogniser, and recognition experiments are currently being conducted [4] to ascertain whether such changes will lead to improved performance in automatic speech recognition.

REFERENCES

[1] S. W. Beet, R. K. Moore & M. J. Tomlinson (1986), 'Auditory modelling for automatic speech recognition'. *Proc. Institute of Acoustics, Speech and Hearing*, **8**(7), 571-579.

[2] S. W. Beet (1990), 'Automatic speech recognition using a reduced auditory representation and position-tolerant recognition', *Computer Speech and Language*, **4**(1), 17-33.

[3] S. W. Beet & I. R. Gransden (1992), 'Optimising time and frequency resolution in the reduced auditory representation', *Proc. ESCA Workshop on Comparing Speech Signal Representations*, ISSN 1018-4554, 101-108.

[4] S. W. Beet & I. R. Gransden (1992), 'Interfacing an auditory model to a parametric speech recogniser', *Proc. Institute of Acoustics, Speech and Hearing*, **14**,.

[5] R. F. Lyon (1982), 'A computational model of filtering, detection and compression in the cochlea', *Proc. ICASSP '82*, 1282-1285.

[6] B. C. J. Moore & B. R. Glasberg (1983), 'Suggested formulae for calculating auditory-filter bandwidths and excitation patterns', *JASA*, **74**(3), 750-753.

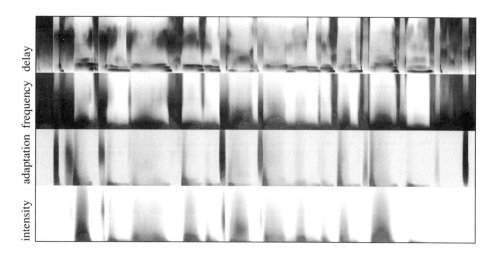

Fig. 1   RAR of 'clean.wav' optimised for resolution of events with characteristic duration of 12.5 ms
         and bandwidth of 400 Hz.

Fig. 2   RAR of 'clean.syl' optimised for resolution of events with characteristic duration of 1.25 ms
         and bandwidth of 40 Hz.

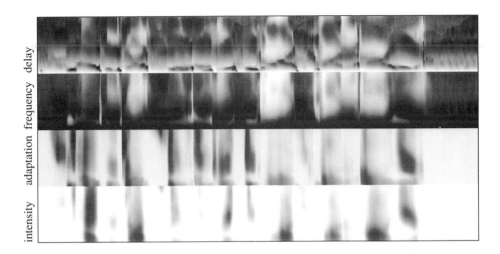

Fig. 3   RAR of 'timit.wav optimised for resolution of events with characteristic duration of 12.5 ms and bandwidth of 400 Hz.

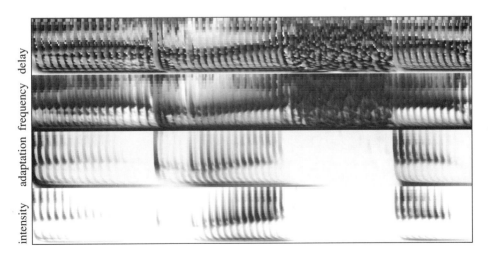

Fig. 4   RAR of 'timit.syl' optimised for resolution of events with characteristic duration of 1.25 ms and bandwidth of 40 Hz.

Physiologically-motivated signal representations for computational auditory scene analysis

15

Guy J. Brown and Martin Cooke

1 INTRODUCTION

Speech is normally heard in the presence of other interfering sounds, so that the auditory system is faced with the problem of grouping together those spectral components which belong to the same acoustic source — a phenomenon named *auditory scene analysis* by Bregman [1]. Computer models of scene analysis may provide a means of improving automatic speech recognition in noise [3, 15], and of performing tasks such as music transcription [10]. This paper describes a number of physiologically-motivated signal representations that the auditory system might use to solve the problem of auditory scene analysis. The representations form the basis for a computer model which implements a grouping algorithm using periodicity, frequency modulation, onset and offset constraints. The system is able to separate speech from interfering sounds with some success.

2 AUDITORY MAPS

Since the discovery of a columnar organisation in the visual cortex by Hubel and Wiesel [6], it has become apparent through physiological studies that the building blocks of the central nervous system are *computational maps*, arrays of cells which are arranged in two or more dimensions. In the auditory system, maps are two-dimensional with frequency and some other parameter represented on orthogonal axes. The value of the parameter at a particular frequency is indicated by the firing rate of the cell at the appropriate position in the neural array. Periodicity, intensity, frequency modulation, interaural time delay and interaural intensity difference all appear to be represented in this manner (see'[2] for a review).

Following the work of Marr in vision [8], we argue that audition should be seen as a series of representational transforms, each of which makes explicit some aspect of the preceding representation. The existence of a rich variety of computational maps in the auditory system is good evidence for such a view, and our approach has been to model auditory maps in order to provide the primitives needed for scene analysis, and to demonstrate algorithms which exploit these primitives effectively.

3 REPRESENTATIONS FOR AUDITORY SCENE ANALYSIS

Bregman [1] identifies two ways in which spectral components are grouped together. Firstly, *simultaneous grouping* separates sounds that occur concurrently into different perceptual streams. We use periodicity, onset and offset maps to provide simultaneous grouping primitives. The periodicity map is used to identify those areas of the spectrum which share a common fundamental frequency, and the onset and offset maps are used to identify spectral components which start or finish in synchrony. Secondly, *sequential grouping* separates sounds that emanate from the same source over time. We use a map of orientation to provide information about the movement of partials, allowing the periodicity representation at one time to be related to the periodicity representation at a later time.

Visual Representations of Speech Signals: Martin Cooke, Steve Beet and Malcolm Crawford (eds.)
© 1993 by John Wiley & Sons Ltd

3.1 Auditory periphery

Mechanical filtering in the cochlea is modelled by a bank of 128 gammatone filters [11], with centre frequencies spaced linearly on an ERB-rate scale between 50 Hz and 5 kHz. Transduction by inner hair cells is simulated by the Meddis hair cell model [9], which provides a representation of firing rates in the auditory nerve that forms the input to the maps.

3.2 Periodicity map

Scheffers [12] has shown that the auditory system is able to use information about the presence of different fundamental frequencies (periodicities) to separate simultaneous voices. In our model, periodicity information is extracted by autocorrelating the output of each auditory nerve fibre, giving the familiar *correlogram* proposed by Licklider [7] and recently revived by Slaney & Lyon [14]. The correlogram is compatible with our definition of auditory maps, having frequency and autocorrelation delay (pitch period) represented on orthogonal axes. The channels of the correlogram can be summed to give a *compound correlogram*, which indicates the likelihood of each pitch period.

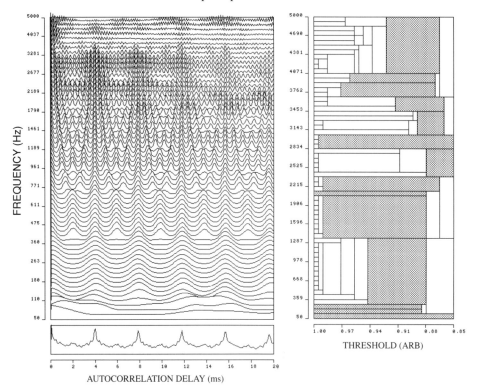

Fig. 1   *left* : correlogram map for one frame of 'clean'. The formation of periodicity segments is shown on the *right* : stable segments, selected by an area stability criterion, are highlighted.

Auditory filters which are responding to the same spectral dominance have a very similar structure in the correlogram, because they share the same fine time structure and modulation pattern. For example, in the correlogram of fig. 1 (taken from 'clean') channels 4-17 are responding to the first harmonic, channels 18-26 to the second harmonic, and so on. Hence, an early opportunity for grouping is to remove this redundancy by combining adjacent channels which have a sufficiently similar structure. The similarity of two channels in the correlogram c_1 and c_2 over T delays can be compared using the energy-normalised metric:

$$sim(c_1, c_2) = \left(2 \sum_{\tau=0}^{T} c_1(\tau) c_2(\tau)\right) \Big/ \left(\sum_{\tau=0}^{T} c_1(\tau)^2 + \sum_{\tau=0}^{T} c_2(\tau)^2\right) \qquad (1)$$

which is unity in the case of perfect synchrony. If the threshold at which adjacent channels are allowed to group is gradually relaxed, *periodicity segments* form which delineate areas of spectral dominance (fig. 1). The display is reminiscent of the acoustic-phonetic segmentation process described by Withgott *et al.* [16]. The "best" segments are selected by choosing the most stable areas in frequency-threshold space, according to a criterion which selects a segment if it has no descendents of greater area.

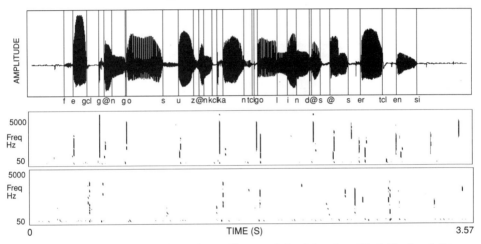

Fig. 2 'clean.wav': *upper*: original waveform with transcription taken from Dix & Bloothooft (this volume, chapter 22); *middle*: onset map; and *lower*: offset map.

3.3 Onset and offset maps

Darwin [4] has shown that a difference in onset or offset time can be used to separate a harmonic from a vowel, a result which reflects a general auditory mechanism that groups components together if they start or end sychronously. Our maps for detecting onsets and offsets are developed in analogy with the mechanism of ON-I cells in the cochlear nucleus [13], which produce a brief burst of activity at the start of an applied stimulus. The cells essentially consist of a leaky integrator (the membrane), an excitatory input and a delayed inhibitory input. A suitable equation for the membrane potential p_{on} of an onset cell is therefore

$$p_{on}(t) = p_{on}(t-1) c_d + gain_{ex} x(t) - gain_{in} x(t - \Delta t) \qquad (2)$$

where $x(t)$ is the (phase-corrected) firing rate of the channel at time t, $gain_{ex}$ and $gain_{in}$ control the relative strengths of the excitatory and inhibitory inputs, and c_d is a decay constant. Offsets are detected similarly, except that the inhibition arrives first at the membrane:

$$p_{off}(t) = p_{off}(t-1) c_d + gain_{ex} x(t - \Delta t) - gain_{in} x(t) . \qquad (3)$$

The delay Δt is a variable parameter which forms the second dimension of the onset and offset maps, allowing control over the scale of features that are detected. For example, onset cells with long inhibitory delays detect slower onsets (e.g. nasals), whereas cells with short delays respond to abrupt onsets (e.g. bursts). Figure 2 shows onset and offset maps for the 'clean' utterance with $\Delta t = 1$ ms.

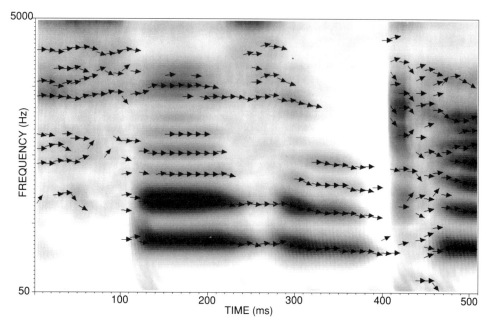

Fig. 3   Auditory nerve rate spectrum for 'clean.syl', with vectors representing the position and
orientation of partials derived from the map of orientation.

3.4 Partial orientation map

Information about the movement of partials through time and frequency is captured by a map of orientation, which convolves the auditory nerve rate spectrum with a number of "receptive fields" of the form

$$F(t,f) = \frac{1}{\pi \sigma_f^2} G(t,f) - \frac{f^2}{\left(\pi \sigma_f^2\right)^2} G(t,f) \tag{4}$$

where $G()$ is a two-dimensional Gaussian, and σ_f is its extent in frequency. This function takes the form of a central excitatory lobe and two inhibitory lobes, and is similar to the receptive fields of line-orientation sensitive cells found in the visual cortex [6]. Within the map, the orientation of the receptive fields is varied along one axis between best sweep rates of ± 20 octaves/s. When a partial is correctly aligned with a receptive field, a peak of activity is registered at the appropriate frequency and orientation in the map. Figure 3 shows the position and direction of movement of partials for 'clean.syl', derived by identifying the maxima in the orientation map at each time slice.

4   MODELLING AUDITORY SCENE ANALYSIS

A strategy for incorporating the maps into a scene analysis algorithm is now described. Firstly, periodicity segments are tracked across time and frequency using the orientation map, giving an explicit representation of partials as shown in fig. 4 for 'clean.syl'.

One way of deciding which partials belong together is to identify the pitch period of each source, and to score each partial against the pitch track. However, this approach requires *a priori* knowledge of how many sources are present at each instant, and is unable to cope with cases where the pitch tracks cross [15]. A better method is to *find the most likely pitch track for each partial, and to decide whether partials belong together by comparing their pitch tracks.* For a partial occupying channels c_1 to c_2 in the correlogram, the likelihood of the par-

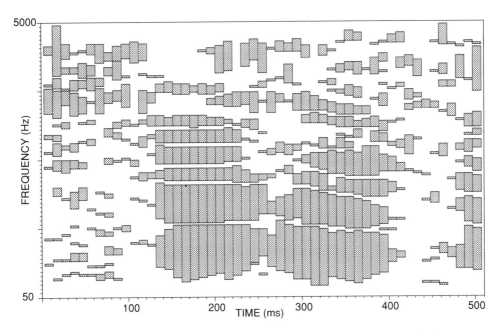

Fig. 4   Representation of partials for 'clean.syl'. Periodicity segments (see fig. 1) are tracked across time using orientation information (see fig. 3).

tial belonging on a pitch period τ is a function of the height of the compound correlogram *sum*() and the average height of the channels in the correlogram *cor*() occupied by the partial,

$$prob(c_1, c_2, \tau) = \frac{sum(\tau)}{c_1 + c_2 + 1} \sum_{c=c_1}^{c_2} cor(c, \tau) . \qquad (5)$$

For each partial, this function is computed at each time frame and the best pitch path is found by a dynamic programming algorithm with Gaussian-weighted distance penalties. Partials which overlap in time are compared pairwise to see if their pitch tracks match, using

$$sim(p_1, p_2) = \sum_{t=1}^{T} \exp\left(\frac{(p_1(t) + p_2(t))^2}{2\sigma^2}\right) . \qquad (6)$$

If the similarity is above a threshold value (0.70), the partials are allowed to group. Onset and offset information is incorporated by adding a constant to the *sim* score when two partials start or finish at the same time and have sufficient energy in the onset or offset maps.

5   RESYNTHESIS

Separation performance can be evaluated by resynthesising a waveform from the partial groups, and assessing its intelligibility and naturalness in informal listening tests. The partial tracks indicate which channels of the filterbank belong to a source at a particular time, and a resynthesised waveform can be obtained simply by summing these time-frequency regions of the (phase-corrected) gammatone filterbank output.

6   RESULTS

The Sheffield signals are not ideal for demonstrating the separation system because the system is limited to separating periodic sounds. Since the 'clean' and 'dirty' signals contain regions of unvoiced speech, it was necessary to manually concatenate the groups that the sys-

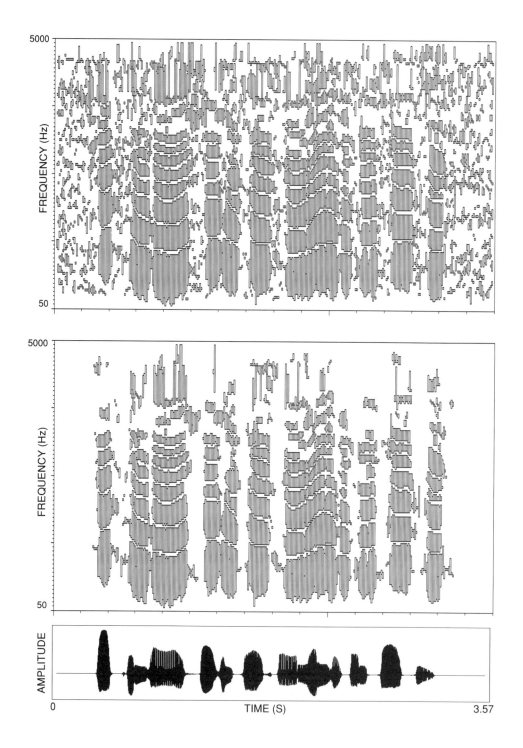

Fig. 5   'clean.wav': *upper* : partials before separation; *middle* : partials after separation; and
lower : resynthesised waveform.

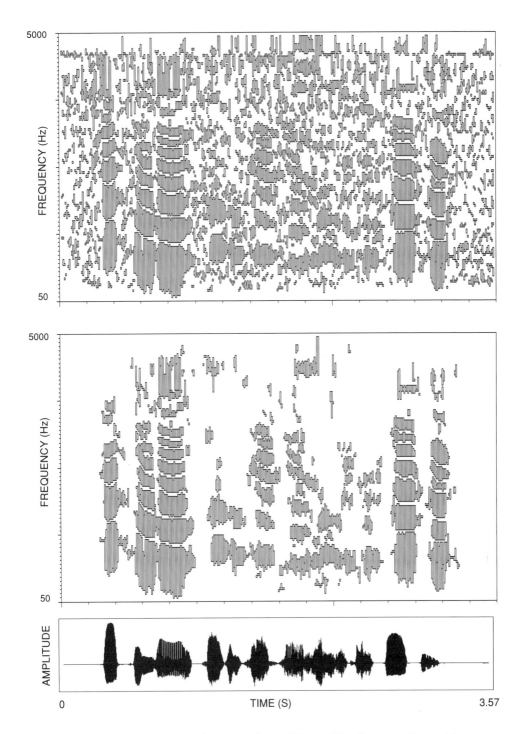

Fig. 6   'dirty.wav': *upper* : partials before separation; *middle* : partials after separation; and *lower* : resynthesised waveform. The resynthesised waveform should be compared with the original in fig. 2.

tem found in periodic regions — to do this automatically is a very complex problem that requires information about, for example, speaker characteristics and spatial location [1].

Figure 5 shows the partial tracks for the 'clean' utterance. After grouping, several large groups have been found which are shown in the middle figure. The resynthesised waveform derived from these groups is shown in the lower figure. The resynthesised speech is highly intelligible and very natural, even though the unvoiced regions are not represented. The partial tracks for the 'dirty' utterance are shown in fig. 6, and although the partial tracks in the noisy region are highly degraded, it is still possible to see the harmonic structure. The groups formed from this representation are shown in the middle figure, and a resynthesised waveform in the lower figure. The resynthesis is intelligible, but less natural, in the noisy region and represents a modest improvement over the original noisy utterance.

7   CONCLUSIONS AND FUTURE WORK

The separation system performs reasonably well. The restriction of the system to the representation of periodic stimuli does not appear to be a serious one, since the resynthesised utterances are of high intelligibility and naturalness. Further work will concentrate on incorporating learned ("schema-driven") processing into the system. Edelman [5] has proposed that computational maps play a central role in learning, and we are about to investigate the use of auditory maps in the formation and application of schemas.

References

[1] A.S. Bregman (1990), *Auditory Scene Analysis*, *MIT Press*, Cambridge, MA.

[2] G.J. Brown (1992), *Computational Auditory Scene Analysis: A Representational Approach*, Ph.D. Thesis, University of Sheffield.

[3] M.P. Cooke (forthcoming), *Modelling Auditory Processing and Organisation*, Cambridge University Press, Cambridge, *UK*.

[4] C.J. Darwin (1984), 'Perceiving vowels in the presence of another sound: Constraints on formant perception', *JASA*, **76**(6), 1637-1647.

[5] G.M. Edelman (1989), *Neural Darwinism: The Theory of Neuronal Group Selection*, Oxford University Press.

[6] D.H. Hubel & T.N. Wiesel (1962), 'Receptive fields, binocular interaction and functional architecture in the cat's visual cortex', *Journal of Physiology*, **160**, 106-154.

[7] J.C.R. Licklider (1951), 'A duplex theory of pitch perception', *Experentia*, **7**, 128-133.

[8] D. Marr (1982), *Vision*, W.H. Freeman, New York.

[9] R. Meddis (1988), 'Simulation of mechanical to neural transduction in the auditory receptor', *JASA*, **79**(3), 702-711.

[10] D.K. Mellinger (1991), *Event Formation and Separation in Musical Sound*, Ph.D. Thesis, Stanford University.

[11] R.D. Patterson, J. Holdsworth, I. Nimmo-Smith & P. Rice (1988), 'SVOS final report: The auditory filterbank', *Report 2341, MRC Applied Psychology Unit, Cambridge*.

[12] M.T.M. Scheffers (1983), *Sifting Vowels: Auditory Pitch Analysis and Sound Segregation*, Ph.D. Thesis, Groningen University.

[13] W.P. Shofner & E.D. Young (1985), 'Excitatory inhibitory response types in the cochlear nucleus: relationships to discharge patterns and responses to electrical stimulation of the auditory nerve', *J. Neurophysiology*, **54**, 917-930.

[14] M. Slaney & R.F. Lyon (1991), 'A perceptual pitch detector', *Proc. ICASSP '90*, 357-360.

[15] M. Weintraub (1985), *A Theory and Computational Model of Auditory Monaural Sound Separation*, Ph.D. Thesis, Stanford University.

[16] M. Withgott, S.C. Bagley, R.F. Lyon & M.A. Bush (1987), 'Acoustic-phonetic segment classification and scale-space filtering', *Proc. ICASSP '87*, 860-863.

Modelling the representation of speech signals in the peripheral auditory system

16

M. F. Cheesman, D. G. Jamieson, S. Krol and I. Kheirallah

1   INTRODUCTION

1.1 Objectives

The response to a standardised CV speech sound (the /ka/ of "can't") of a model of normal and damaged human peripheral auditory systems was compared to that seen with more conventional spectral estimation approaches (FFT and autoregressive modelling-based techniques). Both approaches were applied to the 'clean.dip' and 'dirty.dip' signals.

1.2 Acoustical analysis procedures

Three spectral estimation techniques available in the CSRE system [5] were applied to estimate the spectrum [8,9,12,13] of the speech samples: the fast Fourier transform (FFT), and two autoregressive techniques that use autocorrelation (AC) and modified covariance (MC) methods.

Spectral estimation for discrete signals is most frequently done by FFT. To improve the resolution and spectral fidelity, particularly for short data segments, the AC and MC estimation techniques represent the data by a model for which parameter estimates are obtained, i.e. by linear prediction.

FFT spectral estimates are characterised by many trade-offs in windowing, time-domain averaging, and frequency-domain averaging. These are necessary in order to balance the need to reduce sidelobes, to perform effective ensemble averaging, and to ensure adequate spectral resolution. This technique is computationally efficient, but has many problems associated with the assumptions regarding data outside the measurement interval. In addition, frequency resolution is limited to the reciprocal of the time-domain data length [8].

Autoregressive methods have been designed as alternative spectral estimation procedures that overcome some of the inherent limitations of the FFT approach. Rather than assuming that the data outside the window are zero, the spectral estimates are based on the power spectrum density implied by a model which approximates the actual underlying process. The need for windowing functions can be eliminated, along with their distorting impact. As a result, the improvement over the conventional FFT spectral estimate can be quite dramatic, especially for short records [8].

Speech signals are well approximated by autoregressive models because of the close relation of this modelling approach with the linear prediction analysis, where a speech sample is approximated as a linear combination of previous speech samples. In the autocorrelation method, the signal is windowed and then padded with zeros before the autocorrelation coefficients are calculated. AC is successful, in part, because it generates an all-pole model which is guaranteed to be stable. However, the approach provides limited spectral resolution, as closely spaced spectral lines cannot be resolved with a short data window. Furthermore, the windowing decreases resolution and introduces spectral distortion. In certain situations, the AC method also produces spectral line splitting, where two or more peaks occur when only

Visual Representations of Speech Signals: Martin Cooke, Steve Beet and Malcolm Crawford (eds.)
© 1992 by John Wiley & Sons Ltd

one peak should be present in the spectral estimate [9]. Finally, the AC approach models the peaks in the spectrum better than the valleys.

In the modified covariance method, the operations are carried out on the data directly without any zero padding. The MC method utilises a combination of forward and backward linear prediction for estimation. The MC method works better for short data segments, offering sharper response for narrowband processes. The covariance technique operates on the data directly, whereas the AC approach uses the biased autocorrelation estimates to reduce the risk of ill-conditioning, but at the expense of a degradation of the autoregressive spectral resolution and a shifting of spectral peaks from their true locations [12]. In addition, no spectral line splitting is observed with the modified covariance method [13]. This approach can exactly match an all-pole spectrum from a short section of data, but stability cannot be guaranteed.

1.3 Physiological model

Our peripheral auditory system model is derived from that of Kates [6,7]. It is a digital, time-domain model, concatenating submodels of each of the middle ear, basilar membrane, inner and outer hair cells and the synaptic junctions to the auditory-nerve fibres. The composite model thus simulates the signal transformations that occur at each stage of the system, based on biophysical, biomechanical and electrophysiological observations. The input to the model is an acoustic signal, represented as the pattern of sound pressure at the tympanic membrane. The output of the model is the activity in the auditory nerve.

The middle ear portion of the model follows Lynch *et al.* [11], with the resonance frequency of the filter changed from 800 Hz for the cat to 350 Hz for humans. Basilar membrane (BM) processing is modelled as a cascade of filter sections where each filter has a transfer function chosen to represent the corresponding section of a one-dimensional transmission line, modelled by the corresponding electrical circuit [14,15,16]. At each point on the BM, the output is the cumulative result of previous filter sections, sharpened by a second filter [1] when the response is converted into a neural firing pattern by the inner hair cells (IHC).

The IHC model transforms the mechanical input to the hair cell into the instantaneous firing rate on a single neural fibre. Each IHC is connected to two high-spontaneous rate nerve fibres (50 and 75 spikes/s) and two low-spontaneous rate fibres (5 and 10 spikes/s). The output at each point on the BM is the sum of the outputs of the fibres attached to the IHC, divided by the number of fibres. This output is modified by two feedback loops between the IHCs and the BM and the second filter; the intensity of firing and the peak velocity at the output of the second filter modify the parameters of the BM and the second filters, simulating the action of the outer hair cells (OHCs) [3,4,17]. For the damaged cochlea, the model simulated 50% and 100% OHC loss.

2   METHOD

2.1 Stimuli

We processed two /ka/ diphones 'clean.dip' and 'dirty.dip' through the analysis systems described above. For the FFT and AC procedures, a 128-point Hanning window was used. Both autoregressive methods used a 20-pole representation.

2.2 Application of the model

Sampling rate adjustment. For processing by the auditory model, the sample rate was converted to 40 kHz, using direct digital conversion [10].

Stimulus scaling. Because the intensity of firing depends on the level of the input signal, it is important to ensure that each portion of the signal is appropriately scaled. Here, the root mean square amplitude across the full signal was used to normalise each sample.

Processing. For the auditory model, processing began 50 ms prior to the onset of the /k/ in order to eliminate artifactual onset effects from the neural firing response. The output of the model is the intensity of firing; intensity ranges between the spontaneous firing rate of 35 spikes/s (the mean spontaneous rate for the high- and low-spontaneous rate fibres), to a maximum rate of 1000 spikes/s. Average saturation firing rate is 150 spikes/s. For normal speech, the firing rate rarely exceeds 500 spikes/s. An increase in the level of the input signal results in an increased intensity of firing, but the relation is compressive, so that variations in firing rate can be represented on a linear, rather than a dB scale.

3 RESULTS AND DISCUSSION

In general, the three acoustical methods worked well for the quasi-stationary, voiced portions of the signal and less well for the plosive (/k/) portion, with the AC (fig. 1) and MC autoregressive approaches giving very similar results. The first and second formant energy was visible in both the quiet speech and the speech-in-noise signals. In quiet, the frequency of the formants was a monotonic rising function of time, while for the noisy speech, this monotonicity was lost due to the energy from the noise.

At a global level, there was a good correspondence between the data obtained through the auditory model and the acoustical analysis approaches. All contours of firing intensity displayed a similar, characteristic "standing banana" shape. This shape arises from the simulation of the travelling wave along the basilar membrane from the high-frequency region at the base to the low-frequency region at the apex; thus, this pattern occurs for voiceless as well as voiced speech. The frequency with which these "bananas" occur reflects the synchronisation of the firing activity to aspects of the stimulus. Channels near the apical end of the cochlea respond to the lowest-frequency components of the speech signal; channels closer to the base respond to increasingly higher-frequency components. In general, the speech features seen in the auditory model correspond to those seen in the acoustical models, but with the phase delay associated with this travelling wave.

In voiced speech, the low-frequency bound of these firing rate contours is the frequency of the fundamental and first formant of the vowel (which are close in frequency). Theoretically, the band of fibres (channel) that responds with the slowest periodicity could be used to identify a formant track, although in general it appears to be easier to extract such information from the output of the AC or MC models than from the auditory model. For the frequency channels between the formants, the firing rate appears to be synchronised to the frequency of the formant in the vicinity of the characteristic frequency of the channel. Comparing the lower-frequency channels to the higher-frequency channels, one sees an abrupt change in synchrony to the next higher formant.

Throughout the voiced speech in quiet, at least three formants are apparent. Estimated on the basis of the average firing pattern of the auditory model to the 50 ms of voiced speech shown in the top panel of fig. 2, the formant frequencies are 350, 850 and 1300 Hz. The second and third formant frequencies estimated by this method are somewhat lower than those obtained from the acoustically-based analyses. For the speech in noise, only the lowest formant is clearly evident. For the damaged cochlea, the output of the model (middle and lower panels of fig. 2) produces less timing detail. In the case of 100% OHC loss, the lowest harmonic completely dominates the neural response.

The firing rate is about 100 spikes/s higher for the /k/ burst in "can't" than for the subsequent voiced speech, and the voice-onset-time gap is clearly evident, although a small response is apparent during this gap. In the noisy speech, the /k/ burst is suppressed and no silent interval after the burst is apparent. At the onset of voicing and throughout the voiced part of the signal, the low-frequency components become very obvious.

Generally, the auditory model is more sensitive to sudden changes in the speech signal than are the acoustical analyses, especially the FFT and AC methods. For example, there is a

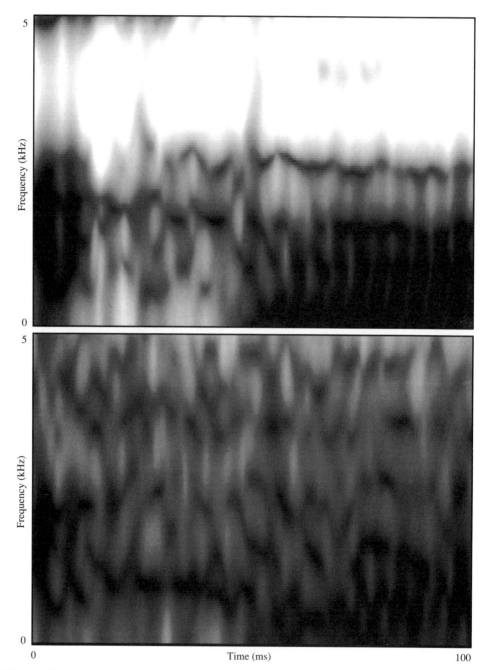

Fig. 1   AC analysis of *upper* : 'clean.dip'; and *lower* : 'dirty.dip.

delay of approximately 3 ms between the energy peak of the /k/ burst found with the auditory model to that found with the MC and AC methods. The auditory model preserves information in the unvoiced part of the syllable following the release burst, in the form of low firing rate, but still-visible components at the higher frequencies, where the synchronisation is low. On

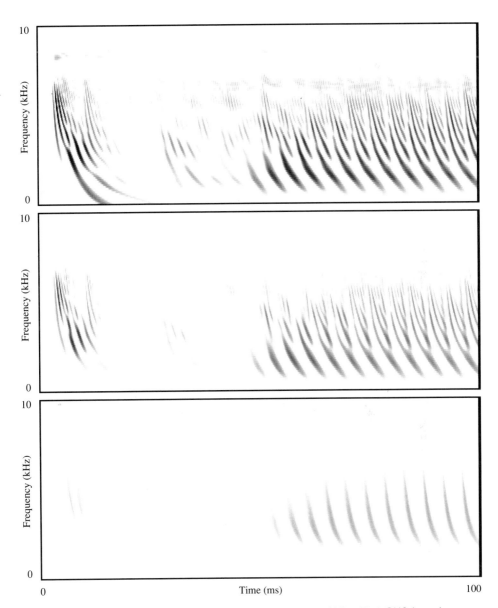

Fig. 2   Modelled output for 'clean.dip': *upper* : normal hearing; *middle* : 50% OHC loss; *lower* : 100% OHC loss. Note the decreased response rate (below spontaneous firing rate) following each period of firing activity.

the other hand, the high-frequency bands clearly visible through acoustical analysis (exaggerated by the use of high-frequency preemphasis) do not appear in the firing rate patterns.

To examine further the response within individual channels of the model, we subjected the output of multiple, individual channels to a conventional AC spectral estimation technique of the type used for fig. 1 (i.e. order 20, after applying a 128 point Hanning window).

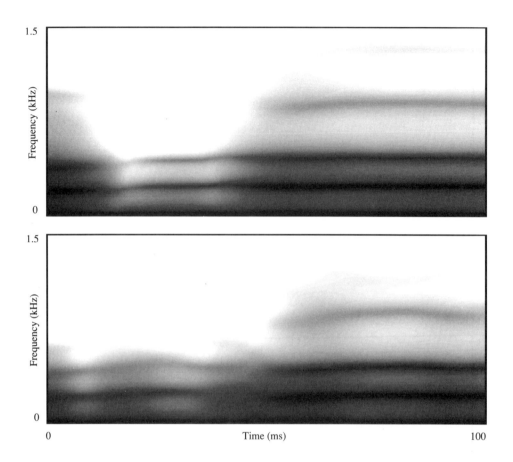

Fig. 3   *upper* : The normal hearing model's output for the channel centred at 205 Hz when stimulated with 'clean.dip'. The first two harmonics of the signal in the region of 225 and 450 Hz are clearly resolved. *lower* : The output for the same channel when stimulated with 'dirty.dip'. While the bandwidths appear to be broader than those seen with clear speech, corresponding to some sensitivity in the channel to noisy portions of this signal, this analysis can be seen to provide a robust representation, as the harmonics of the signal near 450 Hz and near 225 Hz are clearly resolved.

Examples of the results of this analysis are displayed in fig. 3 (for the channel with characteristic frequency (CF) of 205 Hz) and fig. 4 (for the channel with CF = 1511 Hz). Note that a dc component, arising from the strictly positive values of the firing rate, is visible at the bottom of each figure. These figures demonstrate that individual channels are able to preserve the spectral characteristics of the voiced portions of the signal, even in the presence of substantial background noise. Still further spectral detail is recovered when cross-channel integration is added to the model.

Acknowledgements: This work was supported by grants from NSERC, URIF and Unitron Industries Ltd. We are grateful to Ketan Ramji and Lucy Kieffer for their assistance and to Jim Kates for providing code for his auditory models. Correspondence should be addressed to Dr. S. Krol.

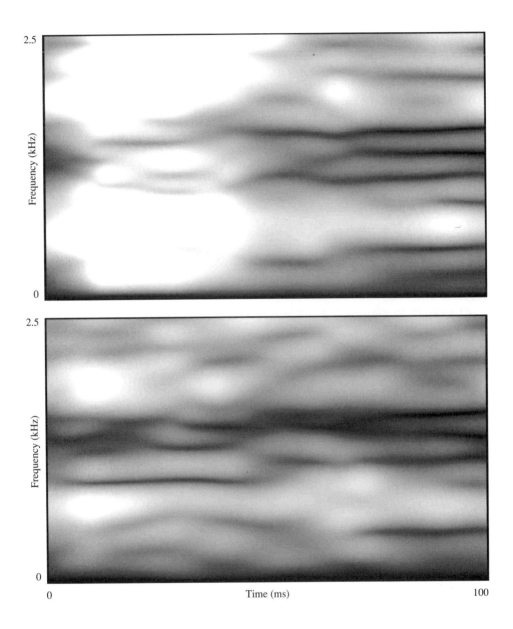

Fig. 4   *upper* : The normal hearing model's output for the channel centred at 1511 Hz when stimulated with 'clean.dip'. Three harmonics of the signal are clearly resolved in the region of the third formant visible in the AC analysis (fig. 1). Harmonics in the region of 450 Hz and 225 Hz are also resolved, corresponding to the first formant which is visible in the AC analysis (fig. 1) and in the output of the CF = 205 Hz channel, displayed in fig. 3. Burst excitation is also visible in this channel. *lower* : Output when the same channel is stimulated with 'dirty.dip'. Harmonics in the F3 region and also in the F1 region remain clearly visible, in contrast to the corresponding AC analysis (fig. 1), although the onset burst is better resolved in the AC analysis.

REFERENCES

[1] J.B. Allen (1980), 'Cochlear micromechanics - a physical model of transduction', *JASA*, **68**, 1160-1670.

[2] J.B. Allen (1983), 'A hair-cell model of neural response', in: *Peripheral Auditory Mechanisms* (eds. E. de Boer & M.A. Viergever), Martinus Nijhoff, The Hague.

[3] J.F. Ashmore (1987), 'A fast motile response in guinea-pig outer hair cells: the cellular basis of the cochlear amplifier', *J. Physiol.*, **388**, 323-347.

[4] C.D. Geisler (1991), 'A cochlear model using feedback from motile outer hair cells', *Hear. Res.*, 54, 105-117.

[5] D.G. Jamieson, K. Ramji & T.M. Nearey (1989), 'CSRE: a speech research environment', *Canad. Acoust.*, **17**, 23-35.

[6] J.M. Kates (1991), 'A time domain digital cochlear model', *IEEE Trans. ASSP*, **39**, 2573-2592.

[7] J.M. Kates (in press), 'Accurate tuning curves in a cochlear model', *IEEE Trans. ASSP*.

[8] S.M. Kay & S. L. Marple Jr. (1981), 'Spectrum analysis - a modern perspective', *Proc. IEEE*, **69**, 1380-1419.

[9] S.M. Kay & S. L. Marple Jr. (1979), 'Sources of and remedies for spectral line splitting in autoregressive spectrum analysis', *Proc. ICASSP '79*, 151-154.

[10] J.S. Lim & A.V. Oppenheim (1988), *Advanced Topics in Signal Processing*, Englewood Cliffs, Prentice Hall, NJ.

[11] T.J. Lynch III, V. Nedzelnicky & W.T. Peake (1982), 'Input impedance of the cochlea in the cat', *JASA*, **72**, 108-130.

[12] S.L. Marple Jr. (1980), 'A new autoregressive spectrum analysis algorithm', *IEEE Trans. ASSP*, **28**, 441-451.

[13] S.L. Marple Jr. (1987), *Digital Spectral Analysis with Applications*, Englewood Cliffs, Prentice Hall, NJ.

[14] L.C. Peterson & B.P Bogert (1950), 'A dynamical theory of the cochlea', *JASA*, **22**, 369-381.

[15] M.R. Schroeder (1973), 'An integrable model for basilar membrane', *JASA*, **53**, 429-434.

[16] J. Zwislocki (1950), 'Theory of the acoustical action of the cochlea', *JASA*, **22**, 778-784.

[17] J. Zwislocki (1980), 'Active cochlea feedback: required structure and response phase', in: *The Mechanics and Biophysics of Hearing* (eds. P. Dallos, C.D. Geisler, J.W. Matthews, M.R. Ruggero & C.R. Steele), Springer-Verlag, Berlin.

Tracking spectral dominances in an auditory model

17

Martin Cooke and Malcolm Crawford

1 INTRODUCTION

This paper describes an analysis of the Sheffield data in which the temporal evolution of spectral dominances in the outputs of an auditory model is made explicit. This representation, known as 'synchrony strands', can be used to provide primitives for a model of auditory scene analysis, and as input to a crude model of large-scale spectral integration, a putative next step before speech recognition.

2 SYNCHRONY STRANDS

The synchrony strand representation and the algorithms for computing it are detailed in Cooke [4]. Here, a brief overview of the computational steps is provided.

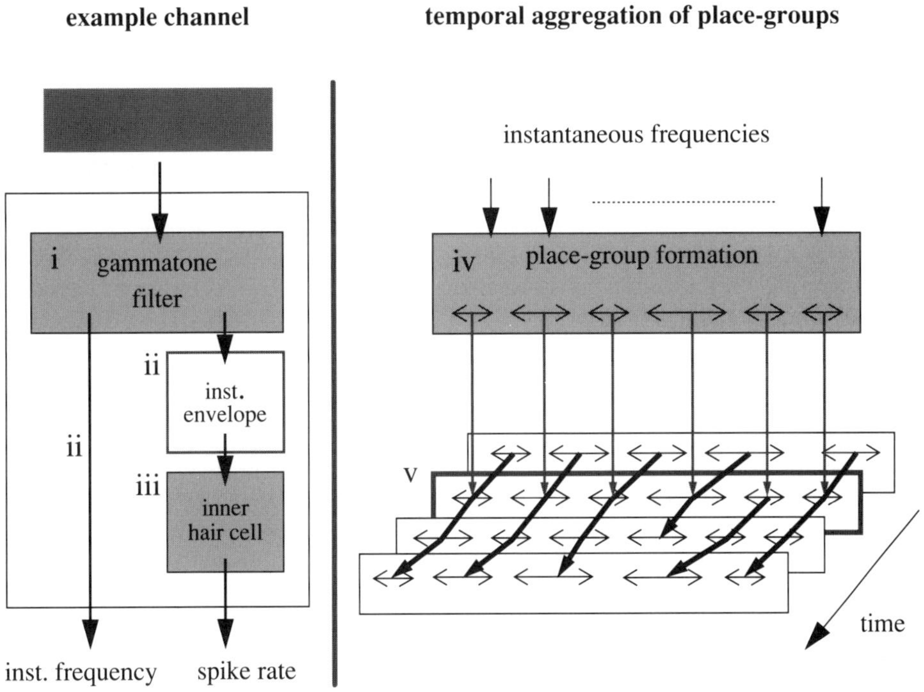

Fig. 1   Steps in synchrony strand computation.

Visual Representations of Speech Signals: Martin Cooke, Steve Beet and Malcolm Crawford (eds.)
© 1993 by John Wiley & Sons Ltd

   i   The signal is processed by a model of the auditory periphery. This consists of a gammatone filterbank (Patterson & Holdsworth [8]), with 250 filters spaced equally along an ERB-rate scale (Moore & Glasberg [7]) to cover the range 50-5000 Hz.

   ii   The instantaneous frequency and envelope at the output of each filter are computed.

   iii The envelope forms the input to a model of the inner hair cell [3]. Its output reflects an averaged firing rate in the auditory-nerve fibre whose best frequency corresponds to the centre frequency of the processing channel. In contrast to models such as that of Meddis [6], the firing rate does not maintain the fine-structure at the output of the previous stage. However, unlike other such models, it is provably capable of modelling additive responses to stimulus increments.

   iv   The instantaneous frequency is median smoothed within a window of 10 ms and downsampled to 1 ms estimates. The frame of estimates across all channels is then processed to determine contiguous ranges of channels (*place-groups*) which appear to be responding to the same stimulus component (note that this scheme is different from the one outlined in Brown & Cooke [2]). For each set of channels grouped in this way, an estimate of dominant frequency and overall firing rate is computed.

   v   Place-groups are tracked across time using a weighted linear approximation to the track, with weights chosen such that frames nearest to the 'aggregation-boundary' have most effect. This results in a collection of 'synchrony strands'.

3   SYNCHRONY STRAND REPRESENTATIONS OF THE SHEFFIELD DATA

Figures 2-5 show synchrony strand displays for the "syllable" sections of the Sheffield data. The frequency axis is linear in ERB-rate and runs from 1.6 to 28.4 ERB (50-5000 Hz) in each case. The instantaneous width of each strand represents its amplitude (the sum of firing rates in all channels grouped into the place-group at that time and frequency). In each display, only those strands which have an average firing-rate above the spontaneous level (50 spikes/s) are shown. Transcriptions of 'clean' and 'spont' were carried out by a far-from-expert non-phonetician (the first author).

3.1 Observations

The first striking feature of these, and many other contemporary auditorily-motivated representations, is the lack of a clear depiction of the first formant, and sometimes also the second. Strands which correspond to harmonic components dominate the display in the voiced regions — the fundamental and the first five or six harmonics are visible. The amplitude of many such strands shows a pronounced onset (corresponding to the onset response of the IHC model), whilst at the higher frequencies a degree of amplitude modulation is apparent (due to the interaction of harmonics within the bandwidth of a filter). This is particularly noticeable on F2, F3 and F4 during many of the voiced parts of 'timit.syl'. Strands do *not* provide a compact representation of unvoiced segments, as shown for example in the initial /s/ in "susan" ('clean.syl', fig. 2). Here, the high-frequency energy concentration is apparent, though it is distributed over a number of strands. Future work is aimed at using a notion of strand bandwidth to allow for characterisation of broadband sources.

Some of the harmonic structure remains in 'dirty.syl', despite the broadband nature of the intrusive source (consider the across-frequency intrusion present during the /k/ closure).

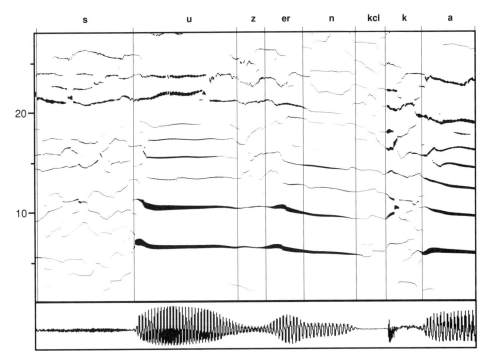

Fig. 2   Representations of 'clean.syl': *upper* : synchrony strands; *lower* : waveform.

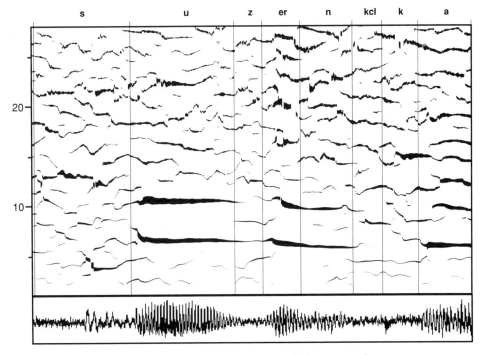

Fig. 3   Representations of 'dirty.syl': *upper* : synchrony strands; *lower* : waveform.

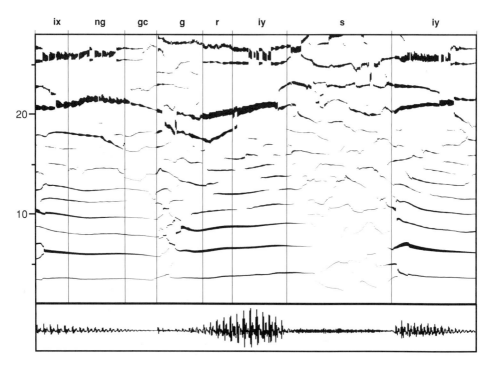

Fig. 4   Representations of 'timit.syl': *upper* : synchrony strands; *lower* : waveform.

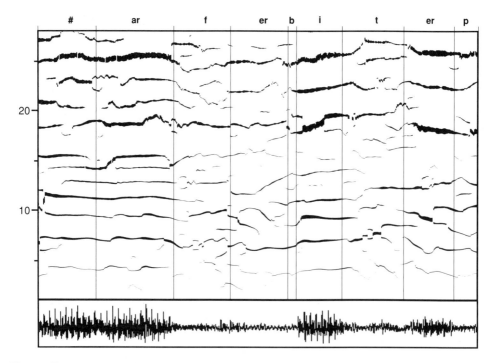

Fig. 5   Representations of 'spont.syl': *upper* : synchrony strands; *lower* : waveform.

The spontaneous utterance 'spont.syl' is depicted in fig. 4. Whilst this is rather noisier than, for example, the 'timit' syllable, similar harmonic and formant structures remain visible, together with amplitude modulation of the higher formants.

We noted earlier the resolution of the first and occasionally higher formants into harmonics: this is important in aspects of auditory scene analysis (ASA). Cooke [3] presents a model of ASA where strands are grouped into higher-level structures on the basis of common harmonicity and common amplitude modulation.

1   LARGE-SCALE SPECTRAL INTEGRATION

The resolution of formants into harmonics also suggests a requirement for some further auditory processing designed to extract the major salient features of the signal, such as the formant frequencies. We have argued previously (Crawford & Cooke [5]) that this stage should come *after* source segregation. The representation used to decode speech should be simple to compute and fairly coarse. Decoding based on the raw representation would be difficult due to the intra- and extra-speaker variability introduced by representation of harmonics. A more likely strategy is to extract the major spectral peaks by smoothing the spectrum such that, for example, F1 is represented as a single dominance. Furthermore, it is likely that this operation is applied wholesale to the whole frequency range, and to all speech segments.

Support for these hypotheses comes from studies of large-scale spectral integration (LSI), such as those of Bladon [1] and Schwartz & Escudier [9]. This processing can be implemented by a simple convolution of strand representations with the first derivative of a Gaussian (equivalent to smoothing and differentiation) of width 4.5 ERB (corresponding to 3.5 Bark). The positive-going zero-crossings in the convolution profile represent the positions of the peaks, which are then grouped across time in the same way as synchrony strands.

1.1 Observations

Figure 6 depicts, on an ERB-rate scale, the non-integrated strands for 'clean.wav' and the strands which result from LSI. We note formant-like structures taking the place of harmonics. Figure 7 shows, on a Hertz scale, the effect of large-scale spectral integration on 'timit.wav', together with a spectrogram of this signal for comparison. Again, it is possible to identify formant-like structures in the integrated representation. These 'auditory formants' do not precisely mirror those seen in spectrograms however; when formants are sufficiently close in frequency, they are likely to be merged into a single auditory formant (e.g. segment /ih/ in 'timit'), whilst a sufficient harmonic separation can result in a 'splitting' of F1 across a pair of dominances (e.g. the /ix/ in 'timit'). Whether this reduced representation is computed by the auditory system remains an open question. However, resynthesis from integrated strands produces intelligible results.

REFERENCES

[1] R.A.W. Bladon (1986), 'Phonetics for hearers', in: *"Language for Hearers"*, (ed. G. McGregor), Pergamon Press, Oxford.

[2] G.J. Brown & M.P. Cooke (1993), 'Physiologically-motivated signal representations for computational auditory scene analysis', this volume.

[3] M.P. Cooke (in press), *Modelling Auditory Processing and Organisation*, to be published by Cambridge University Press, Cambridge, UK.

[4] M.P. Cooke (1992), 'An explicit time-frequency characterization of synchrony in an auditory model', *Computer Speech & Language*, **6**, 153-173.

[5] M. Crawford & M.P. Cooke (1990), 'Speech perception based on large-scale spectral integration', *3rd Int. Conf. Speech Science and Technology, SST '90 (Melbourne)*.

[6] R. Meddis (1988), 'Simulation of auditory-neural transduction: Further studies', *JASA*, **83**, 1056-1063

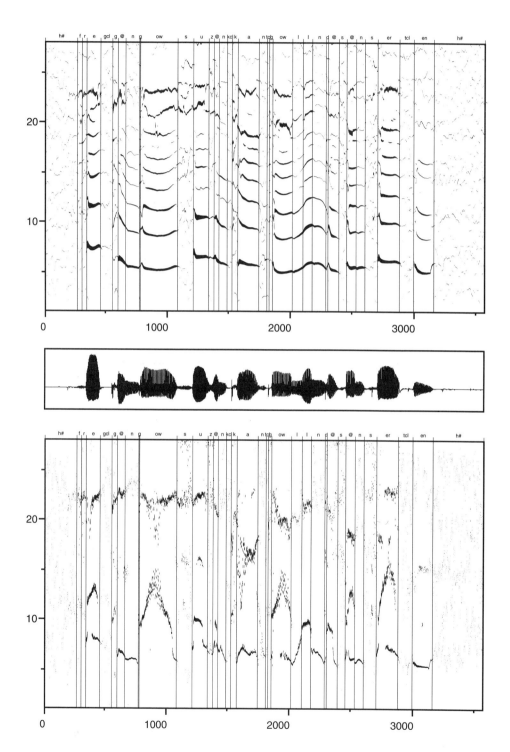

Fig. 6   Representations of 'clean.wav': *upper* : synchrony strands; *middle* : waveform; *lower* : integrated synchrony strands. (Transcription from Dix & Bloothooft, this volume.)

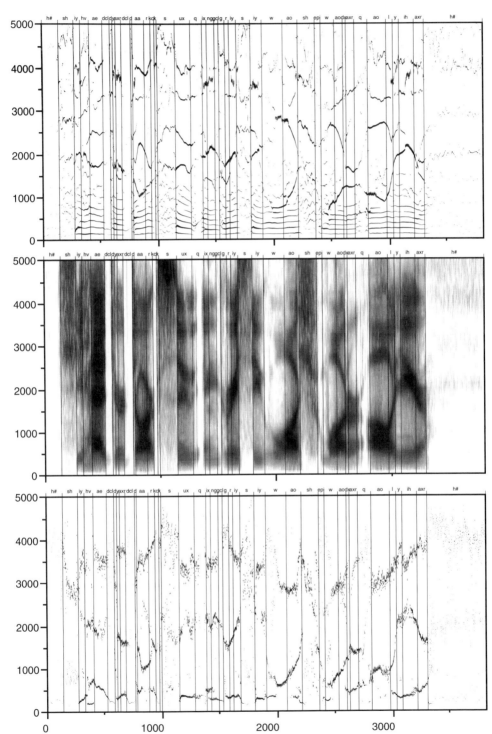

Fig. 7   Representations of 'timit.wav': *upper* : synchrony strands; *middle* : spectrogram; *lower* : integrated synchrony strands.

[7] B.C.J. Moore & B.R. Glasberg (1983), 'Suggested formulae for calculating auditory-filter bandwidths and excitation patterns', *JASA.*, **59**, 750-753.

[8] R.D. Patterson & J. Holdsworth (in press), 'A functional model of neural activity patterns and auditory images', in: *Advances in Speech, Hearing and Language Processing*, (ed. W. A. Ainsworth), Volume 3, JAI Press, London.

[9] J. L. Schwartz & P. Escudier (1989), 'A strong evidence for the existence of a large-scale integrated spectral representation in vowel perception', *Speech Communication*, **8**, 235-259.

Auditory modelling for speech analysis and recognition

18

P. Cosi

1 INTRODUCTION

Cochlear transformations of speech signals result in an auditory neural firing pattern significantly different from the spectrogram, a popular time-frequency-energy representation of speech. Phonetic features may correspond in a rather straightforward manner to the neural discharge pattern with which speech is coded by the auditory nerve. For these reasons, even an ear model that is just an approximation of physical reality appears to be a suitable system for identifying those aspects of the speech signal that are relevant for recognition.

A recently developed joint synchrony/mean-rate (S/M-R) auditory speech processing (ASP) scheme [8] was successfully applied in speech recognition tasks, where promising results were obtained for speech segmentation and labelling [9]. Moreover, results reported elsewhere in the literature show that a combination of the same ASP scheme with multi-layer artificial neural networks produced an effective generalisation amongst speakers in classifying vowels both for English [1] and Italian [2].

The joint S/M-R ASP scheme will be very briefly described and its application to the problem of speech segmentation and labelling, both for clean and noisy speech, will be introduced and analysed.

2 AUDITORY SPEECH PROCESSING

The computational scheme proposed in this paper for modelling the human auditory system is derived from a joint synchrony/mean-rate model proposed by Seneff [8]. The overall system includes three blocks: the first two of them deal with peripheral transformations occurring in the early stages of the hearing process while the third one attempts to extract information relevant to perception.

In fig. 1 a block diagram of the joint S/M-R ASP scheme is displayed together with its mathematical counterpart (for a complete description of the model refer to [8]). The first two blocks represent the auditory periphery. They are designed using knowledge of the well known responses of the corresponding human auditory stages. The third unit attempts to apply a useful processing strategy for the extraction of important speech properties like spectral lines related to formants and also to show enhanced sharpness of onset and offset of different speech segments. The speech signal, band-limited and sampled at 16 kHz, is first pre-filtered through a set of four complex zero pairs to eliminate the very high and very low frequency components. The signal is then analysed by the first block, a 40 channel critical-band linear filterbank whose single channels were designed in order to optimally fit physiological data.

The second block of the model is called the hair cell synapse model. It is nonlinear and is intended to capture prominent features of the transformation from basilar membrane vibration, represented by the outputs of the filterbank, to probabilistic response properties of auditory nerve fibres. The outputs of this stage, in accordance with Seneff [8], represent the probability of firing as a function of time for a set of similar fibres acting as a group.

Visual Representations of Speech Signals: Martin Cooke & Steve Beet (eds.)
© 1993 by John Wiley & Sons Ltd

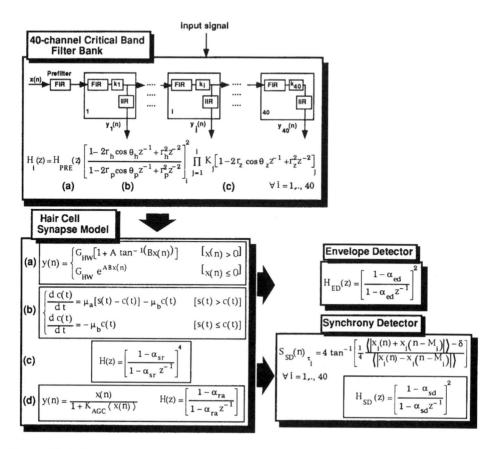

Fig. 1   Block diagram of the synchrony/mean-rate auditory speech processing scheme.

The third and last block of the ear model is a double-unit block with two parallel outputs. The generalised synchrony detector (GSD), which implements the known "phase-locking" property of nerve fibres, represents the first unit and is designed with the aim of enhancing spectral peaks due to vocal tract resonances. The second unit, called the envelope detector (ED) computes the envelope of signals at the output of the previous stage of the model and seems more important for capturing the very rapidly changing dynamic nature of speech. The outputs of this unit should be most important in characterising transient sounds.

The computation time of the joint S/M-R ASP system proposed in this paper is about 150 times real-time on a SUN 4/280. The system structure is suitable for parallelisation with special purpose architectures and accelerator chips. At the present time the model has been also implemented on a floating-point digital signal processor and the computation time is about 10 times real-time [3].

In fig. 2 the output of the model applied to 'clean.syl' (a) from the Sheffield data set is illustrated for the envelope (b) and the synchrony detector (c) modules respectively. In (a), manual segmentation made by an Italian mother-tongue phonetician is superimposed on the speech waveform. The multi-line structure drawn in (b) refers to a particular output of the segmentation procedure which finally produces the target segmentation shown in (c). The use of the GSD parameters allows the production of spectra with a limited number of well defined spectral lines and this represents a good use of speech knowledge according to which formants are voiced sound parameters with low variance. Figure 3 shows the same output resulting from the application of the model to the 'dirty.syl'. It is evident from a comparison of figs. 2c and 3c that the formant structure is well preserved by the S/M-R ASP, even if the speech is corrupted by noise.

3 SPEECH RECOGNITION

Various studies [6,9] suggest the effectiveness of ASP techniques for speech analysis and recognition, especially in adverse speech conditions [6]. Results of the application of this model in previous recognition experiments [1] were also compared with those obtained by using a classical FFT-based front-end. In that particular vowel recognition task the use of auditory model coefficients showed better recognition performance than the use of classical FFT-based coefficients. Furthermore, other results on Italian phoneme recognition experiments [2] provided other evidences in favour of the conclusion that the proposed perception-based auditory analysis could perform better than other acoustic production-based front-end (LPC, MEL-scale cepstrum, etc., ...) in speech analysis and recognition tasks.

4 SPEECH SEGMENTATION AND LABELLING

Following visual inspection of ASP parameters produced in clean and noisy speech analyses, as those previously described in figs. 2b-c and 3b-c, the use of ASP techniques was considered and tested for speech segmentation purposes. We compared results obtained segmenting both 'clean' and 'dirty' sentences of "Fred can go, Susan can't go, and Linda is uncertain", using a semi- automatic segmentation tool called "SONOGRAFIA" [7] which is entirely based on multi-level (ML) segmentation theory [5]. ASP and FFT parameters were used as input to the segmentation system in order to evaluate and compare their performance aligning speech in clean and adverse conditions.

As previously underlined, figs. 2 and 3 show the ML segmentation tree (the "dendrogram" [5]) automatically built by the system analysing the 'clean' (fig. 2b) and the 'dirty' sentence (fig. 3b), using ASP parameters as input. In figs. 2 and 3, the ML structure is superimposed to the envelope output only to have a reference, but it is built considering both envelope and synchrony parameters. The same ML structure, but produced using FFT parameters instead of ASP ones, is shown for the 'clean' (a) and 'dirty' (b) case in fig. 4. The final target segmentation is found with minimal human intervention, which is limited exclusively to fixing the vertical point determining the final target segmentation (corresponding to that found on the horizontal line built at this point), and eventually deleting over-segmentation landmarks forced by this choice. Segmentation marks were always automatically positioned by the system and never adjusted by hand. Inspecting figs. 2 and 4, it is evident that a segmentation vertical point is more easily found in fig. 2b, by reference to ASP parameters, than in fig. 4a, using FFT parameters. Moreover no over-segmentation marks were produced when using ASP parameters, while some of them were forced by the use of FFT parameters without regarding the vertical segmentation choice.

Much clearer evidence in favour of the ASP parameters results by inspecting figs. 3b and 4b referring to the segmentation of the 'dirty' sentence. Even if speech is clearly degraded by quite a relevant noise, ASP parameters lead SONOGRAFIA to compute very clear and reliable segmentation landmarks, while, on the contrary, FFT parameters cause serious problems in finding a possible segmentation line throughout the ML segmentation structure. In other words, throughout the examples we examined, over-segmentation marks (gross errors), always produced by the use of FFT parameters, were totally or heavily reduced by the use of ASP parameters. This result leads obviously to a better starting point for building a real automatic segmentation system [9]. In fact, walking through the dendrogram from left to right, in order to automatically find the optimal segmentation path, clean multi-level structures would surely be more useful than very complicated ones. At present, no attempts have been made to

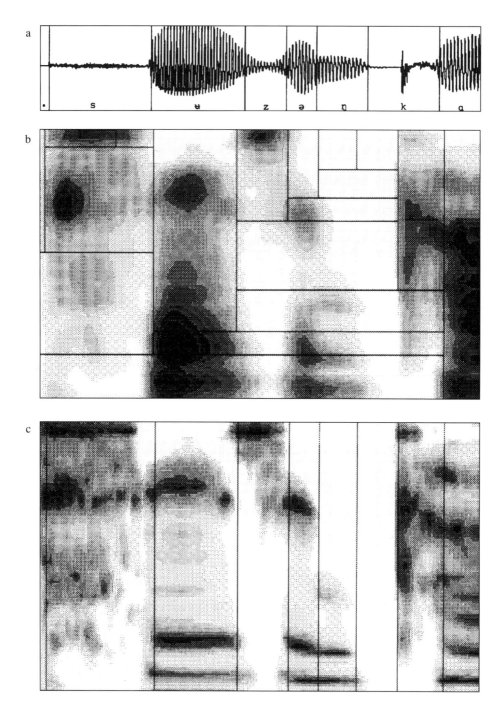

Fig.2   Output of the ASP as applied to 'clean.syl' (*a*), for the envelope (*b*) and the synchrony
          detector (*c*) modules respectively. In a manual segmentation made by an Italian mother-
          tongue phonetician is superimposed on the waveform. Multi-line structure superimposed on
          the envelope output in *b* refers to the "dendrogram", a particular output of the segmentation
          procedure used (see text): the resulting segmentation is shown in *c*.

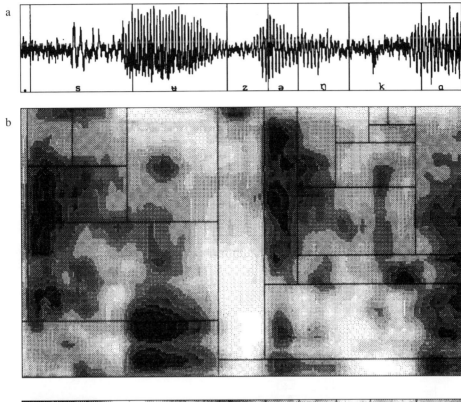

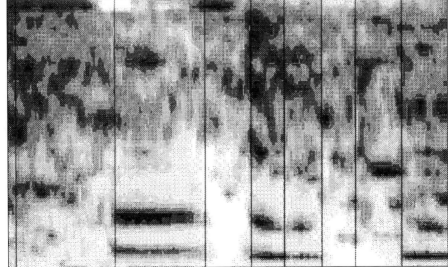

Fig.3   Output of the ASP as applied to 'dirty.syl' (*a*), for the envelope (*b*) and the synchrony
detector (*c*) modules respectively. In a manual segmentation made by an Italian mother-
tongue phonetician is superimposed on the waveform. Multi-line structure superimposed on
the envelope output in *b* refers to the "dendrogram", a particular output of the segmentation
procedure used (see text): the resulting segmentation is shown in *c*.

Fig.4   ML structure produced by the segmentation system using FFT instead of ASP parameters;
          upper: 'clean.syl'; *lower*: 'dirty.syl'.

build such an automatic system; instead, SONOGRAFIA was used, as a very useful semi-
automatic tool, in order to speed up segmentation procedure and to limit human intervention
in fixing segmentation marks.

Finally, speech segmentation discrepancies (fine errors) were computed for both 'clean'
and 'dirty' sentences, comparing SONOGRAFIA semi-automatically produced landmarks
(test segmentation) with those produced by a manual segmentation (reference correct segmentation) made by a phonetician by using audio and visual facilities (see Table 1). Figure 5
illustrates segmentation histograms referring to the application of SONOGRAFIA with ASP
parameters to both the 'clean' and the 'dirty' sentences. Considering a 20 ms error criterion

[4] (i.e. considering an error to be the positioning of a segmentation mark outside a 40 ms interval centred on the correct reference mark) 87% and 90.3% correct segmentation was achieved in the 'clean' and 'dirty' case respectively.

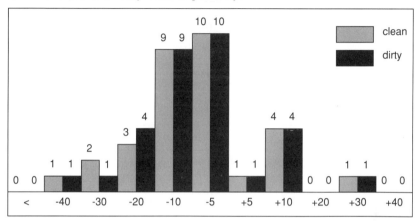

Fig. 5   Segmentation histogram referring to the application of SONOGRAFIA, with ASP parameters, to 'clean' and 'dirty'.

5 CONCLUSIONS

Various results suggest the effectiveness of ASP techniques for speech analysis and recognition. As for segmentation, considering both gross-errors (over-segmentation marks) and fine-errors (segmentation discrepancies) ASP parameters seem to constitute a very effective, hopefully better, alternative to classical speech parameters. In order to verify and make reliable the results presented in this paper (surprisingly higher performance in the noisy speech conditions than in the clean ones) many more experiments need to be performed, but in the mean time these preliminary results could be considered as a very promising starting point for further research.

REFERENCES

[1] P. Cosi, Y. Bengio & R. De Mori (1990), 'Phonetically-based multi-layered neural networks for vowel classification', *Speech Comm.*, **9**(1), 15-29.

[2] P. Cosi, R. De Mori & K. Vagges (1990), 'A neural network architecture for Italian vowel recognition', *Proc. VERBA '90 (Rome)*, 221-228.

[3] P. Cosi, L. Dellana, G.A. Mian & M. Omologo (1991), 'Auditory model implementation on a DSP32C board', *Proc. GRETSI '91 (Juan-les-Pins)*.

[4] P. Cosi, D. Falavigna & M. Omologo (1991), 'A preliminary statistical evaluation of manual and automatic segmentation discrepancies', *Proc. EUROSPEECH '91 (Genova)*, 693-696.

[5] J.R. Glass & V.W. Zue (1988), 'Multi-level acoustic segmentation of continuous speech', *Proc. ICASSP '88*, 429-432.

[6] M.J. Hunt & C. Lefebvre (1988), 'Speaker dependent and independent speech recognition experiments with an auditory model', *Proc. ICASSP '88*, 215-218.

[7] A. Marzal & J. Puchol (1991), 'Sonografia: an interactive segmentation system of acoustic signals based on multilevel segmentation for a personal computer', *ESPRIT-II BRA-ACCOR Progress Reports*, 2.

[8] S. Seneff (1988), 'A joint synchrony/mean-rate model of auditory speech processing', *J. Phonetics*, **16**(1), 55-76.

[9] V.W. Zue, J. Glass, M. Philips & S. Seneff (1989), 'Acoustic segmentation and phonetic classification in the SUMMIT system', *Proc. ICASSP '89*, S8.1, 389-392.

Table 1: Manual segmentation produced by an Italian mother-tongue phonetician of 'clean.wav': "Fred can go, Susan can't, and Linda is uncertain" (SAMPA alphabet).

0, ...	17300, s	29689, 6 (/6U/)	41576, s
4296, f (+/u/?)	19356, }	32225, l	43271, @ (/@:/)
5448, @	22411, z	33639, I (/I~/)	46033, ? k
7246, (/@~/)	22053, @	34868, n	47978, n
9596, e (/e~/)	22763, N	36051, d	50621, ...
10538, N	23814, k	36878, @	57280 <END>
11791, g	25207, A (/A~/)	38030, s (/zx/)	
12612, A	27841,	N 39237, V (/V~/)	
15034, e(/Ae/)	28934, k	40423, n	

On the robustness of two signal preprocessors in the task of semi-automatic label alignment

19

Paul Dalsgaard and Flemming K. Fink

1 INTRODUCTION

In our previous work [e.g. 2,3] on semi-automatic labelling of large speech corpora we have introduced an approach where a self-organising neural network (SONN) functions as a module, which transforms a vector of LPC-derived cepstrum coefficients into a vector of acoustic-phonetic features subsequently transformed into a vector of principal components (PCs). The speech signals were sampled at 8 kHz and frequency limited to telephone band-width. These parameters were used in a dynamic programming algorithm where optimal label alignment is performed on the basis of the following three components: PC parameters; a set of multi-dimensional probability density functions modelling individual phonemes; and the string of phonetic symbols corresponding to the speech signal. The phoneme models were established in the SONN stimulation and calibration session prior to label alignment.

In order to analyse, for example, the influence on label alignment accuracy and robustness against noise corrupting the speech signals, an alternative preprocessing technique has been applied by using Seneff's [6] neurophysiologically-based auditory model (SAM). The reason for choosing this model is twofold. First, in our previous research [4] we have experienced that an auditory model for some noise types is more robust in the task of estimating formant tracks in noise-corrupted speech as opposed to a model using traditional linear prediction techniques. Second, from work on multi-level segmentation it has been observed [7,9] that the outputs from the auditory model show a high degree of dynamic behaviour near time events corresponding to phoneme transitions.

Figure 1 shows the architecture of the label alignment system including the two alternative preprocessors. Both label alignment systems have been trained on the same speech corpus consisting of three spoken passages each of approximately 2 minutes duration taken from the British English part of the EUROM (0) speech database collected within ESPRIT project 2589, 'Speech Assessment Methodology'. A fourth passage — spoken by another talker — was used to test the system performance, where automatically positioned phoneme boundaries were compared to the corresponding manually positioned reference label boundaries.

The results of testing the two systems are reported in this paper where two of the Sheffield signals, 'clean' and 'timit', are analysed. Both utterances were manually segmented and labelled prior to the analyses performed by the two label alignment systems. In addition, a special signal 'timit+noise' was created in order to analyse a signal having a well defined SNR.

2 THE SONN-BASED PREPROCESSOR

The SONN-based preprocessor establishes a method by which a speech signal is transformed into a set of ϑ continuously valued acoustic-phonetic features, which are based on traditionally used articulatory-phonetic features. The process established involves the use of a SONN, which in a training session, firstly, is stimulated by a set of cepstrum coefficients

Visual Representations of Speech Signals: Martin Cooke, Steve Beet and Malcolm Crawford (eds.)
© 1993 by John Wiley & Sons Ltd

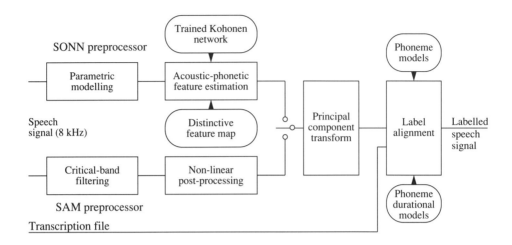

Fig. 1   Architecture of the label alignment system.

describing the speech frame signal such that each neuron (x,y) of the SONN is assigned a cluster vector c_{xy} of cepstrum coefficients, and, secondly, is further calibrated such that each neuron (x,y) is also assigned a vector P_{xy}. The absolute value of the element $P_{xy}(k)$ gives the probability that the kth acoustic-phonetic feature is involved in the speech production process given that neuron (x,y) is firing.

Assigning values to vectors P_{xy} requires a number of definitions linking speech technology and articulatory phonetic concepts. First, a vector N_{xy} is defined by:

$$N_{xy} \equiv [p((x,y) \mid S_1)\, p((x,y) \mid S_2)\, ...p((x,y) \mid S_j)...p((x,y) \mid S_M)]^T \qquad (1)$$

such that elements $N_{xy}(j)$ give the probability that the phoneme with symbol S_j is involved in the speech production process, given that neuron (x,y) is firing. M is the number of phoneme symbols under consideration, $1 \leq j \leq M$. The elements of this vector are given during the supervised calibration process.

Figure 2 identifies the selected set of British English phoneme symbols S_j in terms of their place-of-articulation and manner-of-articulation features (shown on the horizontal and vertical axes respectively). Fifteen vocalic and sixteen consonantal phonemes are individually grouped together with their respective phonetic features as used in traditional phonology [1,5]. The features include vowel (voc), front (fro), central (cen), round (rou), ..., open (ope) for the vowels, and labial (lab), alveolar (alv), velar (vel), nasal (nas), fricative (fri), .., plosive (plo) for the consonants. Furthermore, the phonetic feature voiced (voi) is used to identify all voiced vocalic and some consonantal phonemes, and as such also identifying the remaining consonantal phonemes as being non-voiced. From this figure a ϑ-dimensional distinctive feature framework vector D_j is defined for phoneme with symbol S_j on the basis of traditional phonology. The elements $D_j(k)$ have values +1, –1 or 0. A value of +1 is used to indicate that the kth feature is involved (present) in the speech production process resulting in phoneme S_j, a value of –1 that the kth feature is not involved (absent), and 0 indicates that the feature belongs to the alternative phoneme category (here vowels versus consonants). For English we use $\vartheta = 25$ features including the "feature" silent (sil) which is used to describe the plosive phase in stop consonants and speech pauses such that in general:

$$D_j \equiv [[voi][voc][fro][rou]...[ope][con][lab][alv]...[plo][sil]]^T . \qquad (2)$$

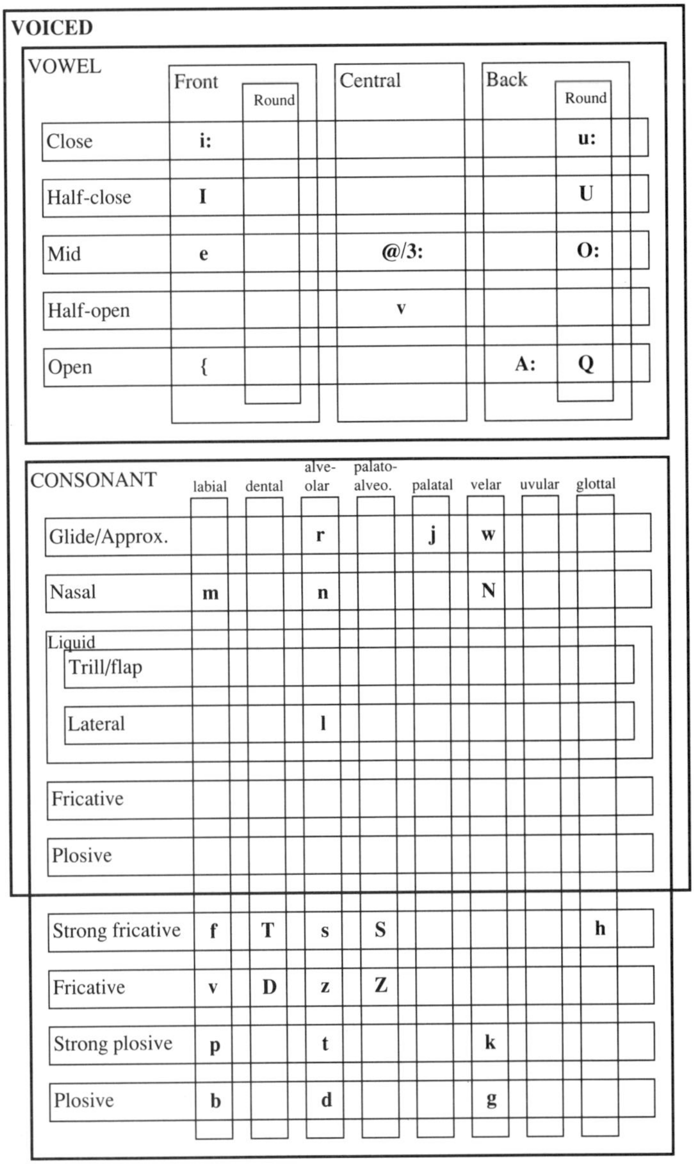

VOICED

VOWEL

	Front	Round	Central	Back	Round
Close	i:				u:
Half-close	I				U
Mid	e		@/3:		O:
Half-open			v		
Open	{			A:	Q

CONSONANT

	labial	dental	alveolar	palato-alveo.	palatal	velar	uvular	glottal
Glide/Approx.			r		j	w		
Nasal	m		n			N		
Liquid — Trill/flap								
Lateral			l					
Fricative								
Plosive								
Strong fricative	f	T	s	S				h
Fricative	v	D	z	Z				
Strong plosive	p		t			k		
Plosive	b		d			g		

Fig. 2   SAM descriptive categories for English vowel and consonant sounds.

Vectors D_j are defined by fig. 2, and the vector P_{xy} is now defined by:

$$P_{xy} \equiv [D_1\, D_2\, ...D_M]^T \cdot N_x . \tag{3}$$

P_{xy} is used during the transformation of the speech signal into the set of acoustic-phonetic features as follows. First, the speech signal is preprocessed into a set of 12 LPC-derived cepstrum coefficients $c(t)$, which are computed every 5 ms with a 10 ms Hamming window. Second, a set $G(t)$ of closest neurons are identified by their minimal Euclidean distance

$d\left(c_{xy}, c\left(t\right)\right)$ between $c(t)$ and the neuron cluster vectors c_{xy} for all neurons of the SONN. Third, elements $\Phi\left(t, k\right)$ of the acoustic-phonetic feature vector $\Phi\left(t\right)$ are calculated as:

$$\Phi(t,k) = W_{G(t)}\left(\sum_{G(t)} \frac{1}{d\left(c_{xy}, c(t)\right)} P_{xy}(k)\right), \quad 1 \leq k \leq \vartheta \tag{4}$$

where the weighting factor $W_{G(t)}$ is given by $W_{G(t)}^{-1} = \sum_{G(t)} \frac{1}{d\left(c_{xy}, c(t)\right)}$.

Ten principal components are derived from the acoustic-phonetic features by a standard technique.

3   THE SAM-BASED PREPROCESSOR

Seneff's auditory model is based on neurophysiological measurements from which much of the behaviour of the inner mammalian ear (e.g. adaptation and masking) is modelled. The ability to model the adaptation functionality is clearly very useful in distinguishing between stationarity and abrupt spectral changes in speech. The masking effect is part of the functionality of the inner ear which in part is related to timing properties.

The auditory filtering is modelled by a 35-channel linear critical band filterbank. The output of each channel is processed by a nonlinear hair-cell-synapse model and Gaussian temporal integration, resulting in a 35-dimensional feature vector, each 5 ms from which 12 principal components are calculated.

The SAM model was employed in the same task of label alignment, as described above using the SONN preprocessor, on the basis of experiments which have demonstrated that the outputs of the SAM preprocessor show clear correlations with the dynamic behaviour in the speech signals as observed, for example, in the spectrogram.

4   OVERALL LABEL ALIGNMENT RESULTS USING THE PREPROCESSORS

The results from label alignment are usually presented in a number of histograms in which the time differences between automatically and manually positioned phoneme boundaries are displayed for individual phoneme transition types (e.g. [2,8]) and boundaries are considered positioned with acceptable accuracy if automatically and manually positioned boundaries are within ±20 ms [7]. Here, however, the results will be demonstrated in a number of figures using the Sheffield signals.

4.1 SONN results on the 'clean' speech signal.

The 'clean' speech signal is submitted to an analysis using the SONN-based system as trained on the EUROM (0) speech database. The results are shown in fig. 3. Before analysis, a label string was established for the 'clean' signal. The label string corresponds to a "broad auditory" transcription of the signal. In this task the listening facility of the label alignment system was used together with the spectrogram as shown in fig. 3. During the automatic part of the label alignment this string was used to constrain the Viterbi search/level building to position the label boundaries within the speech signal as shown in fig. 3. The label string originally given is shown equally-spaced above the spectrogram, and the final boundary positions are shown together with the speech signal. Two of these boundaries have been finely adjusted after the automatic positioning. The two boundaries — /U/-/l/ transition and /u/-/z/ transition (marked with a ☞) — each needed manual interactive repositioning.

Figure 3 shows the result after these adjustments, and it is seen that the interactive labelling of the 'clean' signal coincides very well with the information displayed in the spectrogram. Some of the necessary repositionings may partly (for example at the /z/ boundary) be caused by the unusual 2.8 kHz cutoff in the 'clean' speech signal.

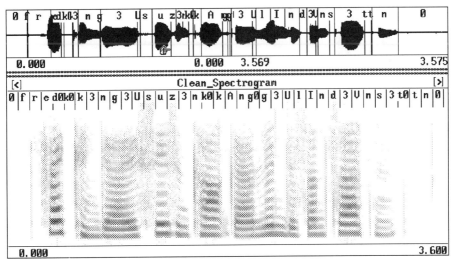

Fig. 3 'Clean.wav', signal and spectrogram.

4.2 SONN and SAM results on the 'timit' speech signal

Results from SONN- and SAM-based alignment are shown in figs. 4 and 5, respectively. The speech signal is the 'timit' signal. The SONN-based label alignment shown in fig. 4 — after some manual interaction — has been verified on the basis of listening, and there is very good agreement between the positioned boundaries and the replayed speech signal. The results from the SAM-based alignment shown in fig. 5 did not require any manual realignment.

4.3 SONN and SAM results on 'timit + noise' speech signal

A special 'timit + noise' signal consisting of the 'timit' signal with additive cocktail-party noise at a resulting SNR of 17 dB was established and is shown in figs. 6 and 7. This signal was established in order to analyse a noisy signal, which — as opposed to the 'clean' signal — is not limited to 2.8 kHz bandwidth, keeping in mind that the SAM-based label alignment system is trained on telephone bandwidth, and that the test material is American English as opposed to the British English training material.

Comparisons between figs. 6 and 7 clearly show that the SONN-based label alignment system is much more sensitive to noise in the speech signals being labelled than the SAM-based system. In fig. 7 only a few segment boundaries are clearly mispositioned. No attempt has been made here to perform manual interactive positioning of boundaries.

5 CONCLUSIONS

The analyses of the noise-free speech signals demonstrate that both systems are able to perform semi-automatic label alignment giving results in good agreement with manually performed reference labelling. The small-size test material used here seems to show that the SAM-based system will need less interactive intervention following automatic labelling. However, to justify this claim a much larger test corpus should be used. The analyses using the two preprocessors have shown that the auditory preprocessor is more noise robust than the preprocessor based on linear prediction.

Integrating auditory modelling in a semi-automatic label alignment system will probably increase the overall accuracy, but more extensive tests need to be performed to justify this expectation. However, a computationally simpler auditory model than the Seneff model used here is required in order to establish a near-real-time labelling system.

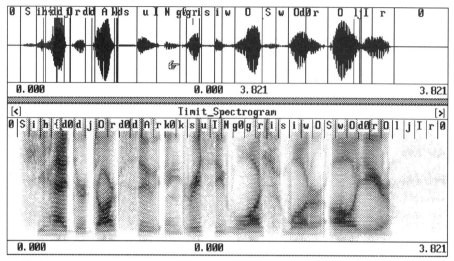

Fig. 4   'Timit.wav' , signal and SONN processing.

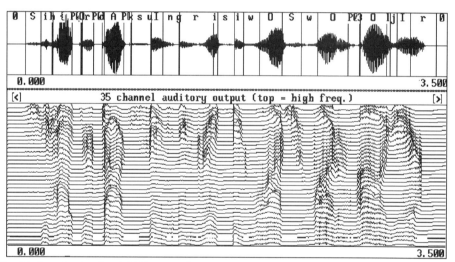

Fig. 5   'Timit.wav' , signal and SAM processing.

Special attention has to be given to proper scaling of the input when using the SAM-based preprocessor, not only in order to avoid internal saturation effects, but also to ensure comparable levels of the principal components used during training and testing.

Acknowledgements: The authors wish to thank William Barry, Allgemeine Linguistik, Universitat Saarlandes, for his assistance in establishing the transcriptions of the speech signals used in this paper, and to our colleague Ove Andersen, Speech Technology Centre, Aalborg University, for his special assistance in integrating the SAM-model into the Interactive Label Alignment software tool. This work is in part supported by the Danish Technical Research Council.

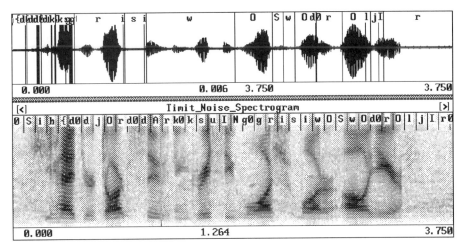

Fig. 6   'Timit.wav' at 17 dB SNR and SONN processing.

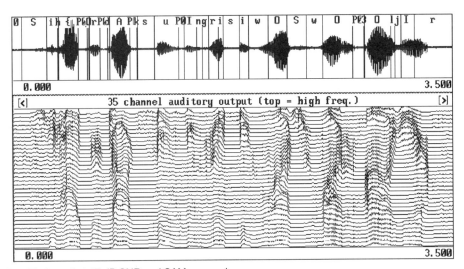

Fig. 7   'Timit.wav' at 17 dB SNR and SAM processing.

REFERENCES

[1] N. Chomsky & M. Halle (1968), *The Sound Pattern of English*, Harper and Row, New York.

[2] P. Dalsgaard & W. Barry (1990), 'Phoneme label alignment in the context of acoustic-phonetic features and neural networks', *Proc. ICSLP*, Vol. 2, 945-949.

[3] P. Dalsgaard, O. Andersen, W. Barry & R. Jørgensen (1992), 'On the use of acoustic-phonetic features in interactive labelling of multi-lingual speech corpora', *Proc. ICASSP '92*, I:549-552.

[4] F.K. Fink & P. Dalsgaard (1989), 'Estimation of formants in noise corrupted speech using auditory models', *Proc. EUROSPEECH '89*, 677-680.

[5] P. Ladefoged (1982), *A Course in Phonetics*, Harcourt Brace Jovanovich, New York.

[6] S. Seneff (1988), 'A joint synchrony/mean-rate model of auditory speech processing', *J. Phonetics*, **16**, 55-76.

[7] H.B.D. Sørensen & P. Dalsgaard (1989), 'Multi-level segmentation of natural continuous speech using different auditory front-ends', *Proc. EUROSPEECH '89*, 79-82.

[8] T. Svendsen & K. Kvale (1990), 'Automatic alignment of phonemic labels with continuous speech', *Proc. ICSLP*, 997-1000.

[9] V.W. Zue, J. Glass, M. Phillips & S. Seneff (1989), 'Acoustic segmentation and phonetic classification in the summit system', *Proc. ICASSP '89*, 389-392.

Time-instantaneous frequency representation

C. Demars

1   INTRODUCTION

Among numerous representations of speech [1,2,8,13] we introduce a new representation based on the concept of *instantaneous frequency*, the *time-instantaneous frequency* representation. We associate with the signal a distribution $T(\omega, t)$, the envelope of the signal at the instant t for the instantaneous frequency ω. Integrating $T(\omega, t)$ gives a distribution of the energy along the instantaneous frequency axis. Section 2 defines instantaneous frequency and introduces the time-instantaneous frequency representation. In section 3 we give some brief implementation details. In section 4 we present some properties of the representation. The final section discusses applications in speech processing.

2   INSTANTANEOUS FREQUENCY VS. TIME REPRESENTATION

2.1 Instantaneous frequency

According to the methodology of Berthomier [3] we associate the so-called *in-quadrature* signal $y(t)$ to the signal $x(t)$ to obtain the complex signal $s(t) = x(t) + iy(t)$. The square of the modulus is the envelope:

$$e^2(t) = x^2(t) + y^2(t) \tag{1}$$

and the argument is the phase of the analytical signal. Instantaneous frequency $\omega(t)$ is the derivative of phase:

$$\omega(t) = \frac{d}{dt}\left(\mathrm{atan}(y/x)\right) = \frac{xy' - yx'}{x^2 + y^2} \ . \tag{2}$$

2.2 Construction of the representation

Definition: As in [4] we associate with the signal a distribution $T(\omega, t)$, the envelope (which is twice the energy of the signal) at instant t for the instantaneous frequency ω. Integrating $T(\omega, t)$ with respect to time gives a function of ω which represents a distribution of the energy along the instantaneous frequency axis. This integration can be done on the whole signal. Done with a sliding window we get a representation, similar to a spectrogram, with a time axis, an instantaneous frequency axis, and energy represented in grey levels (see fig. 1).

Secondary parameters: For each frame we can calculate secondary parameters: for instance, the first moment (mean instantaneous frequency), energy of the frame, the second moment, the ratio of energy on negatives frequencies, (being a derivative, the instantaneous frequency can be negative), this ratio being suggested for a classification of vowels [5] (see fig. 1).

Visual Representations of Speech Signals: Martin Cooke, Steve Beet and Malcolm Crawford (eds.)
© 1993 by John Wiley & Sons Ltd

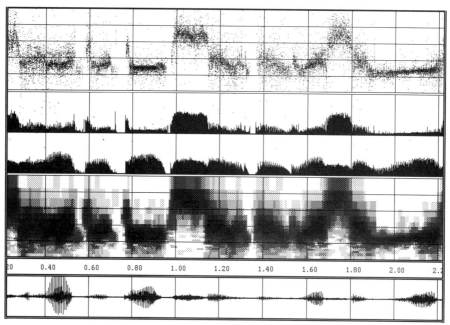

Fig.1   Comparison of different representations of the start of 'timit.wav'; *upper*: time-instantaneous
frequency, linear scale from –2 kHz to 8 kHz, window length 1 ms, no overlap, 512 channels
from –8 kHz to +8 kHz; *middle*: (two black histograms) mean instantaneous frequency (top),
energy (bottom); *lower*: time-instantaneous frequency, Bark scale from –2 kHz to 8 kHz,
512 channels reduced to 24, from –2 kHz to 8 kHz, window length 30 ms, overlap 10 ms.

3   NUMERICAL IMPLEMENTATION

3.1 Analytical signal and instantaneous frequency

The analytical signal can be calculated by one of the following alternatives:

i   *FIR filters*: as output the filters deliver a signal which is in-quadrature with the
input signal in a broad band.

ii *Fourier transform*: the Fourier transform is calculated, the part dedicated to
negative frequencies is set to 0, the remaining part is multiplied by 2, then an
inverse Fourier transform is done to obtain the so-called in-quadrature signal.

iii *Phase-splitting network*: The analytical signal is calculated by a *90* degree
phase-splitting network [7] which, from the input signal, produces two signals
the phase of which is in-quadrature on a large bandwidth.

For instantaneous frequency, the time derivatives can be calculated by the Fourier transform or using FIR differentiators.

3.2 Instantaneous frequency-time representation

The distribution is obtained by a summation: at each instant we have the instantaneous
frequency and the energy of the signal, we add the value of this energy to the energy present
in the corresponding instantaneous frequency channel.

3.3 Complexity

The total number of operations (additions + multiplications) depends on the accuracy
chosen for the derivatives and the quadrature [7]. For the phase-splitting network we choose

filters of the same length N_1, i.e. $2N_1$ operations. For the derivatives we choose FIR filters of odd order N_2; due to the antisymmetry $N_2 - 2$ operations only are needed for the two signals: here, $N_1 = 8$, $N_2 = 32$, i.e. 47 operations for each sample.

4 PROPERTIES

4.1 A brief list

A detailed list of properties can be found in [4,8]. Here we outline only some points:

i *Positivity*: the quantity represented, the envelope, (on a logarithmic or linear scale) at the point (t, ω) is an energy.

ii *Frequency resolution*: the frequency resolution (the number of channels), is, in theory, not limited. It is independent of time resolution.

iii *Time resolution*: the time resolution can be as small as 1 sample.

iv *Linearity*: the representation is not linear. Yet when the signal consists of a pure gliding tone in the frequency band, the distribution is situated only on the frequency line and the method provides a very good melody detector [9,11]. Moreover we can apply a bandpass filter to speech, to calculate the pitch [6, 9]. When the signal consists of two sounds relatively well separated in frequency we can divide the frequency band in two sub-bands and calculate the instantaneous frequency and envelope in each sub-band, the grouping being done at the graphic stage. Yet we consider that it is another form of coding the information and that this coding is good enough in speech recognition [10], and can be good for other tasks, with specific possibilities for the processing of consonant sounds. Let us remember that practically all the members of Cohen's class transform (Wigner-Ville, Rihaczek, Born-Jordan and others, and even spectrograms) are not linear (they are bilinear) and present cross-terms which are not easy to suppress.

v *Window*: The use of recursive quadrature filters means that the windowing is done only for easy processing.

vi *Separability*: The construction of the distribution can be done *independently* on a number N' of samples with $N' < N$, N being the width of the interval treated. Moreover we can calculate the instantaneous frequency, and the envelope of the entire signal; then we construct the distribution for a frame of width N', displacing along the time axis with overlapping or not.

vii *Overlapping*: the use of sliding window with overlap *does not increase the total number of operations*: for the new frame only the calculation for the new points is done.

4.2 Relation to other representations

The moments of order 0 and 1 of $T(\omega, t)$ are equal to the moments of the corresponding Fourier spectrum. The second moment of $T(\omega, t)$ is smaller than the Fourier one. The local moment, at the time t (obtained by integration with respect to frequency) of the Wigner-Ville distribution, and of the Margeneau-Hill distribution, is equal to instantaneous frequency, a general property of Cohen's class distributions, with a particular kernel.

The method was developed for the first time in analogic [3,11]. Its ability to capture fast variations of instantaneous frequency has been demonstrated [9].

5   APPLICATION TO SPEECH ANALYSIS

5.1 The Sheffield signals

Representations with different choices of parameters: We present different representations of 'timit.wav' corresponding to various choices of the analysis parameters: time and frequency resolutions, overlap, number of channels, type of scales.

The upper part of fig. 1 corresponds to an analysis over 512 channels, from –8 to +8 kHz; the display is restricted to –2 kHz to +8 kHz as we observe that, in speech signals, there is very little energy below –2 kHz. Recall that the instantaneous frequency can be negative as it is a derivative and that the part of energy on negative instantaneous frequency seems to be of interest for vowel characterisation. The window length is 1 ms with no overlap. The lower part corresponds to another choice of the parameters of the analysis: the 512 original channels have been reduced to 24, with separate Bark scales on positive and negative frequencies, the window length is 30 ms, with 10 ms overlap in order to be near the usual conditions in the recognition process. The middle part is dedicated to the representation of the first moment of the distribution (mean instantaneous frequency), and of the energy (two of the secondary parameters we can extract from this distribution). Other representations are presented in fig. 2.

Note the following general characteristics: segmentation of different parts of the signal by the overall structure of the distribution in the time-instantaneous frequency space is clear; the temporal events are detected and their general place on the frequency axis is correctly situated.

Comparison with spectrogram: In fig. 3 we present a comparison between the spectrogram (lower part) and the time-instantaneous representation (upper part) of the beginning of 'timit.wav' signal, with the same time-scale, window length (30 ms) and overlap (10 ms). The number of original channels is identical (512), this number being reduced to 16 for the spectrogram for the 0-8 kHz frequencies (the part for negative frequencies being blank), to 20 for the time-instantaneous distribution, for the –2 kHz to +8 kHz, in order to have the same resolution on the positive frequencies (Bark scale). Yet the grey levels which code the energy were manually adjusted separately to obtain the maximum contrast on each picture. Other comparisons are presented in figs. 4 and 5. We observe that the pictures present simultaneously similarities and differences.

5.2 Other applications to speech

A review of different applications to speech processing, and to other domains (bioacoustics, biomedicine, geophysics is presented in [8]. In particular:

- *isolated word speech recognition*: we apply a process of boundary detection on the envelope and of time compression of stable parts. We use a Bark scale, a logarithmic scale on the energy on each of the eight channels. The recognition rate of 92% becomes 99% after linear interpolation on the envelope and the instantaneous frequency [10].
- *pitch detection*: after low-pass filtering, the instantaneous frequency represents the pitch [6].
- *formant representation*: the instantaneous frequency of the two signals obtained by bandpass filtering around the two first formants is calculated [11].
- *speech segmentation*: for continuous speech and acoustic-to-phonetic decoder [14,15,16].

6   DISCUSSION

We have presented a representation based on the concept of *instantaneous frequency*. The number of operations necessary for its calculation is small and does not increase with overlapping. Windowing is possible but not necessary, and the calculation of the visual rep-

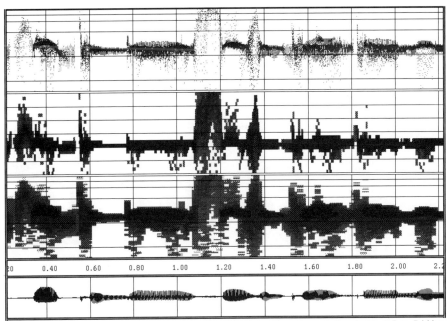

Fig. 2   Comparison of different representations of 'clean.wav': representation from -2.5 to 5 kHz; *upper* : window 1 ms, no overlap, 512 channels, Bark scale; *middle* : window 10 ms, overlap 5 ms, 64 channels linear scale; *lower* : window 30 ms, overlap 10 ms, 512 original channels reduced to 32 channels Bark scale (conditions for the recognition process: 16 channels on 0-5 kHz).

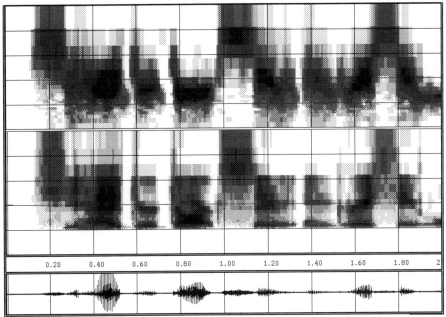

Fig. 3   The start of 'timit.wav'; *upper* : time-instantaneous frequency distribution, Bark scale from −2 kHz to 8 kHz, 512 original channels reduced to 20; *lower* : Bark scale spectrogram from 0 to 8 kHz, 512 original channels reduced to 16. The time scales are the same: window length 30 ms, overlap 10 ms.

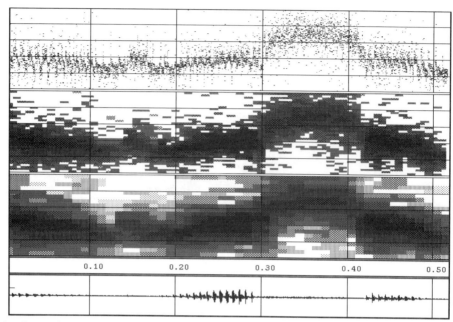

Fig. 4   Comparison of different representations of 'timit.syl'; linear scale −2 kHz to 8 kHz for the representation, −8 kHz to 8 kHz for the analysis; *upper* : 1 ms window, no overlap, 512 channels; middle: 10 ms window, 5 ms overlap, 64 channels; *lower* : 30 ms window, 10 ms overlap, 32 channels (conditions for the recognition process), 16 channels on positive frequencies.

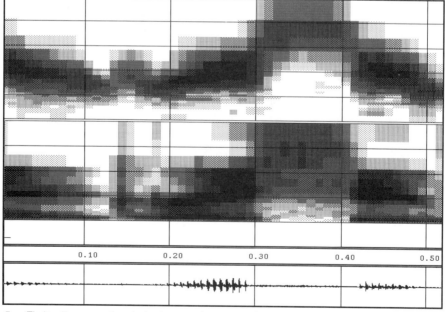

Fig. 5   'Timit.syl'; *upper* : time-instantaneous frequency distribution, Bark scale from −2 kHz to 8 kHz, 512 original channels to 20; *lower* : Bark scale spectrogram 0 to 8 kHz, 512 original channels reduced to 16. The time scales are the same, window length 30 ms, overlap 10 ms.

resentation can be completely independent of the calculation of instantaneous frequency and envelope. The representation is a new means of coding the information in a signal, and various applications have been studied.

In comparing the advantages and drawbacks of this representation with others we have to distinguish:

- the mathematical and physical properties of the continuous, original, representation,
- the properties of its discrete counterpart,
- the properties after different degrees of smoothing in time or frequency, and after channel and energy compression,
- the visualisation of the features the user is interested in (parameters commonly used in recognition, such as mel frequency cepstral coefficients, may not be useful for visualisation), with special attention to the coding of the parameter represented, scales and thresholds.

The comparison of representations of signals is not easy: even if they are simple the quality of the analysis depends on the signal [12].

Acknowledgements: The programs for displaying the graphic representations were developed by P. Blanchet.

REFERENCES

[1] C. d'Alessandro & C. Demars (1992), 'Representation temps-fréquence du signal de parole', *Traitement du Signal*, **9**(2), 153-174.

[2] F. Auger & C. Doncarli (1992), 'Quelques commentaires sur des représentations temps-fréquence proposées récemment', *Traitement du Signal*, **9**(1), 3-25.

[3] C. Berthomier & R. Riguet (1972), 'Calcul analogique de l'enveloppe et de la fréquence instantanée des signaux TBF', *Colloque sur l'utilisation du filtrage par correlation en géophysique et en astronomie*, Lyon.

[4] C. Berthomier (1983), 'Instantaneous frequency and energy distribution of a signal', *Signal Processing*, **5**, 31-45.

[5] C. Berthomier (1983), 'Fréquence instantanée et représentation du signal de parole', *Actes du Séminaire "Traitement du signal de parole" (ENST, Paris)*, 119-124.

[6] C. Berthomier (1979), 'Calcul analogique de la fréquence du fondamental', *Proc. IXth Int. Cong. Phonetic Sciences (Copenhagen)*, 260.

[7] C. Demars (1984), 'Détermination pratique d'un réseau déphaseur à 90 degrés numérique et à large bande', *Onde électrique*, 64(4), 108-113.

[8] C. Demars (1990), 'Représentations temps-fréquence et paramétrisations d'un signal. Eléments de monographie', *Note interne LIMSI 90-9*, 31-42.

[9] C. Demars, C. Berthomier & M. Goustard (1976), 'The ontogenesis of the "Great Call" of gibbons (Hylobates Concolor)', *Recent advances in primatology Vol. I*, Academic Press, London, 827-830.

[10] C. Demars & J-L. Gauvain (1983), 'Application de la fréquence instantanée la reconnaissance des mots isolés', *Actes du Séminaire "Traitement du signal de parole" (ENST, Paris)*, 226-224.

[11] A. Gabison & R. Gendrin (1979), 'Appareil analogique destiné à la mesure en temps réel de l'amplitude, de la fréquence et de la phase instantanées de signaux variant avec le temps', *Ann. Télecom.*, **3-4**, 158-165.

[12] D. L. Jones & T.W. Parks (1992), 'A resolution comparison of several time frequency representations', *IEEE Trans. on Speech Processing*, **40**(2), 413-420.

[13] F. H. Lawatsch & G.F. Bourdreaux-Bartels (1992), 'Linear and quadratic time frequency signal representation', *IEEE SP Magazine*, 21-67.

[14] D. Seggie (1987), 'The use of temporal frequency in speech signal analysis', *Proc. XIth Int Cong. Phonetic Sciences (Tallinn)*, 364-367.

[15] A. Tsopanoglou, J. Mourjopoulos & G. Kokkinakis (1989), 'Continuous speech phoneme segmentation method based on the instantaneous frequency', *EUROSPEECH '89 (Paris)*, 67-70.

[16] A. Tsopanoglou, E.D. Kyriakis-Bitzaros, J. Mourjopoulos & G. Kokkinakis (1991), 'A real time speech decoder using instantaneous frequency and energy', *EUROSPEECH '91 (Genova)*, 1349-1352.

Comparative evaluations of auditory representations of speech

Phillip Dermody, George Raicevich and Richard Katsch

1   INTRODUCTION

There are several ways to evaluate different auditory representations. The first is to determine if a new representation provides improved performance for a specific application. An example of this approach is the investigation of the performance of auditory model representations in machine speech recognition (Cohen [1]; Ghitza [5]). However, it is not clear whether the results of these evaluations are confounded by the interface chosen between the representation and a pre-selected classifier. A second approach to evaluation is to directly compare standard and auditory model representations of particular spectral landmarks such as speech formants (e.g. Fink & Dalsgaard [4]). This approach presumes the primacy of features derived from standard methods and may not show the importance of new features extracted by alternative methods. A third approach attempts to re-synthesise the outputs of different auditory representations and play these to listeners to determine which representation might provide the best signal for distorted speech. Cooke [2] provides an example of this approach. Finally, it is possible to compare alternative auditory representations on performance criteria such as the invariance of the pattern produced in quiet and noise. This approach assumes that the method that preserves the most information across adverse conditions might also provide the most information for an application. The present study is an example of the last approach and compares an auditory model and a standard analysis of quiet and noisy speech samples.

Once a general approach has been chosen there remain several other problems for comparative evaluations of alternative auditory representations because different scales are used for the parameters selected for the representation. The present paper attempts to find a solution to this problem by normalising the output parameters of different representations to allow direct comparisons on a standard speech data base.

2   METHOD

2.1   Description of auditory representations

The comparative evaluations were carried out using the auditory model developed by Seneff [6,7] and a linear predictive coding (LPC) analysis from a standard signal analysis package (Entropic Signal Processing System v. 4.1). The Seneff auditory model was chosen because it provides a full model up to the level of the auditory nerve and is being used in ongoing applications (Seneff [7]). LPC is a standard speech analysis method which approximates spectral information (the LPC spectrum or LPCS) provided in speech formant patterns.

The Seneff auditory model uses a 40-channel filterbank in the range of 208 to 6707 Hz with a filter bandwidth of approximately 0.5 Bark. The linear filterbank (stage 1 of the model) is followed by a nonlinear stage which includes a half-wave rectification; short-term adaptation (based on a threshold and decay mechanism); a low-pass filter (which reduces synchrony to high-frequency components and smooths any square-wave shape produced by the rectifi-

Visual Representations of Speech Signals: Martin Cooke, Steve Beet and Malcolm Crawford (eds.)
© 1993 by John Wiley & Sons Ltd

cation process); and a rapid AGC which also simulates the refractory period of neuron firing. These processes (stage 2 of the model) simulate available physiological data quite well and their output resembles that from auditory nerve fibres described in physiological studies.

The output of stage 2 is either used via an envelope detector (based on calculations of the envelope amplitude across channels) which produces a mean rate spectrum (MRS) or via an alternate module that determines the extent to which the information near the centre frequency of the linear filter dominates the output. This synchrony detector produces information about the dominant periodicity in the response pattern from the stage 2 output. This is used to calculate a synchrony spectrum (SS). The details of the implementation of all the stages are presented in Seneff [6,7].

The choice between the use of the MRS or the SS as the final output of the model is one of the questions addressed in this study. The second question is how to compare either of these analyses with a standard LPC analysis for the same speech data.

2.2 Normalisation of output parameters in evaluations

For meaningful comparative evaluations between different auditory representations it is necessary to consider issues related to scaling. In general it will be necessary to normalise scales of frequency, gain, analysis window integration times (frame rate), and the relative dynamic ranges. Normalising frequency, gain and frame rates is reasonably straightforward. In the present study we used a cubic spline interpolation to convert the output representations of the auditory model and the LPC analysis to the same linear frequency scale between 210 and 5000 Hz. Gain normalisation was achieved by referencing the maximum signal level to 0 dB and scaling on log energy. A high-resolution frame rate of 1.25 ms was chosen for the comparisons.

The normalisation of dynamic range was performed by measuring spectral distances only over the dynamic range that was common to all outputs in the noise conditions (noise represents the worst case for the dynamic ranges). Dynamic range was defined as the difference between the maximum peak level and the minimum valley level across the whole output signal.

2.3 Stimuli and evaluation method

The stimuli consisted of a syllable /kae/ extracted from a spoken sentence. The analysis was performed on the syllable in quiet and with a realistic noise added to it. The speech stimuli are the signals referred to as 'clean.dip' and 'dirty.dip'.

The purpose of the comparative evaluation was to decide which auditory representation provided the most invariant signal extraction in a noise condition compared to a quiet condition. One reasonably straightforward way to carry out this comparison is to use a Euclidean distance metric comparing the spectra in the two conditions. A distance metric used in this way should indicate the extent to which the analysis method preserves the signal components in adverse conditions and thereby provides a figure of merit for different analysis methods whose output parameters have been normalised.

Another way to use distance measures is to compare the distance across each frame and reward analysis methods that produce several frames (segments) during which the signal does not change much. One method that may lend itself to this requirement has been suggested for feedback control systems where the problem of losing a signal becomes more serious the longer the duration of the loss (Dorf [3]). A performance index can therefore be based on the integral of the time multiplied by the absolute error (ITAE). In the present case the error is the distance and we weight the distance measure by the number of contiguous speech frames during which it remains high.

The Euclidean distance measure (EDM) was calculated on the points of each frame across all frames in the analysis using the formula:

$$EDM = \sqrt[p]{\frac{1}{m}\sum\nolimits_{i=1}^{m} |p_y(i) - p_x(i)|^p}$$ (1)

and the ITAE as:

$$ITAE = \sqrt[p]{\frac{1}{m}\sum\nolimits_{i=1}^{m} ETL|p_y(i) - p_x(i)|^p}$$ (2)

where

p_y = signal plus noise
p_x = signal
p = distance power
m = number of points
ETL = error time length.

It should be noted here that in the present study $p = 2$ and that the formula shows that the squared distances were divided by the number of points in the distance calculation to provide a more manageable number for the comparisons.

3 RESULTS

3.1 Spectral analysis

The dynamic ranges for the speech samples in noise as output from the different analyses methods were 31.8, 16.25, and 41.6 for the LPCS, MRS and SS respectively. Because of the very compressed signal produced by the MRS in noise, the distance measures were run on each analysis at 16 dB down from peak. This uses the dynamic range of the MRS as the worst case criterion. An additional distance measure was also run at 30 dB down from the peak to more appropriately compare the LPCS and SS measures over their full range. There should be little difference in the distance measures for the MRS after its dynamic range limit at 16 dB. The quiet and noise spectra are displayed for the MRS at 16 dB down from the peak while the LPCS and SS are displayed at 30 dB down from their peak.

The results of signal analysis for these dynamic ranges for the same signal in quiet and noise are presented in figs. 1-6. Figure 1 shows the LPCS result for the syllable in quiet demonstrating an initial peak around 1500 Hz (which is characteristic of velar stops) followed by a lower-energy portion of the frication in the stop consonant and vowel transition (the diphone) followed by the predominantly low-frequency high-energy of the vowel. A similar pattern is also evident in fig. 3 showing the MRS response but in this case there is a decrease in the dynamic range of the signal as a result of the nonlinearities introduced in the processing of the model. The SS which was designed to enhance the formants by emphasising signals with synchronous output is shown in fig. 5. As predicted, the output shows an increase in the dynamic range of the spectral peaks compared to the MRS.

The LPCS of the same signal in noise is presented in fig. 2. By comparing this result with fig. 1 it is possible to see the spectral peaks of the speech but there is considerable interference from other peaks introduced by the noise. It should be noted here that limiting the dynamic range included in the comparison between the quiet and noise conditions should capture the main speech peaks without also including the lower energy peaks produced by the noise. A similar conclusion can be reached by comparing the analyses from the SS in quiet and noise in figs. 5 and 6.

3.2 Distance metric evaluation

The results for the distance measure are presented in Table 1. These results suggest that the LPCS and SS results produce low EDM and ITAE measures at the very compressed dynamic range compared to the MRS. The results also show that as the dynamic range increases over which the distances are measured there is a predictable increase in the EDM for the

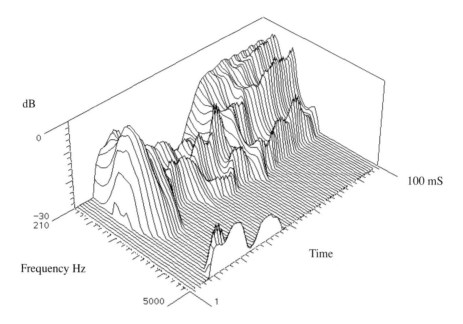

Fig. 1   LPCS analysis of 'clean.dip'.

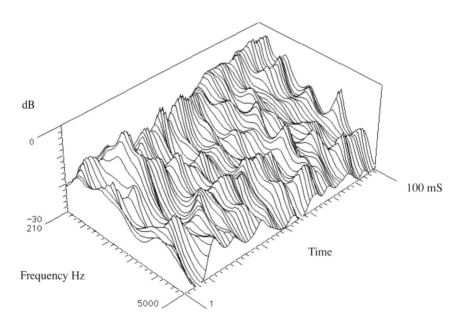

Fig. 2   LPCS analysis of 'dirty.dip'.

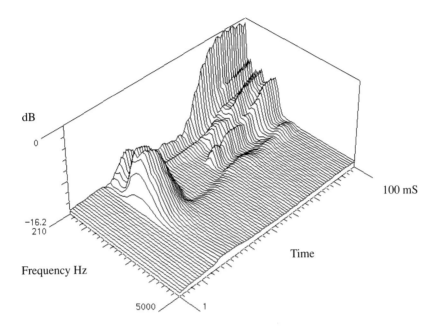

Fig. 3   Seneff model MRS of 'clean.dip'.

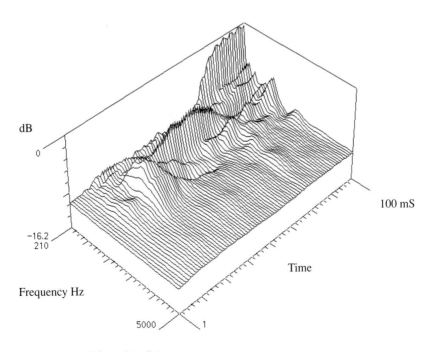

Fig. 4   Seneff model MRS of 'dirty.dip'.

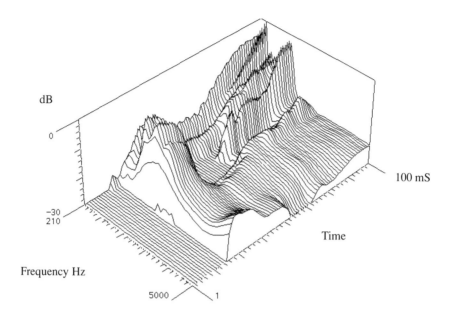

Fig. 5   Seneff model SS of 'clean.dip'.

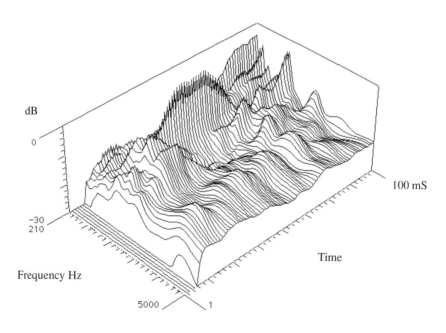

Fig. 6   Seneff model SS of 'dirty.dip'.

Table 1

DR	EDM			ITAE		
	LPCS	MRS	SS	LPCS	MRS	SS
16	1.9	3.9	1.8	9.4	4.1	6.7
30	28.6	167.3	28.0	367.7	169.9	148.8

LPCS and SS but not for the MRS which was at its limit at the 16 dB dynamic range comparison. The difference in the EDM for the LPCS and SS over the 30 dB dynamic range suggests that the SS produces less variability for signals presented in quiet and noise and this conclusion is supported by the ITAE result which indicates that there is less variability in contiguous samples for the SS compared to the LPCS.

4 DISCUSSION

The results of the comparative evaluation of the performance of the analysis methods suggest that the mean rate spectrum produces the most variance between the analysis of speech in quiet and noise conditions while there is only a small difference between the LPC based spectrum and the synchrony spectrum produced from the auditory model. A direct contrast of these analyses seems valid because in this study an effort was made to contrast the different outputs using identical frequency, gain, frame rate and dynamic range for the different analysis outputs on the same speech samples. It should follow that the differences in distance metrics represent real differences in the performance of the techniques.

One issue arising from this study is that the choice of the dynamic range of the auditory representation seems critical. For instance, presumably small spectral distances could be achieved from any analysis method that only included one or two spectral peaks. In other words, if the dynamic range of the representation is too restricted then most analyses might perform fairly well. In the present study the LPCS and SS perform better when only their peaks are included in the comparison. On the other hand, if the full dynamic range of each representation is used then models with a large dynamic range could be disadvantaged because of more chance for increased variability in the spectral analyses over different conditions. As more dynamic range is included in the comparison in the case of LPCS and SS there is a corresponding increase in the variability from quiet to noise conditions. This suggests that the MRS representation may have only limited application because of its severely limited dynamic range.

The present study supports the use of a distance measure on the spectra across different speech in noise conditions as a method for establishing the relative performance of speech analysis methods. Future studies need to provide additional metrics for the differences in the outputs across different signal-to-noise conditions, and to determine the effects of differences in spectrum compression on application requirements for speech processing. The issue of what compression is used in auditory representations may prove to be a critical one and it should be noted that a recent study by Thurston & Norris [8] shows that the representations produced by an auditory model and standard analysis yielded equivalent speech recognition results when the compression of the spectra of the two outputs was matched.

Acknowledgements: We would like to thank Stephanie Seneff for making her model available to us for use in the evaluations and Daniel Woo for his cubic spline interpolation program.

REFERENCES

[1] J. Cohen (1989), 'Applications of an auditory model to speech recognition', *JASA*, **85**, 2623-2629

[2] M. P. Cooke (forthcoming), *Modelling Auditory Processing and Organisation*, Cambridge University Press, Cambridge, UK.

[3] R. Dorf (1980) *Modern Control Systems*, Addison-Wesley, Reading, MA, 124-127

[4] F. Fink & P. Dalsgaard (1989), 'Estimation of formants in noise corrupted speech using auditory models', *Proc. EUROSPEECH '89*, Vol. 2, 677-679.

[5] O. Ghitza (1986), 'Auditory nerve representations as a front-end for speech recognition in a noisy environment, *Computer Speech and Language*, **1**, 109-130.

[6] S. Seneff (1985), 'Pitch and spectral estimation of speech based on an auditory synchrony model', *RLE Technical Report no. 504 Massachusetts Institute of Technology.*

[7] S. Seneff (1988), 'A joint synchrony/mean-rate model of auditory speech processing', *J. Phonetics*, **16**, 55-76.

[8] P. Thurston & D. Norris (1991), 'A comparison of two compression functions used for noisy vowel detection with back-propagation networks', *Proc. EUROSPEECH '91*,Vol. 2, 995-998.

Segmentation by means of temporal decomposition

P.J. Dix and G. Bloothooft

1 INTRODUCTION

Speech can be described as a sequence of distinct articulatory gestures towards and away from articulatory targets, resulting in a sequence of speech events. Since the articulatory system is rather slow, these movements overlap in time. Temporal decomposition (TD), introduced by Atal [1] in 1983, models this overlap by decomposing a time-sequence of speech parameters into a series of time-overlapping interpolation functions and an associated series of data vectors. TD shows a high correspondence between number and positions of the interpolation functions and the phonetic events present in the speech signal. Since it is a speech coding scheme as well, there is an interesting interplay between analysis and synthesis of the speech signal. TD is based on the assumption that the effects of articulatory movements from one articulatory target towards the next are sufficiently slow to be linearly approximated. The overlapping interpolation functions may be seen as expressing the effects of coarticulation reflected in the particular parameterisation employed. Following Atal's notation, a time-sequence of speech data vectors $y(n)$ is linearly approximated by a series of time-overlapping so-called phi functions $\phi_k(n)$ and an associated series of so-called target vectors a_k:

$$y(n) \approx y^*(n) \equiv \sum_{k=1}^{K} a_k \phi_k(n) \quad 1 \le n \le N. \tag{1}$$

In this formula, N equals the number of frames in the given utterance, K is supposed to be approximately equal to the number of speech events in the given utterance, and $y^*(n)$ denotes the approximation of the observed speech data vector $y(n)$ (see fig. 1). We can link segmentation of speech with TD if we associate a segment $[m,n]$ with a rectangular-shaped phi function given by:

$$\phi(r) = \begin{cases} 1 & r \in [m,n] \\ 0 & elsewhere. \end{cases} \tag{2}$$

Thus, TD can be viewed as a generalisation of segmentation, allowing for a more gradual transition from one event towards the next instead of an abrupt division into segments. We have devised a more robust interpolation scheme for TD [3], giving it a geometrical interpretation as an analysis procedure which approximates a path in parameter space by means of straight line segments (see fig. 2). The underlying idea is to have the ending points of the straight line segments correspond to phonetic events and to have the phi functions describe an interpolation between these points. The movement along a straight line segment usually will be non-uniform. Typically, the movement at the ends will be slower than in the middle of the line segment, since the speech signal will be more or less steady at the ending points. The connection between the events found by TD and phonetic events present in the speech signal is somewhat loose. Usually, phonetic events are linked to phonemes, and segmentation of speech is associated with a division of the speech signal into intervals that correspond to phonemes. TD employs a more informal definition of a phonetic event: any distinctive part

Visual Representations of Speech Signals: Martin Cooke, Steve Beet and Malcolm Crawford (eds.)
© 1993 by John Wiley & Sons Ltd

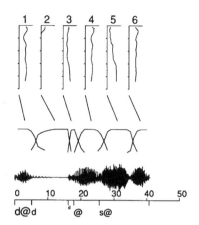

Fig. 1   Example of interpolation by means of temporal decomposition. The phi functions are drawn directly above the oscillogram. The target vectors, in this case filterbank output energies, are drawn at the top. The word that was spoken is /d@d@s@/.

Fig. 2   Our algorithm approximates the path in parameter space as described by the sequence of speech parameters $y(n)$ by means of straight line segments. At the positions of the ending points the actual path $y(n)$ and the approximated path $y^*(n)$ intersect.

of the speech signal fits the definition. This means that in general the number of segments will be larger than the number of phonemes. Evaluation of our algorithm on 660 sentences taken from the TIMIT database gave 5.6% deletions and 34% more interpolation functions than the number of phonemic labels.

2   EXPERIMENTAL RESULTS ON SHEFFIELD DATA

2.1 Segmentation

In order to assess TD's segmentation results, a manual segmentation of the 'clean' sentence "Fred can go, Susan can't go and Linda is uncertain" was made. This segmentation was made on the basis of visual inspection of the oscillogram, auditory feedback, and a spectrogram. The results of this manual segmentation are presented in Table 1. For comparison, segmentations by the ACCOR team (Nicolaidis *et al.* [4]) and Cosi [2] are given as well. Segments from TD were taken equal to the point of intersection of neighbouring phi functions. A simple straight line interpolation procedure was used for this purpose. We may note that, aside from the number, the segment boundaries of the three manual segmentations are usually fairly equally set. Comparison of our own manual segmentation — which is very much in line with the one made by Cosi — and the TD segment boundaries shows that TD has some trouble with plosives: the /g/ starting at 771 ms is missed and the /tcl,g/ pair starting at 1807 ms is taken as a whole. This is probably due to their short duration. With respect to the ACCOR data, TD's segmentation results would be somewhat worse. Most notably the /r/ in 'Fred' and the /n/ in 'and' are missed if we take the ACCOR segmentation as a reference. However, we feel it is fair to say that, except for the two missed plosives, TD got all of the reliable boundaries.

2.2 Influence of noise on TD segmentation.

One can make some general remarks about the influence of noise at the segmental level. Let us define speech segments as acoustically distinctive parts of the signal (for the moment forgetting about any classification). Since noise affects the parameterisation and since the distinctiveness of a segment is related to some metric based on this parameterisation, noise may introduce both insertions and deletions. This introduction of insertions and deletions is very much dependent on the SNR. A high SNR level should have little effect at the segmental level because of continuity properties of both parameterisation and metric. For low SNR levels, a distinction between stationary noise and isolated noise seems appropriate. Essentially, isolated noises are on the same lines as speech, and there is no reason to treat such noises any differently from speech itself. Thus, isolated noise is likely to introduce both insertions and deletions (a deletion results if segments are drowned in noise). Ideally, stationary noise should not introduce insertions (but it may cause deletions). As for the noise added to the clean sentence, we would say it is reasonably stationary and should cause few insertions. In order to get a comparison at different levels of noise we constructed two additional degraded sentences besides the one distributed. A clean sentence was constructed by dividing all samples of clean.wav by a factor two. The prerecorded noise was recovered by subtracting this 'clean' sentence from the 'dirty' sentence. The following sentences were made:

'clean.wav'/2 + α * prerecorded noise; $\alpha = 0.1, 0.5,$ and 1.0.

We note that:

- The first degraded sentence (0.1 times the original noise level) has four phi functions less than the clean sentence, which however causes only one deletion (/d/ starting at 2283 ms). Overall, the results of the analysis seem to be reasonably stable for this small noise level.

- The second degraded sentence (0.5 times the original noise level) has two additional deletions: the /@,n/ pair at 1377 ms is taken as a whole and the same holds for the /kcl,k/ pair at 1483 ms. Funnily enough, the phi function at the position of the /d/ at 2283 ms reappears, which is probably a lucky coincidence.

- The third degraded sentence (same as the 'dirty.wav' sentence) has another deletion: the /n,tcl,g/ triple at 1741 ms is taken as a whole.

It is somewhat difficult to arrive at any conclusions on the basis of a single sentence, but it seems that plosives are more susceptible to corruption than other phones. Because of their lower sound level this could be expected beforehand. We may tentatively conclude that TD seems reasonably stable with respect to adding of moderate noise for phones other than plosives (but once again: it is just a single sentence and one particular type of noise).

REFERENCES

[1] B.S. Atal (1983), 'Efficient coding of LPC parameters by temporal decomposition', *Proc. ICASSP '83 (Boston)*, 81-84.

[2] P. Cosi, 'Auditory modelling for speech analysis and recognition', chapter 18, this volume.

[3] P.J. Dix & G. Bloothooft, 'A break-point analysis procedure based on temporal decomposition', submitted to *IEEE Trans. on Signal Processing*.

[4] K. Nicolaidis, W.J. Hardcastle, A. Marchal & N. Nguygen-Trong, 'Comparing phonetic, articulatory, acoustic and aerodynamic signal representations', chapter 3, this volume.

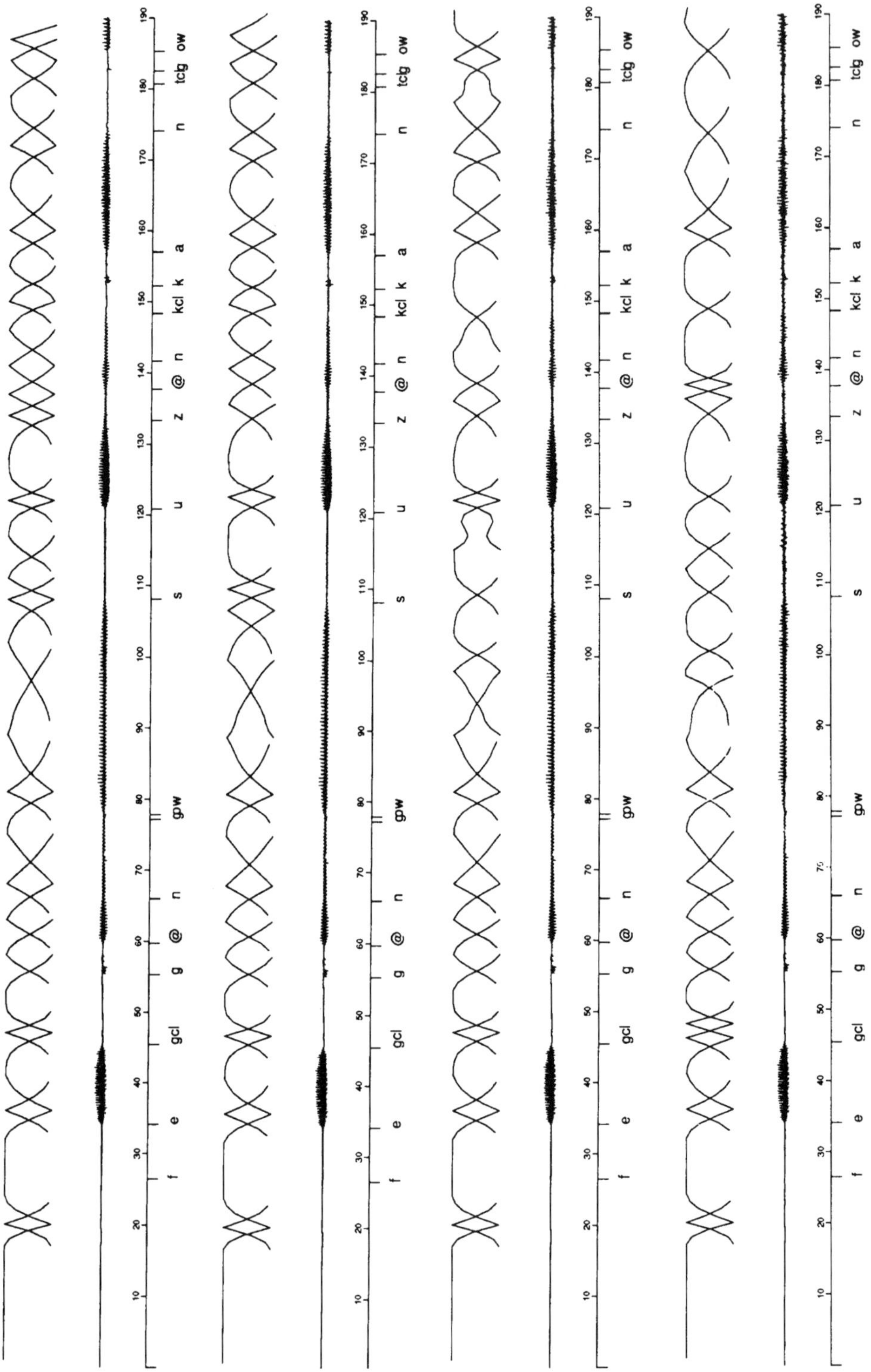
f e gcl g @ n gpw s u z @ n kcl k a n tclg ow

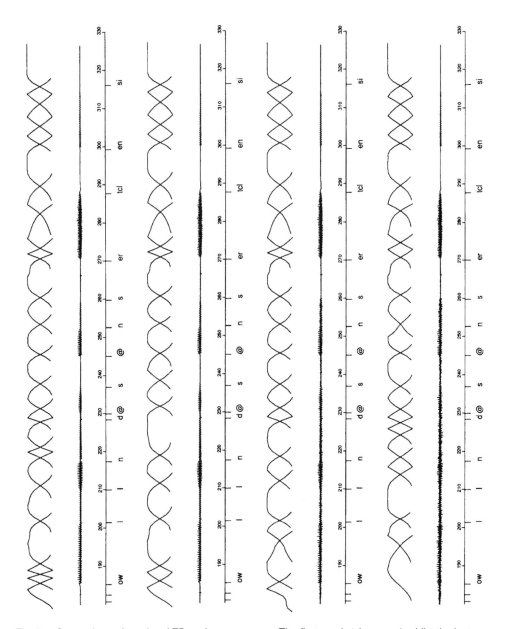

Fig. 3 Comparison of results of TD on four sentences. The first one is 'clean.wav', whilst the last one is 'dirty.wav'. In between are two additional degraded sentences, constructed in order to get a comparison at different levels of noise.

**Table 1: Comparison of three different manual segmentations of 'clean.wav'
("Fred can go, Susan can't go and Linda is uncertain") and TD segmentation results.**

Dix and Bloothooft		Nicolaidis *et al.*		Cosi		TD
	-		-		-	191
f	265	f	265	f	269	212
	-	r	303		-	-
e	341	ε	350	@(+/u/?)	341	346
	-		-		-	375
gcl	454	gok	451	k	453	457
	-		-		-	480
g	552	h	551			557
@	597	ə	597	e(/e~/)	600	609
n	659	ŋ	663	N	659	662
	-		-		-	710
g	771	g	762	g	737	-
			772		-	-
ow	778	əʊ	786	A	788	794
	-		-		-	836
	-		-	e(/Ae/)	940	966
	-		1073		-	1064
s	1081	s	1085	s	1081	1095
	-		-		-	1140
u	1208	u	1211	}	1210	1209
	-		-		-	1234
z	1333	z	1322	z	1338	1326
	-		-		-	1354
@	1377	ə	1389	@(/@~/)	1378	1387
n	1417	ŋ	1422	N	1423	1436
kcl	1483	k	1486	k	1488	1488
k	1523	h	1525		-	1525
a	1570	ɑ	1571	A(/A~/)	1575	1582
	-		-		-	1624
	-		-		-	1704
n	1741	ŋ	1747	N	1740	1745
tcl	1807	k	1797	k	1808	1813
g	1825	h	1825		-	-
ow	1852	ə:	1852	6(/6U/)	1855	1857
	-		-		-	1880
	-		-		-	1907
l	2013	n	2012	l	2014	2019
	-	l	2051		-	-
I	2099	I	2097	I(/I~/)	2102	2111
n	2173	n	2178	n	2179	2185
d	2283	d	2270	d	2282	2279
	-	z	2280		-	-
@	2299	ə	2301	@	2305	2314
s	2368	s	2368	s(/z/)	2377	2379
			2432		-	-
@	2450	ə	2449	V(/V~/)	2452	2456
n	2526	n	2524		-	2535
s	2597		2596	s	2599	-
	-	s	2607		-	2606
er	2700	ə	2707	@(/@:/)	2704	2707
	-		-		-	2735
	-		-		-	2825
tcl	2877	t	2877	?	2877	2898
	-	n0	2953		-	-
en	2992	n1	2997	n	2999	3008
	-		-		-	3114
sil	3160	sil	3161	sil	3164	3158

Speech innovation characterisation by higher-order moments

23

Alessandro Falaschi and Ivo Tidei

1 INTRODUCTION

It is well known that the speech signal can be regarded as a random process which is only locally stationary. The boundaries between different speech events, where two processes with a different statistical description meet, can be considered as the places where the linguistic *innovation* operates (i.e. where an intentional driving phenomenon inserts linguistic information into the acoustic wave). This occurs when one of the following two phenomena holds: either the closure of the glottis interrupts the glottal flow, or an abrupt change in the vocal tract area places a boundary between two different phonemes. These two kinds of discontinuity (which in the following will be referred to as the glottal and syllabic innovations) can be detected by using statistical indicators operating on different analysis window-lengths for the two onset types, i.e. allowing the proper time resolution accuracy. In fact, during transients, the speech signal diverges significantly from a Gaussian assumption: this fact is exemplified in fig. 1, where a discontinuity is shown, together with the global probability density function (PDF) obtained as the mixture of the PDFs of the constituent processes. As a Gaussian process is completely described by its first- and second-order statistics, knowledge of the higher-order moments (HOM) in the non-Gaussian case adds more information to the process description. In particular, the deviation of the HOM estimate from the values obtained in the Gaussian case constitutes a cue for locating abrupt changes in the signal statistics. Discontinuities, or onsets, of the speech wave can thus be detected adopting an hypothesis verification strategy, based on short-term estimates of the first four moments.

Fig. 1   When the analysis window contains two different events, the mixture PDF (solid line) may diverge from a Gaussian assumption.

2 HIGHER-ORDER MOMENTS

Let x be a random process, defined through its PDF, $p(x) = p(x_1, x_2, ...x_n)$, which asserts the probability of observing a set of realisations of the random variable x, taken at the set of instants $(t_1, t_2, ..., t_n)$. The nth-order moment is defined as

Visual Representations of Speech Signals: Martin Cooke, Steve Beet and Malcolm Crawford (eds.)
© 1993 by John Wiley & Sons Ltd

$$m^{(n)}(1, 2, ..., n) = \mathrm{E}\{x_1, x_2, ..., x_n\}$$
$$= \int x_1\, x_2\, ...x_n\, p(x_1, x_2, \ ..., x_n)\, dx_1\, dx_2\, ...dx_n \tag{1}$$

which, for zero-mean processes, coincide with the central moments. If a given process is stationary and ergodic, expectations may be replaced by time averages. These assumptions do not hold during transitional events, but they may be fairly approximated during steady state speech events. Moreover, if we are solely interested in the shape of the process PDF, we only require the zero lag moments:

$$m^{(n)} = \mathrm{E}\{x^n\} = \frac{1}{-j2\pi}\frac{d^n}{dy^n}P(y)|_{y=0} \tag{2}$$

where $P(y)$ is the Fourier transform of the process PDF $p(x)$, i.e. the characteristic function of the process, and the expectation spans over the analysis window, assuming that the stationarity hypothesis holds true. If x is a Gaussian process with zero mean and variance σ^2, so that $P(y) = e^{-2(\pi\sigma y)^2}$ one can obtain:

$$m^{(n)} = (n-1)\,\sigma^2\, m^{(n-2)} \tag{3}$$

so that the HOMs are completely defined by knowledge of $m^{(1)}$ and $m^{(2)} = \sigma^2$. The zero-mean hypothesis gives $m^{(n)} = 0$ for n odd, while for n even it is easily seen that the relation $m^{(n)} = 1 \times 3 \times ... \times (n-1)\sigma^n$ holds.

In the following, we estimate the third and fourth moments over rectangular windows of speech, spanning N samples, and then we normalise the result with respect to the variance estimate. The features used for subsequent classification purposes are thus defined as:

$$\Upsilon = \frac{N\sum\limits_{i=1}^{N} x(i)^4}{\left(\sum\limits_{i=1}^{N} x(i)^2\right)^2} \qquad \chi = \frac{\sqrt{N}\sum\limits_{i=1}^{N} x(i)^3}{\left(\sum\limits_{i=1}^{N} x(i)^2\right)^{1.5}} \tag{4}$$

which are unbiased estimates of the quantities known as, respectively, the *kurtosis* and the *skewness* of x. While the skewness takes a null value for any symmetrical distribution, the kurtosis is exactly 3 for Gaussian variates, smaller than 3 if $p(x)$ has small tails, and greater than 3 if not. The estimation window length N should be defined as a trade-off between different conditions. Large windows are required to minimise the estimate variance, and short windows are required for keeping temporal resolution comparable with the phenomena under investigation.

3   GLOTTAL INNOVATION

Figure 2 gives the $5\log_{10}(\Upsilon/3)$ and χ values for the syllables 'timit.syl' and 'spont.syl'. These analyses show the high sensitivity of the measure to additive noise, confirmed by comparison of figs. 3 and 4. Figure 3 reports the values $5\log_{10}(\Upsilon/3)$ and χ, evaluated for different choices of window length, for the diphone 'clean.dip' utterance. The periodic ripple of these values is clearly related to the pitch period, but its visualisation is heavily dependent on the window length. Figure 4 shows the result for 'dirty.wav'. It is evident that the estimates are no longer able to accurately locate the same events.

4   SYLLABIC INNOVATION

In this case we are looking at events which span a somewhat larger time-frame, so larger windows must be used in order to smooth the glottal innovation contribution. Figure 5 displays the $5\log_{10}(\Upsilon/3)$ and χ values, evaluated with an 80 ms running window on 'timit.wav'. A fairly good segmentation of the signal into syllabic events can be observed. The same analysis has been performed on 'spont.wav' (fig. 6), and the weakness of the proposed cues in presence of additive noise is again shown. Figure 7 compares the estimates obtained for different window lengths, and emphasises the high variance estimate which arises for short windows. Finally, fig. 8 confirms the reduced performance in presence of noise.

5   A COMBINED FEATURE

In order to jointly consider the information given by the log-kurtosis and the skewness, a combined feature as been defined as

$$CF\,(\zeta)\ =\ (\zeta - m_\zeta)^T \Sigma_\zeta^{-1}\,(\zeta - m_\zeta) \tag{5}$$

where ζ is a column vector whose two components are given by the log-kurtosis and the skewness estimates, m_ζ is its mean value, and Σ_ζ is its covariance matrix (whose elements are defined as $\sigma_{ij} = E\{\,(\zeta_i - m_{\zeta i})\,(\zeta_j - m_{\zeta j})\,\}$), when a stationarity hypothesis holds. In order to compute $CF\,(\zeta)$, m_ζ and Σ_ζ must be estimated, as follows:

   i   Estimate m_ζ and Σ_ζ on the all the speech material.
   ii   Fix a threshold α^2.
   iii   Make a new estimate of m_ζ and Σ_ζ based only on those frames with $CF\,(\zeta) < \alpha^2$.
   iv   If the latter estimate differs from the former, go to step iii.
   v   Exit.

We adopted such procedure on a database of 540 isolated words, uttered by a single speaker. A reasonable choice for the threshold is $2 < \alpha^2 < 3$. Figure 9a reports the behaviour of $CF\,(\zeta)$ for 'clean.wav', with m_ζ and Σ_ζ estimated on the single-speaker database. As is evident, no real improvement seems to emerge. Then, we estimated m_ζ and Σ_ζ on the four Sheffield signals. The following table reports the results found for the two cases:

	540 words, single speaker		Four phrases	
m_ζ	0.36	0.02	0.21	0.40
Σ_ζ	0.39	-0.02	0.67	0.19
	-0.02	0.05	0.19	0.21

As is evident, a higher variance is found if statistics are evaluated for very different conditions. Figure 9 reports the behaviour of the $CF\,(\zeta)$ when the latter m_ζ and Σ_ζ estimates are used. The result found for the 'timit' phrase seems to be particularly good, as syllabic boundaries are clearly detected. The other files behave a little worse, either because of reduced bandwidth in the case of 'clean', or because of superimposed noise ('dirty' and 'spont').

6   CONCLUSIONS

The work presented here extends some previous experiments [1] where the invariance of the higher-order moments estimate with respect to a whitening of the speech wave has been demonstrated. At present, utilisation of HOM has been extended to localisation of the glottal innovation process. A method for segmenting speech in syllabic events, on the basis of the joint consideration of the first four moments has been demonstrated, together with a simple algorithm for estimating the parameters of this classifier. Finally, a larger variance has been found when analysing a few multi-speaker and multi-condition recordings, than when a large single-speaker database is considered.

REFERENCE

[1]   G. Jacovitti, P. Pierucci & A.Falaschi (1991), 'Speech segmentation and classification using higher order moments', *Proc. EUROSPEECH '91 (Genova)*.

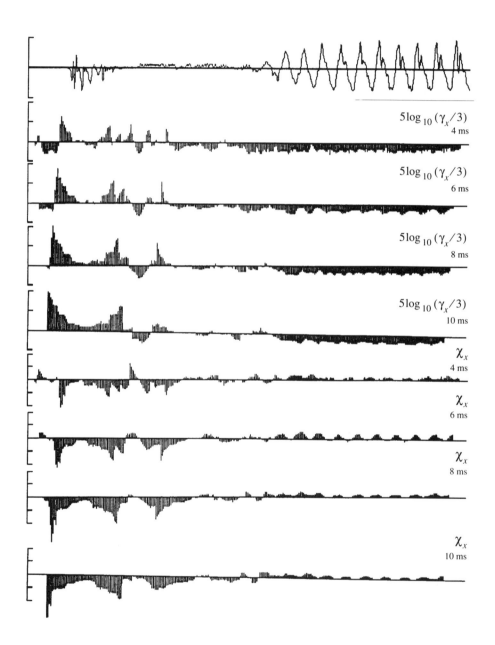

Fig. 2   'clean.dip': log-kurtosis and skewness estimates using different window lengths.

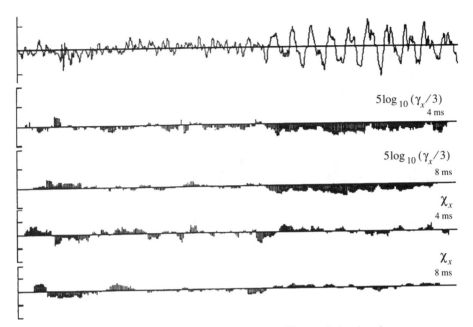

$$5\log_{10}(\gamma_x/3)$$
$$4 \text{ ms}$$

$$5\log_{10}(\gamma_x/3)$$
$$8 \text{ ms}$$

$$\chi_x$$
$$4 \text{ ms}$$

$$\chi_x$$
$$8 \text{ ms}$$

Fig. 3   'dirty.dip': log-kurtosis and skewness estimates using different window lengths.

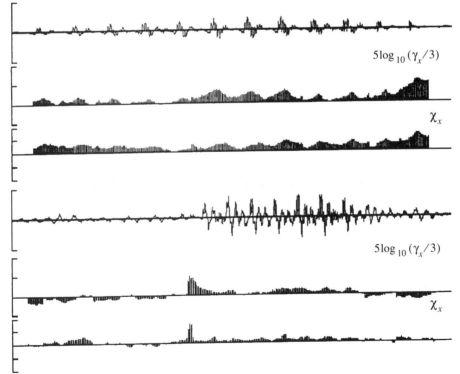

$$5\log_{10}(\gamma_x/3)$$

$$\chi_x$$

$$5\log_{10}(\gamma_x/3)$$

$$\chi_x$$

Fig. 4   *upper panels* : 'timit.dip'; *lower panels* : 'spont.dip': log-kurtosis and skewness estimate using a 10 ms window.

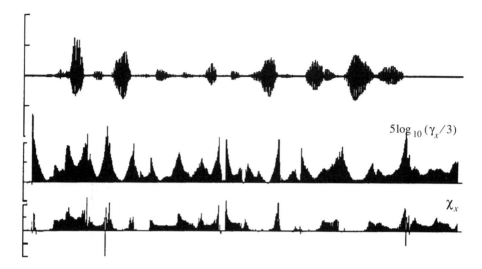

Fig. 5   'timit.wav': log-kurtosis and skewness estimates evaluated using a 80 ms window.

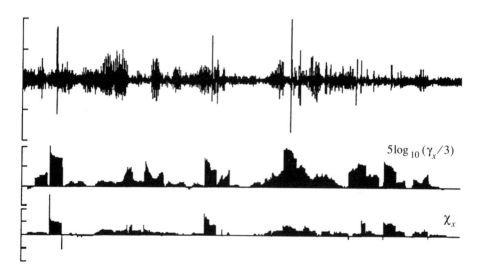

Fig. 6   'spont.wav': log-kurtosis and skewness estimates evaluated using a 80 ms window.

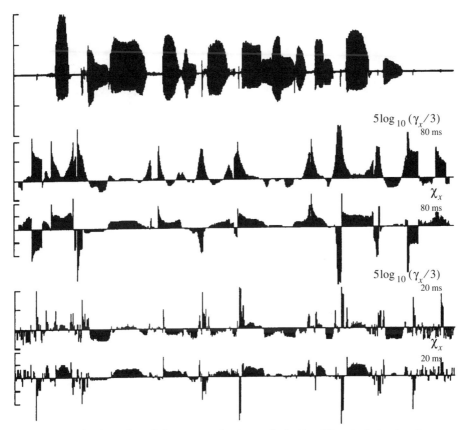

Fig. 7   'clean.wav': log-kurtosis and skewness estimates evaluated for different window lengths.

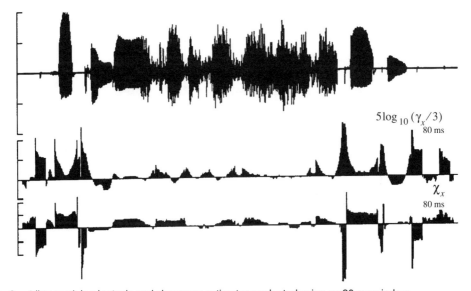

Fig. 8   'dirty.wav': log-kurtosis and skewness estimates evaluated using an 80 ms window.

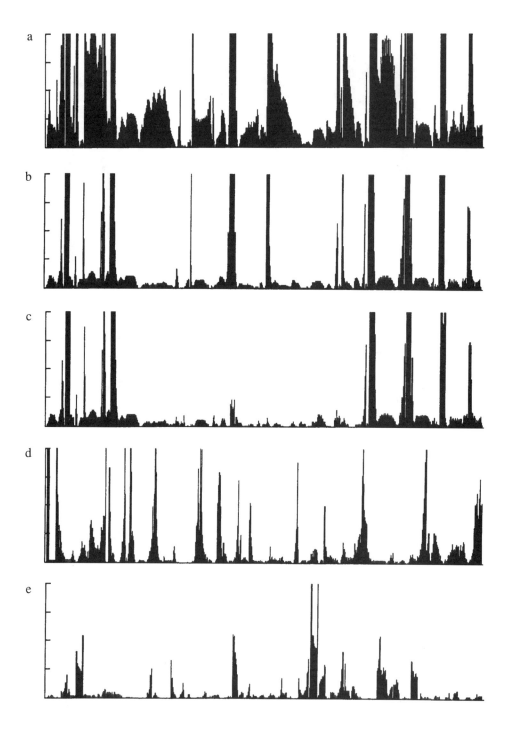

Fig. 9   Combined feature behaviour: in each case, the quantities m_ζ, and Σ_ζ estimated a :
'clean.wav', estimated on 540 words; b-e : 'clean.wav', 'dirty.wav', 'timit.wav'and 'spont.wav'
respectively, all estimated on the Sheffield '.wav' signals.

Distortion maps for speech analysis

M. Falcone, S. Ragazzini and A. Paoloni

24

1 INTRODUCTION

Several speech analyses are possible when considering the time- and frequency-domain evolution of the speech signal, e.g. formant estimation or tracking and signal labelling (usually in phonetic units or in acoustic sub-units). Both tasks are very hard and may result in a high error rate even if executed by a human expert. Further, if we want to locate particular signal zones, we must first define the properties of these zones, then analyse time and spectral representations from this particular point of view.

Let us consider the most common (and probably powerful) time-frequency representation of speech: the spectrogram. It is a common opinion that a phonetician will be able to locate and classify phonemes by looking at this time-frequency representation, but this fact has not been seriously experimented for clean speech, and no positive results have been claimed for noise-corrupted signals.

We must outline that, first, the choice of time and spectral resolution (or generally speaking of the "image filtering parameters") of the sonograms may mask evidence of important features. This is discussed in depth in Riley [7]. So the first problem is to guess these parameters. A second and more important fact is that spectrogram reading is a hard task for the unskilled reader. For these reasons there have been many attempts (often with disastrous results) to realise expert systems or "intelligent-tools" to perform this task automatically.

The visual analysis of a spectrogram representation obliges the operator (or the automatic system) to consider spectral information locally in the frequency domain. Also, if broadband or frequency smoothings are employed, the information to be processed may be redundant for relatively simple tasks such as segmentation or broad classification. This means that a lot of processing is necessary even for simple tasks. Two important factors arise: if the task is intrinsically simple we must filter the information before any decision is taken; and if a task presents some peculiar difficulties we are tempted to use more information than we are able (or allowed) to analyse. In the most optimistic case (the first one) we are overloaded with useless work; otherwise (the second) we are probably doing something wrong.

One solution to this problem is to represent speech in a more suitable form for the specific problem we are considering, instead of defining rules to be applied in spectrogram reading. In this paper we introduce some bidimensional distortion maps of speech signals, and discuss their properties. A brief analysis to outperform an "acoustic" automatic segmentation of speech is presented.

2 IMAGING THE SPEECH SIGNAL: INTRODUCING DISTORTION MAPS AND "INTEGRAL-IMAGING"

Representing speech means to transform the acoustic pressure signal into a "visible" form. From a purely mathematical point of view we may divide representations thus: mono-dimensional functions of the form $y = f(x)$ (e.g. amplitude-time, energy-time, pitch-time,

Visual Representations of Speech Signals: Martin Cooke, Steve Beet and Malcolm Crawford (eds.)

decibel-frequency waveforms and many others) or bidimensional functions, $z = g(x, y)$, as in the case of spectrograms. In this second representation the plane is filled, as x and y move all along both Cartesian axes, and values of the dependent variable z are represented using colours or a grey scale.

It is common opinion that the "visual" or automatic analysis of an image is more difficult than that of a monodimensional function. This is true in many scientific fields and of course also in voice processing, but this does not mean that a decision over plotting such functions (as we will discuss later) is easier than for images.

Let us consider, for example, the sonogram of the 'clean.wav' speech signal. In our analysis, the FFT is computed on a 0.97 preemphasised signal, Hamming-windowed to 512 points and with a window shift of 128 points. All computation is performed in floating point. The results are in dB and scaled into an arbitrary 256 grey scale, where white is the minimum value of the resulting spectrogram and black is the maximum one. Now, consider a fixed time point. In relation to our ability in spectrogram reading, we will be able to say if speech is voiced, vocalic and so forth. If we are not experienced in spectrogram reading the only result we may derive is that in the image there are some zones that look stable in the time domain. In other words, the image can be divided in the time domain in some particular zones, or acoustic "events". This segmentation does not (necessarily) coincide with a phonetic one, and will have a different level of granularity.

Although it seems a easy task, we will have serious problems in the presence of coarticulation, noise and any time a fine comparison between speech parameterisation must be evaluated over a short or long time interval. In this case we may reduce the information along the frequency domain to a scalar quantity, i.e. we may realise an integral representation reducing one dimension of the spectrogram map by computing the distortion (or the distance) of the parameterisation at time $t(n)$ in relation to a different time $t(x)$. This introduces a new dimension because the distortion is computed at each time all along the duration of the signal. So we are back again into an image with both x and y axes representing the time domain, while z (the grey scale) is the distortion value.

This method, introduced in [3], may be seen as a variation of such segmentation techniques [1,2] based on a fixed delay T in the distortion computation $d(n,T)$ that reduces the original representation to a monodimensional function, instead of a continuous $d(n,T)$ map. For a "simple" segmentation task we just analyse the distortion maps in a neighbourhood of the reference point (along the diagonal of the map), but a wider and deeper analysis will reveal more characteristics of the speech signal, of the parameterisation and distortion measure used.

Distortion maps may also be used as "visual" tools for the analysis and comparison of speech parameterisations, or for the analysis of robustness of such parameters, as an alternative to more formal and analytic methodologies [4] dedicated to this task. We call these maps "integral-image" because of the integration and relative loss of local information along a dimension (in the previous example the frequency).

3   COMPUTING THE SPEECH PARAMETERS (THE ESTIMATION PROBLEM)

The parameters we chose in our analysis were mainly derived from linear predictive coding (LPC) theory. Using the autocorrelation formulation of the problem, and Durbin's recursive solution [6] to minimise the mean squared error between the speech segment and the output of the predictor, we found the LPC coefficients of the all-pole model.

The order of the model was set to 12 and the LPC analysis was performed like the FFT one, as described in the previous section. In this way the two spectral representations are comparable.

Directly from the LPC coefficients we obtained other parameters useful for a characterisation of the speech signal, viz. reflection coefficients and vocal tract areas that are strictly related to each other.

To perform a cepstral analysis, on a mel frequency scale, the discrete fourier transform (DFT) was calculated from the speech signal, then the transformed samples were filtered by a filterbank of triangular filters, linearly distributed in frequency up to 1 kHz and logarithmically above 1 kHz [5]. From the filter outputs eight cepstrum coefficients were computed.

The parameterisations analysed are: narrowband spectra, autocorrelations, reflection coefficients, linear predictive coefficients, residual LPC vector, vocal tract area, mel cepstrum and LPC spectrum estimate. At this stage we prefer not to use quantities derived from "estimation" algorithms such as pitch, formants and so forth. For such quantities results are determined by choice of algorithm and thresholds.

4   REPRESENTING 'CLEAN' AND 'DIRTY' USING DISTORTION MAPS

For our analysis we look for pieces of signal having the following characteristics: duration long enough to include more than syllabic and single-word events; short enough to fit the image of the phonetic events into an appropriate space; the signal completely includes the corrupted zone of the 'dirty.wav' file. We found the segments 'clean.syl' and 'dirty.syl' had these properties. Note that all maps are intrinsically square.

Starting from the speech parameterisation discussed in the previous section, we computed the Euclidean distance maps for each single parameter; in addition we also compute the distortion maps for the log likelihood measure, a variation of Itakura-Saito distortion (see fig. 1). We have a total of nine maps for each signal file; some of these are reported in figs. 2-4.

A qualitative 'visual' analysis of these maps reveals the following facts:

- the dynamics of the distortion value are very important and are obvious in the contrast of the map;
- some parameterisations (vocal tract and mel cepstrum) show behaviour dramatically worse than others in terms of their dynamics;
- some parameters give very informative maps (LPC residual); and
- maps, i.e. parameters, may be classified in relation to the precise location of specific zones.

For example, in 'clean.syl', the spectrum (from the signal and from LPC), reflection and LPC coefficients seem to form a class, while autocorrelations and LPC residual seem to have the same behaviour.

All analyses are presented in their "natural" form, i.e. no filtering or processing of the images. Of course, other characteristics may be outlined by image processing. Generally speaking it is also possible to map cross-distortion maps between two signals (aligned using DTW or similar techniques).

5   ANALYSIS AND RESULTS

All the maps were searched for stability zones. For this purpose we set four different thresholds calculated specifically for each map, depending on the minimum and mean values of the distances in the whole map. Starting from the element on the main diagonal of the map, we can define a stability zone when we find that all the elements of this zone are lower than the chosen threshold. We define a right and a left boundary simply by moving from the starting point and searching the stability zone along each column of the map. The information on these local boundaries is stored up after each column analysis in order to obtain bidimensional information, so at the end of the procedure we have four (one for each threshold) sequences that tell us how many bidimensional stability zones we can find in the map. As the results found in this way were dependent on the chosen threshold, we attempted to find more global

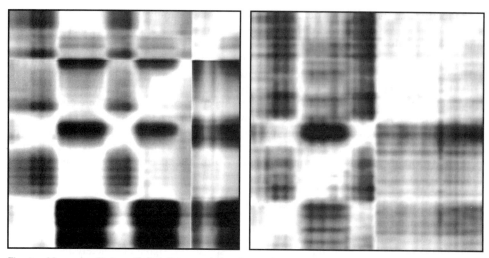

Fig. 1   Map using "Itakura-Saito" distance: *left* : 'clean.syl', *right* : 'dirty.syl'.

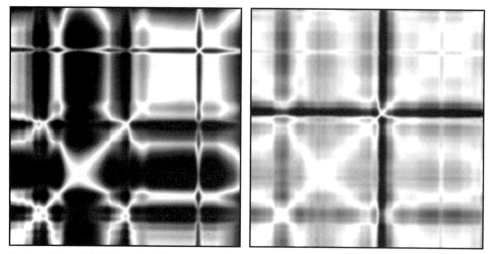

Fig. 2   Map using LPC residual distance: *left* : 'clean.syl', *right* : 'dirty.syl'.

information by correlating every pair of sequences. Some results of this analysis are depicted in figs. 5 and 6.

6   CONCLUSION AND FURTHER DEVELOPMENT

We have discussed the problem of 'imaging' speech signal related quantities, and the importance of the integration of features along a spatial dimension in cases where no local information is needed. The problem of locating stable zones (segmentation?) has been faced. The use of mutual distortion or distance measure imaging has been investigated as a tool to analyse properties and robustness of speech parameterisation. In particular we found that distance evolution of very useful, in speech recognition, parameterisations, such as mel cepstrum and vocal tract area, seem not to have informative behaviour in this representation; on the contrary, unexpected parameterisations such as the LPC residual vectors show very interesting characteristics (unfortunately the printed image may not do justice to high resolution

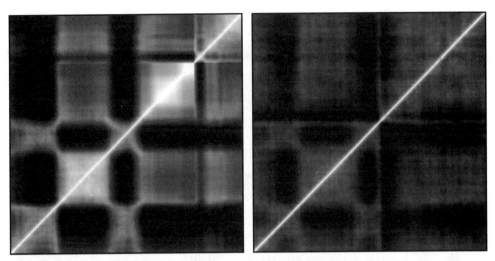

Fig. 3   Map using narrow band FFT distance: *left* : 'clean.syl', *right* : 'dirty.syl'.

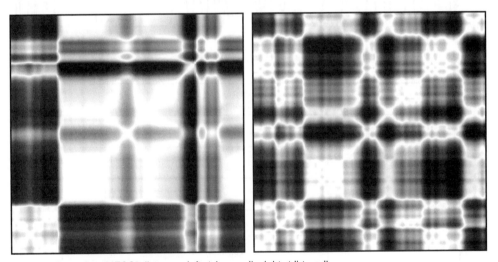

Fig. 4   Map using "MFCC" distance: *left* : 'clean.syl', *right* : 'dirty.syl'.

video images). Future work will process the cross-distortion maps using different distortion evaluation and image processing and filtering to obtain a highlighted vision of specific properties of the speech signal.

REFERENCES

[1] P. Cosi & E. Ferrero (1986), 'The use of spectral distance for speech segmentation', *Proc. RAASR (Roma)*, 137-174.

[2] D. Falavigna & M. Omologo (1990), 'A spectral variation function for acoustic speech segmentation', *Proc. VERBA '90 (Roma)*, 365-372.

[3] M.Falcone & A. Paoloni (1990), 'On the use of spectral shape stability in a phone based segmentation', *Proc. VERBA '90 (Roma)*, 125-132.

[4] M. Falcone & A. Paoloni (1991), 'An acoustical pattern classifier based on n-depth projection on privileged eigenstructures', *Proc. ICASSP '91 (Toronto)*, 3301-3305.

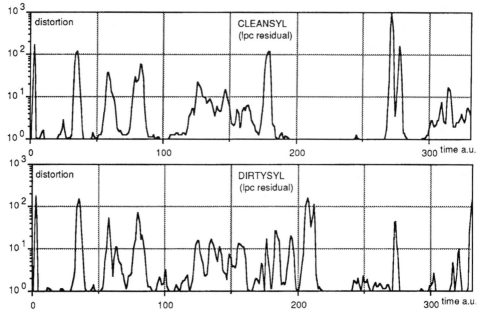

Fig. 5   LPC residual distance measures, 'clean.syl' and 'dirty.syl'.

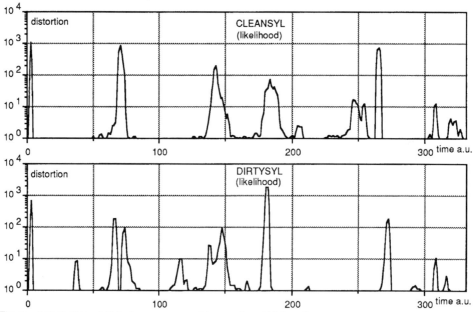

Fig. 6   Log likelihood distortion measures, 'clean.syl' and 'dirty.syl'.

[5] G. Hult & C. Back (1990), 'SAM_REC0 Isolated Word Recogniser', Software Documentation and Users' Manual, *SAM-TVT-003*.

[6] L.R. Rabiner & R.W. Schafer (1978), *Digital Signal Processing of Speech*, Prentice-Hall, Englewood Cliffs, NJ.

[7] M. D. Riley (1989), *Speech Time-Frequency Representations*, Kluwer Academic Publishers, Durdrecht.

Speech analysis using a nonlinear cochlear model with feedback regulation

25

C. Giguère and P.C. Woodland

1 INTRODUCTION

A modular auditory model (AM) has been developed [6] to address two important observations which have been given little attention in speech research. Firstly, there is now ample
experimental evidence that the basilar membrane (BM) motion is highly nonlinear and is a
major source of level compression [8]. The outer hair cells (OHCs) are believed to participate
in this process as mechanical force generators acting on the cochlear partition. Secondly,
there is a complex network of descending paths from the central auditory system (CAS) to
the peripheral ear controlling the processing in the ascending path via feedback loops [3].

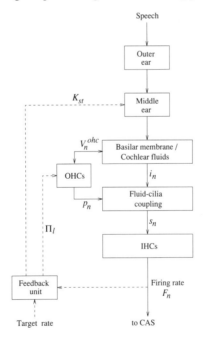

Fig. 1   Block diagram of the peripheral AM.

A block diagram of the AM speech processor is shown in fig. 1. It is closely related to
the physiological mechanisms and anatomical architecture of the peripheral ear. The ascending path of the model is assembled from electroacoustic networks which were selected or
adapted from a set of successful models from the acoustics and hearing research literature
[1,5,9,10,11]. The networks are brought into a unified computational framework using the

Visual Representations of Speech Signals: Martin Cooke, Steve Beet and Malcolm Crawford (eds.)
© 1993 by John Wiley & Sons Ltd

technique of wave digital filtering [4]. This leads to a dual analog/digital representation of the ascending path. A functional feedback unit regulates the average firing rate at the output of the inner hair cell (IHC) module via a simplified modelling of the dynamics of the descending paths. Two feedback systems are considered: the acoustic reflex of the middle ear and the efferent innervation of the OHCs.

2   ASCENDING PATH

2.1 Outer and middle ear

An electroacoustical analogy can be developed for the outer ear if attention is restricted to lateral sound incidence [6]. It consists of a network for the sound diffraction by the head and upper torso in series with a second network for the sound propagation through the concha cavity and auditory canal. The first network is based on Bauer's approximations for the effect of a plane wave striking an acoustical obstacle [1]. The second network is an extension of the transmission line model of Gardner and Hawley [5].

The network of Lutman and Martin [9] was selected for the middle ear module since it incorporates the terminal effect of the acoustic reflex. The stapedial muscle compliance, the contribution of the reflex on this network, is represented by a time-variant capacitor $C_{st}(t) = 1/K_{st}(t)$.

2.2 Basilar membrane and outer hair cells

The BM module is based on the classical transmission line model of cochlear hydrodynamics [11]. The membrane is discretised into $N = 96$ segments of equal length as shown in fig. 2. To establish a correspondence between segment place x_n (mm) and characteristic

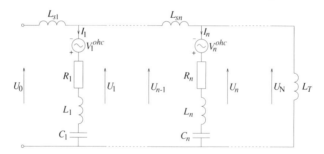

Fig. 2   Transmission line network of the BM-OHCs.

frequency f_n (Hz), the auditory scale of Greenwood [7] is used:

$$x_n = 35 - \frac{1}{0.06}\log\left(\frac{f_n}{165.4} + 1\right).$$
(1)

The end points x_1 and x_N correspond to the maximum f_1 and minimum f_N auditory filter centre frequencies of interest. The passive circuit elements L_{sn}, L_n, C_n and R_n are derived from electroacoustical analogies [6,11].

The force developed by the fast motile mechanism of the OHC cilia bundle [8] is represented by a level-dependent voltage source V_n^{ohc} in each segment as follows:

$$V_n^{ohc}(t) = GR_n\left(\frac{d_{1/2}}{d_{1/2} + |d_n(t)|}\right)I_n(t)$$
(2)

where $G = 0.99$ is a gain factor, $d_n(t)$ is the instantaneous BM displacement and $d_{1/2}$ is a scaling constant. The proportionality of $V_n^{ohc}(t)$ with BM volume velocity $I_n(t)$ ensures that the effect of the OHCs is undamping. The nonlinearity is scaled by assuming that an incident sinusoidal wavefront of 50 dB (SPL) at 1000 Hz is associated with a BM displacement (rms) of $d_{1/2}$ at the place of resonance. The output of the module is the BM particle velocity $i_n(t)$.

Figure 3 is the amplitude response of the BM module as a function of place for a pure-

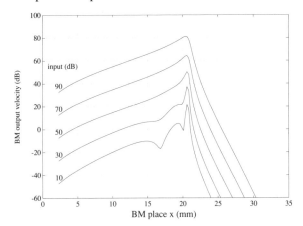

Fig. 3   Amplitude response of the BM-OHC module for a pure-tone of 1000 Hz at different input.

tone of 1000 Hz. At low input levels, the BM is very sharply tuned near the place of resonance ($x \approx 20.6$ mm). At high input levels, the OHC circuit becomes saturated and the BM is more broadly tuned. The gain at resonance is level-dependent. An increase of 80 dB in input level results in a 60 dB increase in output level, a compression of 20 dB.

2.3 Inner hair cells

The three-reservoir model of Meddis *et al.* [10] was selected for the inner hair cell module. A separate IHC is paired to each BM segment using the parameters of a medium-rate fibre. The input $s_n(t)$ to the IHC cilia is assumed to be proportional to the viscous drag of the surrounding fluid, itself a function of BM velocity:

$$s_n(t) \; = \; p i_n(t). \tag{3}$$

The fluid-cilia coupling constant p is scaled to bring the IHC rate and saturation thresholds to 35 and 80 dB respectively. The output of the module is the instantaneous firing rate:

$$F_n(t) \; = \; h c_n(t) \tag{4}$$

where $c_n(t)$ is the cleft contents and h is a constant.

3   DESCENDING PATHS

3.1 Acoustic reflex

The CAS controls the middle ear transmission through a feedback loop, the acoustic reflex (AR). We make the assumption that the reflex is a feedback regulation system [3] whose goal is to maintain the average firing rate constant in the ascending path once it exceeds a threshold. The firing rate $F_n(t)$ is averaged across the entire population of IHCs over non-overlapping detection windows of duration $\delta = 1$ ms. The average firing rate $\bar{F}(\tau)$ $\tau = \delta, 2\delta, 3\delta, \ldots$, is then compared to a target rate F^{ar} of 35 spikes/s representing a high-level command from the CAS to yield a firing rate error function $\Delta(\tau)$:

$$\Delta(t) = F^{ar} - \bar{F}(\tau). \tag{5}$$

$\Delta(\tau)$ is passed through a hard threshold detector to determine the next contraction command $K(\tau)$ to the stapedial muscle:

$$K(\tau)\begin{cases}(0.1\,\mu F)^{-1} & \Delta(\tau) \le 0 \\ 0 & \Delta(\tau) > 0.\end{cases} \tag{6}$$

The gradual build-up of stapedial muscle contraction is approximated by passing $K(\tau)$ into a low-pass filter with a cutoff frequency of 2.5 Hz. The resulting stiffness $K_{st}(\tau)$ is the terminal contribution of the AR on the middle ear network. Maximal stapedial muscle contraction incurs a loss in middle ear transmission below 1000 Hz of up to 15 dB [6].

3.2 Efferent system

The inner ear response is under control of the CAS via the efferent innervation of the OHCs [3,8]. We hypothesise that the control function is achieved by a slow modulation of the spacing between the IHC cilia and the overlying tectoral membrane [2]. In eqn. (3), this amounts to a time- and space-varying fluid-cilia coupling gain $p_n(t)$. We further assume that the goal of the OHC efferent system is to regulate the average firing rate in the ascending path over a limited number of frequency bands. The N output channels of the IHC module are grouped into $L = 4$ contiguous bands, and firing rate regulation is applied independently in each band. The average firing rate, $\bar{F}_l(\tau)$, in band l is then compared to a target rate F^{eff} of 25 spikes/s to yield the firing rate error function $\Delta_l(\tau)$:

$$\Delta_l(\tau) = F^{eff} - \bar{F}_l(\tau). \tag{7}$$

$\Delta_l(\tau)$ is passed through a hard threshold detector to determine the next gain command to the OHCs:

$$P_l(\tau)\begin{cases}-12\,dB\,(re:p) & \Delta_l(\tau) \le 0 \\ +12\,dB\,(re:p) & \Delta_l(\tau) > 0.\end{cases} \tag{8}$$

The gradual build-up of OHC response to efferent innervation is approximated by passing $P_l(\tau)$ in dB into a low-pass filter with a cutoff frequency of 5 Hz. The resulting filtered gain $\Pi_l(\tau)$ in each band represents the terminal contribution of the OHC efferent system. The fluid-cilia coupling gains $p_n(t)$ are then obtained by spatial and temporal interpolation of the filtered gains. Efferent control of the OHCs results in a level compression of 24 dB.

4   SYLLABLE-LEVEL ANALYSES

For time-domain numerical solutions, the networks of section 2 were implemented as wave digital filters [6]. The rate of operation of the filters was 48000 Hz for the 'timit' sentence and 40000 Hz for the 'clean' and 'dirty' sentences. The final time-frequency representations are speech cochleograms obtained by integrating the firing rate $F_n(t)$ with a 2 ms time constant and downsampling to 1 ms frames.

Figure 4 presents the closed-loop cochleogram of 'timit.syl'. The level-dependent filtering by the BM-OHC module contributed to an enhancement and a spectral sharpening in the low-energy portions of the cochleogram. This preserved the phone boundaries while allowing an amplification of the stop release /g/ and fricative /s/, and a better resolution of the formant structure for nasal /ng/, vowel /ix/ and both vowels /iy/. The feedback unit provided additional level compression along both the time and frequency axes. The feedback states K_{st} and Π_l broadly delineate the phone boundaries. An analysis of the efferent gains reveals an enhancement of the stop release /g/ and fricative /s/. In contrast, phones /r/ and /iy/ were reduced in intensity and this also involved the AR system. The feedback systems also improved the continuity of the cochleogram contours at the fundamental and low-pitch harmonics. As a direct result of compression, the cochleogram becomes somewhat devoid of the broad spectral and temporal variations of the utterance. This information is now conveyed by the feedback

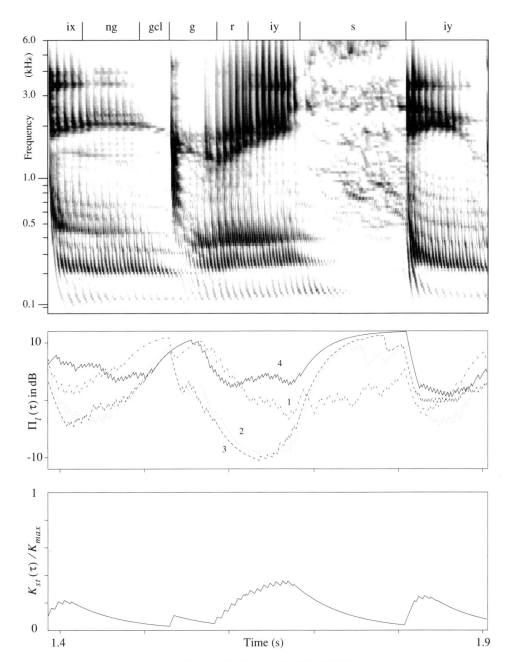

Fig. 4   Closed-loop cochleogram of 'timit.syl' with associated feedback states.

states. They could thus be considered an integral part of the peripheral AM output comple-
menting the cochleogram. .

Figure 5 presents the closed-loop cochleogram of 'clean.syl'. The 2.8 kHz cutoff due to
the Rothenberg mask used during recording has severely reduced high-frequency energy. The

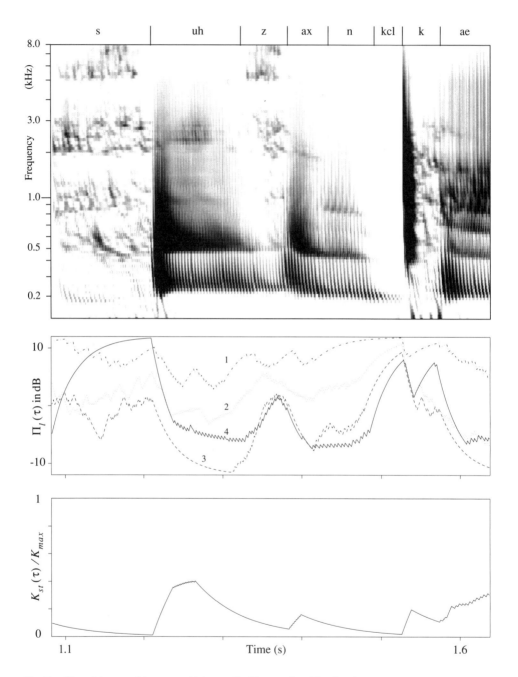

Fig. 5   Closed-loop cochleogram of 'clean.syl' with associated feedback states.

efferent gain Π_1 in the upper frequency band of the cochleogram partly compensates for this loss ($\Pi_1 > \Pi_2 > \Pi_3$). The low-frequency efferent gain Π_4 is primarily sensitive to voicing and shows large temporal fluctuations. Fricative /z/ is distinguished from /s/ by the presence of voicing, i.e. by horizontal cochleogram contours and vertical striations at the level of the

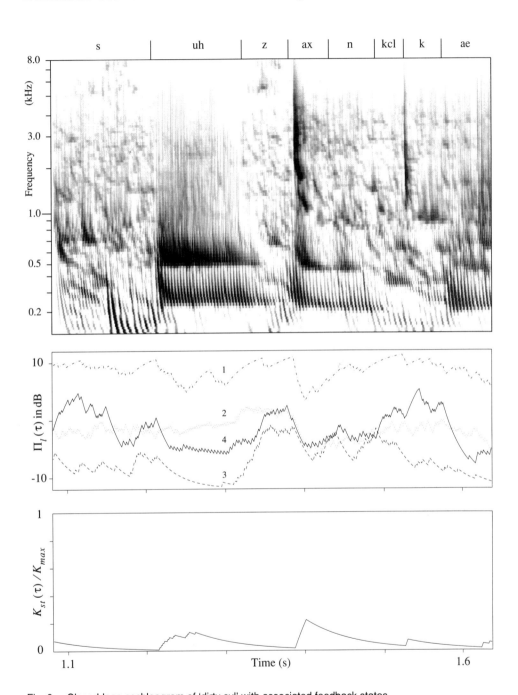

Fig. 6   Closed-loop cochleogram of 'dirty.syl' with associated feedback states.

pitch frequency. The first formant of vowel /uh/ at about 480 Hz strongly masks its upper formants. The low-frequency attenuation provided by the AR prevented further masking. The third formant is seen at 2400 Hz, but there are only traces of the second formant around 1000 Hz. The boundary between vowel /ax/ and nasal /n/ is characterised by an abrupt formant transition at $t = 1.430$ s. The stop release /k/ and the preceding closure /kcl/ are also clearly seen. The terminal vowel /ae/, on the other hand, does not have a well defined formant structure. Rather, the pitch harmonics are individually resolved and there is a broad modulation in their intensities with a peak around 700-1700 Hz.

Figure 6 presents the closed-loop cochleogram of 'dirty.syl'. The laboratory noise had a very deleterious effect on the quality of this cochleogram. The most robust features are the detection of voicing and the low-frequency structure of voiced sounds. The efferent feedback states show much less fluctuation and therefore provided much less compression than in the 'clean' sentence. The most striking consequence is the reduction of the stop release /k/ and of the high-frequency fricative noise. There is also a blurring of the formant transition between vowel /ax/ and nasal /n/. A feedback scheme based on the temporal structure at the output of the peripheral model, as opposed to average firing rate, could improve performance in noise.

Acknowledgements: This model was implemented within the AM software platform of the MRC-APU (Cambridge, UK).

REFERENCES

[1] B.B. Bauer (1967), 'On the equivalent circuit of a plane wave confronting an acoustical device', *JASA*, **42**(5),1095-1097.

[2] H.D. Crane (1982), 'IHC-TM connect-disconnect and efferent control. V', *JASA*, **72**(1), 93-101.

[3] P. Dallos (1973), *The Auditory Periphery: Biophysics and Physiology*, Academic Press, New York.

[4] A. Fettweis (1986), 'Wave digital filters: theory and practice', *Proc. IEEE*, **74**(2), 270-327.

[5] M.B. Gardner and M.S. Hawley (1972), 'Network representation of the external ear', *JASA*, **52**(6), 1620-1628.

[6] C. Giguère & P.C. Woodland (1992), 'A Composite Model of the Auditory Periphery with Feedback Regulation', *Cambridge Univ. Eng. Dept., Technical Report CUED/F-INFENG/TR.93*.

[7] D.D. Greenwood (1990), 'A cochlear frequency-position function for several species — 29 years later', *JASA*, **87**(6), 2592-2605.

[8] D.O. Kim (1986), 'Active and nonlinear cochlear biomechanics and the role of the outer-hair-cell subsystem in the mammalian auditory system', *Hear. Res.*, **22**, 105-114.

[9] M.E. Lutman & A.M. Martin (1979), 'Development of an electroacoustic analogue model of the middle ear and acoustic reflex', *J. Sound. Vib.*, **64**(1), 133-157.

[10] R. Meddis, M.J. Hewitt & T.M. Shackleton (1990), 'Implementation details of a computation model of the inner hair-cell/ auditory-nerve synapse', *JASA*, **87**(4), 1813-1816.

[11] H.W. Strube (1985), 'A computationally efficient basilar-membrane model', *Acustica*, **58**, 207-214

Speech representations in the SYLK recognition project

26

P.D. Green, N.R. Kew and D.A. Miller

1   OVERVIEW OF SYLK

The aim of the SYLK project is to develop a speech recognition front-end which combines statistical and knowledge-based processing to mutual benefit. The project, located at Sheffield University and Leeds University, is funded by the UK IEATP programme.

The SYLK speech recognition approach is unusual in two ways:

- *The syllable, rather than the phone or the word, is chosen as the 'explanation unit'*; i.e. SYLK interprets a spoken sentence as a sequence of syllables, each with a particular structure. The motivation for the choice of the syllable is that much allophonic variation is conditioned by syllable position. The notion of syllable-based speech recognition is, of course, not new: a variety of approaches have been tried (e.g. Allerhand [1], De Mori [7], Weigel [14]). The SYLK acronym stands for 'Statistical SYllabic Knowledge'.

- *Recognition proceeds in two stages: a conventional "first-pass", followed by the application of "refinement tests"* (see fig. 1). The first pass is based on hidden Markov models (HMMs), with models for syllable structure components (section 2). Refinement tests provide a mechanism for using evidence (such as formant transitions) which the first pass cannot make explicit. Each refinement test attempts to capture some piece of phonetic knowledge and use it to improve the first-pass results. Refinement tests are trained and deployed within an evidential reasoning scheme. The result of applying a refinement test is to change the relative probabilities of alternative hypotheses (see fig. 1).

Green *et al.* [9] gives a more detailed account of these ideas. Work on the front-end is reported in Roach *et al.* [12]. See Boucher & Green [4] for details of the evidential reasoning scheme. In this paper we illustrate the processing by SYLK of the utterance 'timit.wav' from the Sheffield data set.

2   THE FIRST PASS

The SYLK first-pass is a conventional continuous-density HMM recogniser developed using the HTK toolkit[1]. Since the aim is to attempt to find the likely syllabic structure of the input sentence, HMMs are trained for a set of 'SYLK symbols': allowed syllable onset, peak and coda types in English. There are about 20 such onsets, 20 peaks and 60 codas. Table 1 contains some examples of these. Training such models requires an appropriately annotated database. Since no such resource exists, we derive training annotations by applying an algorithm based on the maximal-onset principle to the conventional phonetic annotation of the TIMIT database, accepting that this procedure will inevitably introduce some syllabification errors. The training set comprises some 600 utterances from the TIMIT dr1 and dr7 dialect regions. The test set is around 250 dr1 and dr7 utterances. The shibboleth sentences (.sa1 and.sa2) are excluded.

Visual Representations of Speech Signals: Martin Cooke, Steve Beet and Malcolm Crawford (eds.)
© 1993 by John Wiley & Sons Ltd

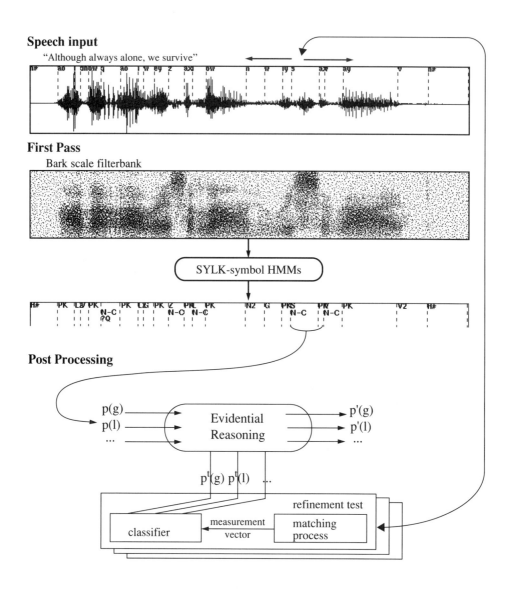

Fig. 1   Recognition in SYLK.

Table 1: Examples of SYLK symbols.

SYLK symbol	represents
T	voiceless-stop-onset /p- t- k-/
TL	voiceless-stop-liquid-onset /pr- pl- tr- kl- kr-/
STL	fricative-stop-liquid-onset /spr- spl- str- skr- skl-/
T2	voiceless-stop-coda /-p -t -k/
ST2	fricative-stop-coda /-sp -st -sk -st/

The representation used as input to the HMM recogniser is a 32-channel Bark-scale spectrogram, subjected to a cosine transform. The HMM topology is three-state, "straight through". Figures 2 and 3 show this representation and the Viterbi SYLK Symbol recognition for the exemplar TIMIT utterance. Since this is taken from a different dialect region (dr5), one can expect performance to be degraded. The overall performance of the first-pass on the SYLK test set is 67.9% correct, 53.5% accurate.

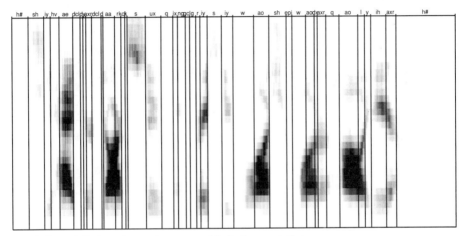

Fig. 2   'timit.wav': Bark-scale spectrogram and timit.phn annotation.

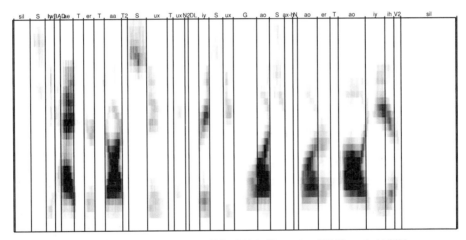

Fig. 3   'timit.wav': Bark-scale spectrogram and Viterbi labelling using SYLK symbol HMMs.

3   ESTIMATING INITIAL PROBABILITIES

Our work to date has been restricted to refining hypotheses for syllable onsets. The refinement process for a given syllable starts from an initial estimate of the probabilities of the various onsets. These probabilities may be obtained from a confusion matrix of first-pass errors or, more sensitively, by a technique which re-applies the first-pass HMMs, following the suggestion of McInnes *et al.* [11]. Each interval between two peaks is considered as a separate utterance consisting of coda-onsets, and a lattice of possible HMM matches, with appropriate probabilities, is obtained (illustrated in fig. 4).

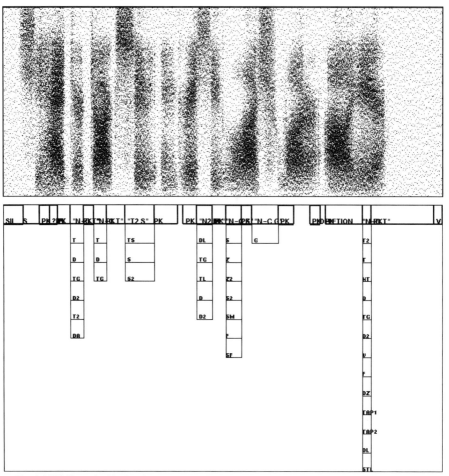

Fig. 4   Partial SYLK symbol lattice for utterance 'timit.wav'.

4   REFINEMENT TESTS

A refinement test is based around a *matching process*, which takes a syllable structure hypothesis H and returns a measurement vector v. In training, v is used as the basis for a statistical classifier which discriminates between the alternative labels for H, or its refinements. When the test is applied, probability estimates from this classifier are combined with existing probabilities by Bayesian updating. The system provides the choice between a Gaussian classifier or a neural-net (multi-layer perceptron) classifier. We are also working on the use of neural nets for evidence-combination.

The SYLK architecture is intended to make the addition of refinement tests as flexible as possible: in particular, there is no restriction on:

- what representations the matching process looks at,
- whereabouts in time the matching process looks,
- the kind of processing the matching process does,
- the level of refinement the test operates at,
- how the test partitions the possible refinements.

Figure 5 illustrates the training of a refinement test (called SON) which attempts to improve the discrimination between those syllable onsets (glides and liquids) where there is a gradual transition into the following peak from onsets where the transition is abrupt. It does this on the basis of maximum slope in sonorant energy.

Figure 6 illustrates formant frequency estimates (derived from a local implementation of Crowe's algorithm [6]) used as the basis for a family of refinement tests which make place-of-articulation distinctions between different refinements of onset SYLK symbols on the basis of asking the question *'where were the formants coming from?'*.

Both tests use techniques developed in earlier work on the 'Speech Sketch' (Green *et al.* [8]): they describe the parametric data in terms of peaks and dips, and then take measurements from these descriptions.

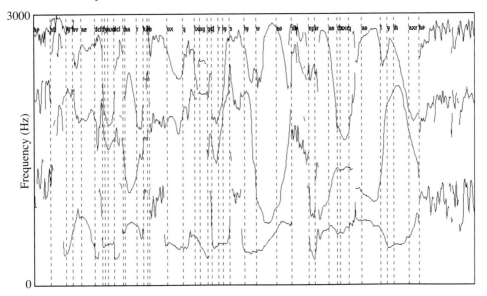

Fig. 6   Formant frequency estimates for TIMIT utterance dr5.mewm0.sa1 derived by Crowe's algorithm.

5   RESULTS

SON, perhaps not surprisingly, makes little impact on the first-pass results. Results based on onsets only are: 40.28% correct after the first-pass, 40.43% correct after SON. This improvement, as measured by the Gillick test (Cox [5]), is not statistically significant.

Since the formant-based tests run over a symbol set different from that used in the first-pass, conventional assessment measures are uninformative. To combat this problem, we use "relative information transmitted" (RIT) (suggested by Smith [13] and further developed in SYLK by Kew [10]) to compare recogniser performance across different symbol sets. The RIT figures given measure the proportion of the information in a correct TIMIT-label transcription which is preserved by the recogniser.

The RIT figure for the first-pass is 0.259 (RIT varies from 0 (bad) to 1 (good) on a logarithmic scale). Table 2 gives figures for several formant-based distinctions, comparing RIT with "ideal RIT" — the resulting figure if the distinction is made reliably.

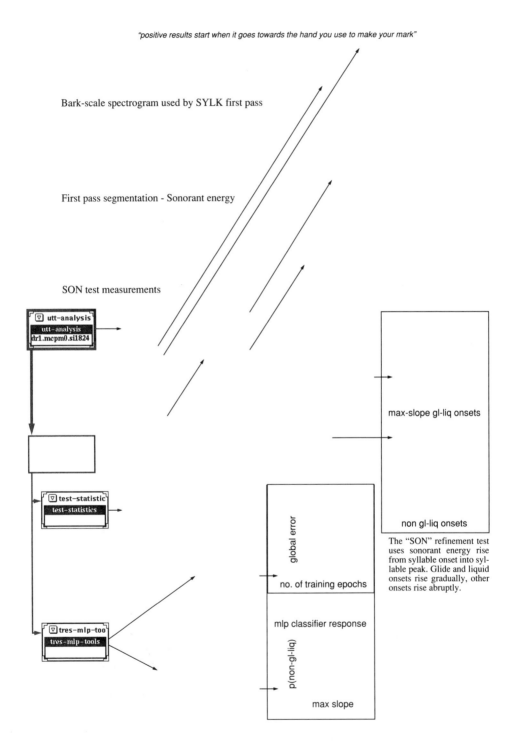

Fig. 5   SYLK analysis tool (SAT); allows: display of speech representations for selected utterances; training of refinement test classifiers; and analysis of refinement test statistics.

Table 2

Distinction	RIT	Best possible RIT	Percentage of available information transmitted
/b d g/	0.306	0.318	88.2
/p t k/	0.339	0.374	69.7
/m n/	0.292	0.305	71.9
/l r/	0.298	0.305	84.4
/w y/	0.300	0.304	92.3

6 THE FUTURE

It has become clear from various studies (e.g. Beet *et al.* [2], Blomberg *et al.* [3]) that using novel representations (e.g. auditory model output) as the input to conventional recognisers does not often give good results. The SYLK architecture is designed to allow any representation to be tried out in a recognition framework without forcing a transformation to fit the frame-by-frame requirements of conventional recognisers. It is our intention to use the auditory work at Sheffield reported elsewhere in this volume as the basis for the next generation of SYLK refinement tests.

Note

1 HTK Version 1.3: A Hidden Markov model Toolkit, available from Cambridge University Engineering Department, Trumpington St., Cambridge, CB2 1PZ, UK.

References

[1] M.H. Allerhand (1987), *Knowledge-Based Speech Pattern Recognition*, Kogan Page, London.

[2] S.W. Beet, R.K. Moore & M.J. Tomlinson (1986), 'Auditory modelling for automatic speech recognition', *Proc. Institute of Acoustics*, **8**(7), 571-579.

[3] M. Blomberg, R. Carlson, K. Elenius & B. Granstrom (1982), 'Experiments with auditory models in speech recognition', in: *The Representation of Speech in the Peripheral Auditory System* (eds. R. Carlson & B. Granstrom), Elsevier Biomedical Press.

[4] L.A. Boucher & P.D. Green (1990), 'Syllable-based hypothesis refinement in SYLK', *Proc. Institute of Acoustics*, **12**(10), 189-195.

[5] S.J. Cox (1988), 'The Gillick test — a method for comparing two speech recognisers tested on the same data', *Speech Research Unit Memorandum 4136*, DRA Malvern, UK.

[6] A. Crowe & M.A. Jack (1987), 'Globally optimising formant tracker using generalised centroids', *Electronics Letters*, **23**(19), 1019-1020.

[7] R. De Mori (1983), *Computer Models of Speech using Fuzzy Algorithms*, Plenum Press, New York.

[8] P.D. Green, G.J. Brown, M.P. Cooke, M.D. Crawford, & A.J.H. Simons (1990), 'Bridging the gap between signals and symbols in speech recognition', in: *Advances in Speech, Hearing and Language Processing* (ed. W.A. Ainsworth), JAI Press, London.

[9] P.D. Green, A.J.H. Simons & P.J. Roach (1990), 'The SYLK project: foundations and overview', *Proc. Institute of Acoustics*, **12**(10), 249-258.

[10] N.R. Kew (1992), 'Information-theoretic measures for SYLK assessment', *SYLK Working Paper #16*, SPLASH, Department of Computer Science, University of Sheffield.

[11] F.R. McInnes, Y. Ariki & A.A. Wrench (1989), 'Enhancement and optimisation of a speech recognition front-end based on Hidden Markov models', *Proc. Eurospeech '89*, Vol. 2, 461-464.

[12] P.J. Roach, P.D. Green, D.A. Miller & A.J.H. Simons (1991), 'The SYLK project: syllable structures as a basis for evidential reasoning with phonetic knowledge', *Proc. XIIth Int. Cong. Phonetic Sciences*, Vol. 4, 482-485.

[13] A.M. Smith (1990), 'On the use of Relative Information Transmitter (RIT) measure for the assessment of performance in the valuation of automatic speech recognition (ASR) devices', *Proc. 3rd Australian Conf. on Speech Science and Technology (Melbourne)*.

[14] W. Weigel (1990), 'Continuous speech recognition with vowel-context-independent HMMs for demisyllables', *ICASSP '90*, Vol. 1, 69-72.

Using cochlear information for speech feature analysis and interpretation

Z. Kačič and B. Horvat

1   INTRODUCTION

During the last decade we have been witnessing a kind of renaissance in the use of neural networks for speech processing and recognition. The likely reason for that is in the failure of standard approaches to yield sufficient speech recognition accuracy. This is particularly true for speaker-independent speech recognition, where speaker adaptation is not possible.

The main problem of almost all complex speech recognition systems existing today is poor recognition accuracy on the level of a recognised word. The inter-speaker and intra-speaker variability of speech (male, female, child, voice under stress, singing, shouting, etc.) causes great feature dispersion of the same recognition unit [3]. Consequently, features of different recognition units inevitably overlap, which results in recognition errors [1]. Neural networks offer much more flexibility in handling the feature dispersion problem, yet the problem of feature overlapping is insoluble for them too [2].

Neural networks use similar organisational principles for information processing as are supposed to be used in the human brain. Still, most of the current speech recognition systems based on neural networks use standard feature extraction methods [3]. This could be one of the important reasons why the efficiency of those systems is currently not much better than the accuracy of the classic pattern recognition approach.

2   ARRAY OF COCHLEAR PERCEPTORS

To avoid feature dispersion and feature overlapping problems, new feature extraction and interpretation methods have to be developed. It is reasonable to expect that such methods should emulate the principles used by human listeners, since humans *can* handle the speaker-independent speech recognition task without speaker adaptation.

The definition of basic information is of crucial importance for the development of a speech recognition system. We have built our technique of speech feature extraction and interpretation on the assumption that the basic information consists of the signal's energy in a particular frequency range, and of its change in a time instant. An input signal is thus described by an intensity pattern and by a pattern of temporal changes. We have further assumed that the observed signal, which we will name a sound event, must have a precisely determined dynamic of both patterns, so that the listener can recognise it. Various sound events may compose a sound scene. Also, in the scene a particular event must be recognisable.

Based on these assumptions we have defined an array of cochlear perceptors (ACP). The number of perceptors corresponds to the number of difference-limens (DL) in frequency in man [4]. Each perceptor responds only in a particular frequency range. The width of the range depends on the perceptor's place in the array. The maximum number of states that a single perceptor can occupy differs and depends on the perceptor's position in the array. It corresponds to the number of DLs in intensity for a particular frequency range [4].

Visual Representations of Speech Signals: Martin Cooke, Steve Beet and Malcolm Crawford (eds.)
© 1993 by John Wiley & Sons Ltd

Since the masking phenomenon prevents some signals passing through the processing stage in the cochlea, it must also be considered in modelling the information that enters higher processing levels. In implementing it we have used the data from Zwicker & Fastl [5]. The array of cochlear perceptors defined in this way has 1077 perceptors and covers the frequency range from 32 to 3400 Hz. The number of states varies from 5, for very low frequencies, to 160 for high frequencies.

The intensity pattern is composed of instantaneous rates of excitation of the perceptors in the array. Similarly, the pattern of temporal changes consists of differences in excitation rates of perceptors between two successive time instants. The pattern of temporal changes is denoted by dots (•) in the diagrams.

In interpreting speech features, the "tracks" of both patterns are used. The number of excited perceptors and their position in the array give us further information about features of a speech unit. For vowels, the intensity pattern is almost stationary. The pattern of temporal changes is thus almost absent and appears only at the starting and the ending point of the vowel. In most consonants the pattern of temporal changes becomes dominant, since the majority of them bear little energy. However, they have a rich pattern of temporal changes.

3   FOCUS OF ATTENTION

The important mechanism used in perception is focus of attention. Its importance is most obvious in visual perception. But focus of attention also plays a significant role in sound perception. However, in modelling perception processes, especially in speech recognition, the implementation of this phenomenon may be found only rarely. The role of focus of attention is significant in localisation and identification tasks. If we use the array of cochlear perceptors, then the patterns of temporal changes represent the main source of information for the implementation of focus of attention. A particular event causes, at its beginning or at its end, simultaneous changes of excitation rate in different groups of perceptors. The main task of the focus of attention is to trace such changes and, in the case of corrupted signals, to select appropriate changes from the sound scene.

4   FEATURE INTERPRETATION AND DATA ANALYSIS

We have focused our analysis on given syllable data ('clean' and 'dirty'). Figures 1 to 4 show normalised energy spectrums and responses of the ACP for each of the two speech fragments.

4.1 The fragment 'clean.syl'

The signal was downsampled from 20 to 10 kHz sampling rate. For spectral analysis, a FFT method with a 25.6 ms Hamming window and a 2 ms frame rate was used. Figure 1 shows the energy spectrum of the signal, whereas fig. 2 shows the response of the ACP. All events (phonemes) can be clearly seen from both figures. However, both fricatives are much more obvious in fig. 2. This is due to increased sensitivity of perceptors in the higher frequency range. Recall that the ACP covers the frequency range from 32 to 3400 Hz.

The duration of the first fricative is about 125 ms. Note the irregularity of the pattern of temporal changes in the area of excited perceptors. This is a general feature of all noise-like signals. Further note the simultaneous appearance of changes in excitation of perceptors at the beginning of the vowel /u/. Its duration is about 140 ms. During this time, the pattern of temporal changes is almost completely absent. It appears again at the end of the vowel. The second fricative is not as intensive as was the first one, but it can still be easily detected in the scene. Again, the pattern of temporal changes is irregular. The fricative is present in the scene for around 26 ms. The next vowel is expressed weakly. There is almost no energy present in the region of the second and the third formant where the perceptors are sparsely excited. The nasal /n/, which follows, can be detected as a prolongation of the vowel /a/. The total duration of the phoneme is about 117 ms. The silence of about 50 ms precedes the velar in /ka/, which is characterised by increased excitation almost through the entire array. Its duration is around 45 ms. A "strong" vowel /a/ follows. It has a clearly expressed energy in the region of all formants. There is a problem with very short events that have little energy, as during the spectral analysis the energy of the neighbouring events smears their real shape.

It would be easy to implement the idea of focus of attention in this scene, since the tracks of temporal changes for particular events are easy to follow.

4.2 The fragment 'dirty.syl'

Analysis parameters were the same as in the previous case. In fig. 3 we can detect most of the events from fig. 1. Among others, two additional events are detectable, both in the region of fricatives. In fig. 4, except for the first two vowels, all other events from fig. 2 are hard to recognise. This happens primarily for two reasons. First, the events added to the scene in fig. 1 include a considerable amount of energy in the region of higher frequencies, which coincide with the energy of fricatives. Second, since we have used the FFT as a spectral estimation method, we have limited ourselves more or less to the analysis of 'clean' signals. In the case of FFT we get the information about the spectral contents of the signal only at predetermined equally-spaced frequency points. Therefore we are not able to handle the problem when the energy appears at intermediate frequencies, because this is determined by the neighbouring frequency points. So we can never be sure whether the energy of both components has in fact increased, or a new component has appeared. If we want to solve this problem we should consider some other spectral estimation methods (e.g. parametric spectral estimation methods).

The purpose of focus of attention in the case of noisy signal should be to search for simultaneous occurrences of intensity changes among perceptors in the array. It should also look for the harmonic property of the signal to detect voiced sounds in the scene. The latter is hard to realise in our case, since the frequency resolution was in all cases around 40 Hz. If some other spectral estimation method were used, then the principle of "gestalt" perception could be implemented at higher levels of processing. With these, the problem of the "cocktail-party" phenomenon might be more successfully addressed.

Furthermore, note that the parameters of the ACP should be further improved to better handle noisy speech. The two most important factors are the intensity sensitivity of the ACP and the masking strategy.

5   CONCLUSION

We have analysed two speech segments, one of which was corrupted by noise. The results have shown that for clean signals the array of cochlear perceptors might be usefully applied in a segmentation problem, whereas for noisy signals further improvements of the parameters of the array have to be made. The principle of focus of attention could be easily implemented in the case of clean signals. Using other spectral estimation methods than the FFT, attention and "gestalt" perception could be combined to extract features from a noisy signal. An adequate speech recognition system is currently under development.

REFERENCES

[1] Z. Kačič & B. Horvat (1988), 'A methodology for efficiency estimation of the speech signal feature extraction methods', in: *Lecture Notes in Computer Science No. 301*, J. Kittler (ed.), Springer-Verlag, Berlin, 636-645.

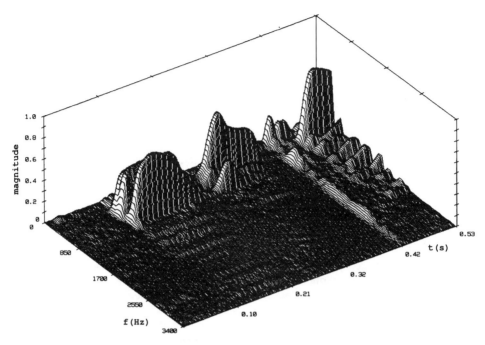

Fig. 1   The normalised energy spectrum of the 'clean.syl' fragment ".. Susan ca.. ".
See text for further explanation.

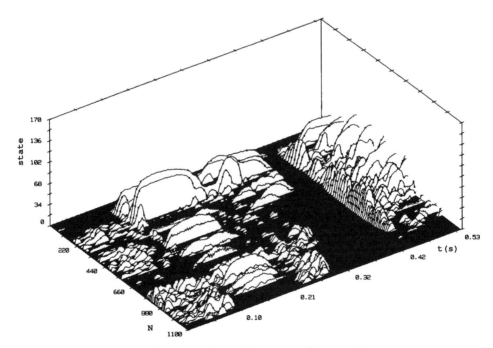

Fig. 2   The response of the ACP on the 'clean.syl' fragment ".. Susan ca ..".

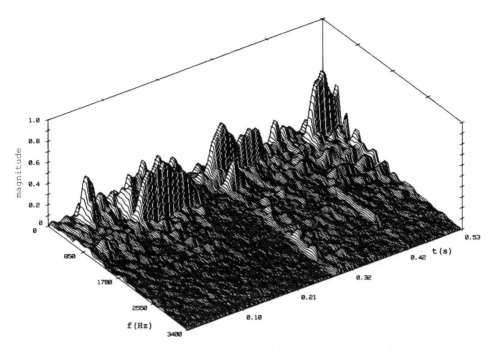

Fig. 3   The normalised energy spectrum of the 'dirty.syl' fragment ".. Susan ca .. ".

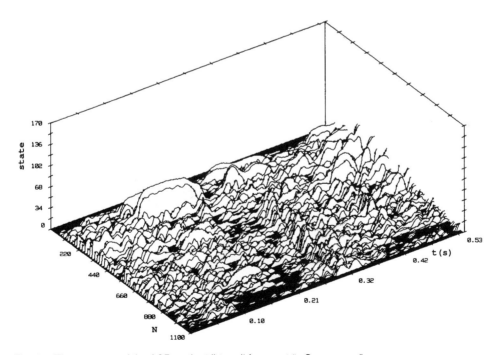

Fig. 4   The response of the ACP on the 'dirty.syl' fragment ".. Susan ca.. .".

[2] R. Lippmann (1987), 'An introduction to computing with neural nets', *IEEE ASSP Magazine*, 4-22.

[3] J. Mariani (1989), 'Recent advances in speech processing', *IEEE ICASSP '89*, 81-84.

[4] S.S. Stevens & H. Davis (1963), *Hearing — its Psychology and Physiology,* John Wiley & Sons, New York.

[5] E. Zwicker & H. Fastl (1990), *Psychoacoustics — Facts and Models*, Springer-Verlag, Berlin.

Temporal factors in speech signals

Richard Katsch and Phillip Dermody

1   INTRODUCTION

The extreme richness of the speech signal has overwhelmed many of the classical techniques of signal analysis. Both the width of the signal when represented in a classical Fourier frequency space and the subtle and rapid temporal variations present have meant that much of speech signal analysis is based on measures which are integrated or averaged over time and frequency. The high bandwidth of the speech signal makes this form of compression convenient, if not necessary, and the results produced have been found to be very useful. The information which has been removed by this process could, however, provide us with additional insights into the nature of the speech signal and contribute additional processing power to models of the peripheral auditory system.

2   WHAT DO WE MEAN BY TEMPORAL FACTORS?

Evidence has accumulated that finely detailed temporal variations are present within the auditory system. The phase locking of auditory nerve fibre firings to the presented stimuli over limited frequency ranges is one example (Dynes & Delgutte [3]). The importance of these details to the way in which speech and other sounds are perceived is not yet clear, but demonstrations of these processes provide an impetus to examine time relationships within the speech signal. Additionally we know that the speech signal has a considerable frequency bandwidth and, at least in part, possesses a rich harmonic structure. This suggests that useful information might be obtained by searching for phase or frequency variation correlations between different frequency regions. In essence we are looking for both "fine structure" within individual time-frequency sections of the signal and co-varying phase or frequency activity across regions. Evidence exists of well correlated amplitude, or energy, variations within the speech signal (Brown & Cooke [1]); however, this is not the focus of our techniques here.

3   WHAT MIGHT WE USE THESE TEMPORAL FACTORS FOR?

We might expect that the information provided by some form of temporal analysis will complement that provided by spectrographic processes. The information provided could show better time resolution which might be useful for automatic segmentation methods which rely for their success on the accurate measurement of the change of signal parameters with time. There is also interest in the ways in which channels within the speech signal can be grouped together for data rate reduction (Brown & Cooke [1]). Measures possessing better time resolution of their variation will make inter-channel comparisons more accurate. Also statistics of channels which are inherently time or phase related such as depth and frequency of FM modulation can be compared.

Visual Representations of Speech Signals: Martin Cooke, Steve Beet and Malcolm Crawford (eds.)
© 1993 by John Wiley & Sons Ltd

4   HOW CAN WE MEASURE THE TEMPORAL FACTORS?

The fundamental problem in measuring temporal aspects of the speech signal is to find a measure which allows a convenient separation of the amplitude and phase information contained within the signal. The speech signal is, of course, strongly amplitude modulated, so our problem is more complicated than one of simple FM demodulation. A technique which has proved useful in this type of situation is that of computing the instantaneous frequency (IF) of the analytic signal associated with the observed time waveform. This requires the computation of the Hilbert transform of the original time sequence. The analytic signal is then the complex combination of the two signals: the original time waveform is the real part and its Hilbert transform is the imaginary part. While this technique has been discussed in detail some years ago (Gabor [4]) and has received some interest recently (Mandel [5]; Seggie [7,8]; Cooke [2]) it does not appear widely used. The theory is well described in the above papers and will not be discussed in detail here. The techniques used in the computation follow those outlined in the papers by Seggie [7,8] which provide the following efficient computational implementation:

   i   Starting with a sampled time signal, remove the dc component of the (real) signal, and set the imaginary part to zero;

   ii   perform complex FFT;

   iii zero the negative frequency components and double the positive frequency components;

   iv   form the Fourier transform of the derivative of the analytic signal;

   v   inverse transform both arrays to give the analytic signal and its derivative;

   vi   compute the instantaneous frequency from the analytic signal and its derivative.

5   USE OF INSTANTANEOUS FREQUENCY FOR PROCESSING THE WHOLE SPEECH BAND

The method of obtaining instantaneous frequency is quite generally applicable to any signal which is band-limited. In practice its use on band limited but still wideband signals such as the entire speech signal produces a signal which appears "noisy". This can be seen in fig. 1. The large excursions evident in the instantaneous frequency waveform are thought to be intrinsic to simultaneously amplitude/phase modulated signals (Seggie [8]). If the waveform is smoothed to remove these rapid variations then the resulting graph shows the variation of average or carrier frequency within the speech token.

6   MULTI-BAND FILTERING FOLLOWED BY INSTANTANEOUS FREQUENCY PROCESSING

One of the objectives of this study is to examine the relationships between temporal variations across different frequency ranges of the speech signal. To provide this frequency separation the time waveform was filtered into a series of 24 bands using the centre frequencies and bandwidths described by Patterson & Holdsworth [6] to design a set of Bessel bandpass filters. The instantaneous frequency technique was then applied to each channel in turn to produce 24 channels of IF measure for each speech token. While bandpass filtering is a common, almost universal, procedure in auditory model and other forms of speech analysis, its use here needs some justification. What, after all, is the point of filtering a signal around a centre frequency and then using a complicated technique to measure its frequency? There are at least two justifications for this. Two completely distinct "frequency" concepts are used here. Filtering, as we have performed it, is an operation defined with respect to the Fourier component frequencies of the signal. Instantaneous frequency, or the rate of change of temporal phase, is not a Fourier-domain concept but is determined by the rate of change of the

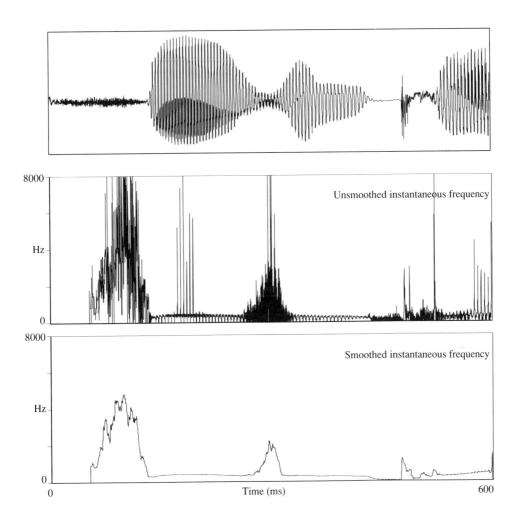

Fig. 1   Representations of 'clean.syl', unfiltered.

inverse tangent of the angle of the analytic signal! Fourier frequency and instantaneous frequency are not simply related. Mandel [5] discusses this in detail. Secondly, the filters we use are not very sharply tuned, with Q factors between about 4 and 10, and so transmit a considerable range of frequencies. From the definition of IF we can expect that it will provide a measure of any frequency or phase modulation present within each band. Covarying modulation should then be evident as simultaneous deviations from the centre frequency and readily apparent on a waterfall display.

The result of this process is applied to two syllable length speech sounds 'clean.syl' and 'dirty.syl' from the Sheffield data set, and the results are shown in fig. 2. The following features are visible. Some degree of correlation appears to be present, particularly at the various acoustic boundaries within the speech sound but there is certainly much apparently uncorrelated activity. Additionally, quite powerful short-term variations of the IF occur within the bands in a similar, but reduced form to the broadband speech analysis. The presence of the

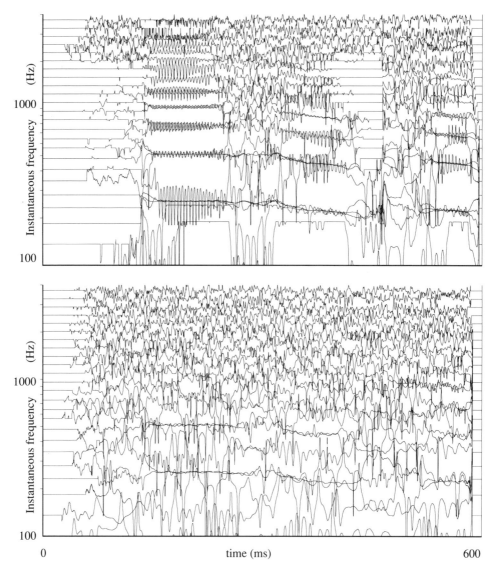

Fig. 2   Instantaneous frequency representations of *upper* : 'clean.syl' and *lower* : 'dirty.syl'.

large, apparently random, spike-type variations requires some explanation. Several options suggest themselves:

   i   Numerical problems within the instantaneous frequency algorithm.

   ii "Real" variations of IF within each band which reflect some phase modulation characteristic of the speech signal.

   iii A by-product of the IF technique not related to phase or frequency modulation — but not a computational deficiency either.

Examination of the real-time waveform and its Hilbert transform suggested that at very low levels the quantisation of the signal could be causing some numerical noise. The instantaneous envelope, which is easily produced as part of the IF computation, was used as a form of discriminator to set the IF to the centre frequency of the filter band when the level was insufficient for reliable operation. This produced virtually no change in the spike peaks. The second alternative seemed difficult to justify on any physical or acoustic grounds. In order to attempt an explanation, a simple synthesis of a two-component sinusoidal signal was generated and its IF computed "analytically". The results are shown in fig. 3. The combination signal was composed of two sinusoids of frequencies 525 Hz with a relative amplitude of 1.0 and 630 Hz with a relative amplitude of 0.9, representing the 5th and 6th harmonic of 105Hz. By interchanging their relative amplitudes the spike polarity can be reversed and a reduction of the lower amplitude is reflected in a lower spike height. The period between the spikes, however, remains constant at the reciprocal of the fundamental frequency of 105 Hz. A point to emphasise is that this variation of IF occurs with no amplitude, phase or frequency modulation of the two-component sinusoids. For comparison these two frequencies are combined in two other modulation schemes; firstly a 90% amplitude modulation of a 525 Hz carrier by a 105 Hz signal and, secondly, phase modulation using the same carrier and impressed signal. The results are shown in figs. 4 and 5.

7   WHAT MIGHT WE USE THIS INFORMATION FOR?

It is clear even from the very limited set of examples presented here that IF variations are present within separate frequency regions of the speech signal and that these variations are correlated between regions in some cases. What is not so clear is how this activity can be usefully interpreted.

Two distinct directions for future investigations are immediately apparent. Firstly, the structure of the spike patterns within individual channels should be investigated and techniques for representing this structure developed. Secondly, inter-channel correlation techniques could be useful in deciding how much of the information present is redundant and how the data representation might be condensed. Combining the information present within related channels both reduces the bandwidth of the signal and also allows for the reduction of competing noise by the use of averaging techniques.

REFERENCES

[1] G.J. Brown & M.P. Cooke (1990), 'A computational model of amplitude modulation processing in the higher auditory system', *3rd Int. Conf. Speech Science and Technology (Melbourne)*.

[2] M.P. Cooke (in press), *Modelling Auditory Processing and Organisation*, to be published by Cambridge University Press, Cambridge, UK.

[3] S.B.C. Dynes & B. Delgutte (1992), 'Phase-locking of auditory-nerve discharges to sinusoidal electric stimulation of the cochlea', *Hearing Research*, **58**, 79-90.

[4] D.J. Gabor (1946), 'Theory of communication. Part III', *Jnl. Inst. Elect. Eng.*, **93**,429-439.

[5] L. Mandel (1974), 'Interpretation of instantaneous frequencies', *Amer. Jnl. Physics*, **42**, 840-846.

[6] R.D. Patterson & J. Holdsworth (in press), 'A functional model of neural activity patterns and auditory images', in: *Advances in Speech, Hearing and Language Processing*, (W.A. Ainsworth, ed.), Vol. 3, JAI Press, London.

[7] D.A. Seggie (1986), 'The application of analytic signal analysis in speech processing', *Proc. IOA: Speech and Hearing*, **8**(7), 85-92.

[8] D.A. Seggie (1987), 'The use of temporal frequency in speech signal analysis', *Proc. XIth International Congress of Phonetic Sciences*, vol. 2, 364-367.

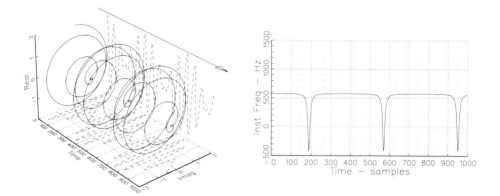

Fig. 3   Two-component summation of 1 x 525 Hz + .9 x 630 Hz; *left* : analytic signal; *right* : instantaneous frequency.

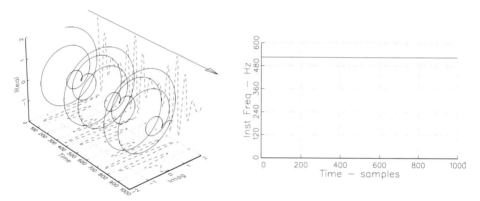

Fig. 4   90% 105 Hz amplitude modulation of 525 Hz carrier; *left* : analytic signal; *right* : instantaneous frequency.

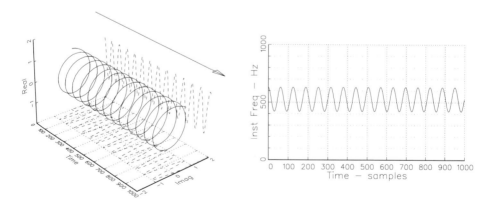

Fig. 5   105 Hz phase modulation of 525 Hz carrier; *left* : analytic signal; *right* : instantaneous frequency.

Phase representations of acoustic speech waveforms

29

Eric Keller

1 INTRODUCTION

Phase representations are commonly used in dynamic systems (Abraham & Shaw [1]). They offer summary glimpses at the complete, repeating behaviour of a given system. Such representations have proven their usefulness in speech kinematics, particularly with respect to their ability to capture phase relationships between interacting (co-articulating) muscular structures (e.g. Kelso & Tuller [4]). In this paper we briefly examine phase representations of acoustic speech signals.

2 METHOD

There are two ways to obtain a phase representation:

i For each sample in the signal, calculate the amplitude difference between the current and the previous sample, and plot this type of velocity against the measured amplitude for the sample. Thus

$$x_k = x(k) - x(k-1), \qquad y_k = x(k) \tag{1}$$

where x_k is the velocity at the current sample derived from the difference between samples $x(k)$ and $x(k\text{-}1)$, and y_k is the amplitude of the current sample obtained from sample $x(k)$.

ii With reference to samples in the signal, calculate an approximation to instantaneous velocity first (e.g. a spline, de Boor [2]) and plot this type of velocity against measured amplitude. Thus

$$x_k = s'(t_k), \qquad y_k = x(k) \tag{2}$$

where x_k in the phase plot represents one point in the first derivative $s'(t_k)$ of a sampled cubic function that approximates the signal's sample path ($s(t_k)$); y_k is the amplitude of the current sample obtained from sample $x(k)$.

The first approach is useful for a rough-and-ready first glance at the phase characteristics of a given signal segment. The second approach is to be preferred for the suppression of quantisation error or for filtering out high-frequency components.

Since phase plots involve velocity as their first parameter, they are different from somewhat similar-looking two-dimensional signal representations popularised some 30 years ago by Lerner [5]. The latter involve as their first parameter either the Fourier or the Hilbert transform (Demars [3]). Despite this difference in derivation, phase plots share some of the interesting properties of Lerner's polar plots, such as their relative lack of sensitivity to temporal parameters like sampling frequency or time scale. A further similarity is that phase plots retain time information without being particularly sensitive to it.

Figure 1 shows the derivation of a phase representation (or "phase portrait") from a time-amplitude plot for a sinusoidal cycle. As the signal rises, velocity first increases and then de-

Visual Representations of Speech Signals: Martin Cooke, Steve Beet and Malcolm Crawford (eds.)
© 1993 by John Wiley & Sons Ltd

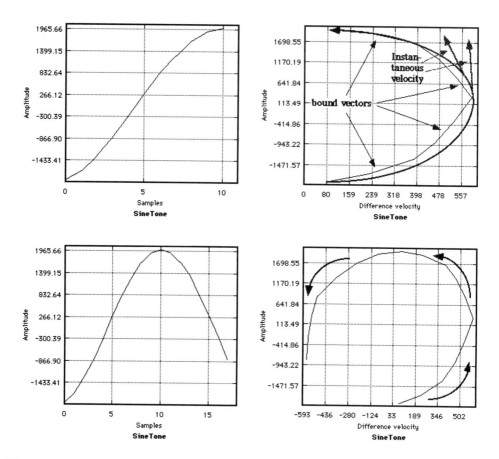

Fig. 1   Time-amplitude and phase representations of segments of a sinusoidal cycle.
In the upper right figure, the rising portion of the sine wave cycle is translated into a phase
portrait by the plotting of bound vectors, or of differences between adjoining samples (thin
line). The assumed underlying smooth phase movement is shown as a thicker line.

creases. In the negative-moving signal, velocity first moves from zero into the negative domain and then back to zero. A circle is thus derived. In dynamic systems, velocity is often
shown on the *y*-axis. However to preserve the similarity to the time-amplitude signal, we have
chosen to show velocity on the *x*-axis and to keep amplitude on the *y*-axis.

In dynamic system terms, the time-amplitude plot shows a *state space* (i.e. a series of successive states of the system), while a phase plot shows a *vector field* (i.e. an area made up of
vectors, or *directions* that the system moves into). In fig. 2, the relationship between time-
amplitude and phase representations is illustrated with respect to a small segment from the
/a/ sound of "can't" in 'clean.dip'.

The superimposition of vectors illustrates well the fundamental tendencies of the sound
pressure system during the production of a vowel. Of particular interest in dynamic system
theory are centres that appear to attract and repel the signal repeatedly (so-called attractor and
repellent basins). At these points, the system shows a loss and regaining of energy. A basin
may act like an attractor at the outer reaches of the system and like a repellent close to its basin. The line between the two areas is known as the *limit cycle*.

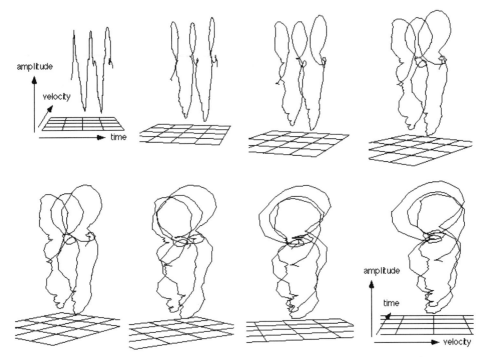

Fig. 2   A segment from the /a/ sound of "can't" in "clean.dip". The plots show that the wave spirals into an apparent centre and then spirals out again. The apparent centre is known as an "attractor" as the signal spirals in and as a "repellent" as it spirals out. Vowels generally show several of these so-called attractor/repellent basins.

3   PHASE PLOTS OF DIFFERENT TYPES OF SOUNDS

Acoustic speech signals are rather distinctive when viewed as phase plots[1]. In figs. 3 and 4, vowels, nasals, unvoiced fricatives, and voiced fricatives are illustrated. On the basis of vector field similarities with the behaviour of well investigated systems, certain dynamic origins of observed patterns may be suggested.

3.1 Vowels

Typical action. A vowel typically spirals towards an attractor and back out towards a larger cycle. There may be one or more attractor/repellent basins.

Presumed dynamics. The vowel phase portrait reflects to a large extent the sound pressure wave imparted by the vocal cords. The phase plot shows typical spring-like behaviour.

Attractors (spiralling inwards). At large amplitudes, this may reflect the progressive loss and damping of energy in the vocal cords.

Repellents (spiralling outwards). (1) Small outward motions may be facilitated by "inverse friction": (2) Larger outward motions may relate to the reinfusion of energy.

3.2 Nasals

Typical action. Similar action to vowels, except that there tend to be fewer attractor/repellent basins.

Presumed dynamics. As for vowels with respect to presumed vocal cord action. If the multiplicity of basins relates to friction and damping, the reduced number of basins in nasals may relate to reduced friction in the nasal vocal tract.

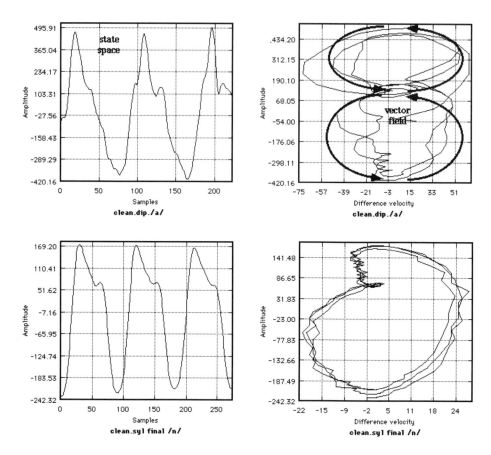

Fig. 3   Signal segments and corresponding phase portraits for different speech sounds.

3.3 Fricatives

Typical action. Strong phase excursions to the lower left and upper right are observed. No attractor/repellent basins are seen.

Presumed dynamics. Near instantaneous amplitude changes are associated with near-instantaneous velocity losses/gains. Voiced fricatives show a combination of the circular characteristics of voicing and the rapid oblique phase excursions characteristic of frication.

4   THE EFFECTS OF NOISE ('clean', 'dirty' and 'spont')

Many types of noise resemble frication. It may thus be possible to distinguish effects of noise from vocalic signals on the basis of their phase characteristics. Different levels of noise are illustrated below by small segments taken from the /a/ sounds found in the signals 'clean', 'dirty' and 'spont' (fig. 5). It can be seen that increased levels of noise are associated with a greater obscuring of vocalic phase characteristics: In noisy conditions, it becomes more difficult to identify attractor/repellent basins, and the outer extent of the phase portrait becomes harder to delineate.

However, a spline[2] operation on the signal prior to the derivation of the phase portrait helps identify vocalic aspects "hiding behind" the noise. In fig. 6, the vowel segments of fig. 5 are shown after interpolation with a tension spline set at a tension coefficient of 0.1.

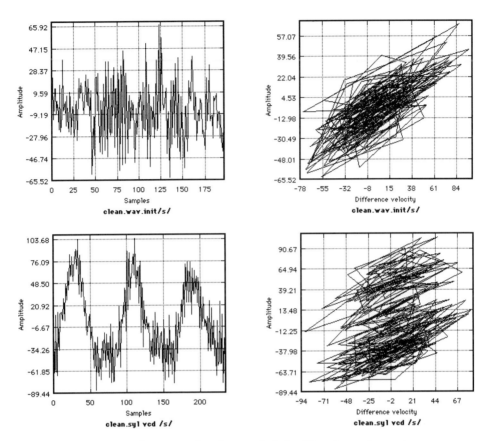

Fig. 4   Signal segments and corresponding phase portraits for different speech sounds.

In fig. 6 it can be readily seen that the splining operation helps reconstitute the vowel's low-frequency characteristics. A splined sound is not necessarily easier to perceive than the corresponding "noise-covered" sound, since high-frequency components are missing. However, splining appears to be a useful technique for rendering speech sounds more amenable to secondary vocalic analyses, such as pitch extraction.

5   CONCLUSION

Phase representations of speech sounds are useful for identifying the essential characteristics of different speech sounds. Vocalic and fricative types of sounds are readily distinguished on the basis of their phase characteristics. In noisy sounds, vocalic low-frequency phase characteristics can be reconstituted with a splining operation. This logic is likely to be of use in the voiced/unvoiced distinction required for pitch extraction algorithms. Further, the study of attractor/repellent basins (typical areas of loss and regaining of sound pressure energy) may provide useful insights into the speech sound's source-filter characteristics.

Notes

1   2D phase representations and splines used here are available in the Signalyze™ software (for availability, communicate with the author). The 3D representations will be part of a future version of Signalyze™. The program uses the phase characteristics described here to effect voiced/unvoiced distinctions in its Temporal Structure Analysis pitch extraction algorithm.

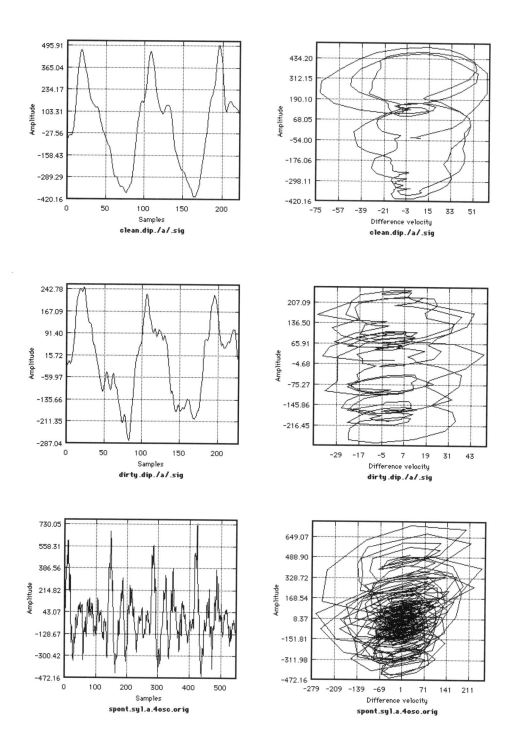

Fig. 5   Signal segments and corresponding phase portraits for the /a/ sound taken from 'clean', 'dirty' and 'spont'. Increasing levels of noise obscure the vowel's phase characteristics.

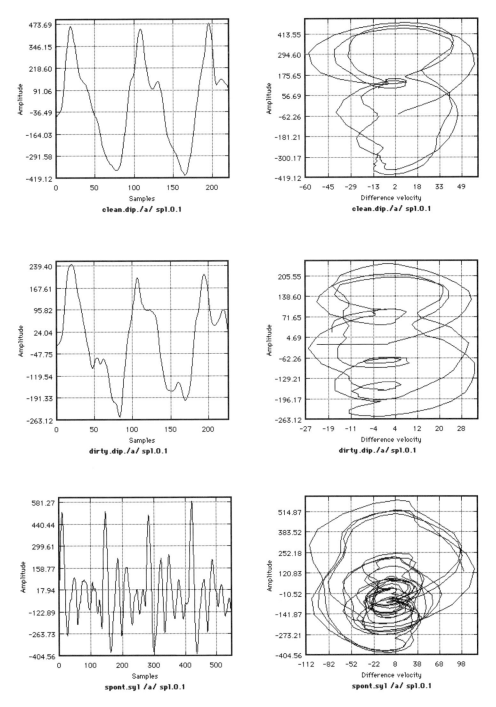

Fig. 6   The same signal segments and phase portraits for the /a/ sound taken from 'clean', 'dirty' and 'spont', but after interpolation with a tension spline, with a tension coefficient of 0.1. The vowel's low-frequency phase characteristics are reconstituted by the splining operation and the vowel's phase characteristics can be inspected.

2   Splines are cubic functions that "follow" a set of points. In a tension spline, the maximal tension is 1.0, which corresponds to a line that crosses the points exactly. Smaller coefficients cause the spline to approximate the points' positions, and to provide a smoother line.

REFERENCES

[1] R.H. Abraham & C.D. Shaw (1984), *The Visual Mathematics Library*, Vismath Volumes 0-4, Aerial Press Inc. Address: Aerial Press Inc. P.O. Box 1360, Santa Cruz, California 95061, USA.

[2] C. de Boor (1978), *A Practical Guide to Splines*, Springer-Verlag, Berlin.

[3] C. Demars (1990), *Représentation temps-fréquence et paramétrisations d'un signal: éléments de monographie*, Document LIMSI: 90-9, Laboratoire d'informatique pour la mécanique et les sciences de l'ingénieur, Orsay, France.

[4] J.A.S. Kelso & B. Tuller (1987), 'Intrinsic time in speech production: Theory, methodology, and preliminary observations', In: E. Keller and M. Gopnik (eds.), *Motor and Sensory Processes of Language*, Lawrence Erlbaum Associates Hillsdale, NJ, 203-222.

[5] R.M. Lerner (1959), *A Method of Speech Compression*, Ph.D. Thesis, MIT, Cambridge, MA.

The use of symbolic speech representations in continuous speech recognition research

30

M.A. de Leeuw and J. Caelen

1   INTRODUCTION

The speech recognition research group at the ICP has chosen an auditory model as the basis for acoustic analysis of the speech signal. Much expertise in the interpretation of the output of this model has been acquired in the past years, to such an extent that it has become very interesting to transfer this knowledge to an expert system for acoustic phonetic decoding. To this aim, expert interviewing sessions have been designed, in which the expert is confronted with short sequences of speech. One of the most critical aspects of the approach is the representation of the data, which are in the form of continuous curves and two-dimensional images (spectrograms). As has been pointed out by many other researchers (e.g. Zue [5]) the spectrogram reading approach tends to shift the speech recognition problem from the auditory to the visual perception domain, without much reduction of complexity. Symbolic representations, however, can be used successfully to obtain reduction of complexity of the representation of speech, without capital loss of information, as will be shown in the following. An interviewing session with a spectrogram-reading expert, using these symbolic representations, is described at sentence level for both the 'clean' and 'dirty' utterances, where diagrams of the syllable level sequence "..Susan ca.." of the 'clean' utterance are provided. Expert performance is discussed at sentence level, notably comparing the 'clean' and 'dirty' utterances.

2   ACOUSTIC ANALYSIS

The auditory model used for the analysis of the speech signal consists of a bank of coupled filters, called channels, whose characteristic frequencies are distributed according to a Bark scale and range from approximately 100 Hz to 7 kHz. It constitutes a nonlinear mechanical model of the basilar membrane of the human ear, as described by Caelen [1]. Due to inter-channel coupling, relatively smooth but accurate spectral slices are obtained, as shown by fig. 1.

Thanks to this property, robust spectral distribution cues can be retrieved from the spectral data, by calculating energy differences between different regions, as discussed by Caelen [3]. The unit for which these calculations are performed is called a frame, usually dimensioned to cover about 10 ms of speech. The spectrogram obtained from the auditory model will in the following be referred to as the *cochleagram*.

Automatic segmentation is performed based on the spectral distribution cues by an adaptive algorithm, yielding a segmentation into infra-phonemic units, so-called homogeneous phones, or phrased differently, resulting in a systematic over-segmentation of phonemes. The algorithm yields segments with a length "proportional" to the stationarity of the speech signal. Transitional parts of speech give rise to short segments (3-5 frames) whereas vowels can produce phones up to several tens of frames. For a discussion of the segmentation model, see [2].

Visual Representations of Speech Signals: Martin Cooke, Steve Beet and Malcolm Crawford (eds.)
© 1993 by John Wiley & Sons Ltd

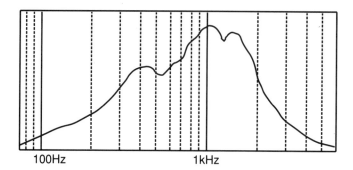

Fig. 1   Burst of phoneme /k/, spectral slice obtained from 'clean.dip' [samples 30536-30664], 6.4
ms (128 point) frame, 256-channel auditory model.

During the first years of use of the model, its output was depicted using characters, representing either energy or amplitude, because this was virtually the only (screen) representation possible with the systems on which the model was implemented. This means that the human expertise acquired in the interpretation of the output of the model is principally based on perception of these character-based representations, which we shall refer to in the following as *symbolic representations*.

3   ACOUSTIC PHONETIC DECODING

Part of the expertise in interpreting cues at phone level has already been transferred successfully to an expert system, giving satisfying "macro class" recognition, as described by Tattegrain [4]. Macro classes distinguished are consonants, stop-consonants, fricatives, vowels, and pauses. Performance of this system is, however, still significantly inferior to the performance of a human expert, reasoning on the same data. This is why expert interviewing sessions have been conceived.

4   EXPERT INTERVIEWING

Human visual perception is essentially as elusive as auditory perception. Visual images of speech can perhaps be manipulated more easily than auditory images. Two different manipulations have been carried out with the representation of cochleagrams and cues for the interviewing sessions undertaken. First of all, the original symbolic representations of cues and cochleagrams have been given a new life, resulting in a discrete representation, which brings computer simulation of the human form of recognition involved a step closer. They have the additional advantage that the human expert is familiar with the character-based representation, as pointed out earlier. Secondly, the time scope of the representations has been limited to the scope of a single phone, despite the original disapproval of the expert, who was not at all confident of being able to recognise such small segments. This scope reduction presents, however, major advantages from a knowledge engineering point of view. It has been shown that coarticulation phenomena can be addressed at this local level by identifying the acoustic phenomena that are "intrinsic" to the phone and those which are "alien". Because the context of the phone is hidden from the expert, this introduces the notion of conditional hypotheses, e.g. "..If this formant comes from the context, then this phone could be an open vowel and the preceding context would be nasal..".

4.1 Cochleagram and symbolic representations

An example of the symbolic representations used is given in fig. 2. The contents of the 'clean.syl' file are shown there, with the '.dip' portions running from frame 151 to frame 161. A "real" 256 channel cochleagram of 'clean.syl' is given in fig. 3, and of 'dirty.syl' in fig. 4

frame	phoneme	art. state		sona-gram	energy curve	energy	low shrill	open closed	sharp flat	compact dispersed	soft sharp	discontin.
108	O	O	CV	.o*#***oo..#.....©.	o	60	|G	|OO	|DD	EEE|	|S	##
109	s	S	FS	..©.......oooo*#oo.	o	56	A|	|O	|DDD	EEE|	|S	###
110	s	S	FS	....ooooo*#*o..	o	56	AA|	FF|	|DDD	EE|		##
111	s	S	FS	..oooo**#**o...	o	58	AAA|	F|	|DDD		|S	#
112	s	S	FS	...o*#oo*#**o...	o	58	AAA|	F|	|DDD			#
113	s	S	FS	.ooo*#*o*#oo....	o	56	AA|	F|	|DD		D|	##
114	s	S	FS	.ooooo#*ooooo.....	o	59	AA|	FF|	|D	|C	D|	#
115	s	S	FS	....o*#*o*ooo..©..	o	56	AA|	FFF|	|D		DD|	#
116	s	S	FC	...o*#****oo..©..	o	58	AAA|	FF|	|DD	E|	D|	##
117	s	S	FC	..ooooooo*#oo..oo.	o	56	AAA|	FF|	|DD		DD|	#
118	s	S	FC	....o#ooo*#oo.....	o	57	AAA|	FF|	|DD		DD|	#
119	s	S	FC	....o*#ooooooo#o.	o	54	AAA|	FF|	|DD		DDD|	##
120	s	S	FC	..ooooo*#**o...	o	54	AAA|	FF|	|DD	|C	D|	##
121	s	S	FC	...oo.o#...oooo#o..	o	54	AA|	F|	|DDD		|S	##
122	u	U	TO	.oo***#***oo..	o	72	|G	|O	|D			####
123	u	U	TO	..oo****#**oo..	o	77	|G	F|	B|	|CC	DD|	##
124	u	U	TO	..oooo**#**oo..	o	78	|G	FF|		|CC	DD|	#
125	u	U	TO	..oooo*#**oo..	o	79	|G	FF|		|CC	DD|	#
126	u	U	TO	...ooo**#**oo....	o	78	|G	FF|		|CC	DD|	#
127	u	U	TO	...ooo*#**o...	o	78	|G	FF|		|CC	DD|	#
128	u	U	TO	..oooo*#**oo...	o	78		FF|		|CC	DD|	#
129	u	U	TO	..oo*o*#**oo..	o	77	|G	F|		|CC	DD|	#
130	u	U	TO	..oo****#**oo..	o	77	|G	FF|		|CC	DD|	#
131	u	U	TO	..oo****#**oo...	o	74	|G	F|		|C	D|	#
132	u	U	TO	.oo****#***oo...	o	73	|G	F|		|CC	D|	#
133	u	U	TO	.oo****#**oo...	o	67	|G			|C	D|	#
134	u	U	TO	..o**#***oo... ©	o	66			|D		DDD|	##
135	s	S	FV	.oo*#*oo... ©. ..	o	60		|O	|D	EE	DDDD|	##
136	s	S	FV	.o#ooo.....©... ..	o	58	A|	|O	|DD	EE|	DDDD|	##
137	s	S	FV	.o#ooo........©. .©.	o	58	A|	|O	|DDD	EE|	DD|	#
138	s	S	FV	..o*#**ooo.....©.	o	63		|OO	|DD	EEE|		##
139	s	S	FV	.oo*#**#**oo..	o	68	|G	|O	|D			##
140	s	S	FV	.oo****#**oo....	o	72	|G			|C		#
141	e	)	TO	.o*****#**oo....	o	72	|G	F|			|S	#
142	e	)	TO	oo*****#**oo....	o	70	|GG				|S	#
143	e	)	TO	o*****#**#ooo..	o	66	|GG		BB|	E|		#
144	e	)	TO	oo***#*****oo..	o	65	|GG		BB|		D|	#
145	e	)	TO	oo***#*****oo..	o	66	|GG		BB|		D|	#
146	e	)	TO	o**#***#**oo.	o	64	|GG		BB|		D|	#
147	n	N	TV	o*#*******oo..	o	64	|GG	|O	BB|	|C	D|	#
148	n	N	TV	***#*****oo..	o	61	|GG	|OO	BB|	|C	D|	##
149	n	N	TV	***#******o..	o	49	|GG	|OOO	B|	E|	|S	##
150	n	N	TV	o**#**o.o#o...	o	38	|G	|OOOO		E|	|SS	##
151	k	K	BF	.o*#**o..o#oo....	o	32		|OOO		EE|	|SS	##
152	k	K	BF	.**#*o.. ..©..©..	o	28	A|	|O	|DD	EEEE|		##
153	k	K	BF	...©..o**#**o..	o	70	A|	|O	|D	EE|	|S	##
154	k	K	BF	...oooo**#oo...	o	68	A|	FF|		E|	|S	###
155	k	K	BF	...ooo**#**oo.	o	58	AA|	FF|	|D	E|	|SS	##
156	k	K	BF	....o#oo***#*oo.	o	60	A|	FF|	|D		|S	##
157	k	K	BF	....oooo**#*o..	o	60	AA|	F|	|D	E|	|S	##
158	a	A	TO	..oo#oo..ooo#ooo..	o	68		|OO		EE|		##
159	a	A	TO	.oo*#ooooooo#ooo..	o	72	|G	|OO	B|	E|	D|	##
160	a	A	TO	..oo#oooooo#oooo..	o	73		|O	B|	E|	D|	#
161	a	A	TO	..ooooooooo#ooooo..	o	74			B|		DD|	#
162	a	A	TO	..ooooooo*#**oo..	o	76			BB|	|C	DD|	#
163	a	A	TO	.....oooo*#*ooo..	o	78			BB|	|C	DD|	##

Fig. 2   Symbolic representation of 'clean.syl'.

below, to show the significant complexity reduction obtained. In the 24-channel symbolic cochleagram, the local maxima of a frame are indicated with a "#" mark and local maxima or minima in the first derivative with an "@" mark. The channel energy outputs have been normalised with respect to the total frame energy, so that the cochleagram reflects the energy distribution in the frequency domain.

The first section of the symbolic cue representations is devoted to the energy curve, which is accompanied by a numeric indication to provide a notion of "absolute" energy level. The dynamic range of the energy curve is coded into about 15 discrete positions (energy lev-

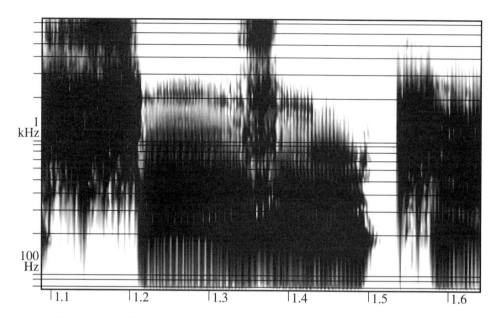

Fig. 3   256-channel cochleagram of 'clean.syl'.

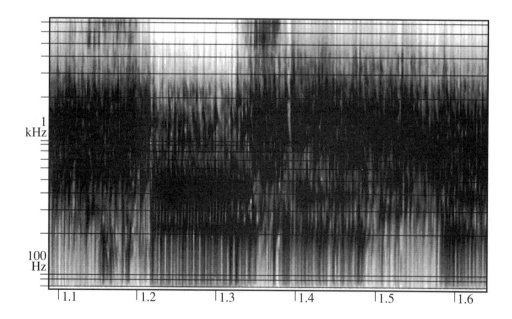

Fig. 4   256-channel cochleagram of 'dirty.syl'.

els below 25 dB and above 85 dB being rare), so that expert observations on the cue form are directed to global-form characteristics, e.g. the energy curve form of the first phone of the 'clean.syl' file (see fig. 2, frames 109-116) is perceived as flat, although there is variation in the energy level.

The energy distribution cues, five in total, are coded into seven levels. The coding mechanisms are adaptive to the speaker; during a recognition session of continuous speech (supposed to be phonetically balanced), the cue representation is progressively normalised with respect to mean and standard deviation of the cues. Because only one sentence was available from the speaker, this procedure has been carried out manually by calculating the cue means and standard deviations for the whole 'clean.wav' file. The 'dirty' segment is thus normalised with respect to the characteristics of the 'clean' section, which seemed the most interesting option. In this way, the 'dirty' phones become representative of a momentary blurring of the cues by accidental (human) background noise.

5   INTERVIEW DESCRIPTION

For the interview, both the 'clean.wav' and the 'dirty.wav' files have been segmented and represented as described above. The blurred phones from 'dirty' (phones 14-31, frames 100-261) have been shuffled together with all the phones (49 phones, 352 frames of 10 ms) of 'clean', thus including the non-perturbed versions of the same frames as those taken from 'dirty'. Note that due to the background noise, segmentation of 'dirty' is not the same as that of 'clean', but comparison of recognition performance by the expert between 'clean' and 'dirty' is nonetheless possible.

The phones were printed on A4 sheets of paper, each containing 6-10 phones. The phones, being in random order, were thus presented in complete isolation from their context and without classification in 'clean' and 'dirty'. Each page was examined in three phases. First, with identity and cochleagram covered, the expert examined phone by phone the energy curve together with the spectral distribution cues, attempting to identify the phones, constructing hypotheses which had to be ordered by likelihood. This is referred to as the cues session, see fig. 2. In a second pass, the symbolic cochleagram was revealed and the phones and their preliminary hypotheses were reviewed, resulting in a final recognition (or not) of the phones on the page. This pass is called the cochleagram session. This form of interview progressively enriches the information presented to the expert and allows comparison of inferences from the cues and those from the cochleagram, which do not necessarily lead to the same conclusion. In a final pass, the evaluation, the identity of the phones was revealed, on the one hand by the uncovering of the labelling, realised by another phonetic expert, and on the other hand by showing the phone in its context, with both the symbolic representation and the 256-channel grey scale cochleagram. In case of doubt, which occurred frequently for the 'dirty' phones, the speech signals concerned were played back.

Before presenting the results, we have to stress that the expert is not at all used to examining English speech, although he showed awareness of differences between French and English during the interview. Secondly, interviewing sessions of this nature have not yet been undertaken for female speakers, for whom the cochleagram tends to show fewer formants. This effect was quite noticeable during the cochleagram sessions.

6   INTERVIEW EVALUATION

The total of 66 phones has been evaluated by assigning one of three different notes to the expert performance on each phone. "Positive" was assigned if the identity of the phone (i.e. either the exact phoneme, or the exact nature, e.g. non-voiced total closure of stop consonant) was the first of the cue hypotheses, without there being more than two candidates *ex equi*; "neutral" if the correct identity was a secondary cue hypothesis or only hypothesised in first position after cochleagram revelation (again with no more than two candidates *ex equi*); and "negative" if none of these demands was satisfied.

Table 1: Recognition results.

Notes	clean	dirty
positive	21[†]	0
neutral	17	5
negative	11[‡]	12[¶]

[†] of which 9 pauses
[‡] of which 5 taken for 'dirty'
[¶] of which 2 taken for 'clean'

Table 1 shows the results of this evaluation. Expert recognition on the 'clean' phones is satisfactory, whereas the 'dirty' phones cannot be satisfactorily recognised. The expert's discouragement during the interviews was noticeable. It should be stressed that nearly all of the 'dirty' phones were recognised as such, about half of them already by disorganisation of the cues. Similarly disorganised phones on the 'clean' side were sometimes mistaken for 'dirty' phones, after which serious interpretation often seemed to be abandoned.

7   CONCLUSIONS

Even though the database used for the interview sessions was not very large, the feasibility of recognition of phones, based on symbolised representations of spectral distribution cues, energy curves and cochleagrams, is clearly demonstrated. This is confirmed by tests already performed on larger databases, not described in this paper. The reduced amount of information involved in the recognition gives a good basis for the development of an expert system for acoustic-phonetic decoding.

The presence of strong human background noise (i.e. voices) is absolutely devastating for the recognition of phones on the basis described. This presence affects the basis of the analysis applied, the spectral distribution of speech energy.

Acknowledgements: The research project described in this article is covered by the EEC SCIENCE program.

REFERENCES

[1] J. Caelen (1979), *Un Modèle d'Oreille. Analyse de la Parole Continue. Reconnaissance Phonémique*, Doctoral Thesis, University of Toulouse, France.

[2] J. Caelen (1986), 'Speech segmenting and kinematics', *Proc. 1986 Montreal Symposium on Speech Recognition*, 223-225.

[3] J. Caelen (1989), 'Indices pour le décodage acoustico-phonétique', in: *Mélanges de phonétique générale et experimentale*, (eds: A. Bothorel *et al.*), Publications of the Strasbourg Phonetics Institute.

[4] H. Tattegrain (1989), 'Phonetic unit localization in a multi-expert recognition system', *Proc. Eurospeech '89 (Paris)*, vol.2, 256-9

[5] V.W. Zue (1979), 'Experiments on spectrogram reading', *Proc. IEEE ICASSP '79*, 116.

Normalised correlation features for speech analysis and pitch extraction

R. De Mori and M. Omologo

1   INTRODUCTION

In many applications of automatic speech recognition (ASR) the acoustic analysis accuracy is a critical issue. When hidden Markov models (HMM) are used (e.g. for large vocabulary speech recognisers), acoustic microsegment models of allophones can be strongly influenced by the acoustic parameter precision, the analysis step and the window size that have been used. Unfortunately, because of the different lengths of acoustic events that occur in speech, appropriate values for such parameters are difficult to establish: a large window can be suitable to better characterise a stationary sound like a vowel, but can produce undesirable bias when applied in the description of an occlusive burst-release. Concerning the spectral description of voiced sounds, another critical issue is the relationship between the size, the offset of the analysis window and the instantaneous pitch period. Furthermore, when the speech signal is corrupted by noise, these problems may become even more crucial: in these cases the characterisation of speech periodicities can be a very difficult task (even if performed by a phonetician through a visual inspection of the signal).

This work discusses the application of a feature which provides detailed periodicity information useful in overcoming these analysis problems. This feature is the normalised cross-correlation (NC) [1] between adjacent speech segments of different length L. Given this lag L, the analysis can be carried out for every speech sample i, evaluating the NC between the speech segments $X[i-L, i]$ and $X[i, i+L]$. The resulting sequence of NC vectors can be well represented as a spectrogram which in this case is called *crosscorrelogram*. This representation is highly informative in analysing the periodicity microvariation of the signal.

In [3] this feature is derived for the development of a very accurate pitch extraction algorithm that can be exploited in a pitch synchronous spectral analysis framework [4]. Moreover, the NC representation can allow a preliminary classification of speech segments, due to some desirable properties that will be described below.

This paper is organised as follows: section 2 introduces the NC representation from the mathematical and the computational points of view; in section 3 some properties are described showing the NC analysis of the given Sheffield sentences; in section 4 an NC-based pitch extraction algorithm is briefly described.

2   NORMALISED CROSSCORRELATION

Given a signal $s(t)$, with zero mean, we define for each instant t_0 two adjacent segments $x_\tau(t, t_0)$ and $y_\tau(t, t_0)$, where the former corresponds to the interval $[t_0 - \tau, t_0]$ and the latter corresponds to the interval $[t_0, t_0 + \tau]$ of $s(t)$ (see fig. 1).

Denoting with $a_\tau(t_0)$ an unknown positive amplitude modulation factor, which reflects the change in the glottal pulse volume, and with $e_\tau(t, t_0)$ an error term that represents the dissimilarity between the two segments, the following relation is assumed:

$$y_\tau(t, t_0) = a_\tau(t_0) x_\tau(t, t_0) + e_\tau(t, t_0). \tag{1}$$

Visual Representations of Speech Signals: Martin Cooke, Steve Beet and Malcolm Crawford (eds.)

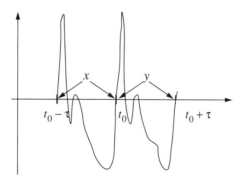

Fig. 1   Example of two adjacent segments of length τ equal to the pitch period centred at time t_0.

In order to find the lag $\tau = T_0$, which corresponds to the instantaneous pitch period at time instant t_0, the dissimilarity between the two segments, expressed in terms of the normalised squared error, is considered:

$$E_\tau(t_0) = \frac{\int_0^\tau [y_\tau(t, t_0) - a_\tau(t_0) x_\tau(t, t_0)]^2 dt}{\int_0^\tau y_\tau^2(t, t_0) dt}. \tag{2}$$

Differentiating $E_\tau(t_0)$ with respect to the variable $a_\tau(t_0)$ to minimise the dissimilarity expressed above, leads to the following maximisation problem (for the sake of simplicity, the following formulae will not include the variable t_0, while x and y will indicate $x_\tau(t, t_0)$ and $y_\tau(t, t_0)$, respectively):

$$T_0 = \frac{max}{\tau} \rho_\tau(x, y) \tag{3}$$

$$\rho_\tau(x, y) = \frac{(x, y)_\tau}{|x_\tau| |y_\tau|} \tag{4}$$

where $(x, y)_\tau$ is the inner product between the $x_\tau(t, t_0)$ and $y_\tau(t, t_0)$ vectors, while $|x_\tau|$ and $|y_\tau|$ denote their magnitudes. $\rho_\tau(x, y)$ is called the normalised crosscorrelation (NC) coefficient for the given lag τ, at instant t_0. Given a set of lags τ, that corresponds to a range of pitch periods expected in speech, (3) provides an instantaneous pitch period estimation.

It is worth noting that:

- $\rho_\tau(x, y)$ does not correspond to an autocorrelation function: for every relative time lag τ, the autocorrelation is computed on the same signal segment of fixed length, higher than the maximum τ. Furthermore, a window is generally applied to the speech segment before computing the autocorrelation [5]. In this sense, an advantage of the NC computation is that no windowing is involved.

- The maximisation procedure (3) corresponds, in a geometric sense, to the minimisation of the angle between vectors x and y, with respect to the lag τ: $\rho_\tau(x, y)$ represents the cosine of this angle. In other words, the magnitude of the vectors does not influence this evaluation, leading to a more robust representation of speech segments involving significant energy variations (e.g. voice onset, occlusive sounds, etc.).

- $\rho_\tau(x, y)$ is influenced by fluctuations of the speech signals, due either to very low frequency noise or to a local non-zero mean: in these cases (4) should be evaluated subtracting the means of x and y from the corresponding segments.

Since this effect generally appears for low-energy signals, a way to reduce it is to add a constant c_τ to each term of the denominator of (4).

- The NC computation, obtained evaluating (4) for every sample and for every lag corresponding to a given frequency range, is not feasible. The computation can be speeded up exploiting, for a given lag, contributions to the terms of (4) that are common to its evaluation at two consecutive samples. Furthermore, simpler computational schemes can be conceived exploiting the high redundancy of the NC representation both in the lag scale and in the time scale. As an example, the number of lags used in the computation of the NC sequences can be reduced, without significant loss of information, to a constant number for each octave; this constant can be fixed according to difference limen-based criteria [2]. Along the timescale, the redundancy is very high for voiced segments, especially inside each pitch period: a time compression can be accomplished either averaging or, in a simpler way, decimating in time the NC representation; an alternative is to apply a preliminary low-pass filtering and decimation stage to the speech signal as described in [3].

3 CROSSCORRELOGRAM PROPERTIES

The NC representation lends itself to an immediate interpretation through a graphic description, similar to a spectrogram and here called crosscorrelogram, where the horizontal axis represents time and the vertical axis represents decreasing lags (i.e. increasing frequencies): at each instant t_0 the NC sequence, obtained computing (4) for each lag τ (see an example in fig. 2), is projected on the crosscorrelogram as shown in fig. 3.

For a perfectly periodic signal of period T_0 the function $\rho_\tau(x, y)$ would have identical maxima at $\tau = kT_0$, where k is a positive integer value. In practice, due to the nonstationarity of the speech signal the NC maxima at multiples or submultiples of T_0 can sometimes exceed the maximum at T_0: this fact can correspond either to a dominant first formant or to abrupt changes of pitch and energy (e.g. voice onset, occlusive bursts followed by vowels, etc.). Generally, during voiced sounds the crosscorrelogram is clear and depicts one or more *stripes*, depending on the fundamental frequency contour. Each stripe corresponds to a part of the NC information related to the range of lags $[kT_0, (k+1)T_0]$, where T_0 is the pitch period. The boundaries of each stripe correspond to the evolution of the pitch period and of its submultiples. With a suitable choice of the lag scale (i.e. of the frequency range), the upper ridge of the first stripe corresponds to the pitch contour. If the lag axis is logarithmically scaled (constant number of lags for each octave) then these stripes are not equally spaced, as depicted in fig. 4.

Inside each stripe there can be other dark and light areas (peaks and valleys of NC) related to the maxima and minima positions of the signal inside a pitch period, as shown in fig. 5.

Other interesting acoustic cues are the width and the position of the NC peaks and valleys. While the most prominent peaks, as already pointed out, correspond to the pitch period and its multiples, the less prominent peaks and the valleys carry information about the relation between the pitch frequency and low-formant frequencies. Also the width of peaks and valleys deserves some investigation: as an example, nasal sounds are characterised by a greater width with respect to vowel sounds, agreeing with the time-domain structure of the signals. Hence, the NC representation can be exploited to preliminarily classify voiced speech segments.

On the other hand, unvoiced signals are characterised by a low dynamic of the normalised crosscorrelation curve (this property can be exploited to perform a very simple and robust voiced-unvoiced decision). In these cases the curve shape is more significant than the maxima values: silence and unvoiced closures are characterised by a flat curve, while fricative and affricate sounds are characterised by an irregular crosscorrelogram curve with some possible

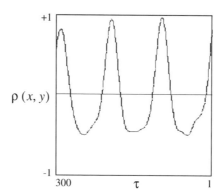

Fig. 2   NC sequence, evaluated in a voiced segment, for different lags τ: peaks correspond (from right to left) to the pitch period and its multiples. The horizontal axis covers the lag range from 300 to 1 corresponding to the frequency range from 66 to 10000 Hz.

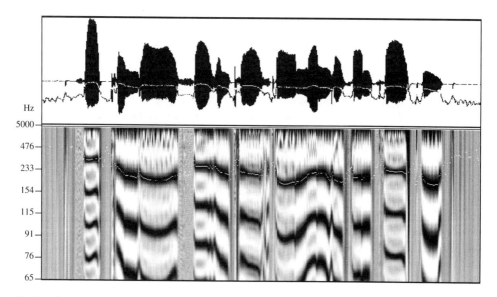

Fig. 3   Analysis of 'clean.wav' ("Fred can go, Susan can't go, and Linda is uncertain", female speaker). *upper* : speech signal and corresponding energy contour; *lower* : the crosscorrelogram — the superimposed white contour corresponds to the pitch evolution.

peaks due to local random high correlations. This fact confirms that the NC representation is not a promising analysis tool for classifying unvoiced sounds.

A further property, evident only using a very low analysis step (less than 1 ms), is related to the correlation between different cycles inside a pitch period and the NC sequences corresponding to high frequencies. An example is given in fig. 6. This property could be useful to a successive, more precise and reliable, parameter extraction, for example through a pitch-synchronised analysis technique.

Finally, it is worth noting that the NC representation is very robust when the speech signal is corrupted by noise. Two examples are given in figs. 7 and 8.

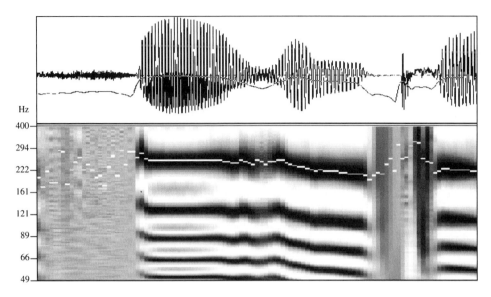

Fig. 4   Analysis of "... Susan ca..." from the sentence shown in fig. 3. The vertical axis is logarithmically scaled: each octave interval is represented by 36 frequencies.

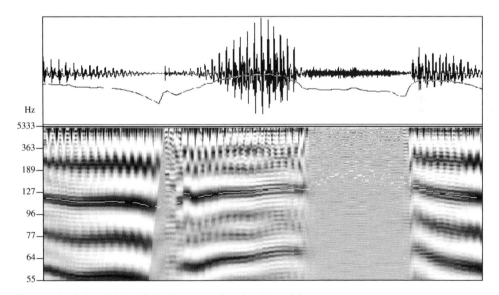

Fig. 5   Analysis of 'timit.syl' ("... in greasy..." spoken by male).

4   PITCH ANALYSIS

The most obvious application where the NC representation can be well exploited is pitch extraction. In [3] pitch tracking is performed selecting for each frame some integer pitch period candidates among the NC local maxima. We have investigated an alternative approach, based on the determination of an optimal path in the crosscorrelogram grid (of $N \times M$ points) which connects an arbitrary point $(1, m_1)$ of the first frame to an arbitrary point (N, m_N) of the last frame. The optimality criterion is based on the following maximisation:

$$D^{\circ} = \max_{m} D(N, m) \tag{5}$$

where:

$$D(n, m) = [C(n, m) + 1]^2 + max \begin{cases} D(n-1, m) \\ D(n-1, m-1) \\ D(n-1, m+1) \\ D(n, m-1) \\ D(n, m+1) \end{cases} \tag{6}$$

and $C(n, m)$ is the crosscorrelation value at time instant n and lag m. In other words, this approach is based on a classical optimal path-finding method, where the path is allowed to make vertical steps in both directions. In some preliminary experiments this technique has provided good pitch tracking (as depicted in several figures of this paper) even if applied to noisy speech signals.

5 CONCLUSIONS

The NC representation offers many desirable properties that allow a robust pitch extraction. Its use can be oriented to an accurate characterisation of voiced speech segments using a pitch-synchronous spectral analysis. The objective of this work was to introduce this representation and to describe its most significant properties. Future work will be devoted to investigating how these properties can be exploited in the classification of speech segments.

Acknowledgements: Discussions with Jordan Cohen have been a source of inspiration for the work described in this paper. This research has been conducted under the IRST project MAIA Advanced Model of Artificial Intelligence.

REFERENCES

[1] J. Cohen, Personal communication.

[2] W. Hess (1983), *Pitch Determination of Speech Signals*, Springer-Verlag, Berlin.

[3] Y. Medan, E. Yair & D. Chazan (1991), 'Super resolution pitch determination of speech signals', *IEEE Trans. on Signal Processing*, **39**, 1.

[4] Y. Medan & E. Yair (1989), 'Pitch synchronous spectral analysis scheme for voiced speech', *IEEE Trans. on Signal Processing*, **37**, 9.

[5] L. R. Rabiner & R. W. Schafer (1978), *Digital Processing of Speech Signals*, Prentice-Hall, Englewood-Cliffs, NJ.

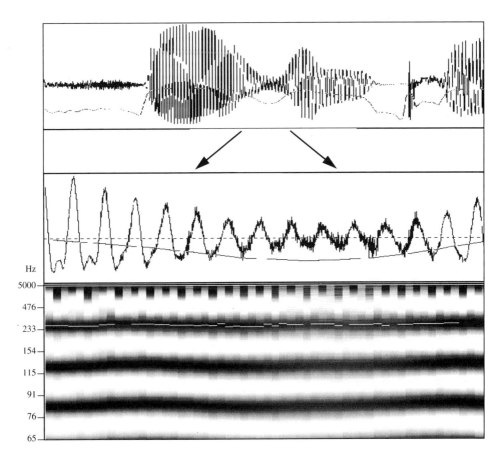

Fig. 6   Detail of the crosscorrelogram for 'clean.syl'. The zoomed portion corresponds to the transition between "u" and "s" in the word "Susan". In this case the vertical axis is linearly scaled. NC peaks, evaluated for frequencies higher than 500 Hz, can be exploited to identify different cycles inside every pitch period.

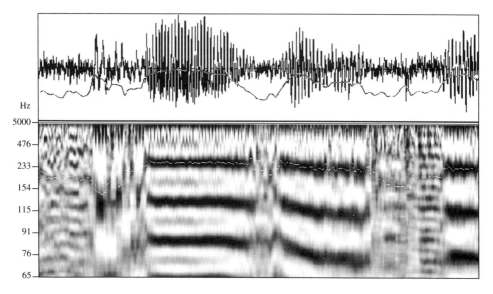

Fig. 7   Analysis of the noisy version of the portion given in fig. 4. The vertical axis is linearly scaled. The figure shows the robustness of the NC representation and of the pitch extraction algorithm.

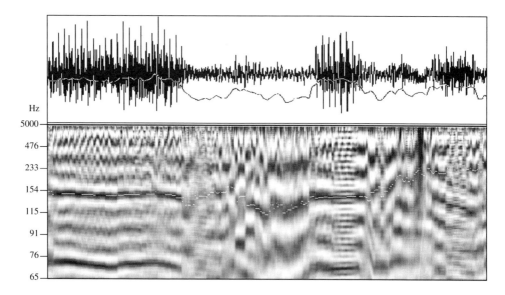

Fig. 8   Analysis of the portion "...half of bitter..." of 'spont.wav' uttered by a male speaker in a public house. Even if speech is distorted by high background noise, the crosscorrelogram still shows the pitch contour.

Auditory representations of speech sounds

Roy D. Patterson, Michael Allerhand and John Holdsworth

1 INTRODUCTION

A computational model of auditory processing has been developed to summarise existing knowledge of human hearing and to provide a platform for further research in a system with a manageable computational load (i.e. currently 50 megabytes per second for real-time operation). Most of the processing is devoted to simulating the operation of the cochlea in a fairly traditional way, that is with a bank of auditory filters and a bank of neural transduction units. The remainder is devoted to two novel processes: firstly, a form of quantised temporal integration introduced to account for the stability of the auditory images produced by periodic sounds; and secondly, a spiral pitch processor that operates on the auditory image and which gives proper weight to the prominence of octaves in pitch perception.

The system is modular and enables the user to examine the auditory representation of sound at the output of each of the processing stages. It is intended for use with everyday signals like music and speech and everyday background sounds like those of engines, motors and fans. These sounds are typically broadband and so the system must have 50-100 filter channels spanning the range 100 - 8000 Hz and it must operate at a sampling rate of 20 kHz or more. As a result, the data rates of the auditory representations flowing from the processing modules are of the order of 1-2 megabytes per second! The only human perceptual system capable of handling anything like this bandwidth is the visual system. Consequently, the software has an integrated set of static and dynamic visual displays, and it processes the sound through to the display automatically. In this paper, we illustrate the operation of the four modules of the auditory model with eight auditory representations of the speech sounds 'clean' and 'dirty'.

2 COCHLEA SIMULATION: AUDITORY SPECTROGRAMS AND COCHLEOGRAMS

The cochlea simulation is composed of two processing modules: a *gammatone auditory filterbank* which performs a spectral analysis and converts the acoustic wave into a multi-channel representation of basilar membrane motion, and a *two-dimensional adaptation* mechanism that "transduces" the membrane motion and converts it into a multi-channel representation of the neural activity pattern flowing from the cochlea to the cochlear nucleus.

2.1 The gammatone auditory filterbank

The gammatone (GT) filter is defined in the time domain by its impulse response

$$gt(t) = at^{n-1}e^{-2\pi bt}\cos(2\pi f_c t + \phi) \qquad t > 0. \tag{1}$$

The name *gammatone* comes from the fact that the envelope of the impulse response is the familiar *gamma* function from statistics, and the fine structure of the impulse response is a *tone* at the centre frequency of the filter, f_c.

Visual Representations of Speech Signals: Martin Cooke, Steve Beet and Malcolm Crawford (eds.)
© 1993 by John Wiley & Sons Ltd

There are three main reasons for choosing the gammatone function as an auditory filter:

- The impulse response (eqn. (1)) provides an excellent fit to the impulse responses obtained from single-unit studies with cats.

- The shape of the magnitude characteristic of the GT filter with order 4 is very similar to that of the *roex(p)* function commonly used to represent the magnitude characteristic of the human auditory filter.

- An *n*th-order GT filter can be approximated by a cascade of n, identical, first-order GT filters, and the first-order GT filter has a recursive, digital implementation that is particularly efficient.

A discussion of the GT as an auditory filter is presented in Patterson & Holdsworth [4]. The parameter b determines the bandwidth of the filter; n is the order and it determines the tuning. When the order is 4, b is 1.019 times the equivalent rectangular bandwidth (ERB). The most recent estimates by Glasberg & Moore [1] indicate that for humans the ERB is a simple function of the centre frequency of the filter, f_c. Specifically

$$\text{ERB} = 24.7 + 0.108 f_c \ . \tag{2}$$

If we assume that auditory filters are distributed across frequency in proportion to their bandwidth, then eqns. (1) and (2) provide a complete specification of a human GT filterbank.

The response of an 85-channel system to the sound 'clean.syl' is presented in fig. 1a. Each line shows the output of one filter; the lowest and highest centre frequencies are 100 and 3200 Hz, respectively. The surface defined by the set of lines is intended to simulate basilar membrane motion in response to 'clean.syl'. When presented on this "syllable time-scale" the display shows what appears to be a fine-grain, auditory spectrogram, that is, a spectrogram with an auditory frequency scale and no temporal integration other than that implied in plotting the filtered waves in this compressed form. When presented on a "diphone time-scale", this auditory representation provides a wealth of detail concerning, for example, the time course of stop consonants and the shape of the resonances that underlie the formants of voiced sounds (Patterson *et al.* [5]).

2.2 Two-dimensional adaptation and feature enhancement

Data from individual inner hair cells indicate that they compress and rectify the basilar membrane motion. They also adapt to level changes rapidly, and there is a lateral interaction in the frequency dimension which results in areas of intense activity suppressing areas of lesser activity. In the cochlea simulation, this processing is performed by a bank of logarithmic compressors and a bank of adaptation units that apply adaptation to the membrane motion simultaneously in time and in frequency. The module converts the surface that represents basilar membrane motion into another surface that represents our approximation to the neural activity pattern (NAP) that flows from the cochlea up the auditory nerve to the cochlear nucleus (Patterson & Holdsworth [4]). The auditory representation of 'clean.syl' produced by the full cochlea simulation is presented in fig. 1b; when presented on this syllable time-scale, the representation is often referred to as a "cochleogram". Note that the compression has increased the relative strength of the second formant of the vowel, and the suppression has sharpened the formants in both the spectral and the temporal dimensions.

The effects of suppression are more readily observed in displays that place more emphasis on the level of activity in the representation, namely spectra. Auditory representations of this form are achieved by short-term averaging of the rectified output of each channel of the filterbank, or each channel of the full cochlea simulation, and plotting the array of average values as a function of filter number (in ERBs). Suppression operates at the diphone time scale and so this analysis focuses on the vowel in the latter half of 'clean.dip' and 'dirty.dip'. When the spectra are calculated from the auditory spectrogram, the results are referred to as 'auditory spectra'; when the cochleogram is employed, the results are referred to as 'excita-

a
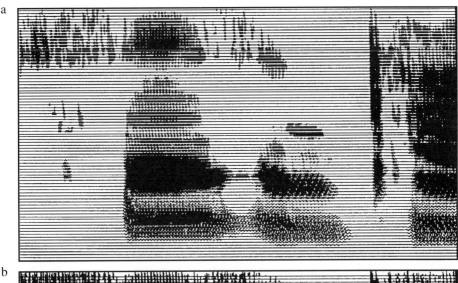

b
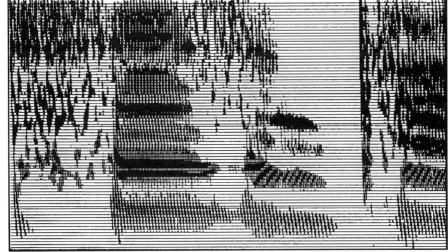

Fig. 1   Two auditory representations of 'clean.syl'. The auditory spectrogram *a* is produced by the gammatone auditory filterbank on its own. The cochleogram *b* is produced by the full cochlea simulation. Each line shows one channel of the analysis. The dark horizontal bands mark the fundamental and formants of the vowels; the formants are sharper in the cochleogram. The fine-grain vertical striations in the vowels are the glottal pulses of the voice pitch; they too are more apparent in the cochleogram. The narrow vertical band is a consonant burst.

tion patterns'. Eight frames of each representation of the vowel in 'clean.dip' are presented on the left in fig. 2, with the excitation pattern in the lower panel; the frames are spaced at 10 ms intervals. In the absence of adaptation and suppression (upper), the level of activity rises continuously throughout vowel onset and the only sharpening in the auditory spectrum is relative — there is a disproportionate rise in level at the fundamental and the formant frequencies as time proceeds. With adaptation and suppression (lower), the rise in level over frames occurs only at the peak frequencies; between these frequencies activity is suppressed as time proceeds, and the resulting excitation patterns have sharper features.

The upper and lower panels on the right in fig. 2 show auditory spectra and excitation patterns, respectively, for 'dirty.syl'. In the auditory spectra the added noise reduces the peak-to-valley ratio of all the peaks and it obscures the smaller peaks. The excitation patterns show that the suppression restores most of the peak-to-valley ratio for the larger peaks. They also reveal that some of the smaller peaks in the mid-frequency range are centred at new frequencies, indicating that they are probably from the added "noise".

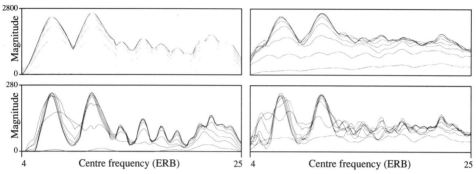

Fig. 2   *upper* : auditory spectra and *lower* : excitation patterns for the latter half of *left* : 'clean.dip'
and *right* : 'dirty.dip' . The fundamental and formants are sharpened in the excitation pattern
during the adaptation.

3   AUDITORY IMAGES: Construction and Processing

The centre section of the vowel in 'clean.syl' is a quasi-periodic sound and so it generates alternating periods of activity and quiescence in the neural activity pattern. But vowels do not give rise to the sensation of rapid loudness fluctuations. Indeed, periodic and quasi-periodic sounds give rise to very stable auditory images, indicating that some form of temporal integration (TI) occurs prior to our initial perception of a vowel. Until recently, it was assumed that a simple low-pass filter could performed the TI and smooth the cochleogram prior to perception. However, if that filter had an integration time long enough to produce stable vowel images for the average male voice, it would smear out temporal features that we hear, for example, the temporal jitter of glottal pulses that helps us distinguish speakers.

3.1 Auditory image construction

Patterson *et al.* [7] have proposed a solution to the TI problem in the form of triggered, quantised, temporal integration. Briefly, a bank of delay lines is used to form a buffer store for the neural activity flowing from the cochlea; the pattern decays away as it flows out to about 50 ms. Each channel has a trigger unit which monitors the instantaneous activity level and when it encounters a peak it transfers the entire record in that channel of the buffer to the corresponding channel of a static image buffer, where the record is added, point for point, with whatever is already in that channel of the image buffer. The multi-channel result of this quantised TI process is the auditory image. For quasi-periodic sounds, the trigger mechanism rapidly matches the TI period to the period of the sound and, much like a stroboscope, it produces a static image of the repeating temporal pattern flowing up the auditory nerve. It also converts the neural pattern of a dynamic sound, like a syllable with a diphthong, into a dynamic image, in which the motion of the formants occurs at the rate that we hear the vowel change.

Auditory images from the sustained portion of the 'ca' vowel in 'clean.dip' and 'dirty.dip' are shown in figs. 3a and 3b, respectively. Each line in the figure shows the contents of an individual channel. Whereas, the harmonics of the vowel sound are evenly spaced across frequency, the width of the auditory filter increases with its centre frequency. As a result, the

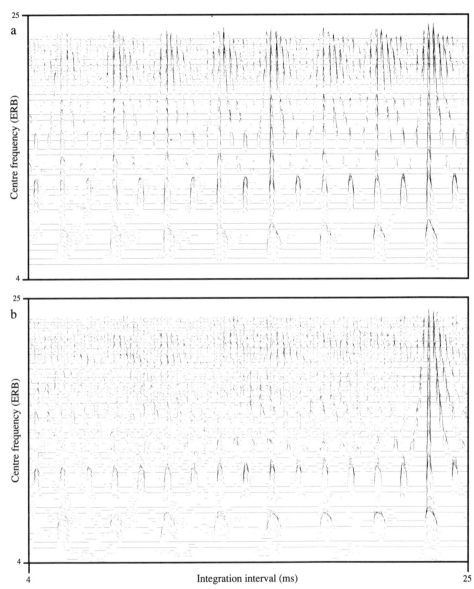

Fig. 3   Auditory images from the sustained part of the vowel in *a* : 'clean.dip' and *b* : 'dirty.dip'
produced by quantised temporal integration. The shape of the repeating pattern in 'clean'
represents the vowel quality information; the spacing of the repetitions represents the pitch
of the vowel. The noise in 'dirty' obscures the upper formants of the vowel at this point in
time.

auditory filter isolates individual harmonics of the vowel in the lower half of fig. 3a. At the
bottom of the figure, the series of evenly spaced humps show the remains of the fundamental
after compression and rectification and adaptation; the spacing of the humps is the period of
the voice pitch. From the fundamental to the middle of the figure, the channels show two,
three or four humps per glottal period for the second, third and fourth harmonics, respectively. The level of the third harmonic is relatively weak indicating that the first formant is below,

and the second formant above, this region. In the upper half of the figure where the auditory filter is broad relative to the harmonic spacing, the formants appear as sets of impulse responses with the longest responses occurring in the centre of the formant and the shortest occurring between formants. It is assumed that the details of the structure of the repeating vowel pattern are the basis of vowel quality and distinctiveness — details that are eliminated by the integration process in traditional speech preprocessors.

The auditory image makes a major distinction between periodic sounds and noises. Whereas the former produce static images with a detailed repeating pattern, noises produce continually fluctuating images with no long-term structure. The auditory image of 'dirty.dip' in fig. 3b provides an example; the added noise dominates the activity in the upper channels and the result is an essentially random pattern in the region away from trigger point at the right-hand side of the image.

Real-time "auditory cartoons" of sounds can be produced by calculating the auditory image every 20-40 ms and then rapidly replaying a sequence of these cartoon frames in synchrony with the sound (a representation originally suggested by Lyon [2]). The auditory cartoons of vowels and fricative consonants can largely be predicted from the examples in fig. 3. A stationary vowel appears as a more or less populated grid of activity in which the spacing of the verticals of the grid represents the pitch of the sound and the position of the activity on the verticals specifies the formants. When the pitch of the vowel decreases, the grid expands towards the left and down; the position of the formants is largely unchanged. Vowel changes are observed as vertical motion in the first three formants, and the motion is largely independent of pitch changes. When the pitch changes rapidly or the formants move rapidly, the features towards the left of the image become blurred and their level drops. Thus, a comparison of portions of the pattern from the left and right of the image provides information about the rate and direction of ongoing changes in the speech. Plosive consonants appear as transients in the auditory cartoon; that is, they appear as a brief flash of activity down the trigger point vertical towards the right of the image.The consonants are distinguished by the distribution of activity along the trigger point vertical and by the aspiration and temporal gaps that surround the plosive burst in time.

3.2 Auditory image processing

Periodic sounds produce regularly spaced peaks in the auditory image (fig. 3a) and the peaks are aligned across channels. Patterson [3] has shown that if we compress the image vertically, extend it horizontally, and wrap the resulting ribbon into a spiral, then repeating peaks fall on a small number of spokes radiating from the centre of the spiral. The pattern of spokes is fixed (i.e. the inter-spoke angles); the orientation of the pattern specifies the pitch chroma of the sound. The details of the operation of the spiral are beyond the scope of this short paper. Rather we will focus on a pattern recognition mechanism developed recently to extract three parameters — that arguably could represent three auditory sensations — from the spiral representation of the auditory image loudness: pitch chroma and pitch strength [7]. The process begins with the calculation of the level of activity in each of 64 equi-angular sectors around the spiral, and the normalised level of activity in each sector. The values are typically calculated every 10 ms and so the analysis is appropriate to all speech time scales.

The sets of normalisation values derived from 'clean.wav' and 'dirty.wav' are presented by the two contours in fig. 4b; 'clean.wav' itself is presented in fig. 4a. Where the contours in fig. 4b overlap, the interference from the noise in 'dirty.wav' is largely inaudible; where they diverge, the interference is most noticeable. This suggests that the normalisation contour is a reasonable candidate for a measure of the instantaneous loudness of sounds. Following normalisation, the spiral pattern processor determines the best-fitting orientation for the spoke pattern and then it estimates the proportion of the activity in the image associated with the best-fitting spoke pattern. The orientation parameter is clearly related to pitch chroma; the

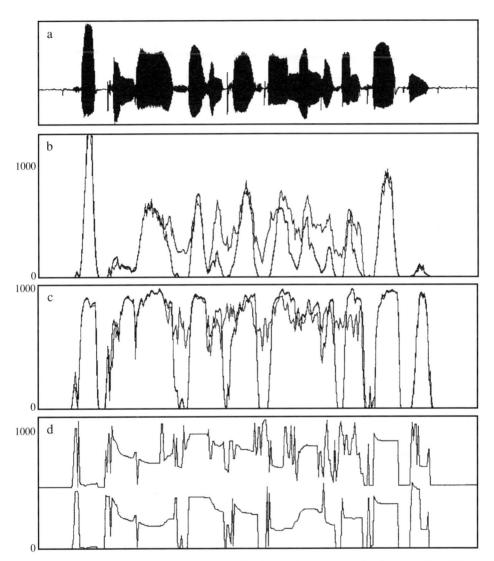

Fig. 4   *a* : 'Clean.wav' along with contours showing *b* : the instantaneous loudness; *c* : the pitch
strength; and, *d* : the pitch of the speech. The upper lines in *b* and *c* show the contour for
dirty.wav, as does the upper trace in *d*.

proportion of activity on the pattern is related to pitch strength, or the degree of voicing when
the sound is speech.

The pitch contours for 'clean.wav' and 'dirty.wav' are presented by the lower and upper
traces in fig. 4d, respectively; the pitch-strength contours are presented in fig. 4c, and as with
the loudness contours, when they diverge, the upper contour is for 'dirty.wav'. The strength
contours show that the onset and offset of voicing in clean speech is abrupt and that strong
voicing can be detected in soft syllables (compare the loudness and pitch-strength contours
for the last syllable). The strength values do not vary from syllable to syllable nearly as much
as the loudness values and so this measure might be a better candidate than loudness for the
initial segmentation of the speech wave.

Turning to the pitch contours (fig. 4d), we find that they are quite similar despite the added noise in 'dirty.wav' (the upper contour). If, for prosody purposes, pitch estimates are limited to the regions where the pitch is changing relatively slowly, the mechanism would be rendered largely insensitive to the presence of the interfering sound. This noise resistance is largely due to the fact that the spiral pattern processor is a multi-channel pitch extractor and it is typically the case that not all of the channels are masked at the same time.

Finally, it should be mentioned that the pitch-height (octave) of multi-harmonic sounds can also be estimated from the spiral auditory image (Patterson *et al.* [6]). The process is somewhat complex but, broadly speaking, the average distance of the peaks from the centre of the spiral specifies the pitch height of the sound.

4   SUMMARY

The paper provides examples of the representations of speech sounds available from an auditory model referred to as AICAP (Auditory Image Construction and Processing). The model simulates basilar membrane motion and VIIIth-nerve activity patterns in response to speech. When the outputs of these modules are plotted on a compressed time scale they provide representations referred to as 'auditory spectrograms' and 'cochleograms' (fig. 1). The effect of neural adaptation and suppression is discussed with the aid of two further cochlear representations referred to as 'auditory spectra' and 'excitation patterns' (fig. 2). The remaining modules provide for the construction of auditory images (fig. 3) and the processing of the spiral auditory image to extract contours for loudness, pitch chroma and pitch strength (fig. 4).

Acknowledgements: The work presented in this paper was supported by the MRC and grants from Esprit BRA (3207) and MOD PE (XR 2239 & SLS/42B/663).

REFERENCES

[1] B.R. Glasberg & B.C.J. Moore (1990), 'Derivation of auditory filter shapes from notched-noise data', *Hearing Research*, **47**, 103-138.

[2] R.F. Lyon (1984), 'Computational models of neural auditory processing', *Proc. ICASSP '84 (San Diego)*.

[3] R.D. Patterson (1987), 'A pulse ribbon model of peripheral auditory processing', In: *Auditory Processing of Complex Sounds* (eds. W.A. Yost & C.S. Watson), Lawrence Erlbaum Associates, Hillsdale, NJ, 167-179.

[4] R.D.Patterson & J. Holdsworth (1992), 'A functional model of neural activity patterns and auditory images', In: *Advances in Speech, Hearing and Language Processing Vol. 3* (ed. W. A. Ainsworth), JAI Press, London (in press).

[5] R.D. Patterson, J. Holdsworth & M. Allerhand (1992), 'Auditory Models as preprocessors for speech recognition', In: *The Auditory Processing of Speech: From the auditory periphery to words* (ed. M. E. H. Schouten), Mouton de Gruyter, Berlin, 67-83.

[6] R.D. Patterson, R. Milroy & M. Allerhand (1992), 'What is the octave of a harmonically rich note?', in: *Proc. 2nd Int. Conf. on Music and the Cognitive Sciences* (ed. I. Cross), Harwood, London (in press).

[7] M. Allerhand, K. Robinson & R.D. Patterson (1991), 'SVOS 5: Application of the SVOS algorithm', *APU technical report*.

[8] R.D. Patterson, K. Robinson, J. Holdsworth, D. McKeown, C. Zhang & M. Allerhand (1992), 'Complex sounds and auditory images', In: *Auditory Physiology and Perception* (eds. Y Cazals, L. Demany & K. Horner), Pergamon, Oxford, 429-446.

The representation of temporal information in time-frequency distributions and the auditory nerve

33

James W. Pitton and Les Atlas

1   INTRODUCTION

Speech processing tools such as filterbanks or the spectrogram are based on a quasi-stationary assumption, and hence subject to trade-offs between time and frequency resolution. As a result of this dependence between time and frequency, these techniques yield only a smooth approximation to the underlying time-varying spectral content of the signal, and cannot simultaneously preserve details of the temporal structure of the waveform. These details may, however, be important for speech analysis and recognition. Time-frequency distributions (TFDs) are a generalised mapping of the signal to the time-frequency domain, providing a joint distribution of signal energy. In these representations, there is no inherent trade-off between time and frequency as in quasi-stationary techniques; the temporal details of speech are resolved independently of frequency resolution. Temporal details that are not available in quasi-stationary representations have also been observed in the auditory system. The auditory nerve simultaneously preserves both spectral and temporal information in its discharge patterns. This simultaneous representation of time and frequency, poorly handled by quasi-stationary techniques such as the spectrogram, is implicitly handled by current auditory modelling approaches [e.g. 7,12]. We propose to *explicitly* represent time and frequency simultaneously through proper TFDs and associated theory. By working from a sound theoretical foundation, the understanding of speech representations and of auditory representations of speech will be advanced (for a detailed introduction to TFDs, see [2] and the tutorial in this volume [5]).

2   BACKGROUND: TEMPORAL INFORMATION IN AUDITORY NERVE FIBRES

The basilar membrane (BM) of the cochlea decomposes a stimulus over a tonotopic mapping determined by distance along the cochlea. Associated with each place along the BM is a best, or characteristic, frequency (CF); this mapping is preserved in the auditory nerve (AN). Each AN fibre reflects the filtering properties of the BM at that fibre's point of innervation. The average rate response of AN fibres reflects the spectral content of the stimulus [11,15], so that the firing patterns of a particular fibre correspond to the time-varying spectral content of the stimulus in the neighbourhood of the fibre's CF. Thus, the AN forms a sort of "biological TFD". In addition, the firing patterns of fibres are affected by the nonlinearities of the auditory system: e.g., the BM's compressive nonlinearity, the rectification of the signal resulting from the transduction properties of the inner hair cells (IHCs), and adaptation effects.

AN fibres have also been shown to phase-lock to the filtered stimulus waveform itself, preserving aspects of the fine-time detail of the input. This effect can be observed in post-stimulus time (PST) histograms, which show the distribution of AN fibre firing time with respect to stimulus onset. PST histograms resemble rectified versions of the BM-filtered stim-

Visual Representations of Speech Signals: Martin Cooke, Steve Beet and Malcolm Crawford (eds.)
© 1993 by John Wiley & Sons Ltd

ulus. This effect has been observed over a wide range of frequencies (up to 4-5 kHz in cats) for single tones and harmonic complexes of tones [4]. For the case of harmonic tone complexes, the Fourier transform of the PST histogram reveals the presence of multiple harmonics of the stimulus, rather than just the dominant frequency. The harmonics present in the histogram spectrum correspond to the stimulus harmonics that lie within the response area of the AN fibre.

In a series of papers [11,15], Sachs & Young explored the responses of cat AN fibres to synthetic vowels. The authors observed that the average firing rate of the fibres saturated at moderately high stimulus intensities, resulting in a broadening of the fibre's response area to the vowel. These results suggest that average firing rate is not a sufficiently robust representation for vowels (although information coded by the small population of low spontaneous rate fibres has not been accounted for). The authors subsequently explored the temporal responses of AN fibres to vowels. It was found that the fibres phase-lock to the individual harmonics of the formants over a wide range of stimulus intensities, providing a robust representation of the vowel spectrum, and preserving the fine time structure of the filtered input stimulus. Other researchers have explored the coding of vowels in the temporal patterns of AN fibres, with consistent results [3,9,13,14]. In particular, Delgutte & Kiang [3] observed that fibres with CFs near a formant frequency encode in their temporal patterns harmonics of the fundamental frequency in the vicinity of the formant. The observed temporal responses are consistent with preservation of the overall temporal structure of the stimulus in the firing patterns; this structure can be observed in the PST histograms of the AN fibres (fig. 3 of [4]). This effect is maintained for stimuli with time-varying frequency components such as formant glides, where phase-locking tracks the instantaneous frequencies of the components [9,14].

3   TEMPORAL INFORMATION IN TIME-FREQUENCY DISTRIBUTIONS

TFDs represent a distribution of signal energy simultaneously in time and frequency; i.e., a time-frequency energy density function. A proper TFD [6] is nonnegative and preserves the marginal distributions of a signal in time and frequency. The frequency content of a signal $s(t)$ is found by computing its Fourier transform, $S(f)$. From this, we have the signal's spectral density function, $|S(f)|^2$, which shows the distribution of signal energy over all frequencies, or the frequency marginal. Similarly, the distribution of signal energy in time, the time marginal, is simply the instantaneous energy of the signal, $|s(t)|^2$. Integrating a proper distribution over all time yields $|S(f)|^2$, and integrating over all frequencies returns $|s(t)|^2$. A TFD which preserves the marginal density functions is said to "satisfy the marginals".

To illustrate the effects of satisfying the marginals in a TFD, it is useful to consider one which doesn't. The spectrogram is undoubtedly the most widely used (and, by that standard, useful) TFD, but it does not satisfy the marginals, and hence it is not a proper distribution. The spectrogram does, however, provide an intuitively satisfying (albeit inaccurate [5]) representation of the time-varying spectral content of a signal. Varying degrees of resolution are obtained with different window parameters. A wideband spectrogram (WB-SG) will more closely resolve temporal details of a stimulus at the expense of frequency resolution; a narrowband spectrogram (NB-SG) yields exactly the opposite. In both cases, though, information in both time and frequency is smeared to some degree, and hence not available in the representation.

Consider, for example, a simple harmonic resonator, modelling a single vowel formant. Figs. 1a-1c show the signal $s(t)$, a WB-SG and a NB-SG, respectively, of this signal. The WB-SG yields the dominant frequency of the resonator, and shows increased energy coincident with the driving function. However, it does not preserve the fine detail seen in the time marginal. The NB-SG, in contrast, resolves the individual harmonics of the resonator, spaced by the fundamental frequency of the driving function, similar to the stationary spectrum. However, it gives no information on how this energy varies in time, e.g. when the driving function occurs. Likewise, the WB-SG does not resolve the harmonic structure evident in the NB-SG.

A proper TFD which satisfies both marginals is shown in fig. 1d. This representation preserves both the long-term harmonic structure of the resonator and the fine-time structure of the individual resonances. There is no misrepresentation of signal energy at high frequencies, nor loss of the periodic driving function. The fundamental frequency is preserved in both the temporal oscillations, as in the signal, and the harmonic spacing of the frequency components, consistent with the spectrum. This principle of simultaneous preservation of time and frequency information is also observed in the firing patterns of AN fibres. PST histograms of AN fibres closely resemble the input stimulus, the fine time structure of which is precisely preserved in the TFD of fig. 1d. The underlying harmonic structure seen in fig. 1d is preserved in the phase-locking of the fibres, though not in the overall rate response.

Figs. 2a and 2c shows a WB-SG and a proper TFD, respectively, for the 'clean' diphone of the Sheffield data. As in the case of the single resonator, the proper TFD clearly resolves the individual harmonics of the speech signal's spectrum, while preserving the fine time detail of the time waveform. This detail is more readily seen in a single channel of the TFD, extracted and plotted as a time waveform in fig. 2d. The spectrogram cannot resolve the individual oscillations of the waveform, and hence yields a smeared approximation of the time-varying energy of this component, as seen in fig. 2b. The bandwidth of the individual harmonics of the WB-SG are also broadened significantly, due to the short duration of the window; using a longer window would have further degraded the time resolution. The TFD does not suffer the trade-off of the spectrogram; hence, both excellent time and frequency resolution are achieved.

4 IMPLICATIONS FOR SPEECH PROCESSING

There are, of course, some fundamental differences between the representation of spectro-temporal information in the AN and in a proper TFD. In the TFD, the magnitude of the signal is preserved in the time marginal, so that all frequency components of the signal may contribute to the temporal structure of the distribution at a given frequency. An AN fibre, however, responds to a filtered version of the stimulus, rather than to the stimulus itself. Only harmonics that lie within a fibre's response area will affect the temporal response. Thus, while the TFD satisfies a "global" time marginal, the AN fibre approximates a "local" marginal, filtered to the vicinity of its CF. Yet both representations preserve fundamental frequency information. There may, however, be an inherent advantage in the modus operandi of the ear. The bandpass filtering performed by the basilar membrane removes the effects of stimuli which are distant in frequency. Since information relating to the fundamental frequency is preserved in the temporal firing patterns, separate channels can be grouped together according to their common fundamental. This technique has recently been used with an auditory model to improve identification of concurrent vowels [8]. A TFD which satisfies the (global) time marginal, however, would not necessarily allow for the separation of components with different fundamentals, since both fundamentals may contribute to the preserved temporal structure. It may be desirable to design a TFD that satisfies such a local time marginal.

Other properties of the auditory system are apparent in the response of AN fibres. Rectification, adaptation, and two-tone suppression can all be observed in the firing patterns. These properties may aid the ear in identifying important cues; for example, two-tone suppression acts to emphasise larger spectral components in a stimulus [10]. It may be desirable for a speech processing tool to reflect these or other properties of the ear, as has been done with the spectrogram [1]. However, it should be remembered that these effects are part of a system whose underlying spectro-temporal behaviour is only now becoming well understood. Applying cochlear nonlinearities to a tool with different spectro-temporal behaviour than that of the auditory system may lead to a misrepresentation or omission of speech features. It is im-

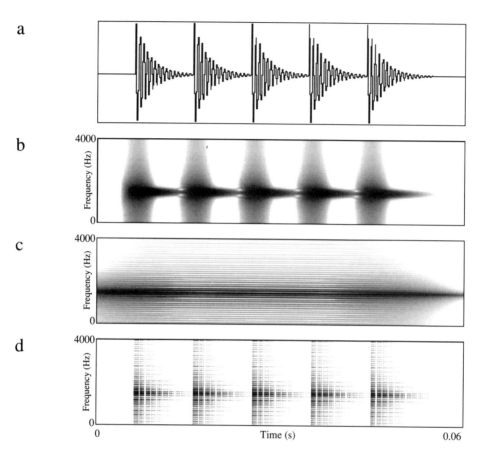

Fig. 1   *a* : time waveform of a single resonator with centre frequency 1500 Hz and fundamental
frequency (pitch) 100 Hz; *b* : wideband spectrogram of resonator, computed using an 8 ms
Hanning window; *c* : narrowband spectrogram of resonator, computed with a 50 ms Hanning
window; *d* : a proper time-frequency distribution of the signal of figure 1a, preserving both
the time and frequency marginals.
The wideband spectrogram reflects a smeared version of the periodic increase in signal
energy coincident with the driving function seen in the waveform (fig. 1a); it does not yield
the harmonics of the fundamental frequency apparent in the narrowband spectrogram (fig.
1c), and it suggests an increase in bandwidth in the neighbourhood of the driving function.
The narrowband spectrogram (fig. 1c) resolves the individual harmonics of the resonator,
but preserves none of the temporal structure of the waveform, and significantly smears the
start and end times of the signal, yielding a much greater total duration. The proper
distribution preserves the individual harmonics of the resonator observed in the power
spectrum with the correct bandwidth. Similarly, the temporal structure of the signal, including
pitch periodicity and overall duration, is precisely preserved.

portant to preserve as much information as exists in the signal prior to applying operations
which perform feature extraction or enhancement. Auditory models, by closely approximating the transduction process, preserve the spectro-temporal properties observed in the auditory nerve. There is no clear consensus, however, on how to best make use of this information
for speech analysis and recognition. This stems from an incomplete understanding of the nature of processing at higher centres of the auditory system, coupled with a lack of experience

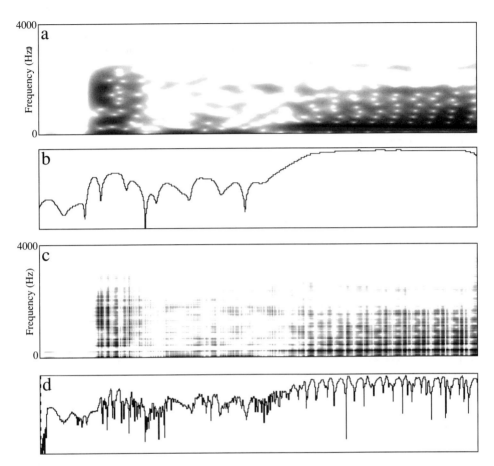

Fig. 2 *a* : wideband spectrogram of the clean diphone 'clean.dip', computed using an 8 ms Hanning
window, displayed on a linear frequency scale from 0 to 4000 Hz; *b* : 220 Hz component from
the wideband spectrogram of 'clean.dip', plotted as log-amplitude vs. time; *c* : a proper time-
frequency distribution of 'clean.dip', computed using the time and frequency marginals of the
signal, and with the wideband spectrogram of figure 2a as the prior estimate (same
frequency scale); *d* : 220 Hz component of the proper distribution of 'clean.dip' vs. time.
Despite its short window length, the wideband spectrogram smears the temporal detail of
the signal, so that one is left with only an approximation of the time-varying energy of the
first formant. The proper TFD does not suffer this drawback; all of the temporal detail
observed in the time signal is preserved in the distribution. Furthermore, each of the
harmonics are clearly resolved, with a bandwidth matching that seen in the frequency
marginal. Thus, both time and frequency resolution are improved over that of the
spectrogram.

in processing temporal information (due to the historical lack of temporally-informative representations). No formalism exists for the representation of temporal information in a speech
representation, and no methodology has arisen for processing this rich source of information.
Current processing is complicated by the very high data rate produced by auditory models,
which makes classification difficult or requires temporal smoothing to reduce the amount of
data. A formalism for the representation of temporal information may provide theoretically
justified methods for reducing the data rate of a TFD.

Acknowledgements: The authors would like to thank Prof. Edward Burns of the Speech & Hearing Sciences Dept. of the University of Washington for many fruitful discussions on this and related topics. This research was funded by the University of Washington Virginia Merrill Bloedel Hearing Research Center, Boeing Commercial Airplane Company, the Office of Naval Research, and the Washington Technology Center.

REFERENCES

[1] Y. Cheng & D. O'Shaugnessy (1991), 'Speech enhancement based conceptually on auditory evidence', *IEEE Trans. on Signal Processing*, **39**, 1943-1954.

[2] L. Cohen (1989), 'Time-frequency distributions — A review', *Proc. IEEE*, **77**, 941-981.

[3] B. Delgutte & N. Kiang (1984), 'Speech coding in the auditory nerve: I. Vowel-like sounds', *JASA*, **75**, 866-878.

[4] J. Horst, E. Javel & G. Farley (1986), "Coding of spectral fine structure in the auditory nerve. I. Fourier analysis of period and interspike interval histograms," *JASA*, **79**, 398-416.

[5] P. Loughlin, L. Atlas & J. Pitton (1993), 'Advanced time-frequency representations for speech processing', this volume.

[6] P. Loughlin, J. Pitton & L. Atlas (1992), 'An information-theoretic approach to positive time-frequency distributions', *Proc. ICASSP '92*.

[7] R. Lyon (1982), 'A computational model of filtering, detection, and compression in the cochlea', *Proc. ICASSP '82*.

[8] R. Meddis & M. Hewitt (1992), 'Modelling the identification of concurrent vowels with different fundamental frequencies', *JASA*, **91**, 233-245.

[9] M. Miller & M. Sachs (1983), 'Representation of stop consonants in the discharge patterns of auditory-nerve fibers', *JASA*, **74**, 502-517.

[10] J. Pickles (1988), *An Introduction to the Physiology of Hearing*, Academic Press, New York.

[11] M. Sachs & E. Young (1979), 'Encoding of steady-state vowels in the auditory nerve: representation in terms of discharge rate', *JASA*, **66**, 470-479.

[12] S. Seneff (1988), 'A joint synchrony/mean-rate model of auditory speech processing', *J. Phonetics*, **16**, 55-76.

[13] S. Shamma (1985), 'Speech processing in the auditory nerve I: the representation of speech sounds in the responses of the auditory nerve', *JASA*, **78**, 1612-1621.

[14] D. Sinex & C. Geisler (1983), 'Responses of auditory-nerve fibers to consonant-vowel syllables', *JASA*, **73**, 602-615.

[15] E. Young & M. Sachs (1979), 'Representation of steady-state vowels in the temporal aspects of the discharge patterns of populations of auditory-nerve fibers', *JASA*, **66**, 1381-1403.

The representation of speech in a computer model of the auditory nerve and dorsal cochlear nucleus

34

Michael J. Pont and Seyed Mashari

1 INTRODUCTION

As a result of a variety of recent investigations (e.g. Sachs & Young [11]; Carney & Geisler [1]) exploring the representation of speech and other complex sounds at the level of the auditory nerve, it has become apparent that some sophisticated processing of the speech waveform occurs even in the auditory periphery. In particular, many physiological studies have been carried out using "animal[1] models" of the human auditory periphery. The justification for such studies is that the representation of speech in the mammalian auditory system can better define the input to the cognitive system than the acoustic signal itself[2]. As Kiang puts it:

"Ultimately, the descriptions of how we process speech or any other auditory stimulus will come from physiology." ([5], p. 418).

Recently, it has become possible to look not just at the auditory periphery but beyond to the nuclei of the auditory brain stem. In particular, there are now many data available relating to the physiology and anatomy of the first "auditory relay station", the cochlear nucleus (CN). All afferent auditory nerve fibres terminate in the CN, and the representation of speech in this nucleus must therefore be of considerable import.

However, while the results of studies of the periphery of the cat may generalise correctly to the human auditory system, we encounter a problem when we consider the cochlear nucleus: even at this relatively low level of the nervous system there are major and significant cross-species differences between humans and other mammals (e.g. Moore [6]).

One way around such a problem is to use a computer model of the system in question. The model can be constructed based on human (post-mortem) anatomical data in conjunction with physiological data from other species, solving many of the problems mentioned above. We have developed such a model, and describe it in detail elsewhere (Pont & Damper [8]). In this paper, we examine graphically the representation in this model of a single sentence, spoken by a female speaker. We briefly describe the model (section 2) and give details of the stimuli used (section 3), before going on (section 4) to detail the simulated physiological responses obtained.

2 THE COMPUTER MODEL

2.1 The auditory nerve and cochlear nucleus

The auditory nerve (AN) is the sole pathway by which incoming auditory information can reach the central nervous system, and all afferent fibres within the auditory nerve terminate in the cochlear nucleus (Palmer [7]). The CN itself consists of two major sub-divisions, dorsal (DCN) and ventral (VCN). Neurons within the DCN have, compared with those of the AN and VCN, particularly complex properties (e.g. Young [12]) which may be important in the processing of acoustic patterns (see Evans & Nelson [4]; Evans [3]). Thus, it may be hypothesised that the VCN plays an important role in the pre-processing of auditory information

Visual Representations of Speech Signals: Martin Cooke, Steve Beet and Malcolm Crawford (eds.)
© 1993 by John Wiley & Sons Ltd

for the purposes of sound localisation while the DCN is involved in the pre-processing of auditory information for speech perception. The focus here will be on the representation of speech within the dorsal division of this nucleus.

The response properties of DCN cells in the cat can be divided into two main classes, Type II/III and Type IV (Young & Voigt [13]). Type II/III units correspond to interneurons within the DCN and Type IV unit axons make up the dorsal acoustic stria (DAS), which projects principally to the contralateral inferior colliculus.

In the present paper, we will focus on the responses of two different groups of model units: the AN units (the "input" to the DCN) and the Type IV units (the "output" from the DCN).

2.2 The original model: version 1.0

Our original computational model (v 1.0) is described fully by Pont & Damper [8]. Briefly, the model is coded in Pascal and simulates afferent neural processing up to the level of DAS. The model consists of two scissile stages simulating (1) the cochlea and AN and (2) the DCN. The model derives its input from a 128-channel cochlear filterbank. Cochlear transduction, rectification, logarithmic compression, and two-tone suppression functions are performed at the first stage of the simulation. The 512 artificial neurons employed model the cell at the level of trans-membrane potential and have interconnections that follow closely those reported in recent anatomical and physiological studies.

2.3 The new model: version 1.1

Knowledge of auditory system morphology and function is accumulating all the time. Clearly, therefore, any computational model must be subject to continual revision. Although version 1.0 of our model is able to reproduce accurately the findings from a number of important physiological studies, it is far from being perfect in this regard. Furthermore, it runs quite slowly and is rather cumbersome to use. We are therefore currently involved in a long-term project extending and enhancing the original model.

To date, for model version 1.1, we have re-coded the original simulation in C and improved the user interface. We have also increased the number of rows from 128 to 200, raising the total number of cells modelled from 512 to 800. However, only the "central" 120 hair cells are driven by filterbank inputs (centre frequencies from 100 Hz to 5 kHz, linearly spaced on a Greenwood scale), the remaining 60 (30 at each edge of the array) being simply spontaneously active. The extra hair cells are added to improve the simulation of DCN cells at the edges of the array (Pont & Mashari [10]). In all other respects, thorough testing of the modified model has confirmed that it functions identically to the original version.

Of course, even with these extensions, it is possible to simulate only a small portion of the auditory nervous system; for example, humans have some 3500 inner hair cells, and the model simulates only 200 in the current implementation. In a crude effort to simulate a larger array of cells, we conduct the probabilistic simulations of the cell responses several times: in the experiments to be described in this chapter, the model was run twenty times for each stimulus.

One final, minor, difference between the present model and that described previously is that we now pre-process stimuli using a version of a filterbank developed by Cooke [2] in place of a similar filterbank developed by Hukin[3].

3   DETAILS OF APPLIED STIMULI

One sentence was used in the present study: "Fred can go, Susan can't go, and Linda is uncertain". The sentence was applied to the model twice. In the first instance, it was applied "in quiet": this is the data file 'clean.wav'. In the second instance, the same sentence was partially embedded in "cocktail-party" noise (recorded in a busy student laboratory): this is the file 'dirty.wav'. In each case, the stimuli were presented at a signal level of "65 dB SPL" (calculated as described in Pont & Damper [8]).

It should be noted that the original data files 'clean.wav' and 'dirty.wav' are sampled at 20 kHz. Since the present computer model requires a sampling rate of 10 kHz, the original data were "down-sampled" by discarding every second sample.

4   MODEL RESPONSES

The responses of the model to the two sentences are shown graphically in figs. 1 and 2. Two different responses are given for each trial: the simulated auditory nerve response (figs. 1a and 2a), and the simulated response of the dorsal acoustic stria (figs. 1b and 2b). For each of the four figures, the x axis is time (milliseconds), and the y axis is 'Simulated Row' (1-2400)[4].

Figure 1a shows the response of the AN units in the model to the 'clean' sentence. The driven activity of the AN units (up to about 120 spikes per second) stands out against the much lower background levels of spontaneous activity (about 10 spikes per second) that these units produce. In the bands of correlated driven activity (visible across a wide range of frequencies), the syllabic structure of the applied sentence is clearly visible.

Figure 1b shows the response of the model Type IV units to the same 'clean' stimulus; this response was recorded simultaneously with that in fig. 1a. The first point to note is that, unlike AN units, Type IV units demonstrate relatively high levels of spontaneous activity (typically about 50 spikes per second), and a driven response that is, predominantly, inhibitory. Thus, where the AN response was a series of excitatory bands, the simulated DCN response is — very roughly — in the form of corresponding series of inhibitory bands.

Looking at fig. 2a, the AN response to the 'dirty' stimulus, is very similar[5] to that for 'clean' (fig. 1a) until — about 1/3 of the way through the simulation — the noise is added. At this time, the average discharge rate response of the model AN units, as expected, shows a tendency to saturate, and the "bands" of driven activity visible in the response to the 'clean' sound are almost invisible. Note also that the effect of the noise lingers after the noise is over (the last third of the simulation); the "fatigue" of the AN units means that the driven response is noticeably less than for the corresponding period in the 'clean' simulation.

Figure 2b shows the response of the model Type IV units to the 'dirty' stimulus. Again, this response was recorded at the same time as the corresponding AN response in fig. 2a. As for fig. 1b the response is largely inhibitory. The most interesting thing about these responses is, however, that while the AN response appears to saturate in the presence of the noise applied during the middle third of the simulation, the response of these DCN units to the 'dirty' stimulus appears, in these graphical representations, to be similar to the response of the same units to the 'clean' stimulus. In particular, though an area of excitation is clearly visible in the mid-frequency area of the applied noise, elsewhere bands of inhibition are still clearly visible at this level.

Clearly, much further work remains to be done in this area. In particular, while we have examined and compared visually the responses of the AN and DCN units in the model to noisy and noise-free speech, a more rigorous analysis is also required. We are currently performing such an analysis using a neural network, an approach that has previously proved very effective (Pont & Mashari [9]).

5   CONCLUSIONS

In this paper, we have provided details of the representation of speech in a computer model of afferent neural processing from the cochlea to the dorsal acoustic stria. We have argued that, while the AN response of the model appears — as expected from previous studies — to saturate in the presence of noise, the representation of the speech sounds at the level of the DCN in the model may show a degree of noise immunity. We have suggested that an analysis of the present results using a neural network might be used to test this hypothesis more rigorously

Acknowledgements: We are grateful to Dr. Martin Cooke (University of Sheffield) for providing us with his filterbank software for use in the experiments described in this paper. Some of the equipment used here was provided by a grant from the University Research Fund (University of Sheffield) to MJP.

Notes

1 Most frequently cats or guinea pigs.
2 Though this is seldom explicitly stated.
3 This change was necessary because the Hukin filterbank is written in Fortran and no suitable compiler was available for our new computer system. However, the version of the Cooke filterbank used here has, for example, Greenwood-spaced filters, and bandwidths precisely as described for our original model. Results using the different filterbanks have, of course, been carefully compared, and no differences have been detected.
4 Figures 1 and 2 each show the activity of 120 simulated neurons over 20 model runs: the "frequency" scale is therefore from 1 to 2400 (2400 = 120 real rows x 20 model runs), corresponding to a frequency range from 100 to 5000 Hz, on a (stepped) logarithmic scale. For example, the first twenty rows of fig. 1a each show the response of the same AN cell model (centre frequency 100 Hz), each row giving the result of a single model run. In each of the four graphs, the presence of a 'dot' at time t and "Simulated Row" sr indicates that a simulated unit at "Row" sr in the model generated an action potential (that is, 'fired') at time t.
5 The response will not be identical: like the biological original, the response of the model is probabilistic and exactly the same response will never be observed on two successive runs.

REFERENCES

[1] L.H. Carney & C.D. Geisler (1986), 'A temporal analysis of auditory-nerve fibre responses to spoken stop consonant-vowel syllables', *JASA*, **79**, 1896-1914

[2] M.P. Cooke (forthcoming), *Modelling Auditory Processing and Organisation*, Cambridge University Press, Cambridge, UK.

[3] E.F. Evans (1975), 'Cochlear nerve and cochlear nucleus', in: *Handbook of Auditory Physiology* (eds. W.D. Keidel & W.D. Neff), Springer-Verlag, New York, 1-108.

[4] E.F. Evans & P.G. Nelson (1973), 'On the functional relationship between the dorsal and ventral divisions of the cochlear nucleus', *Experimental Brain Research*, **17**, 428-442.

[5] N.Y.-S. Kiang (1986), "Comment", in: *Invariability and Variability in Speech Processes* (ed. J.S. Perkell & D.H. Klatt), Lawrence Erlbaum Associates, NJ, 418.

[6] J.K. Moore (1987), 'The human auditory brain stem: a comparative view', *Hearing Res.*, **29**, 1-32.

[7] A.R. Palmer (1987), 'Physiology of the cochlear nerve and cochlear nucleus', *British Medical Bulletin*, **43**, 838-835.

[8] M.J. Pont & R.I. Damper (1991), 'A computational model of afferent neural activity from the cochlea to the dorsal acoustic stria', *JASA*, **89**, 1213-1228.

[9] M.J. Pont & S.J. Mashari (1990), 'Modelling the acquisition of voicing contrasts in English and Thai', *Proc. Inst. Acoustics*, **12**(10), 323-329.

[10] M.J. Pont & S.J. Mashari (submitted), 'An improved computer model of afferent neural processing from the cochlea to dorsal acoustic stria'.

[11] M.B. Sachs & E.D. Young (1979), 'Encoding of steady-state vowels in the auditory nerve: representation in terms of discharge rate', *JASA*, **66**, 470-479.

[12] E.D. Young (1984), 'Response characteristics of neurons of the cochlear nuclei', in: *Hearing Science: Recent Advances* (ed. C.I. Berlin), College-Hill, San Diego, CA, 423-459.

[13] E.D. Young & H.F. Voigt (1981), 'The internal organization of the dorsal cochlear nucleus', in: *Neuronal Mechanisms of Hearing* (ed. J.Syka & H.F. Voigt), Plenum Press, New York, 127-133.

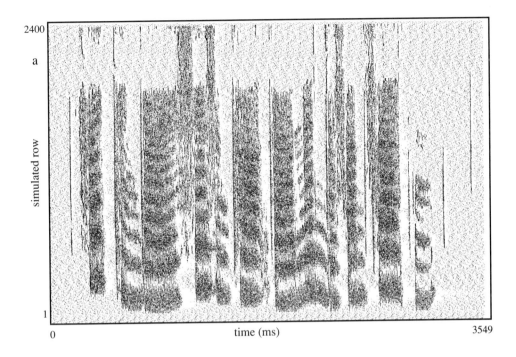

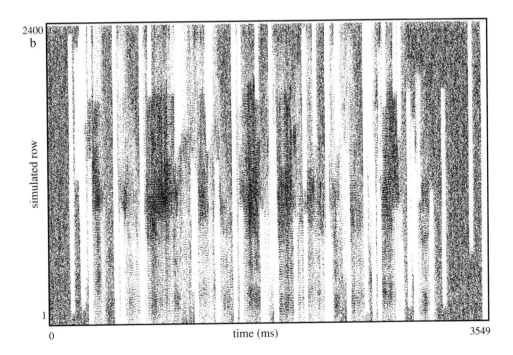

Fig. 1   Response of the model to the 'clean.wav'; *a* : simulated auditory nerve units; *b* : simulated dorsal cochlear nucleus (Type IV) units.

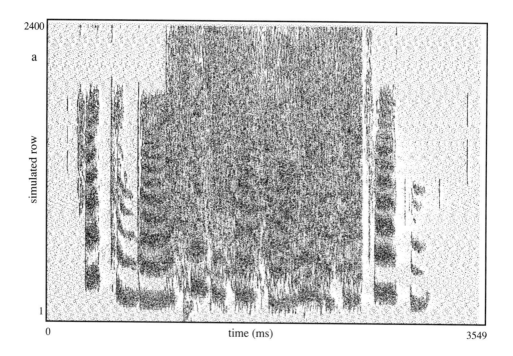

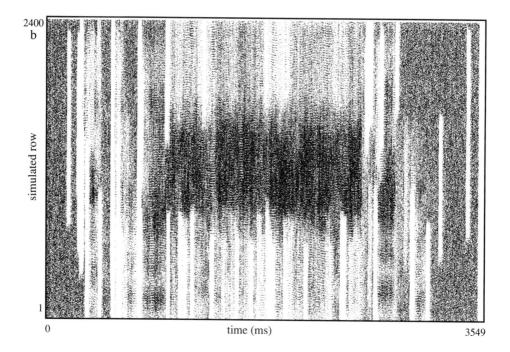

Fig. 2   Response of the model to the 'dirty.wav'; *a* : simulated auditory nerve units; *b* : simulated dorsal cochlear nucleus (Type IV) units.

The state space and "ideal input" representations of recurrent networks

35

Tony Robinson

1 INTRODUCTION

This paper takes the opportunity to present different levels of representation in a recurrent network phone recogniser (Robinson & Fallside [5]) on standard sentences. This recogniser has been shown to give good performance on a standard database (TIMIT), and so one sentence from this database, 'timit', is analysed. A sentence recorded under different conditions ('clean') is also analysed, and recognition is seen to be considerably worse. Analysis for the other two Sheffield sentences ('dirty' and 'spont') has been carried out, but is not presented here as there is sufficient difference in quality between the two analysed sentences.

The first three sections detail the input, internal and output data representations of the network, along with the associated processing. In the next two sections the data representations are given for the sentence from the training database, including a plot of the state space variables. This is followed by two sections analysing the other sentence and computing the input representation which yields an output closer to the assumed transcription of the sentence.

2 THE PREPROCESSOR

The preprocessor used in this system is fairly conventional. A Hamming window of width 256 samples is applied the speech waveform every 16 ms. From this window the following features are extracted:

i   The log power.

ii   An estimate of the fundamental frequency from the position of the highest peak in the autocorrelation function.

iii   An estimate of the degree of voicing from the relative amplitude of the highest peak in the autocorrelation function.

iv   A power spectrum using an FFT which is power normalised then grouped into 20 mel scale bins and cube rooted.

After the preprocessor, all channels are normalised and scaled to fit into a byte using a monotonically increasing function such that every value is eqi-probable. On presentation to the network, these values are expanded into a Gaussian distribution with zero mean and unit variance.

This data will be presented at the top of every diagram, in the order above reading from the bottom up. Thus the top twenty channels on the page form a spectrogram.

3 THE RECURRENT NET

Recurrent networks have been shown to give good estimates of the class conditional probabilities needed for Markov model-based speech recognition systems (Morgan & Bourlard [3]; Robinson [4]). The network architecture used is shown below in fig. 1. Inputs from the preprocessor, $u(t)$, are presented to the network along with the state vector, $x(t)$. A single-

Visual Representations of Speech Signals: Martin Cooke, Steve Beet and Malcolm Crawford (eds.)
© 1993 by John Wiley & Sons Ltd

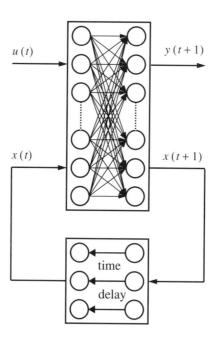

Fig. 1   Recurrent net.

layer network computes the output, $y(t+1)$, and the next state vector, $x(t+1)$. The internal state units are considered to be independent estimators of unknown features.

4   WHY USE A STATE SPACE?

The use of a recurrent network for phone probability estimation differs significantly from other approaches (e.g. the standard discrete, continuous or semi-continuous HMM estimators, or the use of non-recurrent networks) in the use of an internal state. Hence, conventional approaches are memoryless and contextual variation is explicitly modelled using mechanisms such as triphones or gender dependent networks. In contrast, the recurrent network employs an internal state trained by gradient descent for contextual modelling.

The acoustic realisation of a phoneme is known to depend on coarticulation effects from the immediate phonetic context. The triphone approach to modelling this variation assumes that a window including the preceding and following phoneme is sufficient to capture the contextual variation, and so builds a model for every triplet of phonemes which occur in the language. As well as requiring considerable storage for the models, good smoothing techniques across models are needed so that the parameters may be reliably estimated. Connectionist probability estimation normally takes a data-driven approach to this problem by effectively enlarging the window on the observations to encompass the relevant information. However, a simple finite window is both inefficient in terms of the increase in the number of free parameters with window size, and in terms of run-time computation. This limits the window size that can be used although tied weights, such as employed in the time-delay neural network, can reduce these problems. However, a finite window size will always limit the temporal scope of the contextual information. Use of feedback within the network allows the accumulation of information over an arbitrarily long period and avoids the duplication of processing associated with presenting multiple observations as a single input.

In experiments where the gender of the speaker was explicitly presented to the network, no change in recognition rate was observed. Similarly, training two networks for female and male speech, and testing on the appropriate set yielded a drop in performance, apparently because there was not enough data to make a good estimation of the parameters for the female model. In conventional systems, reasonable increases in performance are gained by having gender-dependent models; the lack of similar behaviour with recurrent networks suggests that this information is being successfully held in the internal state.

5   ANALYSIS OF 'timit'

For the 'timit' sentence, the recurrent net is used to produce the activations in fig. 2. The display is in two parts: the top part shows the output of the preprocessor as the input to the network; the bottom part shows the output of the network as phone occurrence probabilities. Target outputs, as provided by the hand labellers, are shown by the shaded regions. It can be seen that the recurrent net closely models the task of the hand labeller. When the maximum likelihood symbol string is extracted with a Markov model, there are the following errors:

i   Two substitution errors: The word "in" is labelled as [ix ng] and recognised as [iy ng], and the word "year" is labelled as [y ih axr] and recognised as [y ux axr].

ii   One insertion error: [v] is recognised between "wash" and "water".

iii   One deletion error: [y] in "had your" is lost.

Four errors in 41 symbols is an unusually low error rate for this classifier. On the full TIMIT test set the error rate is 30.3% (3.7% insertions, 20.5% substitutions, 6.1% deletions).

6   A LOOK AT THE STATE SPACE

The dimensionality of the state space for the recurrent net is 176. For display reasons, only the first 32 outputs are shown at the top of fig. 5. Immediately obvious is a large degree of temporal correlation. The rms difference between successive state vectors is shown at the bottom of the figure, under the dashed line. If each element in the state vector were subjected to additive noise, then the maximum information would be transmitted if the state values were randomly distributed between 0 and 1. Under this assumption the expected rms difference is $\sqrt{1/6}$ or about 0.41. The observed rms difference is 0.07. However, in practice there is no explicit noise added to the state units, so the underlying correlations in the acoustic data and the limited processing capabilities of the (effective) single-layer network give a correlated structure.

Looking at the temporal structure, it can be seen that while there are large changes in the network output, these are not on the whole reflected in all the state units. Thus the rms difference does not give phone boundary information. However, this is to be expected if the contextual information is fully utilised, as the time scale of information to pass through the network is of the order of the mean phone duration, so changes to the state vector will be blurred over the extent of the phone.

7   ANALYSIS OF 'clean'

In contrast to the 'timit' sentence, the same network is used for recognition on the 'clean' sentence. This sentence has been recorded through a low-pass filter with a cutoff of 2.8 kHz. In this case a transcription is not available, so the pronunciations given in Table 1 are assumed. The pronunciations were concatenated and a Viterbi alignment performed with the Markov model. The results are shown in fig. 3, again with target phones shaded. In this case it can be seen that the network output vastly disagrees with the assigned labels; in fact only 35% of the frames agree in labelling. The loss of the high-frequency part of the spectra causes the occurrences of [s] to be recognised as [f], as well as many other errors. However, it can be seen that the boundaries given by the Viterbi algorithm are often aligned with sharp acoustic changes and with a change of recognised symbol.

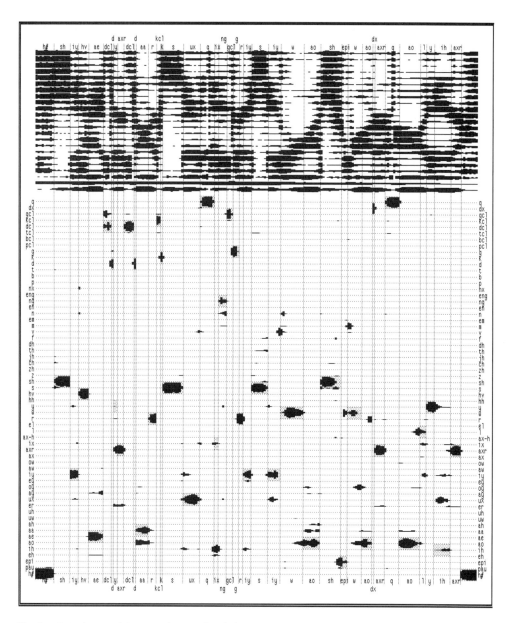

Fig. 2   Actual network input and output for 'timit.wav'.

8   THE "IDEAL INPUT" REPRESENTATION

The "ideal input" representation is that input which minimises the cost function of the network over the whole sentence. This can be achieved by gradient descent in the input space (Linden & Kindermann [2]), and this method has been proposed for speech synthesis by recognition (Fallside [1]). After 300 iterations of gradient decent through the fixed weights no further reduction in the cost function occurred, and the resulting input and output space is as

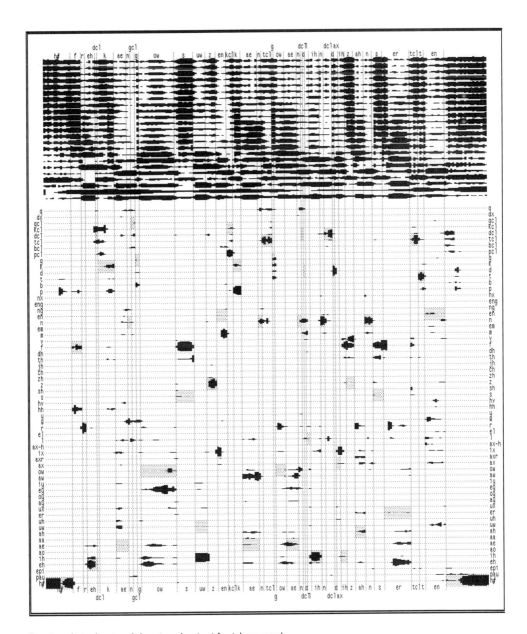

Fig. 3   Actual network input and output for 'clean.wav'.

shown in fig. 4. The frame by frame error rate has been halved from 65% to 32%, although many segments are still incorrect, especially the vowels. Even though considerable change in the input space had occurred, the final output is still worse than for the 'timit' sentence, so it may be concluded that a better input exists than was found with gradient descent. Interestingly, the "ideal input" representation contains many non-speech features in that the normal constraints of smoothness in the time and frequency domains have been relaxed. For instance, in the first [s] there is one frame where a single channel has zero energy.

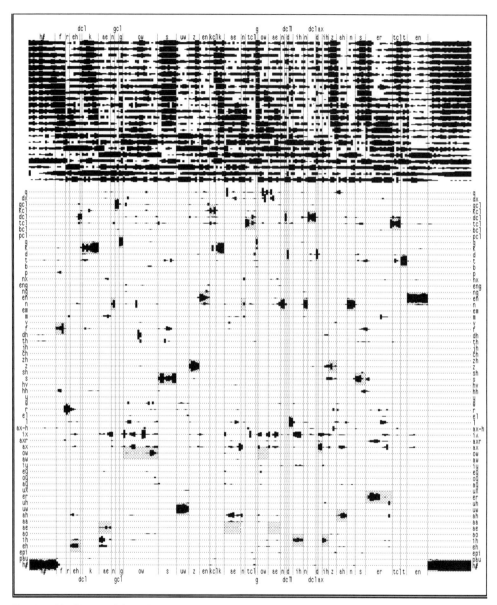

Fig. 4   "Ideal" network input for 'clean.wav'.

9   CONCLUSION

This paper has presented an analysis of the recurrent network on two sentences. Whilst good recognition results are possible on a sentence taken from the training set, this performance shows considerable degradation on sentences recorded under other conditions. This illustrates the need for an acoustic analysis robust to such variations. The "ideal input" has been calculated for one sentence, and found to have several non-speech features. Hence there is considerable scope for improvement of this recognition framework to increase the robustness to recording conditions and to make more accurate models of the speech dynamics.

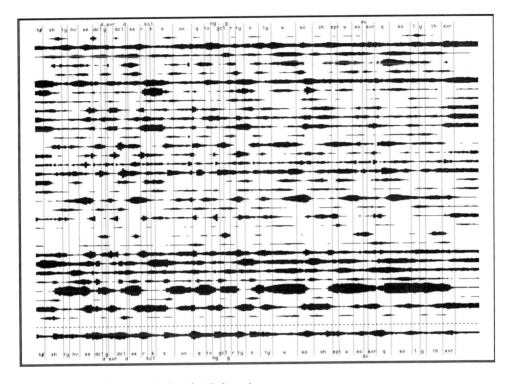

Fig. 5   The first 32 state activations for 'timit.wav'.

Table 1.

SENTENCE-END	h#
Fred	f r eh dcl
can	k ae n
go	gcl g ow
Susan	s uw z en
can't	kcl k ae n tcl
go	g ow
and	ae n dcl d
Linda	l ih n dcl d ax
is	ih z
uncertain	ah n s er tcl t en

Acknowledgements: The author wishes to acknowledge the ESPRIT BRA project Auditory/ Connectionist Techniques for Speech for funding up to October 1991, and the UK Science and Engineering Research Council for subsequently supporting this work.

REFERENCES

[1] F. Fallside (1990), 'SYNFREQ, speech synthesis from recognition', *Proc. ESCA Conf. Speech Synthesis*, 237-240. Also CUED/F-INFENG/TR.54.

[2] A. Linden & J. Kindermann (1989), 'Inversion of multilayer nets', *Int. Jnt. Conf. Neural Networks*, vol. II, 425-430.

[3] N. Morgan & H. Bourlard (1990), 'Continuous speech recognition using multilayer perceptrons with hidden Markov models', *Proc. ICASSP '90*, 413-416.

[4] T. Robinson (1991), 'Several improvements to a recurrent error propagation network phone recognition system', *Technical Report CUED/F-INFENG/TR.82, Cambridge University Engineering Department*.

[5] T. Robinson & F. Fallside (1991), 'A recurrent error propagation network speech recognition system', *Computer Speech & Language*, **5**(3), 259-274.

Nonlinear operators for speech analysis

Jean Rouat

1   INTRODUCTION

Research in speech analysis is recognised as an important aspect of speech processing, with applications in speech coding, speech recognition, etc. Depending on the application, the speech analyser has to extract the most appropriate parameters. This paper will focus on the problem of speech analysis with possible applications in speech recognition.

The automatic "demodulation" of speech with nonlinear operators based on perceptual knowledge is a problem which has not yet been fully addressed, and speech demodulation might assist the researcher in the understanding of speech and/or in the design of a simple and efficient speech analysis.

2   MODULATED TONE PERCEPTION

Since the auditory system does not resolve the higher-frequency components, the temporal features of vowel-like sounds are comparable and hence coded similarly to those of amplitude-modulated tones. Research on automatic demodulation of speech can be motivated by the hypothesis that the human brain has neural cells specialised in amplitude modulation (AM) and frequency modulation (FM) detection (Gardner & Wilson [2]; Tansley & Suffield [12]; Wakefield & Viemeister [13]). More recently, Schreiner & Langner [11] have studied the representation of amplitude modulation in the inferior colliculus of the cat and have shown that it contains a highly systematic topographic representation of amplitude modulation parameters.

3   BASILAR MEMBRANE NONLINEARITIES

Nonlinearity and perception of intermodulation distortion products (f1-f2, 2f1-f2, etc.) are a live issue in hearing research and it is not easy to understand the origin of these nonlinearities. Recently, Ruggero & Rich [10] have observed distortion products on chinchilla basilar membrane by using a laser-velocimetry technique. Their work suggests that the live basilar membrane is a nonlinear system and thus the perception of distortion products could be due to the basilar membrane response and not only to the neural postprocessing.

4   NONLINEAR OPERATORS

Recently, Kaiser [3] proposed a nonlinear operator (called the "Teager energy operator") which is able to extract the energy of a signal based on mechanical and physical considerations. It has been shown (Maragos *et al.*[5]) that this operator is able to track the amplitude of an AM signal or the frequency of an FM signal very quickly. Another nonlinear operator has been proposed (Rouat [9]). This operator, called "Dyn", shows an ability to enhance the AM-FM modulation in speech, and it is interesting to compare it to the Teager energy operator. Figure 1 illustrates the output of Dyn and Teager energy operators. Depending on the application, one can use the Dyn or the Teager operators. The top section of fig. la shows the

Visual Representations of Speech Signals: Martin Cooke, Steve Beet and Malcolm Crawford (eds.)
© 1993 by John Wiley & Sons Ltd

original speech (/a/) of a male speaker (three pitch periods). The second section presents the bandpass-filtered speech (Moore & Glasberg [6]) with a centre frequency of 1400 Hz. The third section shows the output of the Dyn operator on the bandpass-filtered speech. The fourth section illustrates the output of the Teager energy operator on the same bandpass-filtered speech. Figure 1b presents the same output for a /i/ with a centre frequency of 2300 Hz (three pitch periods). Both Dyn and Teager energy operators show the modulated energy pulses characteristic of the speech signal. The Teager energy operator has an output which does not need to be postprocessed when the speech has been properly recorded and bandpass-filtered.

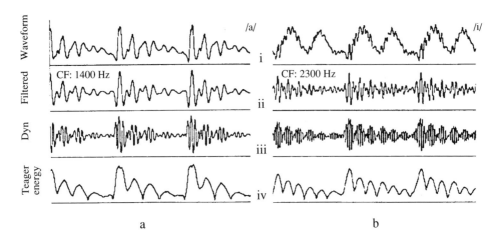

Fig. 1   i : Three pitch periods of /a/ (*a*) and /i/ (*b*) spoken by a male; ii : Vowel from *i* bandpass-filtered with a centre frequency of 1400 Hz (*a*) and 2300 Hz (*b*); iii : Signals from *ii* filtered by Dyn operator; iv : Signals from *ii* filtered by Teager energy operator.

5   THE ANALYSIS OF SPEECH

In this section, we describe how we use the Teager energy and Dyn operators for extraction of amplitude and/or frequency modulation in speech.

5.1 Filtering

The actual version of the analyser comprises a bank of twenty-four filters centred from 330 Hz to 4700 Hz. These filters simulate partially the frequency analysis performed by the cochlea. These are rounded exponential filters with the eequivalent rectangular bandwidths (ERB) proposed by Patterson [7] and Moore & Glasberg [6]. The output of each filter is a bandpass signal with a narrowband spectrum centred around f_i where f_i is the central frequency (CF) of channel i. According to communication theory [1] the output signal $s_i(t)$ from channel i can be considered as being modulated in amplitude and phase with a carrier frequency of f_i.

$$s_i(t) = A_i(t) \cos[\omega_i t + \phi_i(t)]. \tag{1}$$

$A_i(t)$ is the modulating amplitude and $\phi_i(t)$ is the modulating phase. It should be noticed that eqn. 1 is true only for a bandpass signal (bandwidth of $A_i(t)$ and $\phi_i(t)$ small in comparison to f_i, where $\omega_i = 2\pi f_i$).

In the following, channel subscripts i are dropped for clarity.

5.2 AM - FM demodulation

The output of the analog version of the Teager energy operator (Kaiser [3]) to $s(t)$ is given by $\dot{s}(t)^2 - s(t)\ddot{s}(t)$.

It is possible to show [9] that:

$$\text{Teager}(s(t)) = \eta(t) + \frac{\dot{A}^2(t) - A(t)\ddot{A}(t)}{2}(1 + \cos 2\upsilon(t))$$
$$+ \frac{A^2(t)\ddot{\phi}(t)}{2}\sin 2\upsilon(t) \tag{2}$$

where

$$\eta(t) = A^2(t)\left[\omega + \dot{\phi}(t)\right] \tag{3}$$

$$\upsilon(t) = \omega t + \phi(t) \tag{4}$$

and dots represent first and second time derivatives.

The term $\eta(t)$ is related to the modulating amplitude times the instantaneous frequency. Thus, depending on the modulation (AM or FM), the Teager energy operator will automatically demodulate the signal. The other terms in eqn. (2) will be considered as being "noisy" terms (for the purpose of the paper) and are, most of the time, much smaller than $\eta(t)$ when ω and $A(t)$ are large enough.

The output of the Dyn operator [9] to $s(t)$ is given by

$$\text{Dyn}(s(t)) = s(t)\dot{s}(t)$$
$$= \frac{1}{4}\frac{d}{dt}A^2(t) + \frac{1}{2}A^2(t)\sqrt{\left(\frac{\dot{A}(t)}{A(t)}\right)^2 + \left(\frac{d}{dt}\upsilon(t)\right)^2}\cos[2\upsilon(t) + \zeta(t)] \tag{5}$$

with $\zeta(t) = \text{atan}\dfrac{A^2(t)\left[\omega + \dot{\phi}(t)\right]}{\dot{A}(t)}$.

It can be demonstrated (Rouat [9]) that it is possible to extract $(d/dt)(\log A(t))$ (time derivative of the logarithm of the amplitude modulation) and $\dot{\upsilon}(t)/2\pi$ (instantaneous frequency modulation) from the output of $\text{Dyn}(s(t))$ by using standard communication operations (normalisation, envelope detection, etc.) [1], with some restrictions on the speech.

5.3 Speech data

We present the analysis output for 'clean.dip'. This segment contains the sequence /ka/ from the word "can" spoken by a female. The speech has been sampled at 20 kHz after low-pass-filtering. The power of the signal is low because the dynamic range of the quantiser in the A/D converter has not been fully exploited. Thus, the quantisation effect is important and seems to affect the performance.

5.4 Experiment with the Teager energy operator

After filtering, the output of each channel has been processed by the Teager energy operator and the raw data are plotted as three-dimensional images. No smoothing or lowpass-filtering of Teager energy output has been made. In fact, $\eta(t)$ is dominant in eqn. (2) when $A(t)$ and $\phi(t)$ have a bandwidth small in comparison to t and when $A(t)$ and ω are large. But one should be careful since, depending on the speech and for low-frequency channels, the "noisy" terms of eqn. (2) can be large and the Teager energy operator might not always be reliable.

5.5 Experiment with the Dyn operator

The output of each channel has been processed by the Dyn operator. In the first experiment the raw data coming from the Dyn operator is plotted as a three-dimensional image. In a second experiment, the output of the Dyn operator has been postprocessed (lowpass-filtered) to extract the expression $(d/dt)\,(A^2(t))$ from eqn. (5) before plotting the image.

6 ANALYSIS OF THE OUTPUT

Figures 2 and 3 present the output of the 3D analysis of /ka/ using the Teager, Dyn and lowpass-filtered Dyn operators. The horizontal scale is time and the vertical scale is expressed in ERB. The third dimension is the output of the Teager, Dyn or lowpass-filtered Dyn operators. The darkness is proportional to the output value of the analysis. The output of Teager energy operator is positive most of the time, since $\eta(t)$ dominates eqn. (2). Therefore, the white background in figure 2 corresponds approximately to zero. The Dyn output can be negative or positive, giving a grey background on the images for fig. 3. The white portions on the image correspond to negative values of the output analysis. Both operators give a rich representation of the /k/ with a typical "v" shape. The Teager energy operator enhances the high-frequency channels relative to Dyn. With the Teager energy operator the plosive part of /k/ dominates the output of the image. Both Teager and Dyn operators allow an easy detection of /k/. In the two figures, one can observe that the medium-frequency components are not exactly in phase with the low-frequency components, which seems to be typical of the vowel /a/.

7 CONCLUSION

We have proposed a new speech analysis based on nonlinear operators. Results have been presented with the Teager energy and the Dyn operators. These analyses automatically extract information related to an AM or FM signal. With such analyses it seems to be possible to obtain patterns characteristic of phonemes and transitions between phonemes, which cannot be obtained using other speech analysis (FFT, LPC) techniques. From experience on the remaining Sheffield data it seems that the Dyn operator is less sensitive to noise and quantisation noise than the Teager energy operator, but further experiments have to be made on more speech data. The output of Dyn has to be postprocessed in order to obtain the information related to $A(t)\,\dot{A}(t)$ or to the instantaneous frequency. The Teager energy operator does not need such postprocessing to get the information related to $\eta(t)$. In summary, speech analysis experiments have been reported based on two nonlinear operators which are very simple (three point algorithms) and which are able to enhance AM or FM information in speech. We believe that the understanding of the nonlinearity occurring on the basilar membrane is very important to the design of nonlinear analysis enhancing AM and FM components in the speech.

Acknowledgements: This work has been supported by the NSERC of Canada under Grant Nb OGP0042386, by the "Fonds de Développement Académique Réseau de l'Université du Québec", and by the "fondation" from Université du Québec à Chicoutimi. Many thanks are due to S. Lemieux and Y.C. Liu for their programming work.

REFERENCES

[1] A.B. Carlson (1986), *Communication Systems: An Introduction to Signals and Noise in Electrical Communication*, McGraw Hill, New York.

[2] R.B. Gardner & J.P. Wilson (1979), 'Evidence for direction-specific channels in the processing of frequency modulation', *JASA*, **66**, 704-709.

[3] J.F. Kaiser (1990), 'On a simple algorithm to calculate the "energy" of a signal', *Proc. ICASSP '90 (Albuquerque)*, 381-384.

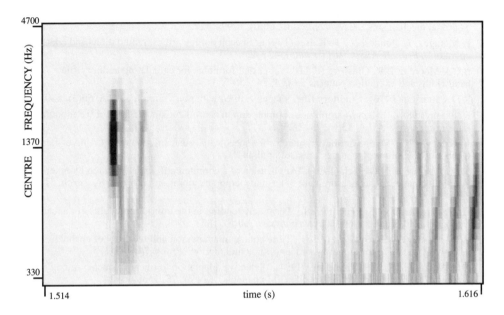

Fig. 2   Teager energy operator output for the segment /k/ /a/ in 'clean.dip'. The output of each
"cochlear filter" has been "filtered" by the Teager energy operator.

Fig. 3   Dyn energy operator output for the segment /k/ /a/ in 'clean.dip'. The output of each
"cochlear filter" has been "filtered" by the Dyn energy operator.

[4] G. Langner & C.E. Schreiner (1988), 'Periodicity coding in the inferior colliculus of the cat. I. Neuronal mechanisms', *J. Neurophysiol.*, **60**(6), 1799-1822.

[5] P. Maragos, T. Quatieri & J.F. Kaiser (1991), 'Speech nonlinearities, modulations and energy operators', *Proc. ICASSP '91 (Toronto)*, 421-424.

[6] B.C.J. Moore & B.R. Glasberg (1983), 'Suggested formulae for calculating auditory-filter bandwidths and excitation patterns', *JASA*, **74**, 750-753.

[7] R.D. Patterson (1976), 'Auditory filter shapes derived with noise stimuli', *JASA*, **59**(3), 640-654.

[8] R. Plomp (1988), 'Effect of amplitude compression in hearing aids in the light of the modulation-transfer function', *JASA*, **83**(6), 2322-2327.

[9] J. Rouat (1991), 'Dyn: a nonlinear operator for speech analysis', Internal report: Université du Québec à Chicoutimi, Dépt. des sciences appliquées.

[10] M.A. Ruggero & N.C. Rich (1991), 'Application of a commercially-manufactured Doppler-shift laser velocimeter to the measurement of basilar-membrane vibration', *Hearing Research*, **51**, 215-230.

[11] C.E. Schreiner & G. Langner (1988), 'Periodicity coding in the inferior colliculus of the cat. II. Topographical organization', *J. Neurophysiol.*, **60**(6), 1823-1840.

[12] B.W. Tansley & J.B. Suffield (1983), 'Time course of adaptation and recovery of channels selectively sensitive to frequency and amplitude modulation', *JASA*, **74**, 765-775.

[13] G.H. Wakefield & N.F. Viemeister (1984), 'Selective adaptation to linear frequency-modulated sweeps: Evidence for direction-specific FM channels?', *JASA*, **75**, 1588-1592.

Speech representation and analysis by the use of instantaneous frequency

37

A. Tsopanoglou, J. Mourjopoulos and G. Kokkinakis

1 INTRODUCTION

Given the time-varying nature of speech signals, most analysis techniques used in this field attempt to achieve optimal results either in the frequency or the time domain. For example, the use of the short-time Fourier transform (STFT) has the obvious advantage of good resolution in the frequency domain but averaged over a single time-domain frame (i.e. window). For this reason, it is advantageous to consider alternative analysis techniques which achieve improved resolution in time and frequency, one of which is based on the use of instantaneous frequency (IF) function and instantaneous envelope (IE) function methods. The use of such techniques in speech can be traced back to the work carried out on contiguous bandpass filters for speech analysis, synthesis and coding [1,5]. A comprehensive presentation and analysis of such techniques is given in [4].

Many aspects of speech analysis can be easily accommodated by using this approach, achieving results comparable to those obtained by the traditional time-to-frequency transform methods. The clear advantage of the IF function-based methods is on the capability of representing frequency dependent time-domain data. However, as is the case with all time/frequency analysis methods, a tradeoff occurs when the signal used is not narrowband. In such a case, the IF function will be the average of all different spectral components contributing to the signal at each specific instant. This problem can be avoided by introducing appropriate division in the frequency domain using a filterbank. However, as is well known, such a choice may lead to other processing artifacts and compromises and also increase significantly processing time and system complexity. For this reason, it is also possible to employ IF analysis in a compromised way, by choosing bandlimited but nevertheless relatively broadband speech input, typically covering the range of 50 Hz to 4.5 kHz.

The advantage of the superior time resolution for IF function-based methods has been shown for many speech applications. For example, speech segmentation/classification can be achieved with this method in a fast and accurate way [6,9,10], avoiding the requirement of using STFT or other parametric analyses. Speech synthesis and coding can also be used following such techniques which manipulate the signal's IE function [5]. Similarly, additive or convolutional signal distortions can be modelled or removed by following such an analysis [8,11]. The analysis of data presented here is directed mainly towards signal segmentation/classification and illustrates most of the points discussed in this section.

2 THEORY

According to the approach adopted here [5], the speech signal $s(t)$, may be approximated by the sum of the outputs of N contiguous bandpass filters whose frequencies are ideally cen-

Visual Representations of Speech Signals: Martin Cooke, Steve Beet and Malcolm Crawford (eds.)

tred at frequencies: $\omega_n = n\Delta\omega$, $n = 1, 2, ..., N$, where $\Delta\omega$ is the frequency increment between two adjacent bands. Then:

$$s(t) \approx \sum_{n=1}^{N} s_n(t) \tag{1}$$

where $s_n(t)$ is the output of the n-th filter band. Each bandpass component can be expressed as:

$$s_n(t) = A_n(t)\cos[p_n(t)] \tag{2}$$

where $A_n(t)$ is IE function $A_n(t) > 0$ and $p_n(t)$ is the instantaneous phase (IP) function. Given that the centre frequency of this band is ω_n, then:

$$p_n(t) = \omega_n t + \phi_n(t) \tag{3}$$

where $\phi_n(t)$ is the "phase deviation" term, often expressed in terms of its derivative:

$$\dot{\phi}_n(t) = \frac{d}{dt}\phi_n(t) \tag{4}$$

which is termed the IF deviation,

$$p_n(t) = \omega_n t + \int_0^t \dot{\phi}_n(\tau)\,d\tau. \tag{5}$$

Similarly, $\dot{p}_n(t)$ is the IF function of the bandlimited speech components. It can be shown [5] that such an analysis is equivalent to short-time speech analysis, so that the IE function, $A_n(t)$, is the magnitude of the short-time spectrum of speech, i.e. $A_n(t) = |S(\omega_n, t)|$ and the IP function, $p_n(t)$, is the angle of the short-time spectrum, both evaluated at ω_n. Following such an approach, the short-time Fourier transform (STFT) must be applied on windowed data, whose duration is T (s), derived from successive frames of $s(t)$. Alternatively, IF and IE functions may be evaluated via the Hilbert transform $\hat{s}_n(t)$, of $s_n(t)$, since it is known that:

$$\dot{p}_n(t) = \frac{1}{A_n(t)}\left(s_n(t)\frac{d}{dt}\hat{s}_n(t) - \hat{s}_n(t)\frac{d}{dt}s_n(t)\right) \tag{6}$$

where:

$$A_n(t) = \sqrt{s_n^2(t) + \hat{s}_n^2(t)}. \tag{7}$$

As was pointed out in [6], provided that

$$\Delta\omega = \omega_n - \omega_{n-1} \leq \frac{4\pi}{T} \tag{8}$$

then $s(t)$ can be reconstructed exactly from the sum of the corresponding products of the phase and amplitude terms in each band.

However, it is also feasible that signal reconstruction is not required and so decomposition of $s_n(t)$ into amplitude and IF function terms can be performed without any prior band splitting operation (i.e. eqn. (1)). Such an approach, given that $s_n(t)$ is broadband but bandlimited, introduces the concept of an IF density (or distribution) function [6] interpreted as follows. This function (at each instant t) gives the number of occurrences of the values of $\dot{p}_n(\omega_n, t)$ over the entire analysis frequency band. As was shown in [2,6] for Gaussian signals, the IF density function displays symmetry around ω_m (the mean angular frequency) and its divergence from this value depends on the signal bandwidth. For non-Gaussian signals, such as speech, it was found [6] that this function is sensitive to signal characteristics and can identify the energy distribution of harmonic components of $s_n(t)$ (for vowel sounds) or the spectral distribution (for non-vowel sounds).

Therefore, in this work, the IF (density) function was usually derived according to eqn. (6), but for the signal $s_n(t)$, i.e. the speech waveform, bandlimited during acquisition between 50 Hz and the cutoff frequency (for the sampling rates appearing at the speech examples, i.e. 16 kHz and 20 kHz). However, in some cases the speech signal was also filtered in narrow bands, in order to increase the accuracy of the IF analysis. It is clear that by following such an approach both envelope and instantaneous frequency functions are estimated as continuous (but discrete time) functions of time. As was noted in [5], the IF function is in principle not bandlimited, but in practice, its variance only becomes large over instances when the envelope function is close to zero $A_n(t) \approx 0$, i.e. during silence or low-amplitude intervals. To avoid such problems, the estimated IF function was smoothed by a "moving average", second order IIR low-pass function, so that $\dot{p}_L(t)$ was generated [9,10]. The filter cutoff frequency was set at 60 Hz, allowing variations slower than 16 ms to appear in the smoothed function. This approach permits the detection of speech waveform changes due to different phonemes, which usually occur at 25-30 ms intervals and rejects unwanted and parasitic IF variations.

3 PRACTICAL ESTIMATION OF SPEECH IE AND IF FUNCTIONS

For efficient estimation of the Hilbert transform, $\hat{s}$, required for estimating both the IE and IF functions, the technique suggested in [1] can be employed. According to this, a two-branch transformation of the speech signal is performed via all-pass filters, easily realised by recursive difference equations. Similarly, the differentiation of both s and $\hat{s}$ was implemented via a 15-point FIR filter [3]. In this way both IE and IF functions are estimated as continuous functions of a discrete time variable. As was discussed in [5], even when s is bandlimited, IE and IF functions may not be bandlimited. In practice, parasitic ripples may often occur for two main reasons:

    i   the broadband nature of the input signal (i.e. simultaneous contributions of different frequencies can appear in IE and IF), and

    ii   the variance of IF becomes large when the IE function is close to zero, $A_n(t) \approx 0$.

To reduce the effects due to the first of these, additional preprocessing can be performed by initial filtering of the signal $s(n, t)$ through a 500 Hz high-pass filter. This process, in effect, removes the signal energy due to the pitch and the first formant and facilitates better tracking for both IE and IF. functions. Furthermore, by smoothing IE and IF functions by a second-order IIR low-pass filter, ripples and parasitic peaks can be removed.

4 ANALYSIS OF DATA

The results here present IE and IF analyses of the 'clean' syllable ("...Susan ca...") spoken by a female speaker and sampled at 20 kHz. Figures 1a-c show the speech signal, the IE function and the IF function respectively. Figure 2 shows the analysis of the 'clean' diphone ("...ca..."). As can be observed, the IE clearly detects the energy contour of the signal (the detection is obvious at syllable or diphone level), and the IF gives an immediate indication of its frequency value (i.e. the combination of pitch/formant contribution for voiced, or spectral content for unvoiced portions). However, as was previously discussed, this is an average (at each instant of time) of the signal's spectral content and this property has disadvantages when signals recorded in the noisy condition are analysed. These results are shown in fig. 3, where, during high-energy phonemes (where the speech signal exhibits high energy level), both IE and IF give relatively accurate results. However, during low-energy segments (voiced or unvoiced fricatives, plosives), IF cannot detect the signal's frequency due to the presence of background noise of a higher level. The detection of IF improves in such a case, if the low-frequency (smoothed) function is derived using a low-pass filter with cutoff frequency set in

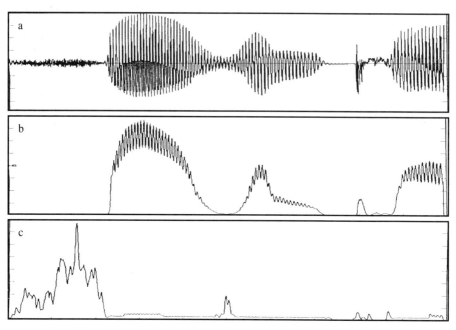

Fig. 1   Representations of 'clean.syl'; *a* : waveform; *b* : instantaneous envelope; *c* : instantaneous frequency.

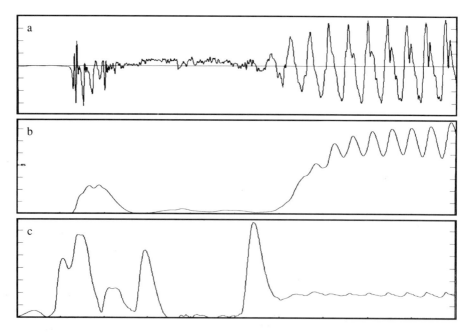

Fig. 2   Representations of 'clean.dip'; *a* : waveform; *b* : instantaneous envelope; *c* : instantaneous frequency.

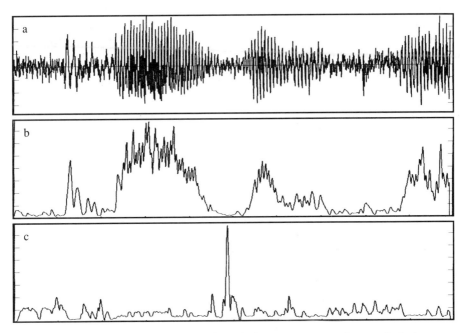

Fig. 3   Representations of 'dirty.dip'; *a* : waveform; *b* : instantaneous envelope; *c* : instantaneous frequency.

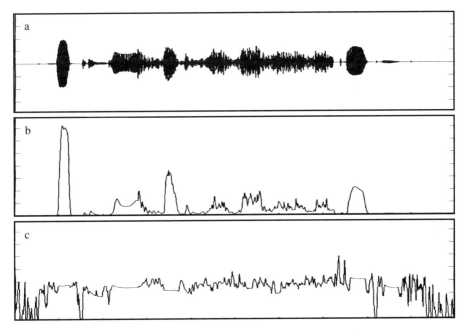

Fig. 4   Representations of 'dirty.wav' after bandpass filtering (500-800 Hz); *a* : waveform; *b* : instantaneous envelope; *c* : instantaneous frequency.

the region of 30 Hz. In general, the combination of IE and IF can be used to give a good indication of the class of a speech segment. For high-energy phonemes IE is robust to noise interference allowing a relatively accurate assessment of the phoneme boundaries. In such cases, the IF function has more or less steady characteristics. Low IE values can indicate fricatives and speech transients, which appear as spikes and high energy values in the IF function. By using the IF distance criterion such speech transients can be more easily detected.

The IE and IF analysis has certain advantages when it is carried out on signals filtered in narrow bands. When for example, a number of frequency bands are employed to analyse the signal, then the features of the IE and IF can be improved in the case when noisy signal has been used. This effectively limits the contribution of interference components in this band. Such results can be observed in fig. 4, for the frequency band 500-800 Hz.

REFERENCES

[1] C. Berthomier (1983), 'IF and energy distribution of a signal', *Signal Processing*, **5**, 31-45.

[2] L. Cohen (1989), 'Time-frequency distributions — a review', *Proc. IEEE*, **77**, 941-981.

[3] C. Demars (1984), 'Filtre de quadrature numérique à la bande', *Onde Eléctrique*, **38**, 5-6, 108-113.

[4] C. Demars (1989), 'Représentations temps-fréquence et parameterisations d'un signal elements de monographie', LIMSI Notes and Documents : **89**,6, 25-31.

[5] J. Flanagan (1980), 'Parametric coding of speech spectra', *JASA*, **68**, 412-419.

[6] D. Friedman (1987), 'Formulation of a vector distance measure for the IF distribution of speech', *Proc. ICASSP '87*, 1748-1751.

[7] Y. Linde, A. Buzo & R. Grey (1980), 'An algorithm for vector quantizer design', *IEEE Trans. Communications*, **28**, 84-95.

[8] J. Mourjopoulos & J.K. Hammond (1982), 'An envelope convolution model for reverberant speech enhancement', *Proc. ICASSP '82*, 1144-1147.

[9] A. Tsopanoglou, J. Mourjopoulos & G. Kokkinakis (1989), 'Continuous speech phoneme segmentation method based on the IF', *Eurospeech '89*, Vol. 2, 67-70.

[10] A. Tsopanoglou, E.D. Kyriakis-Bitzaros, J. Mourjopoulos & G. Kokkinakis (1991), 'A real-time speech decoder using IF and energy', *Eurospeech '91*, 1349-1352.

[11] S. Walsh & P.M. Clarkson (1987), 'Speech enhancement using modelling and replacement of the instantaneous phase signal', *DSP '87*, 279-283.

Speech analysis using higher-order statistics

J. Vidal, E. Masgrau, A. Moreno and J.A.R. Fonollosa

1 INTRODUCTION

Most of the signal analyses made to date have been based on the autocorrelation function or power spectrum. It is well known that these second-order statistics completely characterise a Gaussian process. However, in many applications where non-Gaussian processes or nonlinearities are present, analysis based on the autocorrelation fails to find all the useful information about the process. Cumulants, and their Fourier transform, polyspectra, do contain information about deviations from normality and nonlinearities. There is an increasing interest in their applications to signal processing [6]. Analysis methods based on these statistics are also interesting because they give unbiased results even when the observed signal is corrupted by additive coloured Gaussian noise. For example, we can still obtain unbiased estimation of the LP parameters of the noise provided that it has a Gaussian distribution and the signal is not Gaussian. Therefore, cumulants have found application in those problems where accurate system identification is needed.

Speech analysis using higher-order statistics (HOS) is an almost unexplored area. In [10], third-order cumulants (bispectrum) of some phonemes were studied and used in the voiced/unvoiced decision. In [7], the third-order Yule-Walker equations were used to compute the LP parameters in a robust speech recognition problem. In this paper a new LP method is presented.It can be used either in recognition systems or voice coding applications. The HOS approach is also used in a robust pitch-estimation framework. We will show as well how they are used in signal reconstruction with the help of the Wiener filter.

2 HOS ESTIMATION OF THE LP COEFFICIENTS

As already mentioned, the asymmetry in the probability density function of the voice signal has motivated the use of third-order HOS in speech analysis. However, the use of the third-order cumulant sequence is cumbersome due to the fact that some voiced frames present non-skewed distributions, thus yielding close to zero third order cumulants. This is specially true in female voiced frames like those of the 'clean' recording. Yule-Walker-like equations can be obtained for HOS as well as for the second-order (autocorrelation) but at the expense of a much higher computational burden [9]. The estimation approach that follows is still able to cope with various order statistics while yielding a lower cost algorithm. For a complete review on higher-order estimation approaches see [4].

The speech signal can be modelled by an AR(p) causal model:

$$y(n) = \sum_{i=1}^{p} a(i)\, y(n-i) + e(n) \tag{1}$$

corrupted by another process:

$$s(n) = y(n) + z(n). \tag{2}$$

Visual Representations of Speech Signals: Martin Cooke, Steve Beet and Malcolm Crawford (eds.)
© 1993 by John Wiley & Sons Ltd

The innovation process $e(n)$ is stationary, i.i.d., zero-mean, non-Gaussian. The process $z(n)$ is independent of $e(n)$, zero-mean, Gaussian and of unknown power spectrum. If the AR process is zero-mean and ergodic, its third and fourth order cumulants are defined as [6]:

$$C_{3,s}(i,j) = E\{s(n)\,s(n+i)\,s(n+j)\} \tag{3}$$

$$\begin{aligned} C_{4,s}(i,j,k) = {} & E\{s(n)\,s(n+i)\,s(n+j)\,s(n+k)\} \\ & - E\{s(n)\,s(n+i)\}\,E\{s(n+j)\,s(n+k)\} \\ & - E\{s(n)\,s(n+j)\}\,E\{s(n+i)\,s(n+k)\} \\ & - E\{s(n)\,s(n+k)\}\,E\{s(n+i)\,s(n+j)\}\,. \end{aligned} \tag{4}$$

Moreover, the property that makes cumulants useful is that cumulants of any order are zero for a Gaussian process, so the cumulants of $s(n)$ equal the cumulants of $y(n)$ provided that $z(n)$ are Gaussian. The impulse response $h(n)$ of the linear time-invariant system that generates $y(n)$ satisfies the following recursion:

$$\sum_{i=0}^{p} a(i)\,h(n-i) = \delta(n) \qquad a_0 = 1\,. \tag{5}$$

In [9] it was shown that $h(n)$ can be obtained by means of any weighted sum of cumulant slices (w-slice) of order equal or greater than 2, that is the w-slice:

$$C_w(i) = w_2\,C_{2,s}(i) + \sum_{k=-M}^{N} w_{3j}\,C_{3,s}(i,j) + \sum_{j=-M}^{N}\sum_{k=-M}^{N} w_{4jk}\,C_{4,s}(i,j,k) \tag{6}$$

may yield the impulse response $h(n)$ without previous knowledge of a_i, if the weights w are appropriately chosen. This set of weights has to be such that $C_w(i)$ is a causal sequence. We leave the constants M and N unspecified for the moment. In practice, estimation of the AR parameters needs only $p+1$ samples of $h(n)$, so the set of weights can be estimated by solving the matrix equation: $S_a w = 1$ where S_a is the anticausal w-slice matrix:

$$S_a = \begin{bmatrix} C_{2,s}(-P) & C_{3,s}(-P,j) & \cdots & C_{4,s}(-P,j,k) & \cdots \\ \vdots & \vdots & & \vdots & \\ C_{2,s}(0) & C_{3,s}(0,j) & \cdots & C_{4,s}(0,j,k) & \cdots \end{bmatrix} \tag{7}$$

where w is the weights vector: $w = [w_2, w_{3j}, ..., w_{4jk}, ...]^t$, 1 is the anticausal impulse response: $1 = [0, ..., 0, 1]^t$ and P is an upper bound of the LP order. It was also shown that one solution always exists and it is consistent using the following procedure:

i   Find the minimum norm weights yielding a causal w-slice with $C_w(0) = 1$:

$$w_m = S_a\#1. \tag{8}$$

The minimum norm solution of (8) implies the computation of the pseudo-inverse matrix $S_a\#$. If SVD is used, the solution will always be well-conditioned.

ii   Estimate the causal part of the impulse response using S_c, the causal counterpart of S_a:

$$S_c = \begin{bmatrix} C_{2,s}(P) & C_{3,s}(P,j) & \cdots & C_{4,s}(P,j,k) & \cdots \\ \vdots & \vdots & & \vdots & \\ C_{2,s}(0) & C_{3,s}(0,j) & \cdots & C_{4,s}(0,j,k) & \cdots \end{bmatrix} \tag{9}$$

in the formula $\hat{h} = S_c w$ where $\hat{h} = (\hat{h}(P), ..., \hat{h}(1), 1)^t$.

iii   Solve eqn. (5) by simple back-substitution.

It is worth pointing out that the values of M and N are design parameters, and as they are chosen to consider more cumulant lags, a progressive reduction in variance may be expected, although it depends also on the variance of the estimated cumulants lags being included. The back-substitution approach in step iii suffers from the effect of the accumulation of the variance of the estimated AR parameters as the order is increased. This can be solved choosing deliberately a big value of P and over-determining the system in step iii. In solving the over-determination, least squares has shown to yield better estimates that total least squares.

Regarding the particularities of the speech signal, several comments are in order regarding the application to real signals:

- Signals have been decimated to 8 kHz.

- Since the HOS approach does not guaranty stability like autocorrelation-based methods, unstable AR parameters may be found in noisy environments. Previous windowing of the voice frame alleviates, but not completely avoids, the problem. The Hamming window is used. Even if the final estimation of $h(n)$ turns out to be unstable, it can be windowed with an exponentially decreasing window, in order to bring the poles back to the unit circle.

- Pitch-synchronous analysis seems to be necessary, otherwise estimated cumulants may be biased (especially third-order ones) in frames exhibiting symmetric distributions.

- Results obtained should not differ much from the autocorrelation LP coefficients, but the spectral envelope interpretation is lost since error process power is not being minimised. Note that HOS methods are not optimum in any sense.

- Sample mean estimates of the HOS have a higher variance than sample mean of the autocorrelation sequence. This is expected to influence the LP estimates as well. Since frame length cannot be enlarged indefinitely, improvement will be limited with respect to the signal-to-noise-ratio (SNR).

- In practice it has been found that over-determination in step iii is very useful, reducing the variability of the estimates and putting poles inside the unit circle. Experimentally, the best number of samples P of $h(n)$ to be estimated is one half of the pitch period. The LP order has been assumed to be 10.

- The values of M and N are set to $-P$ and P respectively. Higher values, although involving more cumulant samples, do not significantly improve the results.

- Performance using HOS depends on the estimation method being used, but also on the characteristics of the signal and noise. If third-order cumulants are used, performance is improved as long as the ratio between signal skewness and noise skewness is high. The same conclusion can be reached if fourth-order are used with signal and noise kurtosis.

Bearing this in mind, third- and fourth-order statistics have been used to compute the LP coefficients of one frame in 'clean' and 'dirty'. The pitch period is 4.5 ms and the frame duration is eight periods from sample 32500. To study the characteristics of the noise present in 'dirty', the frame samples of 'clean' were subtracted from the corresponding frame samples of 'dirty'. The values of the variance, skewness and kurtosis of the frame being used are displayed in Table 1, for the whitened speech signal and for the noise. Similar results are encountered for the rest of the recording. Since SNRs are higher for third- and especially for fourth-order than for spectral power, good performance may be expected. Figure 1 (upper panel) shows that the use of third- and fourth-order statistics displaces the formants in 'clean' with respect to the ones found by autocorrelation LP spectrum. This displacement is more evident using only third-order cumulants. However, in the corresponding frame of 'dirty' (lower panel, fig. 1) the use of third- and fourth-order shows less sensitivity to noise. Note the preservation of the 4fourh formant as well as the position of the first three with respect to the spectrum of 'clean'.

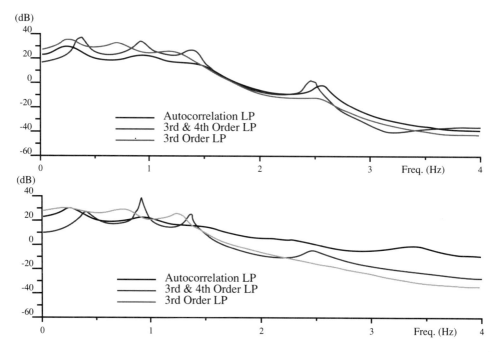

Fig.1   LPC spectrum from *upper* : 'clean' and *lower* : 'dirty'.

Table 1.

	Speech signal	Noise	SNR
Power (second order statistics)	495.4	197.2	2.5 dB
Skewness (third order statistics)	-283.8	163.4	2.7 dB
Kurtosis (fourth order statistics)	284130.0	2222.5	21.0 dB

3   PITCH DETERMINATION

Most pitch-detection algorithms are based on second-order statistics of the signal frame under analysis. Autocorrelation (eqn. (10)) has been widely used in pitch detection applications:

$$r_s(k) = \sum_{i=0}^{L-k-1} s(i)\, s(i+k) \qquad k = 0, \, ..., \, L-1 \tag{10}$$

where $s(i)$ is the frame to analyse, and L its length. Pitch is determined from the index where $r_s(k)$ takes its maximum value:

$$\text{AC} = \operatorname{argmax} r(k) \qquad P_m \leq k \leq P_M \tag{11}$$

where P_m and P_M are the minimum and maximum permitted pitch values.

Autocorrelation is robust against Gaussian white noise but it is not when coloured noise or periodic noise is added to the signal. Moreover, most of these noise types have a symmetric distribution and their third-order cumulants are zero while voiced frames of speech signals have a bispectrum that permits the pitch period to be estimated from these statistics. We have shown [5] that a pitch detector based on third-order statistics is very useful when the signal is corrupted by a wide range of noise types. The method consists of calculating, for each speech frame, a one-slice cumulant:

$$C_{3,s}(0,k) = \sum_i s(i)\, s(i)\, s(i+k) \qquad P_1 \le k \le P_2 \tag{12}$$

and determining the periodicity of this sequence by applying the autocorrelation method over $C_{3,s}(0,0)$ for $k = P_1, \dots, P_2$. We call the resulting method MR.

At least two periods are necessary to determine periodicity. For this reason, P_1 and P_2 are $-P_M$ and P_M respectively. It is possible to calculate more points but this serves either to enlarge the speech window or to calculate the extra cumulant points with few signal values. The choice of limits on the summation (12) is another question to consider. If the signal frame is L, $C_{3,s}(0,0)$ is calculated with L values and $C_{3,s}(0,|P_M|)$ is calculated with $L - P_M$ values. A double-window effect is produced when autocorrelation is applied to determine the pitch, giving fine pitch errors. A good choice is to calculate each cumulant point with $L - P_M$ values ($i = 0, \dots, L - P_M - 1$ for $k > 0$ and $i = -k, \dots, L - P_M - 1 - k$ when $k < 0$).

The pitch-determination algorithm MR has been compared against the autocorrelation method AC. Neither preprocessing (e.g. centre clipping or inverse filtering) nor postprocessing (e.g. smoothing or tracking) were applied to either the AC or MR methods. In this way we compare the characteristics of the basic extractor.

To test the system, we selected sentences 'clean' and 'dirty' of the Sheffield data set. Utterances were down-sampled to 8 kHz. A pattern pitch for the 'clean' utterance was manually derived by a semi-automatic system. Pitch was evaluated in 40 ms frames (320 samples) every 10 ms. This pattern pitch was used as the reference to evaluate the tested methods. Voiced, unvoiced and transitional segments were labelled manually. A transitional segment was defined when the beginning or ending of voicing is in the centre 10 ms of the 40 ms frame. Otherwise it was defined as voiced or unvoiced. As a result there are 210 voiced, 126 unvoiced and 16 transitional frames. Comparison was made with gross pitch errors. We consider a gross pitch error to occur whenever the difference between the detected value and the pattern is greater than 1 ms. Pitch values were searched in a range between 53 and 400 Hz (so $P_m = 20$ and $P_M = 150$). The length of the speech frame was $L = 470$ in order to calculate each cumulant point with 320 samples of speech. This value of L was also used in eqn. (10).

Results. With the 'clean' signal, no errors were detected using the AC method and two errors with the MR method. With the 'dirty' signal, eleven errors where detected with the AC method and two errors using the MR method. These results show that third-order statistics retain important information about speech signals and they are more robust against a wider variety of noise than second-order statistics.

4   SPEECH ENHANCEMENT

It is well known that many applications of speech processing (e.g. speech recognition, source speech coding) which show very high performance in laboratory conditions degrade dramatically in real environments. This is due principally to the low noise robustness offered by standard signal processing algorithms. There are two different ways to solve this problem: firstly, to increase the intrinsic robustness of the processing algorithms and, secondly, to use a preprocessing front-end in order to enhance the speech quality by means a noise reduction or a speech parametric model insensitive to the noise. The solution that we describe in this paper falls into this second class.

Recently, the iterative speech enhancement method based on a sequential MAP estimation of the speech originally formulated by Lim & Oppenheim [2] has been the object of interest [1] and its performance highly improved. This method consists of iterative Wiener filtering of the noisy speech based on spectral estimation of the noise (obtained in non-speech frames) and AR modelling of the speech using second order statistics, i.e. autocorrelation. This speech model is continuously improved using the filtered speech obtained in the preceding iteration. The convergence of the algorithm is highly impaired by the residual noise influence in speech AR modelling. Also, noise-speech coupling causes a spectral distortion and a subsequent loss of the speech intelligibility. This is intensified as more iterations are carried out.

The use of higher-order cumulants for the AR model calculation provides the desired uncoupling between the noise and the speech. It is based on the property that for Gaussian processes only, all cumulants of order greater than three are identically zero. Moreover, the non-Gaussian processes presenting a symmetric probability density function have null odd-order cumulants. Considering a Gaussian or a symmetric p.d.f. noise (a good approximation to many real environments) and the non-Gaussian characteristic of speech (principally for voiced frames) it would be possible to obtain an exact spectral AR model of the speech by using, for example the third-order cumulants of noisy speech instead of the common second-order cumulant.

In our proposed algorithm, an AR model of speech based on third-order cumulants is used for the Wiener filter design in each iteration of the Lim & Oppenheim algorithm. We hope to gain a twofold benefit: first, the convergence of the iterative algorithm is highly accelerated and the number of iterations (and hence the computational complexity) can be greatly reduced (ideally, one iteration is sufficient; in practice, the noise is not exactly Gaussian and the speech is not exactly non-Gaussian, so more than one iteration is required). Also, the spectral distortion — and the subsequent loss of intelligibility — caused by an excessive number of iterations is greatly reduced. Secondly, a non-contaminated AR parameterisation of the speech is obtained directly. This latter result is very useful, for example, in a recognition system based on speech parameterisation [8]. Thus, our final algorithm consists of the following steps:

i   Segment the noisy speech by using a 50%-overlapping Hanning window of N=256 samples (32 ms at 8 kHz sampling frequency).

ii Estimate the noise spectrum in non-speech segments using a smoothing periodogram.

iii Calculate the third-order cumulants of a speech segment using the covariance case defined by the following expression:

$$C(i,j) = \sum_{n=p+1}^{N} s(n-k)\, s(n-i)\, s(n-j) \qquad 0 \le k,i,j \le p. \tag{13}$$

iv Calculate the p-th order cumulant based on AR model by solving [6]:

$$\sum_{k=0}^{p} a(k)\, C_k(i,j) = 0 \qquad 0 \le i \le p,\ 0 \le j \le i. \tag{14}$$

v   Design the non-causal Wiener filter using the estimate of speech and noise spectra.

vi Filter out the noisy speech segment using the Wiener filter designed above by means of an adequate length FFT in order to avoid the aliasing effects caused by the circular convolution. In our case, we use a 512-point FFT.

vii Go to the step iii, $s(n)$ being the filtered signal obtained in step vi.

The algorithm takes one or two iterations for each segment of noisy speech in order to provide a significant enhancement. Additional iterations slightly improve the results obtained only for low SNRs. Finally, the filter responses to all the signal segments are added resulting in the enhanced speech..

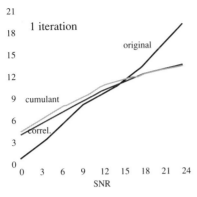
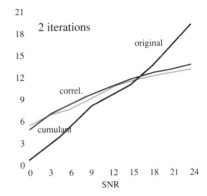

Fig. 2   SEGSNR results.

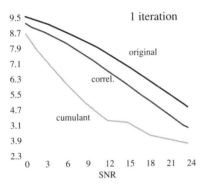
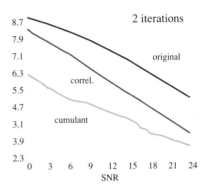

Fig. 3   Itakura results.

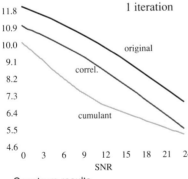
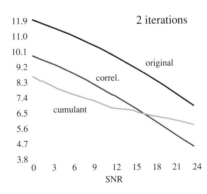

Fig. 4   Cepstrum results.

In order to obtain an evaluation of the proposed algorithm we consider a simple speech enhancement experiment: the 'clean' utterance is disturbed by additive Gaussian white noise with various global SNRs ranging from 24 dB to 0 dB. The performance is evaluated in SEG-SNR terms as with Itakura and cepstrum distances, and the results are compared against those obtained from the standard Lim & Oppenheim algorithm using correlation in the AR model-ling. Figure 2 shows the SEGSNR results obtained after one and two iterations, respectively.

Each figure shows the original SEGSNR values and those obtained using the correlations and the third-order cumulants methods.

Figure 2 demonstrates that both approaches — correlation and third-order cumulants — present similar performance in terms of SEGSNR. Also, the enhancement provided by both approaches is only significant for low SNRs. Figures 3 and 4 show the results obtained in terms of the Itakura and cepstrum spectral distances. In these measures, the enhancement is higher, and the third-order cumulant approach largely outperforms the correlation one. It can be seen that most of the enhancement provided for the cumulant method is obtained after the first iteration. Conversely, the enhancement increases gradually iteration-by-iteration in the correlation approach. After 4-5 iterations, both methods degrade performance. This degradation effect is stronger for the cepstrum distance than for the Itakura one, especially in the cumulant case. This fact is due to the characteristics of these measures: the Itakura distance weights the spectral resonances and these spectrum frequencies are well preserved by both approaches; however, the cepstrum distance looks at the overall spectrum in a more uniform way. Therefore, it is sensitive to the distortion in the valleys and flat zones of the spectrum, and the known peaky effect of the iterative Wiener filtering methods [1] causes high distortion in these zones.

These results show that a hybrid method consisting of 1 or 2 iterations using correlation AR modelling followed by an iteration using cumulant AR modelling can provide optimum performance. We are currently carrying out an exhaustive evaluation of the cumulant and hybrid algorithms using speech degraded with several additive real noises such as car and aircraft cabin, diesel-motor, and office noises. Further results and analyses are presented in [3].

REFERENCES

[1] J.H.L. Hansen & M.A. Clements (1991), 'Constrained iterative speech enhancement with applications to speech recognition', *IEEE Trans. on Signal Processing*, **39**, 795-805.

[2] J.S.Lim & A.V. Oppenheim (1978), 'All-pole modelling of degraded speech', *IEEE Trans. on ASSP*, **26**, 197-210.

[3] E. Masgrau & J.A.R. Fonollosa (1992), 'Enhancement of speech by using higher-order spectral modelling', *EUSIPCO '92 (Brussels, Belgium)*.

[4] J. M. Mendel (1991), 'Tutorial on higher order statistics (spectra) in signal processing and system theory: theoretical results and some applications', *Proc. IEEE*, **79**(3), 278-305.

[5] A. Moreno & J. Fonollosa (1992), 'Pitch determination of noisy speech using higher order statistics', *Proc. ICASSP '92*, 133-136.

[6] C.L. Nikias & M. R. Raghuveer (1987), 'Bispectrum estimation: a digital signal processing framework', *Proc. IEEE*, **75**, 869-891.

[7] K. K. Paliwal & M. M. Sondhi (1991), 'Recognition of noisy speech using cumulant-based linear prediction analysis', *Proc. ICASSP '91*, 429-432.

[8] J.M. Tapia & E. Masgrau (1991), 'Reconocimiento del habla en ambientes ruidosos', *Proc. Congreso URSI '91, (Cáceres, Spain)*.

[9] J. Vidal & J. A. R. Fonollosa, 'Causal AR modelling using a linear combination of cumulant slices', submitted to *Signal Processing*.

[10] B. B. Welss (1985), 'Voiced/unvoiced decision based on the bispectrum', *Proc. ICASSP '85*, 1589-1592.

On the time-frequency display of speech signals using a generalised time-frequency representation with a cone-shaped kernel

39

Hisashi Wakita and Yunxin Zhao

1 INTRODUCTION

In the past decade, substantial efforts have been made to pursue new signal analysis techniques. One such effort is the time-frequency signal analysis technique. In particular, the Wigner distribution has been studied as a tool for nonstationary signal analysis [1], and was often suggested to be applicable to speech analysis. As is well known, the commonly used techniques for spectral estimation of speech signals have problems in resolving closely located formants, tracking rapidly changing spectral peaks, and obtaining spectra for short consonants. As a more effective method to overcome these problems, a generalised time-frequency representation (GTFR) using a cone-shaped kernel was proposed for non-stationary signals [2]. The purpose of this paper is to evaluate this GTFR in its application to acoustic analysis of those speech sounds for which conventional methods fail to give satisfactory results.

2 METHOD

Let $R(t, \tau)$ of a given signal $x(t)$ be given by

$$R(t, \tau) = x(t + \tau/2)\, x^*(t - \tau/2) \tag{1}$$

where x^* denotes the conjugate of x, and let the convolution of $R(t, \tau)$ with a certain kernel function $\phi(t, \tau)$ be given by

$$y(t, \tau) = \int_{-\infty}^{\infty} \phi(t', \tau)\, R(t - t', \tau)\, dt' . \tag{2}$$

Then, the GTFR is given by the Fourier transform of $y(t, \tau)$ as [1]

$$G(t, \omega) = \int_{-\infty}^{\infty} y(t, \tau)\, e^{-j\omega\tau}\, d\tau . \tag{3}$$

Although $G(t, \omega)$ is generally not guaranteed to be a nonnegative function, it can be considered as a generalised energy distribution in the time-frequency space when the kernel satisfies certain constraints, and the value $G(t_1, \omega)$ becomes the instantaneous energy spectrum at $t = t_1$.

When implementing the GTFR for a practical purpose, a certain kind of kernel $\phi(t, \tau)$ is chosen so that a short-time Fourier transform can be performed in (3). The selection of the kernel gives different types of representations. For instance, if a sliding time window $h(t)$, such as a Gaussian window, is chosen so that the kernel is defined as $\phi(t, \tau) = \delta(t)\, h^2(\tau/2)$, the GTFR becomes the pseudo-Wigner distribution. If the kernel is defined for the same time window $h(t)$ as

$$\phi(t, \tau) = h(t + \tau/2)\, h(t - \tau/2) \tag{4}$$

Visual Representations of Speech Signals: Martin Cooke, Steve Beet and Malcolm Crawford (eds.)
© 1993 by John Wiley & Sons Ltd

then the GTFR becomes a spectrogram representation. In this study, a cone-shaped kernel is chosen. It is defined as

$$\phi(t, \tau) = \begin{cases} g(\tau) & |\tau| \geq a|t| \\ 0 & \text{otherwise} \end{cases} \tag{5}$$

where the parameter a adjusts the slopes of the cone and $g(\tau)$ the Gaussian window. The cone-shaped kernel has been shown to give more satisfactory results for various signals than other kernels [2], such as the one for spectrogram representations or the one for the pseudo-Wigner distribution.

3   IMPLEMENTATION

For the discrete case, by defining $t = nT_s$, $t' = pT_s$, $\tau = 2kT_s$, and $2\pi fT_s = 2\pi m/M$ for a sampling period T_s, the GTFR $G(t, \omega)$, is represented by

$$G(n, m) = \sum_{p=-L}^{L} \sum_{k=-L}^{L} \phi(p, k) R(n - p, 2k) e^{-j4\pi mk/M} \tag{6}$$

where $L \leq (M - 1)/2$. By using the kernel as given in (5), the computational form of (6) is given by

$$G(n, m) = 4Re\left[\sum_{k=0}^{L} g(k) r(n, k) e^{-j4\pi mk/M} \right] \tag{7}$$

where

$$g(k) = \begin{cases} 0.5 & k = 0 \\ e^{-2\alpha k^2} & k \leq |k| \leq L \end{cases} \tag{8}$$

and

$$r(n, k) = \sum_{p=-|k|}^{|k|} x(n - p + k) x^*(n - p - k). \tag{9}$$

As seen from (6) and (9), an autocorrelation $r(n, k)$ is first computed, and then the Fourier transform of $r(n, k)$ weighted with $g(k)$ is computed to obtain $G(n, m)$. In implementing the above method, it is to be noted that, due to $\tau/2$ in (1), the value of $G(t, \omega)$ at a frequency f is obtained by the value of the Fourier transform at the frequency $2f$. Thus, the effective frequency band of $G(n, m)$ is limited to $1/4f_s$ for the sampling frequency f_s. Because of this, when a given signal is digitised, the cutoff frequency of the lowpass filter is set to $1/4f_s$ or below. In case it is set to $1/2f_s$ or below, the sampled data can be processed after it is converted into an analytic signal. In applying the kernel in (5) for speech analysis, the slope of the cone is set to $a = 1$, and the α in $g(k)$ is determined so that $g(L) = 0.01$. This kernel function is designed to enhance the spectral peaks and to minimise spectral leakage. Since the positivity of the energy distribution $G(n,m)$ is not guaranteed, the negative values of $G(n,m)$ are set to zero for the sake of display.

4   ANALYSIS

In applying the GTFR to speech analysis, analysis conditions need to be chosen properly. As in spectrogram analysis, a different choice of the window size gives different spectral contents. If a longer window is chosen, obviously the harmonic structure is captured for voiced sounds as in the case of the narrowband spectrogram. To obtain the vocal tract characteristics of voiced sounds, the short-time Fourier transform is applied to a segment of roughly one pitch period. When the pitch period is short, however, a typical problem is encountered due to the uncertainty principle, i.e. the frequency resolution is lost as the window size becomes shorter. In this situation, the wideband spectrogram fails to resolve the closely located formant frequencies. On this issue, the GTFR in this study is definitely superior to the regular spectrogram. In order to obtain the same frequency resolution, the GTFR needs only approximately half the window length required for the spectrogram. Therefore, a much shorter window length can be applied to obtain the time-frequency representation, allowing analysis of shorter speech sounds.

The wideband spectrogram and the corresponding GTFR display for 'clean.wav' are shown in fig. 1 and for 'clean.syl' in fig. 2. For the sampling frequency of 20 kHz, the window size of the GTFR is 81 samples; whereas at the same rate, the window size of the spectrogram is 128 samples. Unfortunately, the 'clean' data is cut off at around 2.8 kHz due to the Rothenberg mask; thus it is hard to see how well the formant peaks are captured by the GTFR method. In order to interpret the result better, the same sentence spoken by a female was analysed. Figure 3 shows the wideband spectrogram and GTFR displays for the "... Susan ca..." portion of the sentence. As can be seen, the GTFR display reveals much clearer spectral peak trajectories than the wideband spectrogram. The vowel /u/ in "Susan" is somewhat fronted in the sentence utterance, resulting in higher F2. Figure 4 shows the spectrogram and the GTFR display of the word "food" spoken by the same speaker. In this case, the F2 of /u/ is in the normal range for the steady-state vowel /u/. Again, the GTFR display shows much sharper spectral peak trajectories and makes it easier to see the transition toward the final consonant /d/. Figure 5 shows the spectrogram and the GTFR display of four vowels produced in the context of "h-d" by a five-year old boy. In these cases, the GTFR display also shows better formant trajectories.

Figure 6 shows an example of the effects of the window size on the GTFR display of the word "pea" spoken by a female speaker. The window size was varied from 257 samples to 41 samples. It is clearly seen that the frequency resolution is degraded as the window size is decreased. This tendency is observed particularly well for the first formant. The frequency resolution of the regular spectrogram with the window size of 128 samples (fig. 6g) roughly corresponds to the one in fig. 6f in which the window size is 41 samples. As is often the case with female speakers, F2 and F3 of /i/ are not clearly resolved in the wideband spectrogram. However, if the window size is properly chosen, the GTFR display can resolve F2 and F3 as shown in figs. 6c-e. Furthermore, the GTFR captures the formant transitions from the consonant to the vowel much better than the spectrogram.

5   CONCLUSION

The analysis method based on the GTFR using a cone-shaped kernel is very promising for acoustic analysis of speech sounds in finding some details of spectral patterns. It was shown that the cone-shaped kernel gives an excellent frequency resolution, particularly in enhancing formant peaks, and allows for a shorter window length without losing much frequency resolution for analysis of shorter sounds. Despite its own problems, the GTFR certainly appears to be a useful tool for such analysis.

REFERENCES

[1] T. A. C. M. Claasen & W. F. G. Mecklenbrauker (1980), 'The Wigner distribution — A tool for time-frequency signal analysis. Part 3: Relations with other time-frequency signal transformations', *Philips J. Res.*, **35**, 373-389.

[2] Y. Zhao, L. Atlas & R. Marks (1990), 'The use of cone-shaped kernels for generalized time-frequency representations of nonstationary signals', *IEEE Trans. ASSP*, **38**(7), 1084-1091.

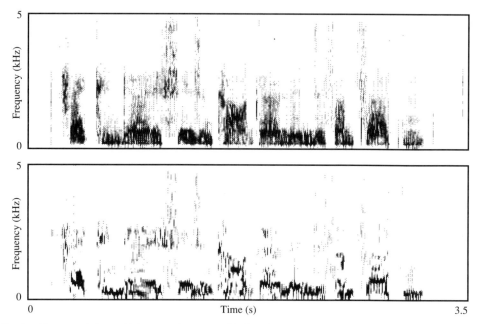

Fig. 1   Representations of 'clean.wav'; *upper* : wide-band spectrogram; *lower* : GTFR display.

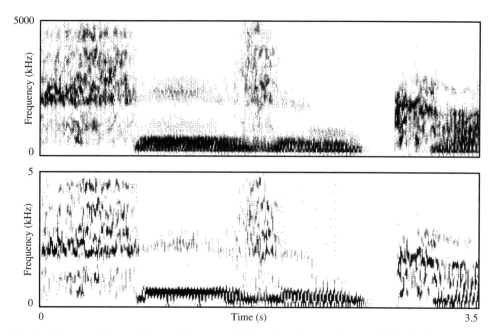

Fig. 2   Representations of 'clean.syl'; *upper* : wide-band spectrogram; *lower* : GTFR display.

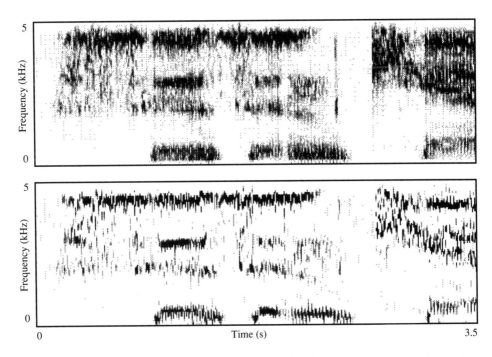

Fig. 3   Representations of "Susan ca..." spoken by a female speaker; *upper* : wide-band spectrogram; *lower* : GTFR display.

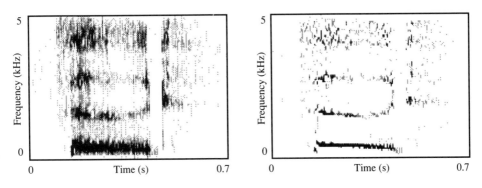

Fig. 4   Representations of "food" spoken by the female speaker in fig. 3; *left* : wide-band spectrogram; *right* : GTFR display.

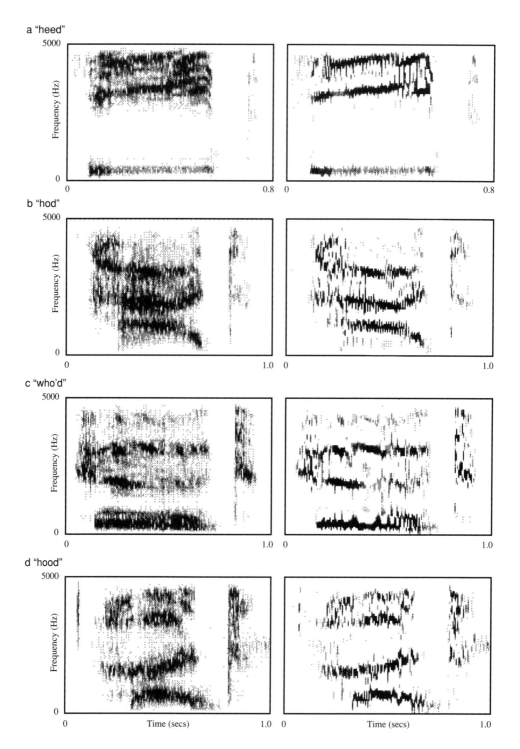

Fig. 5   Analysis results of four utterances by a five-year old boy; *left* : wideband spectrogram; *right*: GTFR display.

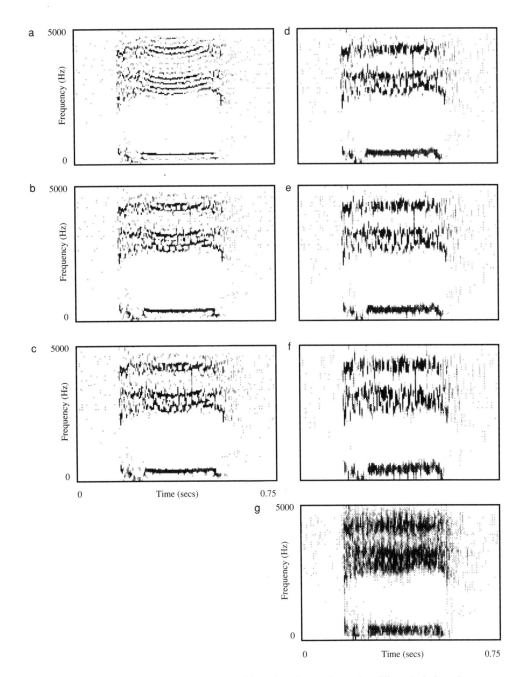

Fig. 6   GTFR analyses for an utterance "pea" by a female speaker using different window sizes;
         a : 257; *b* : 161; *c* : 129; *d* : 81; *e* : 65; *f* : 41; *g* : wideband spectrogram of the same utterance.

Group delay processing of speech signals

B. Yegnanarayana and V.R. Ramachandran

40

1 INTRODUCTION

Speech processing methods for redundancy reduction, parameter/feature extraction and speech enhancement or noise suppression, frequently use spectral magnitude characteristics of a short-time analysis of speech. Computation of the Fourier transform (FT) magnitude in some form or other dominates all these methods, although the signal representation is complete only if both the FT magnitude and FT phase are used. Part of the reason is that the FT phase is not well understood. Even though it is somewhat better understood now [4], it is still not widely used because it is difficult to process the FT phase directly due to wrapping problems (values being in the range $\pm\pi$) in the phase computation via the discrete Fourier transform. The negative derivative of FT phase, or group delay function, can be directly computed from the signal. Therefore, instead of processing the FT phase directly, it can be processed indirectly through the group delay functions.

2 PRINCIPLE OF GROUP DELAY PROCESSING

In this section we discuss the basis for the proposed method of extracting the characteristics of the vocal tract system from noisy speech. The characteristics we are looking for are the formants (resonances) of the vocal tract system. We ignore for the time being the effects of data windows. Let us consider the z-transform representation of speech data $x(n)$ (see fig.1):

$$X(z) = GE(z)/A(z) + U(z) = V(z)/A(z). \tag{1}$$

Since all the coefficients in $V(z)$ and $A(z)$ are real, we can write

$$V(z) = V_1(z) V_2(z) \ldots V_q(z) \tag{2}$$

$$A(z) = A_1(z) A_2(z) \ldots A_p(z) \tag{3}$$

where each of these $V_i(z)$ and $A_i(z)$ are either first- or second-order polynomials with real coefficients. The roots of $V(z) = 0$ may be either inside or outside the unit circle in the z-plane.

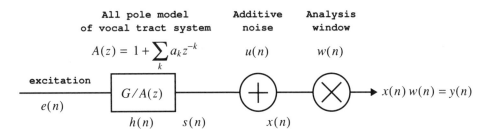

Fig. 1   Model of speech data generation.

Visual Representations of Speech Signals: Martin Cooke, Steve Beet and Malcolm Crawford (eds.)
© 1993 by John Wiley & Sons Ltd

$V(z)$ is mainly contributed by noise or periodic sequence, since in frequency regions where $|A(\omega)|$ is small, $GE(\omega)$ dominates, and in frequency regions where $|A(\omega)|$ is large, $U(\omega)$ dominates [1]. Therefore the roots of $V(z)$ are distributed randomly around the unit circle with most of the roots close to the unit circle. We can show [5] that this produces sharp spikes in the group delay $\tau_V(\omega)$ function of $V(\omega)$.

On the other hand, all the roots of $A(z)$ are well inside the unit circle in the z-plane, and they contribute to a relatively smooth curve in the group delay function $-\tau_A(\omega)$ of $1/A(\omega)$. The locations of peaks in the group delay function correspond to resonances [6]. Note also that, due to additive nature of the group delay functions, the influence of one resonance peak on another is negligible [6].

To extract the resonance information from the group delay function $\tau_X(\omega)$ of $X(\omega)$, we have to suppress the effects of spikes in the group delay function due to $V(\omega)$. To do this, it is necessary to know the locations of the roots of $V(z)$. Since at these roots $|X(\omega)|^2$ has sharp nulls, we can derive a spectrum $|\tilde{V}(\omega)|^2$ (called the *zero spectrum*) having approximately flat spectral envelope and multiply it by the group delay function $\tau_X(\omega)$ to obtain an estimate of the group delay function corresponding to $1/A(\omega)$. The resulting modified group delay function shows peaks corresponding to the resonances of the vocal tract system [1].

3   EXTRACTION OF RAW FORMANT AND PITCH INFORMATION USING THE MODIFIED GROUP DELAY FUNCTION

In this section we describe a procedure to compute the modified group delay function and to estimate the resonance frequencies of the vocal tract system. Given a segment of speech signal, $x(n)$, $n = 0, 1, ..., N - 1$, the group delay function is computed as follows:

Let $X(k)$ and $Y(k)$ be the discrete Fourier transform of the sequences $x(n)$ and $nx(n)$, respectively. The samples of the group delay function are given by [2]:

$$\tau(k) = \frac{X_R(k)\,Y_R(k) + X_I(k)\,Y_I(k)}{X_R^2(k) + X_I^2(k)} \tag{4}$$

where the subscripts R and I refer to the real and imaginary parts, respectively.

Let $|\tilde{V}(k)|^2$ be an estimate of the zero spectrum. This is derived by flattening the magnitude spectrum either by linear prediction or by cepstrum analysis [3]. The modified group delay is given by [1]:

$$\tilde{\tau}(k) = \tau x(k)|\tilde{V}(k)|^2 . \tag{5}$$

The envelope of $\tilde{\tau}(k)$ contains peaks corresponding to the resonances of the vocal tract.

Figure 2a shows a 25.6 ms segment of voiced speech and fig. 2b the corresponding modified group delay function. Figure 2b also shows the smoothed modified group delay function. The frequency locations of the peaks in the smoothed modified group delay function give an estimate of the formant frequencies of the vocal tract system.

The periodic glottal pulse excitation in voiced segments manifests as sinusoids in the frequency domain. In other words, the magnitude spectrum $|X(\omega)|^2$ of a voiced segment contains a sinusoidal component corresponding to pitch, besides peaks due to formants and random fluctuations due to excitation and additive noise. The problem of pitch extraction is simply estimation of the frequency of the sinusoid in $|X(\omega)|^2$ even when there is distortion and noise. We can consider the high SNR portion of $|X(\omega)|^2$ as signal, and compute the modified group delay function for this signal. The peak in the modified group delay function corresponds to pitch period [7]. Figure 2c shows the modified group delay function for the zero spectrum of the voiced segment of fig. 2a.

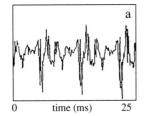 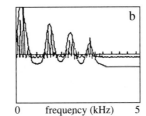 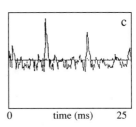

| 0 | time (ms) | 25 | 0 | frequency (kHz) | 5 | 0 | time (ms) | 25 |

Fig. 2   *a* : 25 ms segment of voiced speech; *b* : Modified group delay function of the voiced segment given in fig. 2a. A smoothed modified group delay function is also plotted in the figure to illustrate the locations of the formants; *c* : Modified group delay function of the zero spectrum corresponding to the voiced segment given in fig. 2a. The location of the peak indicates the pitch period.

Figure 3a shows the raw formant data of a male voice obtained for an all voiced utterance of the sentence "we were away a year ago". Figure 4a shows the corresponding data for noisy (SNR = 3 dB) speech. Generally we have noticed that in the unvoiced and noisy regions the peak locations are random. Figures 3b and 4b show the pitch period contours derived using this approach from clean and noisy (SNR = 3 dB) speech data respectively, for a complete utterance. Generally, we have noticed that in the unvoiced and noisy regions the locations of the peaks are distributed randomly in successive frames. Figures 5a-c show the speech data, raw formant data and raw pitch data for a female voice utterance of the sentence 'clean.wav'. The first four highest peaks from the smoothed modified group delay function for pitch extraction are shown in fig. 5c. Figures 6a-c show the corresponding data for 'dirty.wav'. Since it is a high pitched voice and also of poor quality, there are many spurious peaks in the raw formant and pitch data.

The raw pitch data given in figs. 5c and 6c are smoothed using Algorithm 1 given below to obtain an approximate pitch contour as shown in figs. 5d and 6d, respectively. These contours are further smoothed using the Algorithm 2 given below to obtain the final pitch contours shown in figs. 5e and 6e. It is seen that pitch is extracted correctly for most of the voiced segments and the pitch values are random for unvoiced and silence regions of speech. Since it is difficult to decide voiced and unvoiced regions from noisy speech, we have decided to use the final pitch values for all segments. If the values are randomly distributed in successive segments, the corresponding speech will be noisy anyway.

Algorithm 1. To obtain rough pitch contour from raw pitch data, perform the following steps for each frame:

   i   Sort the peak positions P1, P2, P3 and P4 in ascending order.

   ii   Compute the differences D1=P1–0, D2=P2–P1, D3=P3–P2 and D4=P4–P3.

   iii Return the maximum of D1, D2, D3 and D4.

Algorithm 2. To obtain final pitch contour, perform the following steps:

   i   Smooth the rough pitch contour from Algorithm 1 using a moving average of 15 points. The points too far from the moving average value of the previous frame are not used in the moving average computation of current frame.

   ii   Compute the pitch value for each frame by applying the following rules in the given order.

      a   Return the rough pitch value from Algorithm 1 if it is in the 20% neighbourhood of the moving average obtained in step i.

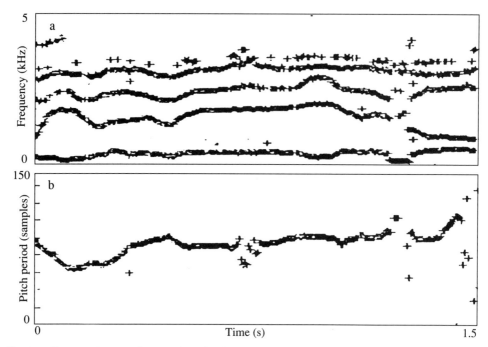

Fig. 3   'Clean.wav'; *a* : raw formant data; *b* : pitch contour.

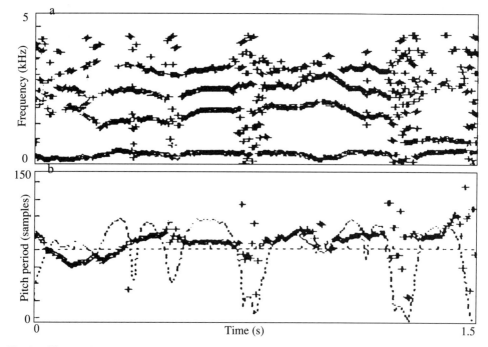

Fig. 4   'Dirty.wav'; *a* : raw formant data; *b* : pitch contour (+), SNR (--).

      b Return the nearest to the moving average, of the differences D1, D2, D3 and D4 (Algorithm 1) if it is in the 20% neighbourhood of the moving average

      c Return the nearest to the moving average, of P1, P2, P3 and P4 (Algorithm 1) if it is in the 20% neighbourhood of the moving average.

      d If twice of nearest point obtained in step c above is in the 20% neighbourhood of the moving average, return the former.

      e If half of nearest point obtained in step c above is in the 20% neighbourhood of the moving average, return the former.

      f If none of the above five conditions is satisfied, return the moving average value.

   iii The final pitch contour is obtained by smoothing above values using three-point median smoothing.

4   SYNTHESIS OF SPEECH FROM RAW FORMANT AND PITCH DATA

We adopt a formant synthesis model for generating speech from parameters. The formant data is used to represent the vocal tract system and the pitch data the excitation component. The raw formant and pitch data have several spurious peaks, especially for noisy speech data. Therefore it is difficult to use this data directly for synthesis. It is also difficult to smooth this data, as oversmoothing may result in unnecessary jumps in formant contours, producing undesirable clicks in the synthesised speech. Likewise direct smoothing of pitch data might produce undesirable jumps in the pitch contour. Hence we used the above two algorithms to smooth the raw pitch data.

A glottal pulse approximating Fant's model is used for each pitch period. Since there is some uncertainty whether a segment is voiced or not, glottal pulse and random noise excitation in proper proportion are used throughout. The gain is computed for each segment using the energy in the high SNR region in the spectrum of each segment. The gain contours for clean and dirty speech are shown in figs. 5f and 6f, respectively.

To represent the vocal tract system, only the peaks up to 2.5 kHz from the raw formant data are used. Typically there is continuity of formants in the voiced regions, apart from several spurious peaks. In the unvoiced and silence regions the formant peaks are distributed randomly across successive frames. The formant continuity is exploited giving a support value for each peak. In synthesis, peaks with poor support will be given larger bandwidths than the one with larger support. Using the formant frequencies and corresponding bandwidths, the coefficients of the corresponding all-pole filter are derived. This filter is driven by the excitation derived from the pitch and gain data to synthesise speech.

Note that the all-pole filter derived from the raw formant data emphasises peaks corresponding to true formants. Thus this filter can be used in several ways for processing noisy speech. We have been able to suppress noise completely with some degradation in the quality of synthetic speech.

REFERENCES

[1] H. A. Murthy & B. Yegnanarayana (1991), 'Speech processing using group delay functions', *Signal Processing*, **22**(3), 259-267.

[2] A.V. Oppenheim & R.W. Schafer (1975), *Digital Signal Processing*, Prentice Hall, Englewood Cliffs, NJ.

[3] L.R. Rabiner & R.W. Schafer (1978), *Digital Processing of Speech Signals*, Prentice Hall, Englewood Cliffs, NJ.

[4] B. Yegnanarayana, D.K. Saikia & T.R. Krishnan (1984), 'Significance of group delay functions in signal reconstruction from spectral magnitude or phase', *IEEE Trans. ASSP*, **32**(3), 610-623.

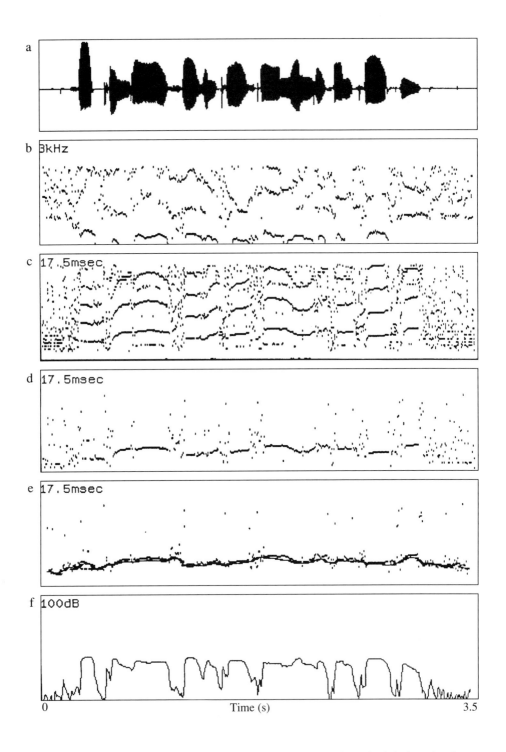

Fig. 5   *a* : 'clean.wav' waveform; *b* : raw formant data; *c* : raw pitch data; *d* : pitch data after first
stage of smoothing; *e* : pitch data after second stage of smoothing; *f* : gain contour.

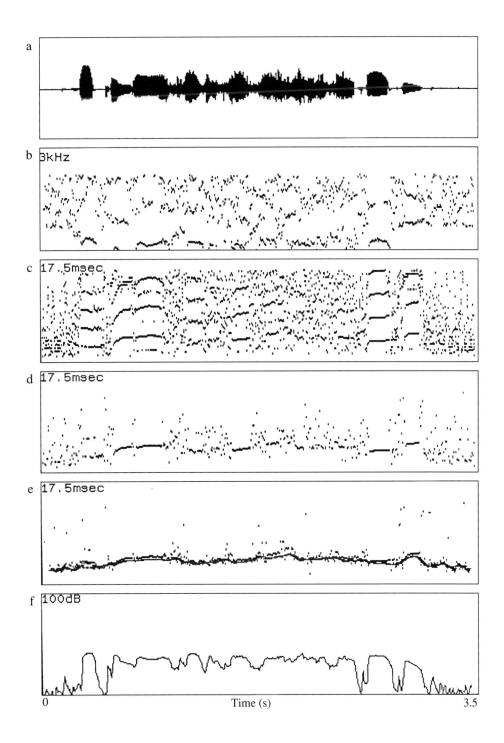

fig. 6   *a* : 'dirty.wav' waveform; *b* : raw formant data; *c* : raw pitch data; *d* : pitch data after first stage of smoothing; *e* : pitch data after second stage of smoothing; *f* : gain contour.

[5] B. Yegnanarayana & H. A. Murthy (1990), 'Spectrum estimation using Fourier transform phase', *Proceedings of Workshop on Signal Processing, Communications and Networking, IISc. (Bangalore, India)*, 44-53.

[6] B. Yegnanarayana (1984), 'Formant extraction from linear prediction phase spectra', *JASA*, **23**, 610-623.

[7] B. Yegnanarayana, H. A. Murthy & V.R. Ramachandran (1990), 'Speech enhancement using group-delay functions', *Proc ICSLP '90*, 301-304.

The effects of noise on connected speech: a consideration for automatic speech processing

41

Keith Young, Stevie Sackin and Peter Howell

1 INTRODUCTION

Most of the authors in this volume have presented analyses of the Sheffield data 'clean.-wav' and 'dirty.wav'. The latter data was obtained by the addition of 1.6 seconds of sounds from a busy laboratory to the 'clean' speech waveform. Whilst there may be situations where it is necessary to analyse a speech signal containing noise of which the speaker was unaware (such as that added by a noisy transmission line), there will be many occasions where the utterance to be analysed was actually produced in a noisy environment.

Numerous studies have been conducted which show that speakers' voices systematically change in a noisy environment. In 1911, Etienne Lombard [14] first described how conversational voice level increases when noise is delivered to a speaker's ear, and returns to its former level when the noise source is removed. Whilst it appears obvious that speakers will increase their vocal effort in order to be heard in noise, many studies have shown persistent increases in speech level, when the speaker, but not the listener, is subjected to noise (such as when the speaker is wearing stereo headphones), and when the speaker has been explicitly instructed to maintain constant vocal effort.

The "Lombard effect", as it is now generally known, was used for many years as the basis for the development of tests for hearing loss [16], but has also been of considerable interest for what it reveals about the dynamic relationship between speech and hearing [12] and is an important consideration for theorists of speech motor control. A thorough review of many of the early investigations on this subject is to be found in Lane and Tranel [12].

Changes in overall level of the speech signal are only one aspect of the effect of noise. Lombard [14] noted that a change in pitch accompanied the change in voice level. Such a change is predictable from the mechanics of glottal excitation [2,11]. Ladefoged [10] reported increases in pitch, a narrower range of pitch variation, and a tendency to use a simple falling intonation pattern for speakers subjected to masking noise over headphones. Ladefoged also observed an effect on length and quality of vowels, and an unusual pattern of nasalisation of sounds.

The effect of noise on speech rate appears to be unreliable. Rubenovitch and Pastier [15] reported some increase in rate under noise conditions, but many investigators have found no effect [1]. Increases in the duration of speech segments have been found by some researchers [17,1,3] but not all. A more recent and detailed study has found an increase in duration for vowels, but a slight decrease in duration for consonants, leading to an overall increase in word duration [9].

Studies which have examined the spectral properties of Lombard speech have produced mixed results for the effect of noise on formant frequencies. There appears to be a tendency for F1 frequency to increase for vowels [9,17], but there is some degree of speaker dependence in this effect which may [17] or may not [9] depend on context. Junqua and Anglade [9] reported rises in F2 frequency under noisy condition for female speakers only, whilst Sum-

Visual Representations of Speech Signals: Martin Cooke, Steve Beet and Malcolm Crawford (eds.)
© 1993 by John Wiley & Sons Ltd

mers *et al.* [17] reported that the effect of noise on F2 was highly speaker and context dependent.

Similar to the effects of noise on speech are the effects caused when a speaker hears her/his own voice echoed back after a short delay. Such situations sometimes occur in real life during long distance telephone calls, when impedance mismatches can cause echo and distortion of the signal. Many studies have shown consistent alterations in speech parameters, including higher fundamental frequencies and increased sound pressure levels when speakers are subjected to delayed auditory feedback (DAF) of their own voices [13,4,6]. Rate tends to decrease [8] and vowels tend to be lengthened [7].

Changes in vocal characteristics due to noise have proved problematic for speech recognition systems [5,17]. This is particularly important, considering that for many important applications, speech recognition must be performed in noisy environments (e.g. fighter aircraft cockpits). The effect of echo on speech recognition systems has not received as much attention, but could be important considering the widespread use of speech recognition systems in telephone dial-up information services. Studies have shown poor recognition rates for Lombard speech when the noise is presented to the speaker via headphones, thus eliminating that noise from the signal to be recognised [5]. Thus, attempting to separate speech from background noise may not prove the best approach to improving recognition in noise [17]. Summers *et al.* argued that if the various aspects of the Lombard effect are systematic and robust, incorporation of this knowledge in speech recognition algorithms could significantly improve performance under adverse noise conditions [17]. Another approach is to attempt to find some representation of the speech signal, such as dynamic (first difference) and acceleration (second difference) features, which may be more invariant across ambient noise conditions [5].

Most laboratory studies of the Lombard effect have concerned themselves with production of isolated words whilst subjects are subjected to continuous white or coloured noise. In this study, we analyse a short sentence, using laboratory noise derived from 'dirty.wav'. This will hopefully suggest an interesting question when examining the various representations of 'dirty.wav' elsewhere in this publication: how would the representation have differed if the additive noise had been present in the speaker's environment? The effect of a short burst of noise in the middle of a connected utterance has not, to our knowledge, been examined in this way before.

2 METHOD

2.1 Subjects

12 native English speakers (5 female, 7 male), a mixture of students, technical and clerical staff from UCL Psychology Department, took part in the experiment.

2.2 Materials

The "noise" used in this experiment was that which had been added to produce the 'dirty' waveform analysed by most of the participants in this volume. It consisted of 1.6 seconds of sound from a "crowded undergraduate laboratory class", sampled at 20 kHz. Three versions of the noise were prepared, differing in amplitude from each other by factors of 2. These samples were replayed to subjects over a Beyer DT 109 headset, which provided approximately 20 dB ambient noise isolation. An intermediate amplifier was set such that peak levels for the loudest noise condition were 104 dB SPL, measured using a Bruel & Kjaer 2203 precision sound level meter in conjunction with an artificial ear. Peak levels for the remaining two noise conditions were measured at 98 dB and 92 dB SPL. Subjects' voices were recorded onto one channel of digital audio tape via an adjustable noise-cancelling microphone attached to the headset and positioned out of the air stream, approximately 4.5 cm from the mouth. The second DAT channel was used for laryngograph recordings. Because of the large variation in voice levels between subjects and our desire to obtain good quality recordings for later digital processing, it was necessary to adjust recording levels on the DAT machine for each subject. However, recording levels were constant during all utterances made by a given speaker. The experimenter monitored subjects over headphones outside the anechoic sound-treated booth where the recordings were made.

2.3 Procedure

The sentence "Fred can go, Susan can't go, and Linda is uncertain" (the 'clean' recording) was replayed to subjects over a loudspeaker inside the booth, followed by a 1 kHz tone of 1 second duration, which was the subject's cue to speak. Subjects had been informed that each time they heard this sequence they should repeat the sentence using a similar intonation to that which they heard over the loudspeaker, and as though they were trying to communicate the information to someone. It was stressed that they should say the sentence exactly the same way and using the same stress pattern, pitch, rate and vocal level on each trial, regardless of any noise which they might hear over their headphones.

Experimentation was carried out in two blocks which ran consecutively. On one of the four trials in each block, nothing was replayed over the subjects' headphones for the duration of their utterance. For the remaining trials in the first block which we shall refer to as the "middle noise" (MN) block, the 1.6 s noise recording was triggered by the experimenter during the subject's production of the vowel in the first word "go" of the sentence, approximately where the added noise starts in 'clean.wav'. The time elapsed between the end of the cue tone, which was audible on the recordings, and the triggering of the noise, was measured by the microcomputer used to control the experiment. Using this measure, we could establish which portion of each utterance was produced whilst noise was being delivered to the subject. In three of the trials for the second or "all noise" (AN) block, the 1.6 s noise was played in a continuous loop over the headphones from the offset of the cue tone until after the subject had finished speaking. Within each block, a different level of noise was used on each of the three non-quiet trials, and the order of trials was randomised.

2.4 Analysis

Data was transferred from DAT, via analogue, to hard disk at a sampling rate of 20 kHz, using a low-pass filter with the cut-off at 7.2 kHz. Excitation periods were obtained from the laryngograph signal using the sample-by-sample differential and instantaneous gradient functions with an automatic threshold determination procedure. This data was then used to calculate fundamental frequency during voiced periods at 5 ms intervals and in LPC analysis to determine formant frequencies. Three segments of the utterance were chosen for analysis, and annotated in the file containing the digitised waveforms. These were:

- *segment 1*: from the onset of voicing of the word "Fred" to the initial burst of "can",
- *segment 2*: from the initial burst of the word "can't" to the burst of the second "go", and
- *segment 3*: from the onset of frication at the start of the second syllable of "uncertain" to the beginning of the final /n/.

For all trials in the MN block, the first segment occurred before the onset of noise, the second during the period when noise was being replayed over the headphones, and the third in the period following the end of the noise. The exact choice of which segments to analyse was governed primarily by reliability of identification. The centre point (as judged by the authors) of the major vowel in each segment was also annotated.

For each annotated segment of each utterance in each block, the following values were obtained:

- *amplitude*: rms amplitude was calculated in 10 ms frames across the segment, and the highest value, expressed relative to 1 volt rms at the DAC input, was used;
- *fundamental frequency*: the mean of three F0 estimation frames centred on the annotated mid-point of the relevant vowel;
- *duration*: the duration (in seconds) of that segment;
- *formant frequencies*: the median of three estimates of centre frequency around the annotated centre point of the relevant vowel for each of the first two formants.

3   RESULTS

The amplitude, duration, fundamental frequency and formant frequency data from each experimental block were analysed by separate repeated measurements and analyses of variance (ANOVAs). The analyses used noise (four levels including "quiet"quiet') and speech segment (three segments) as factors. The segment variable will not be discussed except in the case of significant segment X noise interactions. The significance level for all tests is 0.05.

3.1 Amplitude

Mean peak rms energy frame values for each segment and noise condition in the AN block are shown in fig. 1 (left), where the Lombard effect is clearly visible. Analysis of var-

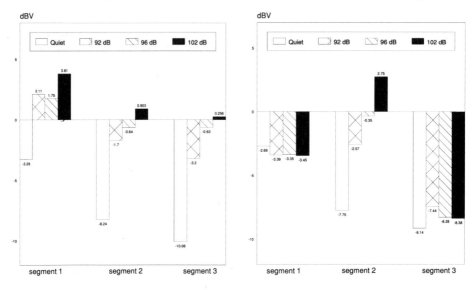

Fig. 1   Mean peak RMS amplitudes of utterances produced in quiet, 92 dB, 96 dB and 102 dB of masking noise; *left* : AN block; *right* : MN block.

iance revealed a significant effect of noise level on speech [$F(3,33) = 57.83$, $p < 0.001$] and an interaction between level and segment [$F(6,66) = 3.79$, $p < 0.01$]. Newman-Keuls analysis revealed that for all segments, voice level in the noisy conditions was significantly higher than in the quiet condition. In the first segment, voice level was not significantly different in the 92 and 94 dB conditions, but was significantly lower in both of those than in the 102 dB condition. The increase in level with each noise level step for the second segment proved not to be significant, but the difference between the 92 dB condition and the 102 dB condition was. In the third segment, the 96 and 102 dB conditions did not differ significantly, but these both showed higher voice levels than the 92 dB condition. The mean increment between noise levels which differed by 6 dB was 1.29 dB: lower than the 3 dB which would have been predicted from the early studies [12,11] but more than that obtained by Summers *et al.* [17].

The MN block showed a main effect of noise on voice level [F(3,33) = 9.53, p < 0.001] and an unsurprising interaction between noise and segment [F(6,66) = 13.48, p < 0.001]. Newman-Keuls analysis showed that no condition was significantly different from any other in segments 1 and 3 (which were always spoken in quiet). However, the Lombard effect is clearly visible in segment 2 (see fig. 1 right). The Newman-Keuls test showed voice level in the quiet condition to be significantly lower than in any of the noise conditions in this segment, with each increase in noise level producing a significant increase in voice level (an average of 2.7 dB per 6 dB increase in noise).

3.2 Fundamental frequency

In the AN block, analysis of variance showed a main effect of noise on F0 [F(3,33) = 8.78, p < 0.001)]. This can be seen in fig. 2 (left). The Newman-Keuls test showed F0 to be significantly lower in the quiet condition than in the noisy conditions, and it was significantly lower in the 92 dB condition than in the 102 dB condition. The difference between individual 6 dB noise steps was not significant. A comparison of figs. 1 and 2 (left) shows the close correspondence between the changes in amplitude and changes in fundamental frequency across conditions.

In the MN block, the main effect of noise [F(3,33) = 2.66, p = 0.065] and the noise X segment interaction [F(6,66) = 2.20, p = 0.054] just failed to reach significance. However, as can be seen in fig. 2 (right), the general trend of increase in F0 with increase in noise is in the expected direction in the middle segment.

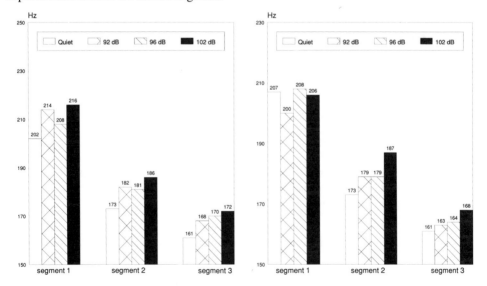

Fig. 2   Mean fundamental frequency at the centre of the vowel in each analysed segment produced in quiet, 92 dB, 96 dB and 102 dB of masking noise; *left* : AN block; *right* : MN block.

3.3 Duration

No effect of noise on duration was found in the AN condition (fig. 3, left). In the MN condition, the ANOVA revealed a marginally significant [F(3,33) = 3.40, p = 0.029] effect of noise. This is particularly surprising, as an effect is not obvious from fig. 3 (right), and the noise X segment interaction did not even approach significance [F(6,66) = 0.85, p = 0.536].

Moreover, Newman-Keuls analysis did not reveal any significant differences between conditions. No explanation for this result is offered, and it will not be considered further.

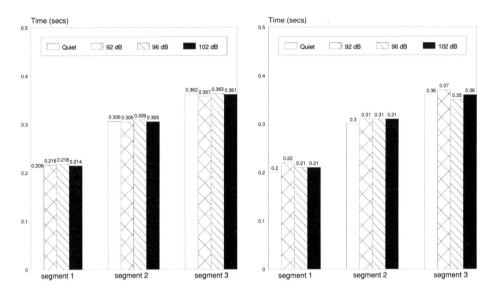

Fig. 3   Mean duration of segments produced in quiet, 92 dB, 96 dB and 102 dB of masking noise; *left* : AN block; *right* : MN block.

3.4 First formant

Mean first formant centre frequencies are shown for each noise condition and each segment in the AN block in fig 4 (left). Analysis of variance showed a significant main effect of noise on F1 [$F(3,33) = 4.79$, $p < 0.01$]. The Newman-Keuls test showed F1 to be significantly lower in the quiet condition than in any of the noisy conditions. The difference between the noisy conditions was insignificant.

F1 values for each segment and noise condition in the MN block are shown in fig. 4 (right). Analysis of variance did not reveal any significant differences between noise conditions. Despite the temptation to conclude that F1 is affected by continuous noise but not by a brief burst of noise, a comparison of the results for segment two in each block shows that the noise effect is least obvious for that segment in the AN block, although there was no significant noise X segment interaction.

3.5 Second formant

No significant effect of noise on second formant frequency was observed in either the AN or MN blocks (fig. 5).

4   DISCUSSION

We have clearly demonstrated how a short connected utterance is affected by noise in much the same ways as has been reported for isolated words. Even a brief burst of noise is enough to elicit significant changes in vocal level. Whilst this may be true, it should not be forgotten that there are other factors involved in the case of connected speech. Most importantly, surprisingly little empirical work has been done on the effect of noise on the prosodic structure of utterances, or on the interaction of the effects of prosody and noise on static features of an utterance. The materials and task used in this study were not appropriate for answering questions in this area. The subjects were asked to use the same prosodic structure

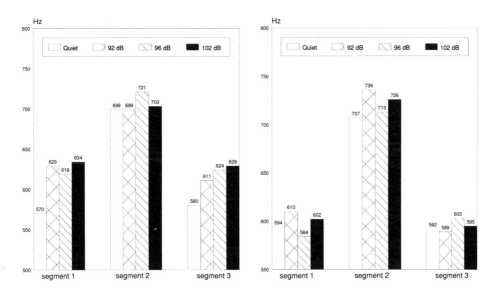

Fig. 4   Mean first formant frequency at the centre of the vowel in each analysed segment from utterances produced in quiet, 92 dB, 96 dB and 102 dB of masking noise; *left* : AN block; *right* : MN block.

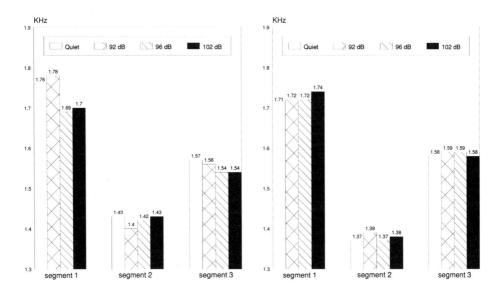

Fig. 5   Mean second formant frequency at the centre of the vowel in each analysed segment from utterances produced in quiet, 92 dB, 96 dB and 102 dB of masking noise; *left* : AN block; *right* : MN block.

regardless of the presence of noise. In a natural task, this constraint would not have been put upon them. The segments analysed were very heterogeneous, differing in prosody, the type of vowel dominating the segment, and position in the sentence. When a noise X segment interaction occurred, the segment factor involved could have been prosody (are stressed vowels more or less affected by noise than unstressed vowels?) vowel type (other studies have shown noise X word interactions for isolated words [17,9]) or length of exposure to noise (the later the segment in the sentence, the longer the speaker had been exposed to noise before uttering it). This is a subject which requires further study using carefully controlled materials.

It is of note that no effect of noise on segment duration was observed in the AN block. This conflicts less with previous work than it may appear. Our 'segments' crossed syllable, and in two cases, word boundaries. Thus it could be that increases in vowel duration reported by others are occurring, but are being balanced by other durational changes.

The effects of noise should be considered when comparing representations of speech spoken in different noise environments. If the representation appears to be altered by the noise, this may be because the talker is altering her/his speech rather than because of an annoying interaction between the speech and noise signals. If a representation of speech appears to be minimally affected by the presence of noise in the speaker's environment, then it could be a contender for incorporation into speech recognition systems for use in adverse noise conditions.

REFERENCES

[1] W.S. Charlip & K.W. Burk (1969), 'Effects of noise on selected speech parameters', *J. Communication Disorders*, **2**, 212-219.

[2] C.G.M. Fant (1960), *Acoustic Theory of Speech Production*, Mouton, The Hague, Netherlands.

[3] J.E. Fricke (1970), 'Syllabic duration and the Lombard effect', *Int. Audiol.*, **9**, 53-57.

[4] R. Ham & M.D. Steer (1967), 'Certain effects of alterations in auditory feedback', *Folia Phoniatr.*, **19**, 53-62.

[5] B.A. Hanson & T.H. Applebaum (1990), 'Robust speaker-independent word recognition using static, dynamic, and acceleration features: Experiments with Lombard and noisy speech', *Proc. ICASSP '90*, 857-860.

[6] P. Howell & A. Archer (1984), 'Susceptibility to the effects of delayed auditory feedback', *Perception & Psychophysics*, **36**, 296-302

[7] P. Howell, T. Wingfield & M. Johnson (1988), 'Characteristics of the speech of stutterers during normal and altered auditory feedback', *Proc. SPEECH '88 (Edinburgh)*, Vol. 3, 1069-1076.

[8] A.W.F. Huggins (1968), 'Delayed auditory feedback and the temporal properties of the speech material', *Z. Phon.*, **21**, 53-60.

[9] J.C. Junqua & Y. Anglade (1990), 'Acoustic and perceptual studies of Lombard speech: Application to isolated words automatic speech recognition', *ICASSP '90*, paper 55.S15b.9.

[10] P. Ladefoged (1967), *Three Areas of Experimental Phonetics*, Oxford University Press, Oxford, 162-165.

[11] H.L. Lane (1962), 'Psychophysical parameters of vowel perception', *Psychol. Monogr.*, **76**, No. 44.

[12] H. Lane & R. Tranel (1971), 'The Lombard sign and the role of hearing in speech', *J. Speech & Hear. Res.*, **14**, 677-709.

[13] B.S. Lee (1950), 'Effects of delayed speech feedback', *JASA*, **22**, 824-826.

[14] E. Lombard (1911), 'Le signe de l'élévation de la voix', *Ann. Malad. l'Oreille. Larynx. Nez. Pharynx*, **37**, 101-119.

[15] P. Rubenovitch & J. Pastier (1938), 'L'épreuve de Lombard appliquées en psychiatrie (contributions à l'étude des réflexes conditionnels)', *Ann. Med. Psychol.*, **96**, 116-121.

[16] W.F. Rintlemann (1979), *Hearing Assessment*, University Park Press, Baltimore, MD.

[17] W.V. Summers, D.B. Pisoni, R.H. Bernacki, R.I. Pedlow & M.A. Stokes (1988), 'Effects of noise on speech production: Acoustic and perceptual analyses', *JASA*, **34**, 936-941.

Appendix:
The Sheffield signals

This Appendix provides details of the four signals which were analysed by participants in the European Speech Communication Association (ESCA) Tutorial and Research Workshop on 'Comparing Speech Signal Representations', held at Sheffield University during April 7-9, 1992.

Three data segments were associated with each of the four signals. The first constituted the whole signal, the second denoted a fragment consisting of a small number of syllables, and the third corresponded to a diphone extracted from the syllable-level file. The precise details of these fragments are provided below.

Signals 'clean', 'dirty' and 'spont' are freely available to anyone interested in comparing their analysis with those presented in this volume, and can be obtained electronically or otherwise by sending a short email (preferred) or letter to one of the editors. The 'timit' signal can be obtained by purchasing the TIMIT CD-ROM.

1   'clean'

This is the utterance "Fred can go, Susan can't go, and Linda is uncertain" spoken by a female and recorded in the Department of Linguistics at the University of Reading. What makes this signal particularly interesting in the context of this volume (and for any future studies) is the existence of simultaneous recordings from devices other than the microphone, including the electropalatograph and laryngograph. A thorough analysis of the information present in the accompanying multi-channel recordings is provided by the tutorial chapter of Nicolaidis *et al.* in this volume.

- *Recording details*. Microphone: Sennheiser MKH20P48 omnidirectional, set to have a flat response; Pre-amp: Symetrix; Anti-aliasing low-pass filter: Kemo 2605, magnitude response 80dB down at 12 kHz.
- *Sampling rate*: 20 kHz.
- *Duration*: 71480 samples (3.574 s)
- *Syllable fragment* ('clean.syl'): ".. Susan ca .." [samples 21640 to 32760].
- *Diphone fragment* ('clean.dip'): ".. ca .." [30280-32320].

2   'dirty'

Human speech perception is highly robust even in the presence of interfering sounds. In order to exercise participants' analyses in such situations, we added broadband 'noise' to the 'clean' signal. This 'noise' was recorded in a busy undergraduate laboratory and fragments of conversation are audible, though unintelligible. Of course, as Young *et al.* point out in this

Visual Representations of Speech Signals: Martin Cooke, Steve Beet and Malcolm Crawford (eds.)
© 1993 by John Wiley & Sons Ltd

volume, adding noise to a speech signal does not replicate real speech production and perception, since no speaker compensation for the intrusion is possible. However, it is often useful, for reference purposes, to have the noise signal available. The spontaneous phrase ('spont'), detailed below, provides a more realistic example of speech in noise.

On computing the mixture, the amplitude of each sample in 'clean' was reduced to half its former level. The laboratory noise is presented at about the same level as the speech signal. For more formal signal-to-noise ratio measurements, it is possible to recover the 'noise' from the mixture as shown, for example, by Dix & Bloothooft in this volume.

3   'timit'

The widely-used TIMIT speech database provides a large number of digitised speech signals on CD-ROM. A single token from this database was selected to facilitate comparison of systems requiring extensive training material. The utterance is a male rendition of the sentence "She had your dark suit in greasy wash water all year" (for TIMIT users, this is the utterance /dr5/mewm0/sa1 — the speaker is from the southern USA dialect region).

- *Sampling rate*: 16 kHz.
- *Duration*: 61133 samples (3.82 s)
- *Syllable fragment* ('timit.syl'): ".. in greasy .." [22170-30444].
- *Diphone fragment* ('timit.dip'): ".. rea .." [25330-26903].

4   'spont'

Visual analyses of spontaneous, natural speech are rarely seen. The automatic recognition of such material, however, represents the ultimate challenge for many systems. We recorded around 30 minutes of conversational speech in a Sheffield bar, from which a short fragment was selected. Out of the background it is possible to make out the utterance "half of bitter, please" followed by a confirmatory "half of bitter?".

- *Recording details*. Microphone: Vision dynamic vocal microphone into a Sony DAT recorder, downsampled using the OROS AU21 A-to-D converter.
- *Sampling rate*: 20 kHz.
- *Duration*: 56001 samples (2.8 s)
- *Syllable fragment* ('spont.syl'): ".. half of bitter .." [10240-20820].
- *Diphone fragment* ('spont.dip'): ".. bi .." [15280-17980].

Index